A PLACE TO GROW OLD

The Meaning of Environment in Old Age

COLUMBIA STUDIES OF SOCIAL GERONTOLOGY AND AGING

Columbia Studies of Social Gerontology and Aging
Abraham Monk, *General Editor*

A PLACE TO GROW OLD

The Meaning of Environment in Old Age

STEPHEN M. GOLANT

New York   Columbia University Press   *1984*

305.06
C 617

Library of Congress Cataloging in Publication Data

Golant, Stephen M.
A place to grow old.

(Columbia studies of social gerontology and aging)
Bibliography: p.
Includes index.
1. Aged—Illinois—Evanston—Social conditions.
2. Human ecology—Illinois—Evanston. 3. Aged—
Illinois—Evanston—Dwellings. 4. Aged—Illinois—
Evanston—Attitudes. 5. Individuality. I. Title.
II. Series.
HQ1064.U6I28 1984   305.2′6   84-5042
ISBN 0-231-04840-8 (alk. paper)

Columbia University Press
New York   Guildford, Surrey
Copyright © 1984 Columbia University Press
ALL RIGHTS RESERVED
PRINTED IN THE UNITED STATES OF AMERICA

To my wife, Dora Kerner

CONTENTS

PREFACE

I have had a longstanding interest in how the attributes of communities, neighborhoods, and dwellings occupied by elderly people influence the quality of their lives. I have been especially concerned about the environmental well-being of what I term the mainstream elderly population. These are relatively healthy, intact persons who live independently in their own homes in ordinary, average houses and apartments in urban and rural communities across the United States. I believe that social and behavioral scientists pursuing gerontological research have paid insufficient attention to this mainstream elderly population, preoccupied as they have been with elderly people in institutions, retirement housing, and other highly distinctive and specialized settings. This research neglect has been particularly evidenced by the dearth of scientific studies investigating how the qualities of the place of residence impinge on the experience of growing old.

I am further troubled by the failure of some scientists, professionals, and advocates to come to grips with the diversity of the American elderly population. Any serious student of aging quickly becomes aware of this population's very heterogeneous composition, a reflection of not only the diversity of people of all ages in modern, western nations, but also of the different rates at which people age—biologically, socially, and psychologically. I have felt that an injustice is being performed by those who arbitrarily lump persons in categories such as "old age," "elderly," and "senior citizens" just because the chronological marker of age 60 or 65 is reached.

The opportunity to carry out serious research on these concerns came in 1977 with my participation (as one of four principal investigators) in a program project grant ("Adult Lives and Patterns of Aging in an Urban Setting") directed by Dr. Bernice Neugarten and funded for over three years by the National Institute on Aging. The project consisted of four component studies having in common their concern with the patterns of social and psychological adaptation of older people living in the social context of a large metropolitan area, Chicago. My study, "Community Ecology and the Adaptation of Older Persons" (#PHFS P01 AG00123) focused on the environmental well-being of persons aged 60 and older in the community of Evanston, Illinois. This book is a culmination of this research effort.

A great many persons were responsible for the successful completion of the research project. I would first like to thank Bernice Neugarten, who was responsible for initiating the program project grant and for encouraging my participation in it. At the time she was professor in the Committee on Human Development (Department of Behavioral Sciences) at the University of Chicago. In my interactions with her, she played many roles: colleague, teacher, critic, ally, and friend. In all these capacities she has made the output of my research better than it would have been. I also benefited from the intellectual exchanges with the other principal investigators in the project, my former Committee on Human Development colleagues at the University of Chicago, Bert Cohler, Gunhild Hagestad, Mort Lieberman, and Mike Czikszentmihalyi. The Department of Geography (Norton Ginsburg, Chair) provided me with a very supportive collegial environment to pursue this research.

The major data source for my investigation consisted of responses by 400 elderly persons (aged 60 and older) to a 90-minute (on average) interview administered in their homes by professional interviewers. All survey research aspects of the study were subcontracted out to the Survey Research Laboratory of the University of Illinois (Chicago) (R. Warnecke was director at the time). Already very experienced in the interviewing of old people, the staff of this organization did a superb job on all parts of the survey, including the sampling design, the final design of the interview schedule, the training of interviewers, pretesting, the administering of the interviews, and the creation of a "clean" data file. Special thanks go to Chuck Sellers, who coordinated these many tasks.

A large number of undergraduate and graduate students at the University of Chicago played important roles in my study. I would like to thank the following persons in particular: Allen McCutcheon, who was primarily responsible for the computer analysis of the survey data; Joseph Maisel, who assisted in the computer analysis and served as coordinator of all aspects of the data analysis; Mary Armstrong, who carried out the data compilation and recording tasks and generally assisted on all aspects of the study; Barbara Sivertsen, who coordinated the day-to-day administration of the grant and who also typed initial drafts of the book manuscript; Chris Muller-Wille, who prepared the graphical material of the book; Rosemary McCaslin, who served as field director for the social service data collected for the study; and Kathi Esqueda, who edited out my worst writing injustices in an initial draft of the manuscript.

A comment about the book's writing: for my own convenience I have frequently used the masculine versions of English pronouns in referring to both male and female elderly persons. Since no sexist connotations were intended, I hope no reader will be offended. I have also not distinguished between widows (widowhood) and widowers (widowerhood). I refer in the book to both male and female persons whose spouses have died as "widows."

Chapter 7 has appeared in I. Altman, M. T. Lawton and J. F. Wohlwill, eds., *Elderly People and the Environment*, vol. 7. Chapter 8 is adapted from an article in the *Journal of Social Issues* (Fall), 38(3):121–133.

This book is dedicated to my wife Dora, who more than anyone else is responsible for my successfully completing it. She has been and continues to be the most salient and positive environmental influence in my own life.

A PLACE TO GROW OLD
The Meaning of Environment in Old Age

Chapter One

An Overview

The expanding body of literature on growing old in America[1] has clarified the social, psychological, and biological changes in a person that produce the patterns and problems of aging. Research has confirmed that old age is distinguished by behaviors and experiences that are a function of a person's stage in life. But this same literature has cautioned that these behaviors and experiences cannot be fully understood or accurately predicted without regard to the total life, cultural, environmental, and sociohistorical contexts of the aging person. People do not begin their lives at age 65. Their attitudes, behaviors, and life-styles are not independent of their lifetime membership in particular racial, ethnic, religious, and socioeconomic groups. Their personalities, habits, and strivings do not emerge unaffected from the pervasive family and societal influences of their youth and early adulthood. Their goals and initiatives cannot fail to be inspired or discouraged by the opportunities and constraints of their environment and culture. Failure to consider the totality of these situational forces inevitably leads to misleading, if not erroneous, interpretations and portrayals of the aging experience.

This book focuses on one broad category of contextual influences—those emanating from the residential environments and human settlements occupied by the majority of noninstitutionalized elderly in the United States. Almost any set of objective indicators shows the sharp differences in the quality of life among various U.S. communities and their neighborhoods and housing structures. Clearly, old people do not live in locations that offer equal opportunities for fulfillment, achievement, and dignity; that have the same potential for satisfying daily needs; and that offer the same resources to alleviate common human stresses. The inevitable conclusion is that it is better, more enjoyable, easier, and less adaptationally costly to grow old in some places than in others.

The implications of these environmental variations for normal and successful aging were addressed formally in the gerontological literature of the late 1960s, with research interest increasing substantially through the 1970s.[2] Today, the main conclusion of this literature does not seem particularly remarkable. Put simply, people do not age in some environmental or situational vacuum, but grow old somewhere and in some place. Individuals grow old in communities, neighborhoods, and dwellings in cities, suburbs, towns, villages, or rural settings; in human-made and natural settings containing buildings, houses, rooms, roads, sidewalks, cars, buses, televisions, appliances, services, stores, organizations, crime, noise, pollution, rodents, insects, weather conditions, and myriad other phenomena of a modern, technologically advanced urban society; in places occupied by populations whose collective attributes define a pervasive social climate; and in the company of individuals who function as family, friends, neighbors, acquaintances, and professionals. These and literally hundreds of others comparable objects and events constitute the residential situation or environmental context in which old people carry out their lives.

Very different types of evidence, from scientific studies to single case journalistic reports, indicated that these environmental phenomena impinged both positively and negatively on the individual aging experience. Most significantly, the evidence implied that because of the physical and sensory deficits associated with old age, the impact of this everyday environment was greater on older than younger people. However, it was somewhat disconcerting—at least for observers seeking a tidy explanation of an environment's impact—that old people who lived in the same place or location did not benefit equally from its advantages or suffer equally from its disadvantages; they did not respond similarly to their environment's opportunities or its constraints. The very same everyday environment was not consistently affecting the well-being of its elderly occupants.

One persistent finding from the gerontological literature promised to improve understanding of this differential environmental impact. It was observed repeatedly that the old population contained a remarkably plural individual membership. Although old age eventually exerted its effects on most people, the magnitude and timing of these influences, and sometimes their very existence, displayed a great deal of variability among individuals. Old people did not equally share in either the afflictions or the joys of old age. They did not uniformly thrive or stagnate after retirement. They did not similarly display stereotypic ailments and bodily declines. Thus, old age did not necessarily bring with it a common set of behaviors, experiences, roles, or physical and mental capacities nor did it eliminate the usual social, economic, racial, ethnic, and personality differences of people living in a modern western urban society.

These observations were highly germane in light of available philosophical and theoretical positions that raised legitimate doubts about an environment's ability to exert uniform and predictable influences on its occupants and users. Proponents of these positions seriously questioned whether the differential impact of an environment could be attributed solely to its variable contextual effects. They assigned comparable importance to the diversity of the human condition as a basis to understand an environment's variable influences. A large literature demonstrated that people dissimilarly perceived and evaluated the qualities and consequences of their residential environment and occupied and utilized its contents in ways consistent with individually defined motives and constraints. In light of the documented diversity of the elderly population—a result of both lifelong and stage-in-life related influences—the environmental properties of a place would therefore be expected to impinge differently on the lives of its elderly residents.

This book presents the results of a research effort that examined these relationships. It had two major tasks: first, to describe the extent to which old persons dissimilarly assessed or experienced the consequences of living in their current residential setting; and second, to distinguish the differences in their personal characteristics that accounted for their variable environmental responses.

These tasks were described and explained at both theoretical and empirical levels. Initially, it was necessary to construct a language by which to describe the variable impact of an environment on its elderly occupants and to propose a theoretical model of individual differences to explain an environment's variable effects. The ensuing empirical investigation produced original findings about the patterns and individual antecedents of the environmental experiences reported by a sample of elderly persons living relatively independent and healthy lives in a midwestern urban community.

To the layperson or the uninformed research scientist, the complexity of such a research effort may not be apparent. It might seem relatively straightforward to demonstrate that a community's quality of life influences the well-being of its elderly population and that these influences depend on the personal characteristics of its residents. However, the researcher who attempts to demonstrate these commonsensical "truths" quickly discovers that the resulting description and verification process is strewn with a dense and often prickly conceptual and methodological thicket. Difficult and never completely satisfactory research decisions must be made as to the selection of the population and the environment for empirical study, the conceptualization and the measurement of an environment's content and qualities, the conceptualization of environmental impact, and the specification of individual differences to account for an environment's variable consequences.

Of course, theoretical and practical guidelines are available to model such tasks, but in light of the alternative philosophical approaches to knowledge and the varying paradigms of scientific disciplines, combined with the researcher's idiosyncratic interpretation and application of these, there is much flexibility regarding the way in which key analytical decisions are handled. Because the book's content and organization rest on these decisions, a brief overview of them follows.

Selection of Population, Sample, and Environment

The analytical inquiry presented is intended to produce insights that can be generalized to all old people and, to a lesser extent, to people of all ages. However, the empirical focus was restricted to relatively healthy, independent, and functionally intact elderly persons (aged 60 and older) who were occupying private households in ordinary houses and apartments located in an unplanned, age-integrated community.

The site of the empirical investigation was a small urban municipality of about 80,000 people located just north of Chicago. It possessed many of the qualities of an older, middle-class suburb, but had the population and land-use diversity and some of the problems associated with older central-city neighborhoods. The elderly population constituted 19 percent of the total population and had a somewhat higher socioeconomic status than the elderly population nationally. However, according to most population and housing indicators, the site included a complete cross-section of the U.S. elderly population. The community also contained elderly people living in retirement hotels, public housing, and nursing homes, but these persons were not considered part of the population universe (for this study).

The data for the empirical investigation were obtained from structured interviews averaging 90 minutes that were administered by professional survey research personnel in the homes of 400 elderly persons randomly selected from this community.

Several considerations guided the selection of the community and elderly population interviewed for this study (chapter 2). Most past research focused on old people who occupied rather specialized, unique, or extremely noxious types of residential settings: nursing homes, retirement hotels, retirement villages, public housing projects, and inner-city transition neighborhoods. Other studies concentrated on old people who had undergone unexpected or dramatic changes in their environmental settings: for example, from slums to public housing; from homes to nursing homes; or from homes to retirement villages. In both cases, these settings were occupied by elderly with relatively extreme personal and social characteristics—they were very sick, frail, depen-

dent, very wealthy, very poor, or isolated. However, within the
United States, the elderly people in any of these situations constitute only a very small segment of the overall elderly population.
In fact, the majority of elderly people are relatively healthy, functionally competent, independent, have family and friends, and live
in ordinary middle-class and working-class communities, neighborhoods, and dwellings. In addition, their present residential
settings do not depart greatly in type or quality from those they
lived in most of their adult lives. Nonetheless the majority of gerontologists concentrated their research on this minority elderly
population. The present investigation thus encountered the para-
dox of studying the majority elderly population while deviating
from the mainstream of research on the aged. This situation raised
a set of theoretical, methodological, policy, and personal issues,
which collectively are referred to as the *scholar's dilemma* (chapter 2).

The discussion of the scholar's dilemma points to the fact that
an elderly population's attributes and place of residence together
can greatly influence the observed impact that an environment has
on an elderly population's well-being. It underlies the importance
of establishing as unambiguously as possible the extent to which
the attributes of an elderly population and its setting under investigation are comparable to those found in other studies. Early
in this book, analyses are undertaken that enable the reader to
judge the generalizability or external validity of the reported empirical findings (chapter 3).

Conceptualization of an Environment's Components and Properties

The selection of a setting and a population is only one of several
ways by which the researcher can profoundly influence a study's
empirical findings. For a place the size of an urban community,
there is an almost unlimited array of alternative languages by
which to describe the form and functioning of an environment's
contents. A diverse group of researchers and practitioners consisting of geographers, social workers, psychologists, architects, rec-

reationists, planners, urbanologists, sociologists, and anthropologists have produced a very large number of taxonomies of an environment's components and properties. Inevitably, any designation of an environment for the purpose of empirical investigation depicts only a selected and limited slice of a far more complex objective reality. This limited portrayal becomes the environment of the researcher because it so strongly reflects his or her scientific and personal values, biases, perceptions, and operational constraints.

Earlier this author criticized gerontological research because of its artificially fragmented depictions of the old person's everyday environment (Golant 1979b), that is, of its failure to encompass the "holistic, many overlapping contexts" (Yarrow 1963:205) of the environments occupied and utilized by old people. Researchers, for example, sometimes focused only on the physical aspects of a dwelling while ignoring its neighborhood social situation, or they considered the suitability of the dwelling but not its community context. When the environment for this research investigation was constructed, the intent was to avoid the fragmentation of earlier studies. The environment was to encompass a wide range of natural, human-made, and social phenomena with which old people were likely to transact in the course of living in an urban community. Additionally, the environment was categorized into three broad types of places or existential spaces previously found to influence old people's well-being: community, neighborhoods, and dwellings (chapter 4).

Conceptualization of Environmental Impact

The researcher seeking to describe or formulate how an environment affects the well-being of its residents can choose from at least five different conceptual approaches (see Nydegger 1977; Lawton 1977b). Further alternatives may be produced using various analytical combinations of these approaches (see chapter 4).

One approach depends primarily on objective indicators of an environment's qualities. The nature and degree of environmental effects usually depends on some social institution or organization defining desirable or acceptable objective standards of quality. Environmental impact represents an objectively defined measure of an environment's deviation from such norms as ascertained by an outside "expert." The actual impact this discrepancy has on an individual or a population is inferred indirectly.

A second approach relies on one or more of an individual's "inner" or intrapsychic states as an indicator of environmental impact. These intrapsychic states describe the person's attitudes or feelings about himself as measured by mood, depression, self-concept, continuity of self, sense of helplessness, morale, or life satisfaction. It is presumed that an individual's environmental context influences the formation, reinforcement, or change of these self-attitudes or self-feelings.

A third approach focuses on an individual's physical and psychophysiological symptoms. These are indicated by the person's judgments or feelings about his physical health or physiological functioning, such as self-reports of fatigue, headaches, poor appetite, or poor health. When these symptoms are viewed as impact measures, it is presumed that the individual's environmental context impinges on these feelings or judgments. A variant of this approach uses objective indicators of a person's mental and physical functioning (such as physicians' ratings).

A fourth approach concentrates on the degree of fit that exists between individuals and their environments. An individual is conceptualized as having demands or needs, and the environment as having resources to meet them. Environmental impact assessments then depend on the degree of congruence between these demands and supplies (see chapter 4).

Environmental impact as formulated in this study (chapter 4) clearly differs from these four approaches, although it has some similarities to the fourth approach. Impact is not defined simply on the basis of the deviating properties of an external preperceptual event or object nor solely on an individual's physical or mental states, but on the interaction of the two. Impact is contingent upon an individual's subjective accounts of what it is like to live in a place perceived to have certain qualities or properties. An individual's expressions of grief, excitement, difficulty, fatigue, satisfaction, pride, fear, likes, dislikes, and plans for moving behavior are examples. More formally, environmental impact refers to the likelihood of individuals cognitively associating certain outcomes or consequences with their subjectively interpreted environmental transactions (or information). Examples include the fear linked with a possible home break-in, the fatigue linked with walking long distances, or the satisfaction linked with knowing that services are available. Such subjective outcomes and their varying likelihoods of occurrence constitute the *dynamic properties* of an individual's environmental experiences. Thus, the differential impact of an environment is exemplified by the unequal likelihood that old persons feel lonely in their dwellings, know about (are aware of) a particular service, enjoy the social composition of their neighborhood, feel proud of their house, perceive the buildings on their street as attractive, fear walking in their neighborhood, dislike their neighbors, believe they need social services, feel satisfied with their community, feel capable of walking long distances, and so on.

As was true when the components and properties of the residential environment were constructed, the researcher is confronted with a literature offering a vast number of ways to conceptualize the environmental outcomes experienced by an individual. For this study, their selection was based on eclectic criteria. A broad sampling of both beneficial and harmful environmental outcomes were conceptualized and measured, drawing from a very diverse, yet representative set of outcome classifications (chapter 4).

Conceptualization of Individual Differences

A theoretical model of individual differences was constructed to explain, in part, the variable impact of a residential environment or human settlement on its elderly occupants (chapter 5). Its contents and organization were guided by the interactionist's position (as interpreted by Bowers 1973) that an environment can be viewed as a function of an individual in two senses.

In the first sense, the environment is a function of the individual, because persons vary as to how they *know* their environment. That is, individuals differ according to how they perceive, interpret, structure, and evaluate information from their environment. Seven mental and behavioral states of the individual were conceptualized to explain why old people do not similarly know their environment and thus are unlikely to have the same environmental experiences. It was proposed that individuals differ as to their awareness of environmental opportunities and constraints; their salient needs—as manifested by their demands of the environment; the amounts of benefits or harms they associate with their environmental demands; the expectations and aspirations they have for achieving their demands; their overall feelings of congruence with their environment; their abilities and motives for remembering earlier environmental experiences; and their abilities or competence to satisfy their needs or achieve their goals. Three sets of individual variables were constructed from which it was possible to infer the presence of these states. These variables also allowed inferences about whether the observed individual differences were likely to have existed throughout adulthood or only in old age (chapter 6).

The environment is considered to be a function of the individual in a second sense. As a result of their variable activity and residential behaviors—termed *behavioral relationships*—individuals select, modify, and maintain different spatial and temporal contexts in which to satisfy their everyday needs and goals. Individuals vary as to how long they live in their dwellings, neighborhoods, or communities; as to what parts or components of their environment—such as its places, districts, streets, facilities, stores, establishments—they actually visit, use, and temporarily occupy; and as to the frequency or regularity with which they engage in such behaviors. The important result is that individuals, although *occupying* the same environment are not being *exposed* to the same environment. Because they do not transact with the same envi-

ronmental content, they do not have the same potential for satisfying (or not satisfying) their needs, leading in turn to their experiencing very different outcomes or consequences. This
interindividual variability of behavioral relationships also implies variable motivations and constraints associated with their
initiation. For instance, some decisions to remain in the same residence reflect the absence of choice; some old people rarely leave
their dwellings because they enjoy solitude; and some old people
are active because they seek novelty and excitement. The result is
that individuals can differ considerably as to how they perceive
and interpret the consequences and outcomes of their behavioral
relationships. Thus, the very same pattern of environmental activities can be interpreted positively by some individuals, but
negatively by others. Two sets of individual variables were constructed to describe the activities and residential behaviors of old
people (chapter 7).

Empirical Investigations

Two major sets of empirical analyses are summarized in this
book. The first provides a descriptive account of the residential
environment's variable impact, examining the likelihood that old
people have environmental experiences with similar content and
consequences. These analyses specifically consider the extent to
which particular experiences lead old people to express preferences and plans to relocate from their present dwellings. These
environmental experiences are examined in three distinctive territorial contexts, the community, neighborhood, and dwelling
(chapter 8), and in response to both the physical (chapter 9) and
social (chapter 10) qualities of the residential setting.

The second set of empirical analyses seeks to explain this variable environmental impact. The proposed individual differences
distinguishing old people according to how they know and behave in their environment are assessed as possible influences
(chapters 8, 9, and 10).

Toward Improved Understanding

The overall purpose of this book is to inform and enlighten its readers about a subject that up to now has received inadequate attention. It differs from other treatments of old age in its concern for how the qualities of a human settlement impinge on older people's well-being, its interest in studying these effects from the point of view of old people themselves, its strong emphasis on identifying the differences that exist among old people, and its focus on the mainstream American elderly population who occupy ordinary houses and apartments in average working- and middle-class places. Compared with other research efforts, much more attention is also given to the theoretical and methodological foundations on which the empirical investigation is built. In this regard, a greater effort is made to share with the reader some of the difficult conceptual and operational decisions confronted by the researcher.

Like most of the literature on old age, the book's primary motivation is to elucidate the nature and problems of aging and old age. However, unlike many other efforts that have limited their investigation to elderly persons, it continually questions whether the individual-environment relationships discovered are really a product of old age or simply a reflection of individual differences typically found among younger populations. Like other research on old age, its findings also have implications for the formulation of public policies and planning strategies—though this is not its major purpose. However, unlike some others, care is taken to warn of the dangers of oversimplified and indiscriminate interpretations of its research findings for practical applications.

Chapter Two

Selecting a Population and Setting: The Scholar's Dilemma

The empirical investigation reported in this book was carried out in Evanston, Illinois, a small urban middle-class community just north of Chicago. Its focus on a relatively healthy and independent population of elderly (aged 60 years and older) who live in an ordinary, unplanned community was a departure from most previous research on the residential environments of old people. Most earlier studies had restricted their focus to the minority segments of the elderly population. Studied were the poor, the sick, the least vigorous, the isolated, and the wealthy populations of elderly who occupied relatively unique social and physical environments, such as nursing homes, public housing projects, skid row neighborhoods, and retirement or leisure villages. These investigations had widespread applications and acceptability, and became the most usual type of gerontological inquiry into the quality of the elderly population's environment.

Unintendedly, this past emphasis has resulted in a greater justification being required to study the majority elderly population who occupy average, middle-class and working-class neighborhoods and communities across the United States. An investigation of the environmental issues relevant to this larger elderly population often requires a more formal, coherent, and rigorous rationale as to its theoretical and policy applications. Moreover, its research questions and methods are more likely to undergo careful scrutiny. This is despite the fact that much less informa-

tion about the everyday lives and environments of this mainstream elderly U.S. population and about the types and impact of
its environmental transactions are available.

This somewhat topsy-turvy state of affairs results in what this
chapter identifies as the "scholar's dilemma," referring to the intellectual and practical challenges of presently undertaking research on the majority elderly population in the United States. This
discussion is followed by a description of the source of the "problem," namely, the research site and population on which the empirical investigations are based. The chapter concludes with a brief
review of the methods and survey instruments used to collect the
data for these investigations.

The Scholar's Dilemma

Previous Research Emphases

Gerontologists, especially in the late 1960s and 1970s, demonstrated a considerable amount of analytical interest in the physical and social environments occupied by old people. Researchers
seeking to better explain or understand the aging process reeval-
uated many of their earlier theories and models in their consideration of the importance of situational and environmental variation and change.[1] In turn, planners and policy makers became
interested in the elderly population's residential environment if
only because it represented a mutable component susceptible to
improvement and modification (Yeates 1979). There is always a
risk of overgeneralizing about the population and environmental
emphasis of past research. However, generally speaking, its investigations were distinguished by the following four features.

First, many of their studied environments were specially created for or adapted to the housing needs and demands of old people. Examples included low-rent public housing for the elderly,
retirement housing, and nursing homes. The deliberate orientation of these housing environments to the older person was man-

ifested by their having one or more of the following attributes: low (below housing market) rents, an age-segregated population, a highly controlled administrative environment, special architectural and locational design features, on-site leisure or recreation-oriented facilities, and on-site food, medical, and social service facilities. The environments studied also had a limited territorial context. For instance, an investigation of how a new apartment unit in a high-rise public housing project affected individual well-being would fail to consider the potential significance of the people and services in the neighborhood or community.

Second, by virtue of their special features, only certain groups of old people were likely to select these settings as their homes or to be selected by them, that is, meet their entrance criteria. Consequently, these groups could be distinguished by life-styles (personality makeups, style of living, role emphases, etc.) and personal resources (health, finance, etc.), which tended to be consistent with their occupied residential environments. For instance, when a nursing home was studied, it was not just a particular environment but also a particular elderly population under investigation, whose members were distinguished by their more severe physical or psychological impairments. Similarly, when a retirement village was studied, more than just a specially planned social situation and material environment were under investigation. Additionally, the focus was on old people whose life-styles purposely favored an age-segregated retirement community and whose higher financial status and better health enabled them to qualify for entry. So, too, it was never just a specially designed low-rent public housing project under investigation but also an elderly population with sufficiently low incomes to qualify for occupany, and for whom public housing actually represented a viable and preferable situation.

Third, the residential environments under investigation were disproportionately dominated by elderly persons who had recently moved. The focus of much environmental research, whether intended or not, involved old people who had experienced the positive and negative behavioral and emotional adjustments usually connected with a major relocation of residence. Of frequent interest were old people who recently entered low-rent housing, retirement residences, or nursing homes. By definition, these elderly had in common their recent departure from a very familiar and long-occupied environment and their entry into a new and different one.

The residential environments studied that were not specifically designed for or oriented to elderly persons were distinguished by a fourth feature: they were, by most objective standards, noxious places to live. They included, for example, dwellings in dilapidated condition, with nonfunctioning plumbing, electrical, and heating systems, and that were rodent-infested, cramped, unsafe, and generally uncomfortable. These dwellings were often located in inner-city, service-deficient, declining, or unstable neighborhoods, often with very high crime rates. By virtue of the relatively unpleasant qualities of the buildings, it was highly probable that only select groups of elderly persons would live in them—the poor, unemployed, unmarried, black, socially isolated, or lonely.

The Population and Environmental Reality

On first glance, this past research appears to have considered a rather diverse set of environmental settings and elderly populations. Along certain dimensions of attributes, this is undoubtedly true (Golant 1980). However, in light of the housing and neighborhoods occupied by the majority of the U.S. elderly population, the characterization of this population and environmental focus as highly restricted is not unreasonable. That is to say, the environmental reality of the mainstream U.S. old population differs substantially from that portrayed in the research literature.

The majority of old people in the United States are living in unplanned, age-integrated, noninstitutionalized housing and neighborhoods that were not built with their age-specific needs or resources in mind. The elderly are mainly homeowners, rather than renters, and both groups tend to occupy older, but relatively stable, neighborhoods. Unlike younger populations, and the elderly subjects of past research, the majority of elderly people, especially homeowners, are not likely to have moved recently, but instead have spent a considerable portion of their lives in the same dwelling and in the same state. This is especially true of the elderly occupants of rural America. Although elderly persons have lower incomes than younger people, the majority do not appear to spend an extremely large proportion of their incomes on their housing rents or mortgages. Both elderly owners and renters (especially the latter) occupy housing with some structural deficiencies; however, the majority of them occupy standard (in good condition) dwellings. Large concentrations of old people still occupy central cities and rural areas, but this traditional pattern has been changing. A large and steadily increasing percentage of elderly now reside in suburban locations of metropolitan areas. Although a sizable percentage of the elderly population receive inadequate incomes, the majority of the elderly population have incomes above the poverty level and benefit from numerous discretionary programs that provide them with age-entitled discounts on a wide array of services, facilities, and programs. The majority of elderly persons are healthy; nevertheless, by age 75, they are likely to suffer from the normal functional impairments of old age. As a result, many older people permanently and periodically suffer from mobility restrictions; however, the majority are not confined to their dwellings and are usually able to carry out most of the usual activities of daily living.

The following facts lend support to the above-stated generalizations.

—In 1978 about 6 percent of the elderly population (age 65+) lived in old-age institutions, although there was about a 25 percent probability of an elderly person eventually residing in an institution sometime during his or her lifetime (U.S. Bureau of the Census 1979; Kastenbaum and Candy 1973).

—In 1977, about 700,000 elderly persons, or 3 percent of the elderly population, occupied federally subsidized (U.S. Department of Housing and Urban Development) rental housing (Welfeld and Struyk 1979).

—In 1974, about 4 percent of the U.S. elderly population occupied some type of retirement residence, including retirement hotels, retirement villages, mobile home parks, congregate housing facilities, and retirement apartment complexes (Lawton 1980; Golant 1980; Mangum 1982).

—In 1978, about 72 percent of households headed by older persons occupied their own homes (U.S. Bureau of the Census 1979). Of this homeowner group, 84 percent did not have any mortgage debts; 38 percent of elderly renters and 30 percent of elderly homeowners with mortgage debts spent more than 35 percent of their incomes on housing expenses (Struyk and Soldo 1980:58–59).

—During the period 1965 to 1970, about 27 percent of elderly-headed households moved from one residence to another. In 1970, 58 percent of elderly-headed households had lived in their present dwelling for more than 10 years (U.S. Bureau of the Census 1973).

—In 1977, 6 percent of U.S. elderly renters and 3 percent of elderly homeowners lacked complete plumbing facilities; 5 percent of elderly renters and 2 percent of elderly homeowners had incomplete kitchen facilities; 2 percent of elderly renters and 0.03 percent of elderly homeowners had unusable or unreliable heating facilities during the previous winter months; 6 percent of elderly homeowners and 2 percent of elderly renters had two or more maintenance deficiencies (for example, leaking roofs, wall holes or cracks, floor holes, areas with broken plaster and peeling paint); and 8 percent of elderly renters and 9 percent of elderly homeowners had evidence of rats or mice. Certain subgroups of older people, especially blacks and the poor, were far more likely to have housing deficiencies than others; and the rural elderly were more likely than the urban elderly to live in poor-quality housing. In general, both since World War II and during the very recent period of 1974 to 1976, elderly households experienced an improvement in their housing quality (Struyk and Soldo 1980).

—A relatively small percentage of elderly persons report the existence of bothersome conditions in their neighborhoods. Most complaints focus on neighborhood street noise and crime. Less frequently cited problems include the existence of excessive amounts of traffic, trash, litter, and junk. In all, 25 to 30 percent of renters rate their neighborhood as "fair" or "poor" whereas 12 to 13 percent of homeowners give such ratings (Struyk and Soldo 1980:54).

—In 1977, within U.S. metropolitan areas (SMSAs) a larger percentage of the elderly population lived outside of central cities in the suburbs or in small, low-density communities surrounding the suburbs (see table 2.1). The growth of the elderly population has been greatest in these suburban or fringe areas. Within suburban areas, the greatest growth has occurred in the oldest neighborhoods, primarily as a result of middle-aged cohorts aging in place (Golant 1980). In nonmetropolitan areas the greatest growth of the elderly population occurred in those counties containing at least one place with more than 25,000 people (table 2.1). Larger growth rates also were experienced by counties that only re-

Table 2.1. Size, Distribution, Growth, and Concentration of Noninstitutionalized Total Population and Population Aged 65 and Older in Central Cities, Suburbs, and Nonmetropolitan Areas, 1970 and 1977

Residential Category	1970 Number (in 1000)	1970 Percent[a]	1977 Number (in 1000)	1977 Percent[a]	Percent Change 1970–1977
		Total Population			
Total United States	199,819	100.0	212,566	100.0	6.4
Metropolitan Areas	137,058	68.6 (100.0)	143,107	67.3 (100.0)	4.4
Central Cities	62,876	31.5 (45.9)	59,993	28.2 (41.9)	−4.6
Suburbs	74,182	37.1 (54.1)	83,114	39.1 (58.1)	12.0
Nonmetropolitan Areas	62,761	31.4	69,459	32.7	10.7
In counties with:					
A place of 25,000 or more	15,845	7.9	17,547	8.3	10.7
A place of 2,500 to 24,999	39,725	19.9	43,331	20.3	9.1
No place of 2,500 or more	7,191	3.6	8,582	4.0	19.3
In counties designated metropolitan since 1970	8,373	4.2	9,980	4.7	19.2
Unchanged nonmetropolitan counties	54,388	27.2	59,479	28.0	9.4

Table 2.1. *(continued)*

Residential Category	1970 Number (in 1000)	1970 Percent[a]	1977 Number (in 1000)	1977 Percent[a]	Percent Change 1970–1977
	Population Aged 65 and Older				
Total United States	19,235	100.0	22,100	100.0	14.9
Metropolitan Areas	12,344	64.2 (100.0)	13,846	62.7 (100.0)	12.2
Central Cities	6,640	34.5 (53.8)	6,842	31.0 (49.4)	3.0
Suburbs	5,704	29.7 (46.2)	7,004	31.7 (50.5)	22.8
Nonmetropolitan Areas	6,891	35.8	8,254	37.3	19.8
In counties with:					
A place of 25,000 or more	1,511	7.9	1,998	9.0	32.2
A place of 2,500 to 24,999	4,479	23.3	5,244	23.7	17.1
No place of 2,500 or more	902	4.7	1,012	4.6	12.2
In counties designated metro- politan since 1970	843	4.4	1,179	5.3	39.9
Unchanged nonmetropolitan counties	6,048	31.4	7,075	32.0	17.0
	Percent of Total Population Aged 65 and Older				
Total United States	9.6		10.4		
Metropolitan Areas	9.0		9.7		
Central Cities	10.6		11.4		
Suburbs	7.7		8.4		
Nonmetropolitan Areas	11.0		11.9		
In counties with:					
A place of 25,000 or more	9.5		11.4		
A place of 2,500 to 24,999	11.3		12.1		
No place of 2,500 or more	12.5		11.8		
In counties designated metro- politan since 1970	10.1		11.8		
Unchanged nonmetropolitan counties	11.1		11.9		

SOURCE: Bureau of the Census. "Social and Economic Characteristics of the Metropolitan and Nonmetropolitan Population, 1977 and 1970." *Current Population Reports.* Series P-23, No. 75, 1978.

NOTE: Table excludes inmates of institutions and armed forces residing in barracks. Boundaries of metropolitan area and central cities as defined in 1970.

[a] Percentages in brackets indicate the intrametropolitan distribution of the population.

cently (since 1970) were reclassified from nonmetropolitan to metropolitan areas. The largest concentrations of old people (that is, old people as a percentage of the total population) were found in central cities of SMSAs and in nonmetropolitan counties containing places with a population of between 2,500 and 25,000. Although

most of the growth of elderly populations in suburban
and nonmetropolitan (rural) areas is due to younger
population cohorts aging in place, there is a substantial
movement of elderly in-migrants to these areas (Longino
1982). In the decade 1960 to 1970, for example, U.S. central cities experienced a net migration loss of about
678,000 elderly persons (Golant, Rudzitis, and Daiches
1978).

—In 1976, 15 percent of the elderly population had income levels that put them below the poverty level.
Black elderly and those living alone or with an unrelated person were particularly likely to be below the
poverty level. Higher concentrations of the elderly poor
were found in central cities and rural nonfarm locations
(Struyk and Soldo 1980;26). There is also a smaller
though increasingly significant population of elderly in
older suburbs, who are facing old age without sufficient
resources to cope successfully with the complexities of
day-to-day living (Gutowski 1978). Because this population is usually dispersed over a wider geographic area,
its problems or needs are often less visible.

——In 1975, 14 percent of elderly men and 36 percent
of elderly women lived alone (U.S. Bureau of the Census
1976).

—In 1972, 18 percent of the elderly population who
lived alone and 15 percent of those living with a spouse
had some limitation in their mobility (National Center
for Health Statistics 1974, and Lawton 1980:67); however, 25 percent of the elderly who lived with a relative
(other than a spouse) or a nonrelative experienced some
limitations in their mobility. The comparable percentages of elderly persons whose mobility restrictions were
so severe that they were confined to their dwelling were
5 percent, 4 percent, and 9 percent, respectively.

The Rationale of Past Research

The demonstration of a discrepancy between the actual and the
portrayed status of the elderly population does not in any way
lessen the significance of past research. Its findings both ad-

vanced the scientific knowledge of environment-behavior relationships in old age and had notable impact on planning and policy pronouncements. Thus, despite the restricted population and
environmental focus of past studies, it is difficult to suggest that
other types of investigations necessarily should have had priority.
This is not a surprising conclusion if the basis for past research is
considered.

The old-age institution offered an excellent, carefully controlled quasi-laboratory setting in which to observe the manifestations of old age. Much research was required to design opti-
mum approaches for successfully caring for the chronically ill and
impaired elderly and to disentangle the effects of biological, social, and psychological processes of aging. Because the institution
constituted a radically different residential environment than
previously occupied by the old person, these research efforts also
afforded an excellent opportunity to study how relocation affected an old person's social and psychological well-being (Lieberman 1975). Independent of these theoretical issues, the quality
of the institutional environment was the object of considerable
public concern. Frequent reports by journalists and public interest groups emphasized the critical inadequacy of the medical,
nursing, and personal care found in these settings. Thus, social and
behavioral scientists had strong practical incentives for documenting the abuses of these places.

Whereas the nursing home environment was often studied to
assess the deleterious effects of relocating to a very controlled, dependent, and often inhospitable environment, the public housing
environment was studied for just the opposite reasons. Because it
offered a much improved and inexpensive housing opportunity to
old people who previously had occupied physically and socially
deficient residential settings, the public housing environment was
investigated for its positive impact on older people's well-being
and independence. Clearly, the documentation of this "improvement" (Carp 1966) was essential for advocates of government-
subsidized housing programs for the elderly. The focus on public
housing also drew attention to the substantial number of U.S. elderly who, because of their occupancy of poor quality housing,

would greatly benefit from the life-supporting and enriching attributes of these planned residential accommodations. In light of
their usually age-segregated social situations, these housing complexes also offered excellent natural settings in which to study the
effects of an age-homogeneous social environment on old people's
social behavior patterns and general well-being (Rosow 1967).

Social workers, journalists, and various public service groups,
in their different capacities, were all concerned with the pervasive negative effects of an urban way of life on certain groups of
old people. Every large city contained neighborhoods that were
virtual display cases for the social injustices found in a modern,
wealthy society. The poor and isolated elderly living in deplor-
able housing situations were obvious targets of such commentar-
ies. In the late 1960s, when social scientists were especially interested in identifying and "solving" social problems, it became
important to demonstrate by scientific research procedures the
bleak living circumstances of these minority elderly populations.
Again, a by-product of this research was the legitimization of the
arguments by critics who demanded greatly expanded housing and
service public programs to alleviate these social ills.

The interest in old people's poor housing situation was motivated by a less obvious factor. The social and behavioral sciences
had a long-standing interest in examining causal linkages between environment and individual well-being. The extremely
noxious environments occupied by some elderly persons provided
relatively clear-cut scientific support for the proposition that the
social, physical, and psychological well-being of old people could
be adversely affected by their environment or situation. Thus, this
research provided evidence—even if at times less rigorous than
desired—that adapting to old age was made more difficult when
transactions with a harmful and nonsupportive residential environment were part of the older person's daily routine.

Demographic trends also constituted a sound rationale for the
interests of past research. From 1900 on, there has been a steady
increase in the proportion of the aged 65 and older population that
is 75 years and older. It is expected that about 44 percent of the
65 and older group will be 75 and older in the year 2000, com-

pared with 38 percent in 1975 (U.S. Bureau of Census 1976). Because of its greater likelihood of severe functional impairments, this old-old group (Neugarten 1974) is more likely to demand the kinds of life-maintenance supports found in the specialized environments of the congregate housing facility and the nursing home. In light of these trends and projections, the research interest in the qualities of these environments and their impact on the well-being of their elderly occupants was justified.

The Scholar's Dilemma

The existence of a strong rationale for this past research does not eliminate its inherent limitations. There has been a failure to adequately portray the environmental experiences and behavior of the disproportionately large population of elderly who are relatively healthy, coping relatively successfully with old age, and are living in ordinary independent households. So entrenched is the orientation of gerontological research toward the minority segment of the elderly who occupy unrepresentative environments that the greater burden of research justification shifts to the investigator who chooses to study the mainstream elderly population. This is a diverse population representing a broad cross-section of income, class, racial, and ethnic groups. It occupies a wide range of age-integrated and unplanned dwellings and neighborhoods in stable, viable, middle-class and working-class communities found in cities, suburbs, and towns throughout the United States. Paradoxically, the researcher who declares an interest in studying such a representative population of elderly must confront some important intellectual issues—collectively which can be referred to as the "scholar's dilemma."

The most tangible expression of the scholar's dilemma emerges from the inevitably more "positive" findings of research focused on the majority population. Because it is not considering extremely noxious residential environments and vulnerable elderly populations, or environments with major social, psychological, and material deficiencies, this research is simply less likely to document the personal and environmental problems that sometimes afflict the elderly. As a consequence, the researcher runs the considerable risk of being accused of trying to casually dismiss the difficulties of old age in American society. Thus, the emphasis on the more positive and less dramatic aspects of aging is sometimes labeled as a form of research neglect.

Trenchant criticism is especially likely from those persons and organizations whose professional raison d'être depends on identifying and alleviating the impairments and problems of old people. The reporting of relatively positive findings can be construed as a suggestion that society is adequately meeting the needs of its old population or, worse, that many existing programs and services offered by the social welfare environment are perhaps not needed. Such research findings are likely to generate "letters to the editor" or editorial replies that emphasize the long list of old people waiting for public housing or the considerable numbers of old people who are isolated because of poor transportation, or the poor care and deficiencies found in long-term care facilities, and so on. It is hard to fault the concerns of these involved professionals. Much consensus exists regarding the inadequacies of the present social welfare environment and of the nonoptimum use of existing public resources. Moreover, in a period of limited and very competitive program funding, legitimate fears exist that any suggestion of the positive well-being of the elderly may be construed as a rationale for reducing the flow of funds to elderly-related programs. So, too, professionals who express their concern over positive findings often are daily confronting the problems of old people in their work experiences. The old population who utilize social welfare services (with the exception of such age-entitlement services as Social Security and Medicare) is a highly select group representing a small fraction of the elderly population at large. However, the continual exposure to these needy elderly cannot help but have a conditioning effect on professionals and staff. It is understandable that they should come to believe that the minority elderly persons they see everyday are, in fact, representative of the majority of the U.S. elderly. Exceptions to such generalizations often become very personal in nature: "Of course,

my parents or my relatives are not typical of the old people I usually see . . ."

A second and less obvious expression of the scholar's dilemma
is the greater difficulty of drawing unequivocal conclusions about
environmental impact from the study of "average" elderly populations and their environments. In contrast, the earlier-referred-
to investigations of extremely noxious housing facilitated generalizations about an environment's negative impact. So too, studies of old people as recent occupants of unfamiliar and different
dwelling environments—whether better or worse than their previous residences—were also more likely to evoke more extreme
behavioral and experiential responses. From a methodological
perspective, few gerontological researchers would deny the appealing neatness of experimental designs that were carried out in
the relatively self-contained environments of nursing homes or new
public housing projects occupied by "captured" populations of elderly. Such conceptual and methodological clarity is less likely to
characterize research on the mainstream elderly population. The
task of defining the boundaries and content of the environment is
more difficult. The abstracting of environment-behavior concepts
and relationships is less obvious. Sampling frames and designs are
necessarily more tentative in natural environmental settings, and
interview completion rates are likely to be lower on the average.
In turn, judgments as to the internal and external validity of
methods and findings are more equivocal.

A final set of issues emerging from the scholar's dilemma involves the impact that research findings have on the public at large,
the communication media, and old people themselves. As already
shown, gerontological research is effective in identifying and ex-
posing the environmental abuses, the wretched conditions, and
social injustices suffered by many of today's elderly population.
To the extent that this education of the public and the media has
led to improved living environments and social conditions (for example, through their influence on public policies), the benefits of
this research are obviously considerable. In contrast, the utility of
research focused on a relatively healthy and independent elderly
population may be questioned.

However, there is an alternative interpretation. It can be argued that important benefits also result from the dissemination of more positive research findings. This conclusion derives from findings of a well-designed, well-executed, and frequently quoted national survey that found "beyond a doubt . . . the image of older people held by the public at large is a distorted one tending to be negative and possibly damaging" and that the "media, with coverage of the elderly poor, the elderly sick, the elderly institutionalized and the elderly unemployed or retired, may be protecting and reinforcing of the distorted stereotypes of the elderly and the myths of old age" (Louis Harris and Associates 1975:193). Certainly, a multitude of factors underlie the image of the elderly held by the public and communicated by the media. It is not unreasonable to propose, however, that researchers of the aged have contributed to these images. Thus, the restricted emphasis of gerontological research could convey a one-sided and excessively negative portrayal of the status of the elderly in the United States (for example, Butler 1975).

A concern for the researcher's impact, in this instance, is especially urgent because there exists a theoretical basis for expecting a relationship between the public and mass media's negative portrayal of the elderly, on the one hand, and the old person's negative self-image and lower psychological well-being, on the other. An individual's assessment of his or her status and achievements is undoubtedly a personal affair. However, for some individuals, this evaluation will more likely be influenced by other persons and social institutions. Kuypers and Bengston argue, for example, "that an elderly individual's sense of self, his ability to mediate between self and society, and his orientation to competence are related to the kinds of social labelling and valuing he experiences in aging" (1973:47). Because of the ambiguities of what constitutes successful aging in American society and because old people may have fewer primary reference groups with whom to discuss and reinforce the favorable aspects of growing old, they are more likely to be susceptible and vulnerable to the opinions of the mass media. Consequently, the dissemination of a negative and unrepresentative image of old age increases the probability of corresponding negative belief acceptance by old people. Theoretical propositions from communications research suggest in fact that old people who are more often dependent on the mass media are also those likely to be the most vulnerable, lonely, and socially isolated (Atkin 1976).

The implications of the above reasoning are clear. The preoccupation of research on the injustices and problems of older people in American society is obviously based on legitimate and needed rationales. However, the danger exists, even though the causal linkages are only tentative, that the persistent reporting of such research findings will contribute to the negative stereotypes of old age communicated by the mass media and held by the public at large, which, in turn, will contribute to the negative images old people hold about themselves.

The issues that constitute the scholar's dilemma deserve far more extensive and rigorous analysis than space allows here. However, the purpose for their introduction is modest: to sensitize the reader to the rationale and broader implications of the environmental and population focus of this book. These issues go beyond the inherent strengths and weaknesses of problem formulation and methodology. There is no simple right and wrong or appropriate and inappropriate when judging an environmental focus. Every emphasis has its own virtues. Gaps in knowledge and understanding do emerge, however, when one focus is excluded or neglected at the expense of the other. It is for this reason that the issues of the scholar's dilemma have been raised: to suggest an imbalance of research emphasis that needs redressing. Important insights will be lost if research does not focus on the majority elderly population who are living in average, everyday environments found throughout the United States. The research site of this study—Evanston, Illinois—was selected because of the need to shift the environmental emphasis of past research.

Research Site of Study

The Personality of a Community

Evanston, a city of about 80,000 people, is located on the shore of Lake Michigan about 13 miles north of downtown Chicago. Although it shares its southern boundary with the northern limits of Chicago, Evanston is often referred to as an older suburban middle-class community set among a very wealthy group of suburbs. However, several investigations of the overall social, economic, and political fabric of Evanston have emphasized the difficulty of stereotyping the community as either a city or a suburb. For this reason it is sometimes identified as a schizophrenic city, its personality split between suburb and city (Northwestern University 1972:45).

By national standards, Evanston must be considered an old and aging community. In 1970, just over 14 percent of its population was older than age 65 and 19 percent older than 60; in 1950, the figures were 10 percent and 15 percent, respectively.

As a middle-class suburb, Evanston's population had a higher socioeconomic status than the U.S. population. The median income levels of its families and its unrelated individuals were higher; a higher percentage of its population was in the upper-income brackets; and a higher percentage of its population was employed in upper-status occupations and had achieved higher educational levels. The middle-class status of Evanston population was also reflected in its housing. A national comparison showed that Evanston's dwellings had considerably higher median values and rents. Although, for a suburb, Evanston's housing stock is quite old (the majority of its dwelling units were built before World War II), it has, in large part, been carefully maintained and progressively upgraded.

Although primarily a middle-class suburb, Evanston contains population groups and housing that are inconsistent with the usual suburban image. A relatively high percentage of its population lives alone, made up of higher than average percentages of widowed and never-married persons. Evanston is occupied by a sizable black population that has grown considerably in the past decade (1960–1970). It is also the home of larger than average concentrations of foreign-born persons. Although representing a minority of the population, a substantial percentage of persons in Evanston have income below the poverty level and formal education not beyond elementary school. Evanston's housing also does not conform neatly to a suburban image. Because of its older housing stock, a sub-

stantial percentage of its dwellings have minor structural deficiencies. Compared with the U.S. housing stock, a relatively low
percentage of its dwelling units are owner-occupied, and there is
a relatively high incidence of condominiums and larger apartment buildings. In addition, a relatively large number of its housing units are found in group quarters, that is, in retirement hotels
and student dormitories.

Other aspects of Evanston defy the usual suburban stereotypes.
The community contains, for example, a complete range of social
services and retail and commercial facilities. Its small geographic
size and the availability of bus transit make its downtown district
accessible in less than 20 minutes from most of its neighborhoods. A commuter train service also links Evanston to downtown Chicago, and other bus lines connect with suburban transit
systems. With the location of a large, nationally renowned private
university (Northwestern University) within its boundaries, Evanston also receives the benefits of various cultural and educational activities.

Despite its diversity, Evanston does not contain the range of
neighborhoods found in a large city or metropolitan area. For example, one does not find large concentrations of run-down, deteriorated, or abandoned housing and the accompanying pockets of
extreme population poverty and social deviance. At the other end
of the spectrum, one does not find the extreme homogeneity of
house type and land use or the continuous low-density sprawling
suburban tract housing.

Evanston's Elderly Population and Its Housing:
National Contrasts

Consistent with the middle-class status of its community, Evanston's elderly population possesses a higher socioeconomic status than the elderly nationwide. Evanston's aged 65 and older
residents have higher educational and income levels, are more
likely to be in the labor force, and in upper-status occupations.
Although Evanston's elderly are less likely to own their homes,

consistent with their higher economic status, they are more likely to occupy higher valued dwellings and, on the average, pay higher rents. The higher than average socioeconomic status of Evanston's elderly should not be interpreted as an indication of the absence of poverty, poor education, low-status occupations, or inexpensive housing arrangements. Substantial percentages (from 16 to 36 percent) of Evanston's elderly population have very low incomes, little formal education, blue collar jobs, and occupy low-priced housing.

National comparisons also show that Evanston's elderly are more likely to be female, to have never married, and to be living alone. Ethnic and racial contrasts are also notable, and higher than national percentages of Evanston's elderly are black and of foreign heritage (i.e., foreign born or parent(s) foreign born).

Population Universe, Sample, and Data Source

The Population Universe

The focus of the research investigation reported in this book is on persons aged 60 and older occupying independent households in unplanned, age-integrated housing in the Evanston community. It excluded old people who occupied retirement residences, public housing, and old age institutions.

Sampling Design

Eligible respondents (in population universe) were identified by the administering of a telephone screening instrument to a systematic random sample of the Evanston community's population. It was determined that the Evanston community had unique telephone prefixes and that only 5 percent of the households had unlisted or unpublished numbers. A high proportion of these were found in group quarters (nursing homes, retirement residences, and university dormitories) that had been excluded from the study's universe. The 1977 Haines reverse telephone-address directory (at the time, just recently issued) was used as the sampling frame.[2] A systematic random sample of 2,656 telephone numbers was selected from the estimated 25,895 households with telephones. The probability of selection was .1026. The administration of a telephone screening instrument to this sample yielded 608 eligible respondents (a 79.2 percent completion rate).[3] The screening instrument consisted of four questions and averaged less than three minutes to complete. They were administered during the first two

Table 2.2. Disposition of Eligible Sample

	Sample	
Category	N	%
Completed interviews	400	66
Refusals[a]	173	28
Non-contacts[b]	5	1
Unavailable[c]	30	5
Total Eligible	608	100

[a] Eligible respondents who refused to be interviewed.
[b] Eligible respondents could not be reached at their address.
[c] In households with both eligible and noneligible respondents, the eligible respondent was unavailable.

weeks of October 1977. In implementing the telephone screening sampling procedure, there was a minimum of ten callbacks.

An attempt was made to administer personal interviews in the homes of each of the 608 eligible respondents. There was a minimum of five attempts to make contact and two attempts were made to administer the personal interview to respondents who initially refused to be interviewed. When there were more than two eligible persons in the same household, the person who initially received the interviewer was interviewed. If the eligible respondent(s) in the household refused to be interviewed, was unavailable, or could not be reached, no substitution was made.[4] A total of 400 personal interviews were completed, representing about 6 percent of Evanston's elderly-occupied households. The disposition of the eligible sample is shown in table 2.2.

Data Source

Professional interviewers administered face-to-face structured interviews (over 90 percent of the questions were close-ended) to each of the 400 elderly persons in the sample. Elderly persons required an average of 90 minutes to respond to all the questions. The interviews were administered from October 1977 to January 1978. Two pretests of the interview schedule were earlier administered to 30 and 16 elderly respondents, respectively (not included in final sample), during the months of June and August 1977.[5]

Chapter Three

Representativeness of Research Site

The previous chapter indicated that a study's findings are shaped by the objective qualities of the research site and that research sites differ in their objective qualities. When observed patterns and their proposed underlying processes are dependent on the studied environment or situation, a scientific rationale exists for establishing the correspondence between environments (Patterson 1977; Bowers 1973). The external validity of a study's empirical findings depends on how generalizable they are to other environmental settings and their occupied populations (Campbell and Stanley 1963; Fishbein and Ajzen 1975).

Such an evaluation requires more complex environmental comparisons than those in the previous chapter in which simple statistical profiles of the Evanston community were compared with U.S. indicators. The successful completion of this task requires the conceptualization of an objective environment with properties that facilitate multivariate comparisons with other objectively defined environments.

This chapter offers a conceptualization of the Evanston community's environment that includes properties derived from three sources: the researcher's values, the sociocultural system, and the local settlement conditions. To investigate the generalizability or applicability of findings from the Evanston community to other places, three different sets of empirical analyses were carried out. The first examined how the objective quality of life in the Evanston community compared with that in other local city, suburban, and rural environments; the second considered how the internal spatial structure of Evanston's environment compared with that of other urban communities; and the third considered how the neighborhood environments in Evanston occupied predominantly by old people compared with those in other residential communities.

Functionally Relevant Ecological Environment

A Conceptualization of the Environment

To start, it is necessary to identify one of the two principal ways in which the environment is conceptualized in this book. The term *ecological environment* refers to a molar objective environment or situation that has an empirical reality, independent of thinking and perceiving human beings, and that is capable of being described in rational, detached terms by a scientific observer. The adjective, *ecological,* emphasizes that this objective environment is typically occupied by people—it is literally the home of people. The description of the ecological environment as *functionally relevant* emphasizes that its objects and events and their properties have the *potential* of evoking, reinforcing, or modifying an individual's or population's behavior or experiences (see chapter 4). Several social and behavioral scientists have similarly conceptualized the environment, although they have not used the same terminology (Chein 1954; Craik 1970; Perin 1970). In practice, the functionally relevant ecological environment—henceforth referred to simply as the *environment* or objective environment—will coincide with the spatial and temporal boundaries of the research investigation's site.

Derivation of Objective Environment's Properties

The properties of the environment are derived from three sources: the researcher's values; the sociocultural system; and the local settlement conditions.

The Researcher's Values

Considerable discretion for the portrayal and measurement of the environment rests with the researcher who selects the parts and properties to be studied and abstracts the concepts and relationships to be analyzed. In the final analysis, the most important determinant of an environment's functional relevance is the values of the researcher. He decides to study nursing homes or ordinary communities, to study its aesthetic qualities or eating facilities, to study attributes denoting beauty as opposed to efficiency, to evaluate unidirectional or reciprocal relationships, and so on. Certainly, in considerable part the values of the researcher reflect the theoretical viewpoints and philosophical thinking that dominate accepted scientific paradigms. However, such paradigms are susceptible to criticism and modification, and the opportunity exists for the researcher to cast his own interpretation on their contents. Because of the researcher's own creativity, biases, values, or misjudgments, the specification of an environment's properties may become a very idiosyncratic operation. For this reason, it is essential to reveal the motives and limitations of the researcher's analytical decisions. This was a rationale for the previous chapter's focus on the factors leading to the selection of the Evanston community as a research site.

The Sociocultural System and Local Settlement Conditions of the Environment

The properties of an environment are derived from two other sources: its sociocultural system and its local settlement conditions. These are rather crude and gross categories when one judges the conceptual criteria defining their content and organization, but they adequately summarize the major sources of variation among environments.

The *sociocultural system* comprises an extended geographic space defined at a particular point or period in time, with boundaries that usually enclose a country or politically defined territory. It includes institutions and organizations that assume forms and functions according to agreed upon social, political, economic, and natural goals, the manifestations of which are a recognizable and coherent material culture—settlements, buildings, art forms, landscapes, etc. It is occupied by a population distinguished by its relatively uniform total way of life. These occupants share common symbols and language and utilize similar standards of perceiving and predicting; and their actions are guided by similar rules, laws, and morals. They share similar life goals, purposes, and preferences and employ similar adaptive strategies for surviving and enhancing the quality of their lives.

The focus on a community in midwestern United States in the late 1970s precludes from consideration the sociocultural diversity of the countries of the world and of the United States' historical past. Also precluded from analysis are the numerous geographic pockets of subcultural diversity found within the country. Consequently, the contemporary community focus of this study considerably restricts the range of environmental variation and stringently confines the functional relevance of the research environment.

Within the same sociocultural system, environments will be distinguished by their *local settlement conditions*. Drawing on the conceptual perspective of Doxiadis (1968), settlement or ekistic units include rooms, dwellings, dwelling groups, neighborhoods, villages, rural areas, towns, cities, suburbs, metropolises, conurbations, and regions. The denotation of an environment *qua* human settlement enables an especially broad characterization of its features. These may include such aspects as its population composition, activities, social values, organizations, institutions, and its adapted spaces—a term coined by Lynch and Rodwin (1958) to refer to "any part of the environment which has been modified by man to facilitate his activities, whether by enclosure, improvement of the floor, manipulation of the shape, provision of fixed equipment, etc."

Though the Evanston community can be identified unequivocably as part of the contemporary U.S. sociocultural system, such ease of assignment is less apparent when characterizing Evanston as a human settlement. While the previous chapter concluded that

Evanston is a middle-class community, it left ambiguous its city-suburban orientation, its overall quality of life, and the spatial organization and attributes of its residential areas and other adapted spaces. The task of the rest of this chapter is to specify how the Evanston community *qua* human settlement differs from other settlement areas.[1] These analyses, in turn, will facilitate assessments of the generalizability and applicability of the study's empirical findings to other environmental research settings.

The Relative Quality of Life in the Evanston Community

In establishing a conceptual and methodological basis to evaluate the representativeness of a settlement's objective quality of life, two major tasks were defined: (1) to select a set of geographic reference zones against which Evanston's quality of life could be compared; and (2) to identify and measure a set of quality of life indicators describing the community and the defined place referents.

Constructing a Set of Geographic Reference Zones

The first task, to define a set of geographic reference zones that would provide a situational context with which to compare a community's quality of life, was the most difficult, if only because adequate guidelines were largely unavailable. Merely measuring the objective quality of life of the Evanston community was insufficient, because it would not provide comparisons with a representative set of other communities or areas. A comparison of Evanston's quality of life with that of its neighboring communities, although of some local pragmatic value, would not be based on any conceptual framework, nor would it result in a set of empirical findings with generalized meaning outside the immediate research context. A comparative analysis of a national sample of U.S. communities, although preferable, would represent a major investigation in itself and was precluded by time and money considerations. The compromise was to define a set of geographic reference zones within the boundaries of the Standard Metropolitan Statistical Area (SMSA)—i.e., metropolitan region—in which Evanston is located.[2]

Two considerations influenced the decision: (1) A majority of the population in the United States lives either in SMSAs or within commuting distance of their boundaries (Berry and Gillard 1976); therefore, it was feasible that other community studies could utilize the reported methodology. (2) The SMSA contains communities that are representative of a wide range of U.S. environmental settings.[3]

The most frequent intra-SMSA geographic comparisons are those between the central city and the remaining area of the SMSA, variously referred to as its suburbs, fringe, or balance. However, this is not only a crude areal classification but it also has little theoretical basis.[4] Although "city" and "suburb" are potentially useful labels to differentiate residential environments, unless carefully defined, any quality of life generalizations will be ambiguous. In addition, the SMSA typically consists of some territory and people more accurately described as "rural" than "suburban." To overcome these potential difficulties, it was necessary to construct a more rigorously defined continuum of city-suburban-rural zones within the SMSA. If this task was completed successfully, other community studies would have a standard for constructing a comparable set of geographic spatial referents.

The following guidelines were followed to divide the SMSA into a set of geographic reference zones: (1) the zones should consist of *spatial units* for which objective quality of life data are readily available without considerable expense or time required for extraction or recording; (2) the spatial units should be described by attributes that enable their differentiation along a city-suburban-rural continuum; (3) these attribute measures should have conceptual significance beyond the locational context of the particular SMSA; and (4) the set of *zones* constructed from these spatial units should have measures of city-suburban-rural attributes that vary along a roughly linear scale.

The most extensive and readily accessible data sets that describe communities and their populations in the SMSA are available for central city and county spatial units. The Chicago SMSA consists of the central city (city of Chicago) and six counties (Suburban Cook,[5] Dupage, Lake, Kane, Will, and McHenry) (see figure 3.1). To define a city-suburban-rural dimension along which to categorize these spatial units, four sets of attributes were selected: size and density, land use, economic base, and functional linkages.

The rationale behind their selection is outlined in detail elsewhere (Golant and McCutcheon 1980). So, too, is a description of the analysis that enabled four geographic reference zones, the central city, and the inner, middle, and outer suburbs, to be distinguished. The attributes of these four zones defined a city-suburban-rural unidimensional scale. That is, moving from the central city to the outer suburbs, the number of urban places decrease; the built-up residential land uses give way to rural, agricultural, and vacant land uses; the people are increasingly likely to be employed in primary industries; the population densities decline; and the functional (journey to work) ties to the central city decline. For convenience in the following descriptions, the outer suburbs zone will be identified as part of the "suburban" continuum even though several of its structural attributes indicate it is more rural in character.

Selecting and Measuring a Set of Quality-of-Life Indicators

Eleven general categories of indicators were identified in order to depict the objective quality of life in the Evanston community and the four geographic reference zones. Within these 11 categories, 92 specific quality-of-life indicator variables were selected.

The indicators were formulated such that a high numerical value implied a less desirable quality of life, whereas a low numerical value implied a more desirable quality of life. It was assumed that a place with a more desirable quality of life had the following characteristics: (1) it was economically stronger (lower unemployment, more diverse economic base, lower short- and long-term

Figure 3.1. Central City and Suburban Zones in Chicago Metropolitan Area

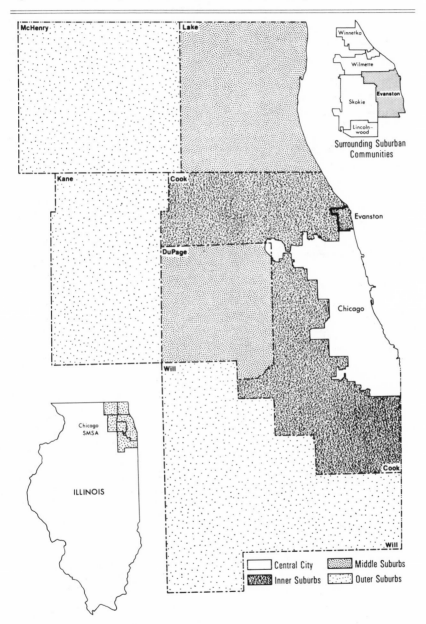

debt); (2) it had a younger, more physically intact housing stock with fewer vacancies; (3) its dwellings were less crowded; (4) it had more services available (medical, retail, repair, recreation, municipal, transit); (5) it was safer (lower crime rate, fewer traffic accidents); (6) it was more likely to have experienced recent growth (population, retail, manufacturing); (7) it was occupied by a population of higher economic status; (8) its population had a higher educational and professional status; (9) it had greater incidence of intact and married families and households; (10) its population was in better physical health (lower age-specific death rates); and (11) its population was in better mental health (lower suicide rate, lower mental health admissions).

The number of indicators selected to measure each quality-of-life category reflected both data availability and category complexity. Each indicator variable describing Evanston and the four

Figure 3.2. Graphed Mean Standard Score Measures of Objective Quality of Life Categories

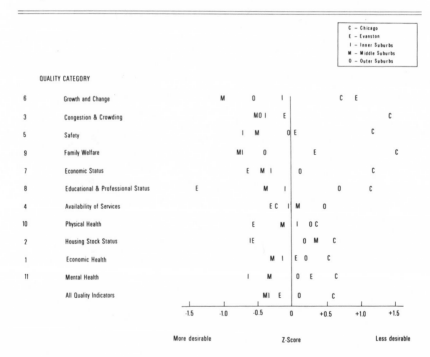

geographic reference zones was transformed into standard (Z) scores. Because simple *a priori* weighting guidelines were not available, each quality-of-life category was given equal statistical weight by averaging the standard scores of the indicators within each quality-of-life category. This resulted in 11 quality-of-life (mean standard scores) measures describing each of the four geographic reference zones and Evanston (figure 3.2).

Simplified Structure of 11 Quality-of-Life Measures

Although conceptually distinct and worthy of separate attention, the quality-of-life categories nevertheless will be statistically related. A geographic zone that scores high on one of the 11 average quality-of-life measures also is likely to score high on others. To shed greater light on these associations, two complementary multivariate techniques were used: cluster analysis (diameter method—Anderberg 1973) and Guttmans-Lingoes smallest space analysis (Lingoes 1972). Both use a matrix of proximity relationships as input to their algorithms.

Euclidean distances (in standard scores) were calculated (in five dimensional space) between all nonredundant pairs of quality-of-life measures. (The solutions resulting from these two algorithms are diagrammed in Golant and McCutcheon 1980.) Together, the statistical approaches suggest three major clusters of indicator measures: cluster A—growth and change (item 6), congestion and crowding (item 3), safety (item 5), and family welfare (item 9); cluster B—economic status of population (item 7) and educational and professional status of population (item 8); and cluster C—economic health of area (item 1), mental health of population (item 11), housing stock status (item 2), availability of services (item 4), and physical health of population (item 10).

This simplified structure expedites an interpretation of how Evanston's quality of life compares with that found in the four city-suburban zones.

Cluster A: The four measures included in this cluster sharply differentiate the "desirable" qualities of life of the suburbs from the "undesirable" ones of the central city. The suburbs are less crowded and congested, more likely to have experienced growth, more likely to have intact families, and are safer than the central city. In three of the four categories, Evanston occupies a middle position between the most desirable suburbs and the least desirable city. However, Evanston, which has experienced little growth in recent years, ranks as a less desirable place than either the central city or the suburbs in the category of growth and change.

Cluster B: The two quality-of-life measures included here clearly distinguish the higher socioeconomic status of Evanston's population from that of populations in the other suburbs and Chicago. The central city's population has the lowest status, whereas the suburbs occupy an intermediate position between Evanston and the city. The middle suburbs are occupied by populations with a higher socioeconomic status than the inner suburbs, followed by the outer suburbs with the lowest status of suburban population.

Cluster C: The quality-of-life measures in this cluster are distinguished by their low statistical variability compared with the measures in the other clusters. In particular, the five geographical zones are the most homogeneous with respect to the availability of services. In three of the five categories (physical health, availability of services, and housing stock status), Evanston ranks as the most desirable place. The central city is the least desirable place in four of the five categories; however in two—economic health and mental health—Evanston is ranked as less desirable. In four of the five categories, the outer suburbs emerge as the least desirable suburban zone.

Evanston: The Quality of Life of a City or a Suburb?

An overall characterization of how these three clusters of quality-of-life measures differentiated Evanston from the central city and suburban zones required further cluster and smallest space analyses.

A proximity matrix of Euclidean distances was calculated between all nonredundant pairs of geographic zones, including Evanston (in eleven-dimensional space) (see figure 3.3). A full description of the statistically derived two-dimensional spatial configuration (solution) of Evanston and its reference zones is found in Golant and McCutcheon (1980). Summarizing briefly the results, the analyses identified three distinctive clusters of places: Evanston, the suburban zones, and the central city. Evanston had

Figure 3.3. Smallest Space Analysis of the Quality of Life in Evanston Community and Geographic Reference Zones

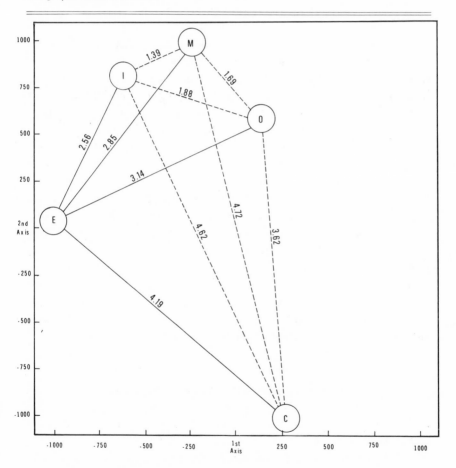

Numerical values between circles are euclidean distances between the respective geographic locations

a quality of life that was more similar to the suburban zones than to the central city. Its quality of life was most similar to that found in the inner suburbs in which Evanston was geographically located. However, its distance (geometric) to the central city was only about one and one-half times its distance (geometric) to the suburban zones, indicating that Evanston's quality of life was not so different from that of the central city (figure 3.3).

Summary and Conclusions

The findings of this analysis support the "split personality" interpretation of the Evanston community given by other studies. However, the construction of a clearly defined and replicable city-suburban-rural continuum and the multidimensional depiction of a place's quality of life enable a more complete and rigorous portrayal. Although in the aggregate the quality of life of Evanston's environment is more similar to that of a closer-in (to the city) suburban community, it has sets of attributes that approximate the quality of life found in both large cities and rural areas.

Evanston's environment is most similar to the city with respect to its (slower) population growth, its (greater) availability of services, and its population's (poorer) mental health. It is more similar to the older close-in inner suburbs with respect to its (lower) levels of crowding and congestion, its (higher) economic status, and its (better) housing stock status. It is more similar to the outer suburbs—primarily more rural areas—in terms of its (higher) levels of safety, (higher) family welfare status, (weaker) economic health, and its population's (poorer) mental health.

The Internal Structure of Evanston's Environment

The multidimensional complexity of Evanston's environment has so far been described only in aspatial terms, that is, as an undivided geographic entity. However, an environment's parts and properties are not locationally or spatially distributed in a homogeneous or random fashion within the community setting. Rather, an environment contains subareas (such as neighborhoods) that differ from each other along predictable dimensions of attributes (for example, the socioeconomic status of its population or physical quality of its housing). Consequently, the environments of research settings will differ from each other because of disparities in their internal spatial organization. In fact, it is possible that greater systematic environmental variability will exist among subareas within a community than between different community settings. Therefore, a judgment of the external validity of findings obtained from analyses of ordinary community environments requires further assessment of the representativeness of their environments' internal spatial organization or structure. Two analytical procedures are required. First, the major dimensions of attributes over which subareas differ must be identified; second, generalizations concerning their spatial organization, arrangement, or patterning must be discerned.

Background: Factorial Ecology Studies

Beginning with social area analysis (Shevky and Bell 1955) and continuing with factorial ecology analysis (Dogan and Rokkan 1969; Johnston 1976; Rees 1970; Schneider 1975), a large literature has described and interpreted the locational variability of the population, housing, and land use characteristics of urban communities. In the United States, such studies have usually focused on larger cities and metropolitan areas, using tract data from the Census Bureau to analyze internal differences. Concurrently, a considerable body of evidence has been compiled by urban economists, urban sociologists, and urban geographers demonstrating that the characteristics of a subarea is in part a function of its distance to the central city's downtown or central business district (CBD). Most existing theories and models of urban spatial structure and growth (such as the Burgess concentric zone theory, Hoyt's sector theory, the family of spatial location equilibrium theories) depend on assumptions and generalizations concerning how environmentally defined residential subareas are located relative to their CBD (for an extensive review and bibliography, see Rees 1979).

Methodology

For this research, the use of the census tract as a spatial unit of analysis was precluded by the fact that the Evanston community is divided (by the U.S. Census Bureau) into only 17 tracts. This necessitated the use of census blocks to record the community's internal environmental diversity. Although the large number of data units (639 blocks) made for a very detailed grid to assess internal variation, it also resulted in a more limited data base, because block statistics are fewer in number and less comprehensive. The choice of variables to serve as objective indicators of Evanston's internal diversity was influenced by two factors: precedents established in a large literature investigating the internal structure of the cities (see Bourne 1967; Herbert and Johnston 1976), and the availability of published data.

The data were collected from three major sources: the published decennial census (U.S. Census 1972a); a housing quality study by a consulting firm contracted by the City of Evanston Planning Department in 1976 to carry out a survey (via assessments by trained enumerators) of the extent of physical deficiencies in Evanston's dwellings; and land use maps compiled in 1970 by the City of Evanston Planning Board from which block information was manually extracted.[6] The number of variables included in the final analysis was smaller than actually collected. Variables that measured a conceptually similar characteristic or that were judged invalid because of definitional or measurement weaknesses were excluded. Care also was taken to avoid recording all possible variable categories or levels for any one environmental characteristic. Thirty-two census blocks, each containing less than five occupied units in 1970, were excluded, leaving a total of 607 census blocks in the analysis.

The final data set for the first statistical procedure consisted of

28 variables that summarized the population, housing, and land use characteristics of each census block in the Evanston community (table 3.1). Two variables measured how the racial composition of the population and the value of owned units had changed between 1960 and 1970. A 28 by 28 variable Pearson r correlation matrix was calculated and served as input to a principal-factor analysis. In this statistical solution, communality estimates are given by the squared multiple correlation between a given variable and the rest of the variables in the matrix. These are then reestimated by an iterative convergence method described in Nie et al. (1975:480). The principal factors were then rotated to the varimax criterion.

In the second statistical procedure, census block standard scores (using all factor loadings) were calculated for each of the computed factors (seven in total).[7] Each census block's relative location was then described by two measures: (1) its distance from Evanston's downtown district, or CBD; and (2) its distance from the downtown, or CBD, of the central city of its SMSA (in this case, the downtown of Chicago). Each of these measures served in turn as dependent variables in a standard linear multiple regression analysis that included the seven newly created factors (sets of factor scores describing 607 census blocks) as independent variables $(F_1, \ldots, F_7)$.[8]

When reporting the findings of these two procedures, census blocks are sometimes referred to as neighborhoods. This is for semantic convenience only, as little theoretical justification exists for such a label.

Findings—Procedure 1

The varimax rotated solution yielded seven factors that explained 66 percent of the common variance of the correlation matrix. These factors can be regarded as seven new statistically derived independent variables that summarize much of the spatial variation in the 28 characteristics describing Evanston's population, housing, and land uses (table 3.1).

Table 3.1. Principal-Factor Analysis of Evanston's Population, Housing, and Land-Use Characteristics (in census blocks), 1970

Variables Describing Census Blocks	I Housing Tenure Status	II Racial Occupancy Status	III Land Use	IV Housing Age & Condition	V Owner-Occupied Housing	VI Renter-Occupied Housing	VII Age of Population	h² Variance Explained
1. Percentage population under age 18	-.46	—	—	—	—	—	-.55	.74
2. Percentage population black	—	.90	—	—	—	—	—	.83
3. Percentage housing units with female head	—	.54	—	—	—	—	—	.36
4. Percentage housing units with only one person	.47	.46	—	—	—	.42	—	.52
5. Percentage housing units with roomers or boarders	—	—	—	-.30	—	—	—	.39
6. Percentage housing units owner-occupied	-.77	—	—	—	—	—	—	.81
7. Percentage housing units with over 1.01 persons/room	—	.78	—	—	—	—	—	.64
8. Percentage housing units in 1-unit structures	-.84	—	—	—	—	—	—	.91
9. Percentage housing units in 10- or more-unit structures	.58	—	—	—	—	.39	—	.58
10. Percentage residential structures built before 1900	—	—	—	.64	—	—	—	.58
11. Percentage residential structures built after 1929	—	—	—	-.78	—	—	—	.71
12. Percentage residential structures needing major repairs	—	.50	—	—	—	—	—	.41
13. Percentage residential structures needing minor repairs	—	—	—	.61	—	—	—	.54
14. Percentage housing units lacking plumbing facilities	—	—	—	—	—	.31	—	.17
15. Average number of rooms in owner-occupied housing units	—	—	—	—	.84	—	—	.88
16. Average value of owner-occupied housing units	—	-.45	—	—	.77	—	—	.85
17. Average number of rooms in renter-occupied housing units	—	—	—	—	—	-.78	—	.71
18. Average contract rent of renter-occupied housing units	—	-.47	—	—	—	-.41	—	.53
19. Percentage population in group quarters	—	—	—	—	—	—	.53	.35
20. Percentage land area in residential land uses	—	—	-.79	—	—	—	—	.68
21. Percentage land area in commercial, office land uses	—	—	.72	—	—	—	—	.65
22. Population per square mile	.69	—	—	—	—	—	—	.58
23. Average land value, 1976	.45	—	.35	—	—	—	.31	.59

24. Number of traffic accidents, 1967	—	.31	.37	—	—	—	.46	
25. Heavy traffic locations	—	—	.36	—	—	—	.13	
26. Proximity to coal-burning apartments	.48	—	—	—	—	—	.28	
27. Change in percentage housing units nonwhite: 1970 minus 1960	—	—	—	—	—	—	.10	
28. Percentage change in average value owned units: 1960–1970	.42	—	.52	—	—	—	.51	
Eigenvalues	5.83	3.65	2.51	1.27	.98	.70	.56	15.5
Factor contributions (in percentages)								
To explained (common) variance[b]	37.6	23.5	16.2	8.2	6.3	4.5	3.6	100.0
To total variance	22.1	14.4	10.1	5.9	5.2	4.1	3.7	65.5

[a] Final communality estimates were reached by an iterative convergence method (16 iterations were required). All loadings are from the "simple structure" solution resulting from rotation of principal-factors to a normal varimax position. To facilitate interpretation of the tables, loadings lying in the range $+.30 > a_{ij} > -.30$ have been omitted.

[b] These are percentages of the total common variance of the 28 variables used in the analysis (the common variance equals the sum of the commonalities or the sum of the eigen values over all positive factors).

Factor 1, *Housing Tenure Status*, explains 38 percent of the common variance in the correlation matrix. It identifies how neighborhoods occupied by owners differ from those occupied by renters. Blocks with positive standard scores are more likely to be occupied by renter-occupants, particularly those in larger apartment buildings. The occupants in these neighborhoods are more likely to live alone, and families with children are less prevalent. Typically, these neighborhoods have higher population densities and higher land values, and they are likely to contain or be in proximity to coal-burning apartments.

Racial Occupancy Status, factor 2, explains 24 percent of the common variance in the correlation matrix. This factor differentiates neighborhoods occupied by predominantly white populations (negative standard scores) from those with predominantly black populations (positive scores). The black neighborhoods are more likely to contain households headed by women or occupied by roomers and boarders. These households are more likely to be crowded (more than 1.1 persons per room), and the buildings in which they live are more likely to need major repairs. Both the rents and the house values are lower in these areas.

Land Use, factor 3, explains 16 percent of the common variance and differentiates neighborhoods according to whether their land uses are residential or nonresidential. Blocks with positive standard scores have a higher proportion of their area devoted to commercial and office land uses and have higher land values and population densities. Also, the values of these residential properties are likely to have increased significantly during the past decade. These neighborhoods are also likely to have heavier traffic volumes and a greater incidence of traffic accidents.

Factor 4, *Housing Age and Condition*, explains 8 percent of the common variance in the correlation matrix and distinguishes neighborhoods on the basis of the age and structural condition of their buildings, independent of their racial status. Blocks with positive standard scores are more likely to contain older buildings with minor structural defects.

Factors 5 and 6, *Owner-Occupied Housing* and *Renter-Occupied Housing*, explain 6 percent and 5 percent respectively, of the common variance in the correlation matrix. Regarding factor 5, blocks with positive factor scores contain owned units that are larger and higher-valued. Regarding factor 6, blocks with negative factor scores contain rented units that are usually larger in size (have more rooms), have higher rents, fewer plumbing deficiencies, and are less likely found in larger apartment structures.

Finally, factor 7, *Age of Population*, explains only 4 percent of the common variance. It distinguishes neighborhoods containing families with younger children from those occupied by elderly populations (who are sometimes occupying group-housing facilities such as retirement hotels). The variable "percentage population aged 62 and older" was excluded from this analysis so that it could serve as a dependent variable in a subsequent analysis. If it is included, it loads highly on this factor, but without it, a weaker "age" factor emerges.

Findings—Procedure 2

The regression of each relative location variable on the seven variable dimensions yields the following two sets of findings (table 3.2).

Table 3.2. Spatial Organization of Neighborhood Ecological Dimensions

	Dependent Variables		
Independent Variables	Distance of neighborhood to downtown Evanston	Distance of neighborhood to City of Chicago border	Percentage of neighborhood population aged 62 and older
Variable Name	Beta Weight	Beta Weight	Beta Weight
(F₁) Housing tenure status	−0.16	−0.43	0.15
(F₂) Racial occupancy status	−0.39	−0.03	−0.26
(F₃) Land use	−0.08	0.04	0.08
(F₄) Housing age and condition	−0.43	0.15	−0.04
(F₅) Owner-occupied housing	−0.10	0.21	−0.06
(F₆) Renter-occupied housing	−0.31	0.09	0.19
(F₇) Age of population	−0.17	−0.12	0.42
	$R^2 = .54$	$R^2 = .26$	$R^2 = .35$
	N = 607 blocks	N = 607 blocks	N = 607 blocks

A neighborhood's distance from its own community's downtown is substantially related to three factors: its racial occupancy status, the age and condition of its housing stock, and its renter-occupied housing status. Distance is more weakly associated with a neighborhood's housing tenure status and the age of its population. Specifically, with increasing distance from downtown Evanston, neighborhoods are occupied by:

(1) White as opposed to black populations in higher valued, better-quality housing (F_2)
(2) Newer housing, owner-occupied, with fewer structural defects (F_4)
(3) Larger sized, renter-occupied (two or more persons) housing units charging higher rents (F_6)
(4) Owner-occupied, single-detached housing units in areas with low population densities and land values (F_1)
(5) Higher proportions of child-rearing households (F_7)

The two remaining factors have almost no association with distance to Evanston's downtown. However, the signs of F_3 and F_5 indicate that commercial rather than residential land uses are more likely to characterize blocks closer to the downtown; and that with increasing distance, owned units become smaller and lower in value.

The second set of findings reveals that the environmental characteristics of Evanston's neighborhoods are more weakly associated with their location relative to downtown Chicago. However, the four strongest relationships indicate that with increasing distance from the central city's (Chicago) downtown, the neighborhoods are occupied by:

(1) Owner-occupied, particularly single-detached, units in areas with lower population densities (F_1)
(2) Higher-valued and larger owner-occupied units (F_5)
(3) Older units in need of minor repairs (F_4)
(4) A higher proportion of child-rearing households (F_7)

Summary and Conclusions

Two related conclusions can be drawn from the preceding analyses. First, with respect to its own CBD, Evanston's pattern of neighborhood environments is a microcosm of that found in larger urban places. That is, with increasing distance from Evanston's CBD, population densities become lower, the housing is owned rather than rented, more housing space is available, and housing is newer and in better condition. Predictable, too, are the locational patterns of the population distinguished by their stage in life and racial characteristics: With increasing distance from the community's CBD, child-rearing households and white neighborhoods become more prevalent.

Second, neighborhoods' locations relative to their own CBD, rather than Chicago's CBD, better predict their environmental characteristics. This finding lends support to the argument that Evanston experienced the social and economic development of an autonomous community and was not simply a spatial extension of the City of Chicago's development and growth. As in the previous quality-of-life objective indicators analysis, these conclusions are not clear-cut. Like other older communities located within a metropolitan area, Evanston's neighborhood structure can be explained, albeit more weakly, as a function of its location relative to Chicago's downtown center.

Elderly Locational Concentrations and Neighborhood Environment Indicators

Thus far, findings have been presented concerning the representativeness of Evanston's overall quality of life and the spatial organization of its neighborhood environments. A third set of inquiries is necessary to ascertain the linkage between the attributes of neighborhood environments and the residential locations of old people. This will enable generalizations about whether old people in Evanston occupy neighborhoods with attributes comparable to those of neighborhoods occupied by old people in other urban communities and places.

Two analyses are carried out to examine this question. The first assesses the age-segregated status of residential locations occupied by Evanston's elderly. The second analysis evaluates how the environmental attributes of different neighborhoods vary according to the size of their elderly population concentrations.

The Age-Segregation of Evanston's Old Population

Background

The spatial segregation of two populations occupying census tracts or blocks is most frequently measured by the index of dissimilarity[9] (Duncan and Duncan 1955a and 1955b; Taeuber and Taeuber 1969). As a statistical index, it is not without methodological weaknesses and interpretative difficulties (Zelder 1970; Jakubs 1977; and Zelder 1977). However, its use here enables statistical comparisons with several other studies. The segregation index can range in value from a high of 100.0, indicating a maximum degree of age-segregation between two populations, to a low of 0.0, indicating a minimum degree of age-segregation.[10]

Taeuber and Taeuber (1969:34) computed indexes of dissimilarity between whites and nonwhites occupying blocks in 207 U.S. central cities in 1960. The index values ranged from 60.4 to 98.1, with only a few cities having values below 70. Lieberson (1962:122) computed segregation indexes between foreign-born and native whites occupying census tracts in 10 midwestern and eastern U.S. central cities in 1950; the indexes ranged from 35.9 to 40.8. Kantrowitz (1973) reported comparable findings. Duncan and Duncan (1955b:498) computed indexes of dissimilarity of all possible pairs of major occupational groups of population who occupied census tracts in the City of Chicago in 1960. Dissimilarity measures ranged from 54 (between sales-persons and laborers and between professionals and laborers) to 13 (between sales-persons and managers). When the residential distribution of each occupational grouping was compared with the total population distribution, the indexes ranged from 35 for laborers to 13 for clerical workers. Comparable findings were reported by Fine, Glenn, and Monts (1971). Poole and Boal (1973) obtained a street-by-street segregation index of 70.9 between Catholics and Protestants in Belfast.

Cowgill, in an unpublished paper, computed indexes of dissimilarity between the population aged 65 and older and the rest of the population occupying census tracts in 72 selected U.S. central cities in 1970; the index values ranged from 10.8 to 37.7. He also computed comparable indexes for 241 metropolitan areas (SMSAs) and these ranged from 15.2 to 44.4 (Cowgill 1978; see also Clark 1975). Rees (1979) computed indexes of dissimilarity between the population aged 65 and older and the rest of the population occupying census tracts in 13 U.S. urbanized areas; the index values ranged from 14 to 29. Rees (1979) also concluded that of all of the age groups, the most spatially segregated was the over 65 group in 12 of the 13 urban areas.

Methodology

Data summarized by census blocks enabled the computation of an index of dissimilarity between the populations under and over age 62 in the Evanston community. The block segregation of populations could also be analyzed by race, but not simultaneously by age (U.S. Census 1972a). However, by census tracts (U.S. Census 1972b), indexes were computed (over 17 tracts) among the following age groups (under 18, 18–24, 25–44, 45–59, 60–74, older than 74).[11]

Findings

The index of dissimilarity between Evanston's population aged 62 and older and under age 62 occupying census *blocks* is 31.4. This implies that at the minimum, 31.4 percent of the aged 62 and older population (*or* the under age 62 population) must shift census blocks to achieve equal residential distributions. (Note that it is a one-way shift of one population or the other, and not a simultaneous exchange of residences.) Predictably, the segregation index computed for the same populations as occupants of census tracts is lower, 17.2 (see note 10). As a way of comparison, the index of dissimilarity calculated between the total black and white populations in Evanston's census tracts is 85.0.

The matrix of dissimilarity indexes (calculated over census tracts) yields the following generalizations:

(1) the younger the population (excluding the population under age 18), the more segregated its residential locations from the older population will be, whether the older population is defined as 60 and older, 60–74, or 75 and older.

(2) The young-old (aged 60–74) population is more segregated from the old-old (aged 75 and older) population than it is from the late middle-aged (aged 45–59) population.

(3) The old-old (aged 75 and older) population is more segregated from younger population groups (all ages) than it is from the young-old (aged 60–74) population.

Summary and Conclusions

A comparison of these age-segregation patterns with those reported by Cowgill and Rees indicates that Evanston's older population occupies less age-segregated residential locations. Consistent with other studies, the segregation of the elderly from the young was found to be much weaker than the segregation of blacks from whites or of the foreign-born from native populations. Findings concerning the age-segregated status of the young-old and the old-old populations, although potentially useful for assertions concerning representativeness, will have to await other studies for verification.

Elderly Residential Concentrations and Neighborhood Environments

Background

Only a few studies have considered how the population and housing attributes of neighborhood environments vary according to the size of their elderly residential concentrations. Smith and

Hiltner (1976) concluded that central city elderly residents were usually located in older neighborhoods (census tracts) in greater proximity to the downtown; and these neighborhoods were more likely to contain lower-valued housing and apartments and multiple-family dwelling units. Pampel and Choldin (1978) found that census blocks with higher concentrations of elderly people were also occupied by higher percentages of households headed by primary individuals, lower percentages of husband-wife households and children under 15, higher percentages of institutional group housing, and lower percentages of minority occupied housing. Rudzitis (1982), analyzing census tract and community area data in the Chicago Metropolitan Area, also found smaller percentages of black residents in elderly-dominated areas. He further reported that higher concentrations of old people were located in lower status areas, although not necessarily poverty areas. The unemployment rates in these areas were relatively low and the labor force population tended to be in working-class and white-collar occupations. These were also stable areas, as indicated by their low population mobility rates, and they tended to have a higher percentage of foreign-born and second-generation ethnic residents. Findings similar to the above can be discerned from studies of the internal structure of cities in which "stage in life" emerges as a persistent ecological dimension underlying the residential differentiation of populations (for a review, see Timms 1971).

Methodology

The presence of elderly residential concentrations in Evanston was measured by the variable, "percentage of neighborhood (block) population aged 62 and older." It served as a dependent variable in a standard multiple linear regression analysis, with the seven factors as independent variables (F_1, . . . , F_7). To help interpret the findings of the regression analysis, simple (zero-order) correlations were also computed between the neighborhood elderly concentration variable and each of the original 28 neighborhood characteristics.[12]

Findings

Larger elderly population concentrations were most strongly associated with two neighborhood factors: "age of population" (F_7), and "racial occupancy status" (F_2). They were more weakly associated with the factors "renter-occupied housing" (F_6) and "housing tenure status" (F_1) (table 3.2). The age and condition of the neighborhood's housing stock were negligibly related.

These relationships were elucidated by examining how the original set of neighborhood characteristics correlated with the size of elderly population concentrations. Larger concentrations of old people were found in neighborhoods occupied by people living alone, that had higher population densities, larger-sized rental buildings, and smaller than average-sized accommodations, and were located on higher-valued land. Smaller concentrations of older people were found in neighborhoods that were occupied by blacks, households containing younger families and their children, crowded households, and households with roomers and boarders.

Summary and Conclusions

It can be concluded that age-segregated *neighborhoods* are more likely than age-integrated neighborhoods to have a lower family status, to be dominated by whites, and have higher population and residential densities. However, these findings may say more about the old people themselves who live in age-segregated neighborhoods. Because of the small areal unit studied—the census block— the area occupied by a relatively large percentage of old people will tend to assume the characteristics of this old population. From this perspective, old people living in age-segregated or age-homogeneous neighborhoods are more likely *themselves* to be white, unmarried, and living alone and to occupy land uses with the characteristics described above. In both instances, these generalizations are consistent with those found in other research.

Chapter Four

Conceptualization and Measurement of the Experiential Environment

This study conceptualizes the environment in a second way, from the subjective perspectives of individuals who are engaged in behavioral and cognitive transactions with its objects and events (Stokols 1978:259).[1] In contrast to the objectively defined environment described by the detached scientific observer, the depiction of the subjectively defined environment depends on reports by residents of their perceptions, feelings, and evaluations. These responses provide two categories of information. First, they reveal the *content* of the environment that individuals are aware of and with which they transact. This is exemplified by responses that reveal residents' knowledge of their community services, buildings, land uses, people, events and their varied denotative features and attributes. Second, they reveal individuals' personal accounts and assessments of the *outcomes* or *consequences* of their environmental transactions. This is exemplified by responses that reveal residents' expressions of grief, excitement, fear, satisfaction, fatigue, likes, dislikes, plans for action, or the lack of them. These subjective reports of an environment's content and consequences are referred to here as the individual's *environmental experiences* or *experiential environment*.

This study treats a description of an individual's environmental experiences as equivalent to a description of an environment's impact on an individual. Thus, environmental impact becomes contingent upon the outcomes or consequences individuals associate with their everyday environmental transactions.

This chapter outlines in both conceptual and operational terms the essential components and properties of the experiential environment, and identifies precedents for the formulation. It concludes with an empirical analysis that describes the structure of the environmental experiences reported by Evanston's elderly population.

Conceptualization of the Experiential Environment

A full description of the individual's or population's environmental experiences involves the specification of three analytically distinctive components: content, dynamic properties, and structure (Leff 1978).

The Content of the Experiential Environment

The content of the experiential environment includes "all the actual things or ongoing events" (Leff 1978:112) that individuals are aware of and transact with in their environment.[2] It includes information about an unlimited variety of social, physical, and natural objects and events "such as particular people, activities, buildings, vegetation, weather conditions, media messages, and so on" (Leff 1978:112).

It is postulated that the content of the experiential environment has eight defining characteristics. The first six are borrowed and slightly modified characteristics introduced by Ittelson (1973) to describe the nature of the perceptual environment. The last two characteristics are identified by Jessor and Jessor (1973) as properties of their "perceived environment." The first characteristic defines the content of the experiential environment as a potential source of stimulus information (Gibson 1960) (as distinct from a source of stimulus energy), that is, "information from, and about, the environment within which the individual functions" (Ittelson

1973:9). Second, it "surrounds, enfolds, engulfs" (p. 13) the individual *qua* participant; it is omnipresent in that its information is always spatially and temporally present. Third, it is always multimodal (p. 13), that is, it offers potential information to many of the individual's sense organs, often simultaneously (p. 14). Fourth, it "always provides more information than can possibly be processed" (p. 14) by the individual. Furthermore, it always represents "instances of redundant information, of inadequate and ambiguous information, and of conflicting and contradictory information" (p. 14). Fifth, it "cannot be passively observed"; it "defines the probabilities of occurrence of potential actions, . . . demand qualities which call forth certain actions, and . . . offers differing opportunities for the control and manipulation of the environment itself" (p. 14). Sixth, it "call[s] forth actions, but not blind, purposeless actions. . . . It possesses the property . . . of providing symbolic meanings and motivational messages which themselves may affect the directions which action takes" (p. 15). Seventh, it has a *"temporal extension,"* a dynamic through time. Perceived environmental attributes may evidence systematic or predictable changes over time" (Jessor and Jessor 1973:33). Eighth, its properties may be aligned along a "generality-specificity" dimension: "certain aspects . . . are more pervasive and relatively enduring, others may be rather specific and momentary" (p. 33).

The Dynamic Properties of the Experiential Environment

The dynamic properties of an experiential environment refer to the subjectively defined impact that transactions have on an individual. Two properties of these transactions can be distinguished: their meanings and their meaningfulness.

Transactions differ according to their *meaning* for the individual, that is, according to the types of their subjectively interpreted outcomes, effects, or consequences. These outcomes impinge upon various social, psychological, or physiological needs of individuals, thereby influencing various aspects of their mental and behavioral well-being. Most importantly, the outcomes or meanings of transactions can be distinguished according to whether they are beneficial or harmful. (In subsequent chapters reference to the *type* of experience will refer to its meaning for the individual.)

Transactions also differ according to their *meaningfulness*, that is, according to the likelihood, frequency, or extent that their outcomes are experienced by individuals. Therefore, a full depiction of the environmental experiences of a person requires a description of not only their subjectively interpreted outcomes but also their frequency or extent of occurrence.

The Structure of the Experiential Environment

The structure of the experiential environment refers to the organizational complexity or diversity of an individual's experiences. Certain experiences are more likely to occur in association with others because of their similar content and dynamic properties. The number and diversity of these distinctive groupings of experiences define the structural complexity of an *individual's* experiential environment. It is also possible, however, to speak of the structure of a *population's* experiential environment, because the patterns of experiences reported by different individuals will share certain regularities. Thus sets of experiences reported by a population can be distinguished from others by virtue of their similar contents and/or dynamic properties.

Precedents for an "Experiential Environment"

The concept, environmental experience, possesses properties that are embodied in John's (1976) categories of a human organism's higher level of information processing and content, namely, subjective experience, self, and self-awareness. The individual's subjective experience "derives from information about the content of consciousness" (p. 4). It is a process that "merges sequential constellations of multisensory perceptions, memories, emotions, and actions into a unified and apparently continuous event, or experience" (p. 4). During the lifetime of an individual, memories of these diverse past subjective experiences are accumulated, resulting in an individual's acquiring a personal history or "self" (p. 5). By virtue of an individual's cognitive or thought process, this store of memories can be activated, analyzed, and modified long after the original basis for their occurrence. Thus, these processes enable the individual to represent such experience memories in symbolic terms and in a form that may bear only slight resemblance to informational interpretations that actually occurred.

In general, the conceptualization of an environment from the perspective of individuals experiencing it, rather than in physicalistic or objective terms, has several precedents in psychology. This approach is broadly consistent with the transactionalist functionalists' (as in the works of Mead, Dewey, Bentley, and Ames) rejection of a dualistic separation of the mind and some external environment (Tibbets 1972). (However, the study's subsequent conceptual and methodological approach diverges from this viewpoint in that a distinguishable "knower" is recognized.) More specifically, environments defined by perceiving and thinking individuals are exemplified by Koffka's (1935) "behavioral environment," Lewin's (1951) "psychological environment," Murray's (1938) "beta environmental press," Roger's (1951) "phenomenal field," Gibson's (1960) "effective stimulus," and Ittelson's (1973:11) "perceptual information."

Koffka's distinction between a geographical environment and a behavioral environment illustrates the alternative environmental perspectives:

> For in reality there are . . . two very different environments to be distinguished from each other, and the question has to be raised: In which of them has molar behavior taken place? . . . Let us therefore distinguish between a *geographical* and a *behavioural* environment . . . our difference between the geographical and the behavioural environment coincides with the difference between things as they "really" are and things as they look to us, between reality and appearance. And we see also that appearances may deceive, that behaviour well adapted to the behavioural environment may be unsuited to the geographical. (1935:27, 28, 33)

And continuing:

> We should discover that objects which have quite similar phys-
> ical dimensions (e.g.: two men that resemble each other) may af-
> fect the organism entirely differently and give rise to different
> reactions. (p. 117)

This study's depiction of the dynamic properties of the experiential environment bears similarity to the theoretical approaches of psychologists Lewin and Murray. Lewin (1951:12)
emphasized the importance of finding methods of representing
persons and environment in common terms as part of one situation. He conceived of individuals as having, on the one hand, needs,
values, or goals and, on the other hand, a subjective or psychological environment containing regions of positive or negative val-
ences with the potential of satisfying these needs or goals or, more
specifically, of releasing tension in the individual's system. According to Lewin, individuals move toward or away from these
goals depending on the direction or strength of the (valence) forces
acting on them.

Murray conceived of the individual as having hypothetical (that
is, nonobservable) needs, functional in the sense that they are
identified with various goals or purposes toward which the individual strives. An individual's environment was classified according to how well its objects or events related to these needs and
goals, for example, "in terms of the kinds of benefits (facilitations,
satisfactions) and the kinds of harms (obstructions, injuries, dis-
satisfactions) which it provide[d]" (1938:118). He referred to the
tendency of objects or situations in the environment to exert these
positive or negative effects in concert with an individual's needs
as "environmental press."

More contemporarily, the treatment presented here is similar
to the systems information theoretic view of meaning referred to
by Buckley:

> What is relevant to an organism and its behavior is not simply
> some external event, or solely some internal state, but rather the
> transaction whereby certain aspects of the external "stimulus"

are "sampled" by the organism and matched against selected internal states. The "meaning" of the stimulus is not something "in" it, or something "in" the organism, but the *relationship* between the two. (1967:54)

At a more operational level, the conceptualization and measurement of environmental experience is closely aligned to the expectancy-value models of attitudes, intentions, and behavior constructed by Rosenberg (1956) and Fishbein (1963). Particularly applicable is Fishbein's concept of belief strength. This refers to the subjectively defined probability that an object (in this study, some part of the everyday environment) is cognitively related to some attribute (in this study an outcome or consequence). Illustrations of this relationship are provided later in this chapter.

Environmental Impact: Alternative Approaches

Chapter 1 briefly reviewed how impact as conceptualized in this study differed from four other approaches: first, an objective indicator perspective from which impact is depicted as some objectively defined deviation in environmental quality from some normatively established standards; second, an intrapsychic perspective, from which environmental impact is depicted as a function of an individual's self-assessment of his inner states, for instance, morale or self-concept; third, a physical or psychophysiological perspective, from which environmental impact is depicted as a function of the individual's self-rated health or physiological functioning; and fourth, an individual-environment congruence perspective.

The last perspective deserves further attention because it shares similarities with this study's interactive state approach. Its general conceptual structure is outlined by French, Rodgers, and Cobb (1974). The individual makes demands of his environment, and the environment supplies resources to meet these demands. Congruence or goodness-of-fit then depends on discrepancies between demand and supply. Demand and supply components are further distinguished according to whether they are based on objective or subjective assessments. Two research groups have conducted empirical studies of old people's environmental congruence. Kahana, Liang, and Felton (1980) assessed the extent that individual preferences (or needs) for environmental attributes in a home for the aged were consistent with commensurate objective indicators of these attributes. Here, impact is defined as the degree of congruence between an individual's perceived environmental needs and the available environmental resources (as objectively defined). The researcher's interpretation of this "impact" further depends on assumptions about the magnitude and direction (i.e., undersupply or oversupply) of the deviations necessary to yield negative personal outcomes. Nehrke et al. (1981) have measured the environmental attribute perceptions and preferences reported by elderly persons occupying a Veteran's Administration retirement home. Congruence was assessed by subtracting individual preference ratings from weighted (by importance) environmental perception ratings. Thus, impact is defined as the difference between subjective assessments of environmental supply and subjective assessments of personal need.

The congruence approach to environmental impact requires the assessment of two components—demand and supply—in order to establish the existence of a gap or discrepancy. In contrast, this study by its *description* of environmental experiences looks not to the components underlying the gap, but to the measurement of the gap itself. In this sense, the occurrence of negative outcomes or consequences indicates incongruence.

Operationalizing the Experiential Environment

The Researcher's Behavioral Environment

Earlier chapters have pointed to the influential role of the researcher in the selection of the functionally relevant ecological environment. Another important instance of this influence is the researcher's conceptualization and operationalizing of the experiential environment's content and dynamic properties. Only a small spatial and temporal segment of an individual's experiential environment can be studied in a particular empirical analysis. The nature of this segment is left to the discretion of the researcher. Thus although the content of the experiential environment is identified by the respondent in subjective or personal terms, it is the researcher who defines the objects, attributes, and consequences that will be the focus of the investigation. It is ultimately the *researcher's* behavioral environment (the subjectively defined environment specified by Koffka 1935) to which a sample of persons are asked to respond. In this sense, the experiential environment is as much the constructed reality of the researcher as it is the reality of the respondent (Polanyi 1946:24, 74).

In the context of a survey research interview methodology, the researcher assumes this influential role through his ability to include or exclude interview questions (items) for a respondent to answer. In Barker's (1968:141–143) terminology, the researcher generates an "operator data system" whereby he regulates the data input (the questions) to the units (the people) he is investigating, and thus imposes limitations on the data output received from them.[3]

This is illustrated by the researcher's control over the potential meanings or outcomes that the individual can assign to his environmental transactions. If the researcher does not conceptualize excitement and sadness as possible transaction outcomes, the individual cannot report being excited or sad. On the other hand, emotional outcomes such as fear, anxiety, anger, and pride can be built into the questions given to the respondent. For example, question stems might include: Are you proud to live in . . .? Are you ever afraid of . . . ? How often have you felt angry or annoyed . . . ? Researcher control of experiential meaning is also exerted by the selection of the environmental content presented to the respondent. For example, if the conceptualization of objects does not include the pet dog or cat or the social service, the individual's experiential environment will not include them. This is critical because transactions with certain objects and events are more likely to lead to certain outcomes than others. For example, being robbed is closely linked with an individual's loss of physical or psychological security and with personal helplessness; the enjoyment of friends is linked with the benefits of companionship, interpersonal understanding and relatedness.

This discussion might be interpreted as a critique of the survey research schedule as a form of data input presentation. This instrument's usually structured and close-ended question format, allows so much researcher control that it is sometimes thought to stifle the full expression of a respondent's thoughts and feelings. Rather, the above observations are intended to suggest the strengths of the interview schedule as a methodological device to record the individual's experiential environment. Although it is certainly true that the interview schedule allows the researcher considerable influence over the design of the presented environment and the individual's responses, it also unmercifully exposes the workmanship upon which this reality is based. Herein lies its strength: the researcher's manipulative role and, in turn, his scientific and personal biases concerning the environment are largely revealed. Thus, other researchers can scrutinize his workmanship and, where appropriate, replicate the most valuable and reliable portions. In contrast, in other data-collecting research methodologies the researcher is often unable to articulate his imposition on the respondent's reality. Although the researcher's role as an "operator" may be more subtle or less formal, resulting in more nonreactive data measures (Webb et al. 1966), it is the researcher who ultimately must decide what to ask, who to listen to (and how often), where to ask, what to listen to, what to watch, and, most difficult, which data selections to make—often using undisclosed guidelines—from the invariably large mass of respondent communications. To analyze these data, he must then impose some weighting and order to their content and dynamic properties. Particularly worrisome is the researcher's failure to be sufficiently sensitive to his reality-constructing role (Cantril 1950). A more devastating weakness is that the reader of the reported data often has no way of scrutinizing or replicating the researcher's construction of reality. As Polanyi observed in his discussion of the reality of science:

> Viewed from outside as we described him the scientist may appear as a mere truth-finding machine steered by intuitive sensitivity. But this view takes no account of the curious fact that he is himself the ultimate judge of what he accepts as true. His brain labours to satisfy its own demands according to criteria applied by its own judgment. . . . While all the time, far from being neutral at heart, he is himself passionately interested in the outcome of the procedure. (1946:24)

To allow the scrutinization of this researcher's construction of reality, the following sections describe the considerations that entered into the operationalization of the content and dynamic properties of the experiential environment of Evanston's elderly population.

The Content of the Experiential Environment

Alternative Classifications of Objects and Events

The researcher who must "select" an experiential environment's content is confronted with literally hundreds of possible variables and an infinite number of variable combinations to describe its objects and events. Furthermore, so that other researchers can compare the selected objects and events with those in their studies, he must describe, classify, and structurally order them using a conceptual language that is not unique to the immediate environment or population under investigation (Craik 1970:15).

Taxonomies of the objective environment are numerous (Rapoport 1977:65–80). Environmental displays, social situations, a city's spatial structure, places, ekistic units, and neighborhood units are variously described by properties or attributes such as degree of human influence, physical-social-cultural aspects, social and institutional scale, architectural design, and types and degree of stimulus uncertainty (figure 4.1). Moreover, these diverse exam-

Figure 4.1. Alternative Conceptualizations of Objective Environments

Craik (1971) Places	Doxiadis (1968) Ekistic (Settlement) Elements	Chermayeff and Alexander (1963) Realms of Privacy	Craik (1970) Environmental Displays
Physical-spatial properties	Nature	Urban—public	Geographical scale
Organization of entities and components	Man	Urban—semipublic	Degree of human influence
Traits	Society	Group—public	
Behavioral attributes	Shells	Group—public	
Institutional attributes	Networks	Family—private	
		Individual—private	

Lawton (1970) Ecological System	Lynch and Rodwin (1958) Urban Form	Foley (1964) Internal Structure of City	Geddes and Gutman (1977) Properties of Physical Environment
Individual	Element types	Normative or cultural aspects	Spatial organization
Physical environment	Quantity	Functional organizational aspects	Circulation and movement systems
Personal environment	Density	Physical aspects	Ambient properties
Suprapersonal environment	Grain		Visual properties
Social environment	Focal organization		Amenities
	Generalized spatial distribution		Symbolic properties
			Architectonic properties

Rosow (1961) Housing	Saarinen (1976) Territorial Organization of Space	Moos (1974) Human Environments	Perry (1929) Neighborhood Unit
Social pathology and efficiency	Personal space and room geography	Ecological dimensions	Size
Livability	Architectural space	Behavior settings	Boundaries
Neighborhood structure and integration	Small towns and neighborhoods	Dimensions of organizational structure	Open spaces
Aesthetics	City	Characteristics of milieu inhabitants	Institutional sites
	Large conceptual regions	Psychosocial characteristics	Local shops
	Nation	Reinforcement characteristics	Internal street system
	World		

Webber (1964) Internal Structure of City	Wohlwill and Kohn (1976) Stimulus Uncertainty	Sherif (1967) Social Situation	Shevky and Bell (1955) Social Areas
Spatial flows of information, money, people, and goods	Diversity	Participating Individuals	Social rank (economic status)
Locations of physical channels and the adapted spaces that physically house activities	Complexity	Activities or tasks	Urbanization (family status)
Locations of activity spaces	Novelty	Setting or circumstances	Segregation (ethnic status)
	Incongruity	Relationship of participants to situation	
	Surprisingness		
	Ambiguity		

ples do not begin to exhaust the various conceptual languages that
have been used to dimensionalize the components of the environment and its properties. Within the field of architectural psychology alone (see, for example, Broadbent 1973; Heimsath 1977; and
Sanoff 1973), one is confronted with dozens of taxonomies depicting the attributes of buildings and their landscaping. As further
evidence of the possible taxonomic alternatives and the combinations they produce, the reader is referred to the "dictionary" of
Sells (1963) in which more than 250 stimulus factors contributing
to behavior variance are listed. In addition, more recent conceptualizations of the objective environment have been sensitive to
the stage-in-life specific behaviors of people. Good examples are
found in the environmental psychology literature on children
(Altman and Wohlwill 1978) and elderly persons (Windley, Byerts,
and Ernst 1975). More general discussions of the significance of
stage in life in environment-behavior and environment-society
models are in Doxiadis (1974) and Land (1975).

A factor complicating the selection of objective attributes concerns the very basis for verifying their objectivity. As Wohlwill and
Kohn pointed out:

> The issue may seem to be substantially clouded by the fact that
> in environmental research the assessment of stimulus variables
> must typically be carried out by recourse to ratings by indepen-
> dent judges, rather than by strictly objective measurement.
> Variables such as "complexity," "incongruity," "unity," and the
> like are difficult to specify in strictly physical terms. (1976:47)

In summary, little theoretical or empirical agreement exists regarding the nature of objects and their properties that should be
potentially included in an individual's experiential environment.
The absence of such consensus increases the likelihood that a researcher will impose his own values when selecting environmental content. The result is a plethora of diverse and unconnected
researchers' behavioral environments. However, even the achievement of a consistent conceptual language to characterize the environment does not solve the dilemma raised by Wohlwill and
Kohn (1976). Replication and verification studies remain neces-

sary as long as there is difficulty in obtaining strictly objective measurements of an environment's properties.[4]

The Selection of Objects and Events for Empirical Study

The selection of objects and events for this investigation was guided by the need to characterize the old person's environment as a residential place or human settlement and to portray it in a holistic, integrated manner.

Initially, environmental areas were *territorially* classified according to their physical scale in geographic space. A nested hierarchy of places was defined: community (TC), neighborhoods (TN), and dwellings (TD) (figure 4.2).

As figure 4.1 indicates, much more detailed conceptualizations of the territorial organization of human settlements exist, but these three categories of residential space are sufficient for the present research goals. The seminal reference work on this topic is by Doxiadis (1968, 1974), but the reader is also referred to the synthesis by Saarinen (1976). Further discussion of the conceptual significance of these settlement categories appears in later chapters, especially chapter 8, which focuses on the territorial experiences of elderly people.

The contents of these territories were further categorized into social and physical components and properties—a distinction persistently made in the social and behavioral sciences literature. The simultaneous focus on both physical and social aspects was designed to avoid the artificial fragmentation of the environment found in other studies (Golant 1979b). The goal was to identify a reasonable cross-section of a human settlement's content transacted with by old people in the course of their everyday lives. Nonetheless, emphasis was placed on the physical environment because of this researcher's greater interest in its impact on individual well-being.

Four subcategories of *physical* objects/events were distinguished and are roughly aligned along a continuum ranging from a low to high degree of human or societal influences (Craik 1970).

Figure 4.2. Conceptualization of Environment for Evanston Investigation

Territorial Objects

TC	Community
TN	Neighborhood
TD	Dwelling

Physical Objects and Events

NEp *Natural Environment:* Conditions of temperature, humidity, precipitation, insects, and rodents.

BEp *Built Environment:* Form and functioning attributes of physical components and spaces developed or adapted for human occupancy and use as, for example, parks, parking lots, buildings, rooms, TVs, appliances, pictures, landmarks, billboards, lights, transportation, circulation, communication systems, and open spaces.

UEp *Urbanized Environment:* Crime, noise, pollution, traffic congestion.

SWp *Social Welfare Environment:* Attributes of organized social and medical services and facilities, municipal services and facilities (police and fire protection).

Social Objects and Events

SSs *Social Situation:* People as neutral objects, distinguished by such characteristics as age, sex, education, and so on; the composition of a population group distinguished by their similarities and differences in sex, age, race, social status, and so on.

PEs *Personal Environment:* People distinguished by their potential for satisfying human relationships in their roles as friends, acquaintances, relatives, family, and professionals.

LSs *Recent Stressful Life Events:* People associated with potentially stressful events as divorce, illness, or death.

The natural environment (NEp)—the lowest order subcategory (least human influence) of physical objects—includes those features of the environment that exert their original presence even in the light of man's manipulation of his environment. Thus, weather (both inside and outside of buildings) and biological forms (insects, rodents) and their various manifestations are contained in this category. The next level—the built environment (BEp)— includes all physical components and their spatial and aspatial attributes that have been developed or adapted for human occupancy and use (Lynch and Rodwin 1958). This depiction of the built environment is very similar to that outlined by Geddes and Gutman (1977:152–157). The third subcategory—the urbanized environment (UEp)—includes the natural and built environments as modified by more macroscale processes, such as industrialization and modernization. Several concomitant conditions of an urbanized society are included, such as crime, noise, pollution, and traffic congestion. At the highest end of the physical environment continuum is the fourth subcategory of the environment—the social welfare environment (SWp). The provision of organized social welfare services occurs only at a relatively advanced and complex stage of society whereby the individual and his family alone cannot cope with all the life tasks necessary for their well-being (Golant and McCaslin 1979a).

The set of *social* objects and events are divided into three subcategories, roughly ordered along a continuum depicting their influence on the individual's social self. At the lowest level is the social situation (SSs), a term borrowed from Sherif (1967). Its application here is restricted, however, to a limited number of Sherif's social factors, namely:

> The characteristics of . . . individuals, such as the number of persons, their ages, their sex, their educational, occupational, economic, and social attainments.
>
> The composition of the total participants in the social situation in terms of their similarities and differences in age, sex, homogeneity as to religion, class, and so on. (p. 120)

Thus, social situation refers to people merely as a collection of emotionally and instrumentally neutral objects, distinguished by their compositional attributes. In direct contrast the personal environment (PEs) differentiates persons according to the extent to which their human relationships have social and psychological significance to an old person. The third subcategory includes social events distinguished by their potential for contributing to stressful disruptions in the individual's personal relationships, including, for example, death, divorce, family departure, and so on (see Paykel et al. 1971; Uhlenhuth and Paykel 1973).

The Dynamic Properties of the Experiential Environment

Alternative Classifications of Environmental Transaction Outcomes

There are probably as many possible classifications of the meanings or outcomes of an individual's environmental transactions as there are classifications of objects. Figure 4.3 offers a representative set of such typologies, although in several instances the respective authors did not intend that their classifications be interpreted as denoting environmental effects or outcomes. In any case, these typologies should be viewed as illustrative rather than definitive.

These classifications should give insights as to why the possible sets of outcomes are so numerous. There is no agreement regarding the types of individual states or functions with which the environment is interacting to produce the various possible outcomes. For example, the classifications of Sweeney et al. and Mehrabian and Russell emphasize an individual's emotional states as outcomes; those by Maslow and Murray focus on the satisfaction of traditional conceptions of motives and needs; and the classification of Kasl lists different types of organic and social pathological symptoms. Spivak's classification differs considerably from the others in that it lists archetypal places, depicting spatial and environmental requirements of settings necessary to support the needs and drives of individuals at different developmental stages of their lives. Here, the setting outcomes reflect the ability of the environment to facilitate certain types of human functioning. Within each of the above classifications there are further variations reflecting whether the transactional outcomes emphasize physiological needs, social needs, or ego-integrative needs. These and other classifications also differ in terms of whether the need categories are hierarchically ordered in some respect. The best known example of such a hierarchically organized system is Maslow's classification of needs, which argues that lower order needs must be satisfied (for example, security) before higher order needs can be fully realized (for example, self-actualization).

In addition, the classifications differ according to whether the outcomes of environmental transactions focus on an individual's intrapsychic states (for example, self-esteem, self-respect) or on interactive states that involve environmental referents. The classifications of Murray and Maslow are clearly of the former type. However, several classifications, including those by Spivak, Sargent et al., Montgomery, and Windley, specify consequences in environment-behavior terms. In these examples, what is affected is an individual's territorial integrity, shelter, privacy, and sense of place. The classifications also differ in a manner not entirely obvious from figure 4.3. This is in whether the effects or consequences emphasize the benefits or positive aspects of the environment as opposed to its harms or negative aspects. Although exceptions exist, it is a fair generalization that social science research has been preoccupied largely with the negative effects of the environment on the individual (Kasl 1977).

Finally, the classifications differ in terms of whether the outcomes can be measured in primarily objective terms. Inconsistency exists both within and between classifications. Maslow's "survival" can clearly be measured in objective or behavioral terms, but not his "esteem" or "self-actualization," which would appear to require an individual's subjective assessments. The outcomes of Mehrabian and Russell's classification can be measured only in subjective terms, whereas those of Spivak, Boal, and Kasl are likely to be detected by behavioral observations.

In light of this potpourri of possible environmental transaction outcomes, it is not surprising that the current literature does not offer a consistent or systematic set of research findings. Notable, however, is the theoretical-empirical research of Mehrabian and Russell (1974) concerned with the impact of real-world or naturalistic settings on human behavior. In seeking an approach to parsimoniously describe an individual's response to his environment, they have argued that "there exists a limited set of basic emotional (connotative, affective, feeling) responses to all stimulus situations, independent of the sensory modality involved" (p. 17). They proposed a set of three such emotions—pleasure, dominance, and arousal—whose derivations can be compared with the

Figure 4.3. Alternative Classifications of Environmental Transaction Outcomes

Boal (1976)	Dalkey (1973)	Dalkey and Rourke (1973)	Geddes and Gutman (1977)
Defense	Physical and mental health	Novelty/boredom	Survival
Avoidance	Status	Peace of mind/anxiety	Security
Preservation (of heritage, identity)	Affluence	Social-acceptance/loneliness	Comfort
Attack	Activity	Comfort	Safety
	Sociality	Relaxation	General physical well-being
	Freedom	Dominance/dependence	Satisfaction
	Security	Challenge, stimulation	Activity and performance
	Novelty	Self-respect, self-awareness	
	Aggression	Privacy	
		Involvement	
		Companionship	
		Achievement, prestige, status	
		Individuality/conformity	

Golant (1976a)	Hinkle (1977)	Kasl (1977)	Leighton (1959)
Independence	Life span of individual shortened	Disease states	Physical security
Security-economic	Disability or impairment	Illness and sick-role behavior	Sexual satisfaction
Security-physical	Cultural information acquisition impaired	Social deviance	Expression of hostility
Security-emotional	Social role acquisition restricted	Social effectiveness and competence	Expression of love
Environmental mastery	Social opportunities restricted	Addiction	Securing recognition
Positive self-image	Performance or activities restricted		Expression of spontaneity
	Displeasure or dissatisfaction		Place orientation
			Securing and maintaining group membership
			Sense of belonging to a moral order

Maslow (1954)	Mehrabian and Russell (1974)	Misra (1970)	Montgomery (1972)
Survival	Pleasure	Relatedness-love	Independence
Security	Arousal	Transcendence-creation	Safety and comfort
Belongingness	Dominance	Rootedness	Wholesome self-concept

Growth, self-actualization   Frame of orientation   A sense of place
                                                                              Relatedness
                                                                              Environmental mastery
                                                                              Psychological stimulation
                                                                              Privacy

Murray (1938)	Sargent et al. (1958)	Schorr (1970)	Spivak (1973)
Achievement	Degree of relevance	Self-perception	Shelter
Affiliation	Amount of stress	Health	Sleep
Aggression	Degree of support (at any level)	Satisfaction	Mate
Dominance	Situational aspects of conflict	Stress	Groom
Autonomy	Opportunities for self-realization, growth, autonomy	Sense of individuality	Feed
Harm avoidance	Congruence of situations with needs, interests, capacities	Psychological disorders	Excrete
Order	Degree of situational mutability	Social interaction patterns	Store
Rejection			Territory
Seclusion			Play
			Route
			Meet
			Compete
			Work

Sweeney et al. (1970)	Thomas (1923)	Windley (1977)	Withey (1962)
Anxiety	Security	Territorial (integrity)	Restriction
Fascination	Recognition	Privacy	Impotency
Anger	Response from others	(Obviating) sensory deficits	Isolation
Bliss	New experience	(Increasing) cognition, environmental awareness	Irrationality
Fear		(Fulfilling) environmental dispositions	Conflict
Helped		(Facilitating) social interaction	Nonacceptance
Helplessness		(Facilitating) mobility	Discomfort
Goodness		Environmental segregation vs. integration	
Guilt			
Pride			
Shame			
Hope			
Hopelessness			

semantic differential measures developed by Osgood, Suci, and
Tannenbaum (1957).

Their system is attractive because of its conceptual and operational clarity; however, it is vulnerable to the same criticism that
was levied at the semantic differential system. This concerns the
tendency of (response) judgmental scales to behave differently depending on the concept (stimulus object) presented—what is termed
concept-scale interaction (for a brief discussion, see Fishbein and
Ajzen 1975:73–79). It is unreasonable to expect that pleasure from
an aesthetically attractive building is equivalent to the pleasure
obtained from a rewarding human relationship. By the same reasoning, an individual's submissiveness in the face of neighborhood criminal activity is unlikely to be equivalent to an individual's submissiveness (as reflected in restricted activity) in the face
of inadequate neighborhood transportation facilities. More generally, the complexity and diversity of human responses to the environment—as suggested by the admittedly unwieldy set of classifications in figure 4.3—are not encompassed in the Mehrabian
and Russell response typology.

The Selection of Environmental Transaction Outcomes for Empirical Study

The outcomes or consequences identified in several of the previous typologies (figure 4.3) were drawn on to operationalize the
meanings of an old person's environmental transactions. A listing
of hypothetical pairings of experiences and consequences examined in the study's empirical analyses is outlined in table 4.1 and
appendix A. The proposed outcomes or consequences were designed to capture the diversity of human responses to the everyday environment. Taking such a catholic approach is not without
scientific costs. Rigorous guidelines did not govern the selection
of the outcome categories. For example, experiences were not systematically distinguished for their potential of producing physiological as opposed to social outcomes, emotional versus instrumental satisfactions, or of satisfying intrapsychic rather than
interactive needs. However, particular care was taken to include

experiences with outcomes that had both potentially positive and negative influences on an individual's well-being. Thus, on the one hand, the studied environment was to have the capacity of contributing to an individual's physical and emotional comfort, achievement, leisure, companionship, and security, and, on the other hand, of contributing to his helplessness, restricted activity, anxiety, fatigue, and insecurity. This effort was guided primarily by a thorough familiarity with the literature on the needs of aging individuals and on the impact of residential environments on people's well-being (see, for example, Kasl 1977).

A potentially more serious criticism is that the hypothesized outcomes or consequences of environmental transactions often can only be inferred. For example, the older person's report of feeling too hot in the dwelling during the summer is associated with the consequence of physical discomfort—a not too remarkable inference. However, it is also associated with the consequence of helplessness under the assumption that few individual coping strategies are available to alleviate this environmental stress. The making of such analytical inferences necessarily gives a degree of tentativeness to some of the conclusions reached in the study's empirical analyses.

The Likelihood (Meaningfulness) of Environmental Transaction Outcomes (Meanings)

Four broad categories of response measures were constructed to operationalize the likelihood (meaningfulness) that individuals associate certain outcomes or consequences (meanings) with their environmental transactions. These included affective (feeling or emotional) responses, evaluative or judgmental responses, designative or awareness responses, and behavioral responses.[5]

Affective Responses. Questions eliciting this category of response inquired how frequently an individual had experienced feelings or emotions toward a particular object or event. The majority of questions in the study's interview schedule were in this category. The following questions and their codes are representative:

Table 4.1. Content, Structure, and Dynamic Properties of the Residential Experiential Environment

Object Category	Experience Items and Factors	Factor Loading[a]	Hypothetical Conseqences
	Factor 1. Satisfaction with community facilities, services, and people		
BEp	Satisfaction with places to have fun or relax in community	.679	Relaxation, leisure, spontaneity, physical and emotional comfort
SWp	Satisfaction with community services	.647	Physical and emotional comfort, peace of mind, self-maintenance, security, control
BEp	Satisfaction with stores in community	.515	Physical and emotional comfort, peace of mind, self-maintenance, security, control
PEs	Satisfaction with friends in community	.495	Involvement, familiarity, relatedness, belongingness, social acceptance
BEp	Satisfaction with dwelling's nearness to desired community places	.490	Physical and emotional comfort, peace of mind, spontaneity, security, control
SSs	Satisfaction with people in neighborhood	.326	Peace of mind, lack of conflict, social acceptance, reputation, pleasure
	Factor 2. Enjoy type of people in neighborhood		
SSs	Enjoyment from social class of people in neighborhood	.704	Peace of mind, lack of conflict, social acceptance, reputation, pleasure
SSs	Enjoyment from age composition of people in neighborhood	.611	Peace of mind, lack of conflict, social acceptance, reputation, pleasure
SSs	Enjoyment from race of people in neighborhood	.525	Peace of mind, lack of conflict, social acceptance, reputation, pleasure
SSs	Satisfaction with people in neighborhood	.341	Peace of mind, lack of conflict, social acceptance, reputation, pleasure
PEs	Enjoyed talking with storekeepers or clerks	.339	Spontaneity, novelty, involvement, relatedness
PEs	Enjoyment from visiting with neighbors	.289	Familiarity, relatedness, social acceptance, companionship, interpersonal understanding
	Factor 3. Concern and worry about crime		
UEp	Worry about being attacked when walking	.757	Fear, anxiety, insecurity, helplessness, restriction, submissiveness
UEp	Afraid to go out at night because of crime	.704	Fear, anxiety, insecurity, helplessness, restriction, submissiveness
BEp	Poor street lighting discouraged activity	.418	Helplessness, restriction, submissiveness
UEp	Concerned that thief might break into home	.300	Fear, anxiety, helplessness, insecurity, submissiveness
BEp	Type of transportation most frequently used	-.279	Restriction, anxiety, helplessness
BEp	Trouble walking because of sidewalk conditions	.258	Restriction, anxiety, helplessness, fatigue, physical discomfort

Factor 4. Annoyed at neighbors' care of property

BEp	Annoyed because neighbors neglect property	.728	Loss of reputation or status, anxiety, emotional discomfort, helplessness, displeasure
BEp	Annoyed because other neighborhood buildings less attractive	.698	Loss of reputation or status, anxiety, emotional discomfort, helplessness, displeasure
UEp	Annoyed because streets or sidewalks have litter	.400	Loss of reputation or status, anxiety, emotional discomfort, helplessness, displeasure
SSs	Satisfaction with people in neighborhood	-.277	Conflict, anxiety, loss of reputation or status, helplessness, displeasure
UEp	Annoyed by polluted air	.252	Loss of reputation or status, physical discomfort, helplessness, displeasure

Factor 5. Accessibility difficulties and restrictions

BEp	Places not within walking distance	.639	Restriction, physical discomfort, helplessness
BEp	Had difficulty getting laundry done	.457	Restriction, fatigue, physical discomfort, helplessness
BEp	Had difficulty getting transportation in community	.376	Restriction, anxiety, physical discomfort, helplessness
BEp	Annoyed because no place to rest while grocery shopping	.279	Restriction, anxiety, fatigue, physical discomfort, helplessness
BEp	Tired just from getting to places in community	.276	Fatigue, physical discomfort, submissiveness, restriction
BEp	Type of transportation most frequently used	-.265	Restriction, anxiety, helplessness

Factor 6. Good time from activity

BEp	Had good time in community	.689	Leisure, variety, freedom, pleasure
BEp	Had good time in own neighborhood	.645	Leisure, variety, freedom, pleasure
BEp	Felt good about doing something different in community	.299	Novelty, change, freedom, self-satisfaction, impulsiveness

Factor 7. Bothered by noise and dirt

UEp	Bothered by traffic and airplane noises, loud TVs	.551	Anxiety, physical discomfort, helplessness, displeasure
UEp	Bothered by people talking loudly outside dwelling	.474	Anxiety, physical discomfort, helplessness, displeasure
UEp	Annoyed by dirt and soot on windows	.467	Anxiety, loss of status, emotional discomfort, visual restriction, displeasure
UEp	Annoyed because streets or sidewalks have litter	.369	Loss of reputation or status, anxiety, emotional discomfort, displeasure
BEp	Had difficulty getting transportation in community	.317	Restriction, anxiety, physical discomfort, helplessness

Table 4.1. (continued)

Object Category	Experience Items and Factors	Factor Loading[a]	Hypothetical Consequences
	Factor 8. Has memories of possessions and place		
TN	Has thought about good memories of neighborhood	.736	Emotional comfort, self-satisfaction, achievement, sense of identity, belongingness
BEp	Has thought about memories of personal possessions	.518	Emotional comfort, self-satisfaction, achievement, sense of identity, individuality
	Factor 9. Bothered and restricted by bad weather		
NEp	Has postponed plans because of bad weather	.702	Restriction, anxiety, helplessness
NEp	Bothered by snow and cold weather	.446	Restriction, anxiety, physical discomfort, helplessness
BEp	Tired just from getting to places in community	.383	Fatigue, physical discomfort
	Factor 10. Feeling bored and lonely		
PEs	Felt bored in dwelling	.665	Boredom, loneliness, helplessness, emotional discomfort
PEs	Have felt lonely	.570	Loneliness, isolation, social rejection, anxiety, emotional discomfort
	Factor 11. Feelings of dwelling restrictions		
BEp	Frequency food or drug items home-delivered	.668	Dependency, physical comfort, peace of mind, self-maintenance, restriction
UEp	Nervous walking because of heavy traffic	.381	Fear, anxiety, helplessness, restriction
BEp	Tired just from getting to places in community	.311	Fatigue, submissiveness, physical discomfort, restriction
BEp	Attractiveness of building	−.259	Emotional comfort, self-satisfaction, achievement
	Factor 12. Grocery store as source of enjoyment		
BEp	Estimated blocks to nearest grocery store	.775	Security, peace of mind, self-maintenance, dominance
PEs	Enjoyed talking with storekeepers or clerks	−.309	Spontaneity, novelty, involvement, relatedness
	Factor 13. Discomforts in dwelling		
BEp	Annoyed because appliances have broken down	.439	Physical discomfort, helplessness, anxiety, submissiveness, displeasure
NEp	Felt dwelling was too hot in summer	.432	Physical discomfort, helplessness, anxiety, submissiveness, displeasure
NEp	Felt dwelling was too cold in winter or autumn	.356	Physical discomfort, helplessness, anxiety, submissiveness, displeasure
BEp	Trouble walking because of sidewalk conditions	.300	Anxiety, fatigue, helplessness, restriction, submissiveness
BEp	Attractiveness of building	.249	Loss of reputation or status, anxiety, helplessness, emotional discomfort

Factor 14. Availability of practical and emotional support

PEs	Instrumental social supports	−.604	Physical comfort, independence, physical security, peace of mind
PEs	Expressive social supports	−.477	Interpersonal understanding, self-confidence, emotional comfort, peace of mind, companionship

Factor 15. Feel lack of privacy

PEs	Felt lack of privacy in dwelling	.699	Anxiety, restriction, lack of privacy, emotional discomfort, helplessness
BEp	Feel dwelling too small	.398	Anxiety, boredom, restriction, crowding, helplessness, displeasure

[a] To facilitate interpretation of the factors, only items with loadings greater than .250 are reported here.

During the past summer, did you feel that your (house
or apartment) was too hot (even with air conditioning)?
    Most of the time.................................. 4
    Some of the time................................ 3
    Only occasionally. 2
    Never... 1

In the past few months, how often have you felt annoyed because the other buildings in your neighborhood
are not as attractive as yours?
    Many times. 4
    A few times. 3
    Only once or twice. 2
    Never... 1

Using the terminology of Fishbein and Ajzen (1975), these two
examples measure the individual's belief strength, that is, the
probability that an object is associated with some attribute.[6] In
this study, the attribute usually refers to an outcome or consequence that is identified in the question or is to be inferred. In the
first example, it is the likelihood that the house (object) is hot (attribute) from which an old person's physical discomfort and his
helplessness in the face of an uncontrollable environment can be
inferred. In the second example, it is the likelihood that the relative unattractiveness of neighborhood buildings (object) is associated with annoyance (the attribute), from which the consequence of loss of status can be inferred.

Evaluative or Judgmental Responses. All questions eliciting this
category of response inquired about the individual's evaluation or
judgment of a particular object or event. Only a small percentage
of questions were of this type. The following questions and their
codes are representative:

In the *past few months,* when you have looked at your
building from the outside, have you thought it looked
    Very attractive.................................. 1
    Somewhat attractive 2
    Somewhat unattractive 3
    Very unattractive 4

Here is a card that I want you to use to tell me how satisfied you are with each of the following things. This is how we will use it. If you point to the largest circle, or no. 7 (show and point to circles), it means you are *completely* satisfied. If you point to the smallest circle, or no. 1, it means you are *completely* dissatisfied. If you are neither completely satisfied nor completely dissatisfied, point to one of the other circles. That is, the less satisfied you are with something, the smaller the circle you should pick. If you pick the middle circle, no. 4, it means that you feel neutral, that is, just as satisfied as you are dissatisfied. Now, how satisfied are you with . . .

The places to have fun or relax
in Evanston? 7 6 5 4 3 2 1
The friends you have in Evanston? 7 6 5 4 3 2 1
The neighborhood you live in? 7 6 5 4 3 2 1

These responses may be interpreted as measures of the strength of the relationship between the object(s) (building, places, friends, neighborhood) and one or other of the attributes at either end of the scale(s) (attractive-unattractive, satisfied-dissatisfied). From this perspective, these responses also provide a measure of belief strength (see Fishbein and Ajzen 1975:53–79).[7] For interpretative purposes, however, the important assumption is that a stronger (or more polar) evaluation or judgment implies a greater likelihood/unlikelihood of an outcome or consequence. In the above questions, responses coded as 4,1,1, and 1 would imply that the individual's transactions with building, places (to have fun), friends, and neighborhood are very likely associated with unpleasant personal outcomes.

Designative or Awareness Responses. Questions eliciting this third category of response inquired about the likelihood that particular objects or events were part of the individual's experiential environment, implying that the individual was aware of or attended to their properties. Only a small percentage of questions were of this type. The following questions and their codes are representative:

In the past few months, have you had such things as
food or drugstore items delivered to your home?
Many times   4
A few times   3
Only once or twice   2
Never   1

During the past year did a close relative or a close
friend die?
Yes   1
No   0

This type of question also provides equivalent measures of belief strength, even though the consequences are not identified in
the question. In the first example, the stronger the likelihood of
food (object) being delivered to the home (attribute), the greater
the likelihood also of such hypothesized outcomes as physical
comfort, peace of mind, and dependence (on the service).[8]

Behavioral Responses. Questions eliciting this category of response inquired how frequently some aspect of an individual's overt
behavior was influenced by transactions with a particular object
or event. Only a small percentage of questions were of this type.
The following questions and their codes are representative:

Do you have trouble walking on the sidewalks in Evans-
ton because they are in bad condition?
Most of the time   4
Some of the time   3
Only occasionally   2
Never   1

When the weather is bad, do you postpone your plans to
go some place in Evanston?
Most of the time   4
Some of the time   3
Only occasionally   2
Never   1

These questions also provide measures of belief strength. They
describe the probability that overt behavioral outcomes such as

"trouble walking" or "postponed plans" (attributes) are associated with bad sidewalks and bad weather (objects or events).

Empirical Analysis of the Structure of the Experiential Environments of Evanston's Elderly

An empirical analysis was carried out to discern the structural organization of the environmental experiences reported by Evanston's elderly population. The analysis had three specific purposes. First, and most simply, the reader is introduced to the array of different environmental experiences reported by the Evanston sample of old people. It offers, therefore, an overall portrayal of the content and dynamic properties of the environmental experiences constructed by the researcher and reported by the respondent.

Second, the computed factor analysis solution indicates the structure or organizational complexity of these experiences. That is, it shows which experiences—distinguished by their content and meanings—were most closely related (or unrelated) to each other, thereby facilitating answers to questions such as: How many independent sets or dimensions of experiences are necessary to effectively describe the diversity of the older population's experiential reality? Does the organizational complexity of the experiential environment mirror the categorical diversity of the objects and events to which old people were asked to respond, or the dissimilarity of the meanings or outcomes they associated with different environmental transactions? For example, do *social* experiences tend to group together, or do experiences resulting in *fear* tend to group together?

Third, the analysis provides an empirical rationale for subsequent more detailed investigations of selected experiences. It is impossible to thoroughly analyze the patterns and individual antecedents of all the experiences reported by the Evanston elderly. One basis for excluding environmental experiences for detailed study is if their contents or dynamic properties are similar to others.

Factor Analysis of Experiential Environment

Methodology

Approximately 112 items in the interview schedule were designed to measure old people's responses to their environment. All
items were scored as interval-level (primarily ordered-metric) scales
or as dummy variables. The majority of the scaled items consisted of four- or five-point measures (the satisfaction items consisted of seven-point measures). A final principal-factor analysis
was performed on 64 of the original 112 experiential items.[9] An
item was excluded from the reported factor analysis for the following reasons: (1) in preliminary factor analyses it did not load
significantly (factor loadings of less than 0.25) on any of the first
20 rotated factors; (2) it was extremely skewed or, in the case of
two-category dummy variables, one of the categories described only
a very small number of persons (many of the stressful life events
were excluded for this reason); (3) it was very highly correlated
($r = > .65$) with another item (several of the territorial experiences
were excluded for this reason); or (4) it measured a very similar
concept as another item and it was expected that a statistically
artificial factor would be created by its inclusion.

Admittedly, researcher discretion is involved in this item dele-
tion process, and the researcher's familiarity with and understanding of the data will inevitably influence the final judgment.
The potential impact of such decisions should not be minimized.
In a statistical procedure such as factor analysis, changing the
number of variables, and thus the pattern of intercorrelation relationships, can alter the final solution considerably. To minimize
this risk, several factor analyses were carried out using somewhat
different sets of variables. The factor structure reported here was
representative of solutions derived in several of these preliminary
analyses.

The analysis yielded 23 principal factors with eigenvalues over
1.00, explaining 64 percent of the total variation in the 64-by-64
correlation matrix. These were then rotated to a normal varimax
position in order to yield a pattern of loadings that maximally

Table 4.2. Statistical Contributions of Varimax Rotated Residential Experience Factors

Factor No.	Factor Labels	No. of Items	Eigen-values	Factor Contributions[a] (in percentages)	
				To explained (common) variance[b]	To total variance
1.	Satisfaction with community facilities, services, and people	6	4.57	16.3	8.0
2.	Enjoy type of people in neighborhood	6	3.86	13.8	6.8
3.	Concern and worry about crime	6	2.09	7.5	4.0
4.	Annoyed at neighbors' care of property	5	1.80	6.4	3.7
5.	Accessibility difficulties and restrictions	6	1.56	5.6	3.3
6.	Good time from activity	3	1.39	5.0	3.0
7.	Bothered by noise and dirt	5	1.28	4.6	2.8
8.	Has memories of possessions and place	2	1.09	3.9	2.6
9.	Bothered and restricted by bad weather	3	1.01	3.6	2.4
10.	Feeling bored and lonely	2	0.93	3.3	2.3
11.	Feelings of dwelling restriction	4	0.90	3.2	2.3
12.	Grocery store as source of enjoyment	2	0.82	2.9	2.2
13.	Discomforts in dwelling	5	0.80	2.9	2.1
14.	Availability of practical and emotional support	2	0.74	2.6	2.0
15.	Feel lack of privacy	2	0.72	2.6	2.0
	Total: 15 Factors	59[c]		84.2	49.5

[a] Final communality estimates were reached by an iterative convergence method (44 iterations were required). All loadings reported are from the "simple structure" solution resulting from rotation of principal-factors to a normal varimax position.
[b] These are percentages of the common variance of the 64 variables used in the analysis. Only 15 of the 23 varimax rotated principal factors were considered interpretable and reported here. The remaining eight factors explained the remaining 15.8% of the common variance and 14.1% of the total variance.
[c] There were only 50 unduplicated items which loaded on 15 factors.

differentiated among the factors. Only 15 of these 23 factors were considered interpretable; these accounted for 50 percent of the total variation in the correlation matrix and 84 percent of the common variation (that is, the variance explained by the 23 varimax rotated factors—see tables 4.1 and 4.2). To facilitate interpretation of these 15 factors, only items with loadings greater than .250 are reported in table 4.2. Fifty of the original 64 experience items loaded on at least one of these 15 factors.

Findings

The experiences grouped in factor 1 (with one exception) differentiate old people according to how satisfied they are with aspects of their community. Four of the five experiences involve responses to the physical environment, especially its built aspects. The other experiences, although social in nature, involve people only as neutral objects (that is, as members of a social situation). Together, these experiences contribute to the physical and emotional comforts, self-status, leisure, self-maintenance, and sense of belonging needs of old people.

The six experiences grouped in factor 2 have in common their measure of old people's enjoyment (or lack of) of the other people living in their neighborhood. This factor indicates that reports of satisfaction with the population in the neighborhood are associated with reports of enjoyment with its compositional attributes: race, age, and social class. Such satisfaction is also related to old people's enjoyment of their personal relationships (visiting) with their neighbors. An enjoyable neighborhood social situation leads to individual outcomes such as peace of mind, lack of conflict, and social acceptance. The hypothesizing of "reputation" as an outcome of these experiences derives from evidence that residents of a neighborhood judge their own social status to be a reflection of the social composition of their neighborhood (Berry et al. 1976).

Factor 3 contains a closely connected set of worries and concerns about the criminal activity in the urbanized environment. It is expected that old people who are concerned about a home break-in or afraid of being criminally attacked while walking or going out at night feel more helpless, insecure, fearful, anxious, and submissive and restrict their activity as a result. The other items loading on this factor, although not directly related to crime, also involve experiences that can contribute to old people's anxiety, helplessness, and sense of restriction. For example, poor street lighting discourages activity at night, and poor sidewalk conditions make walking difficult; and a dependence on walking or public transit increases old people's exposure to possible street crime.

Factor 4 also groups physical environment experiences that involve transactions with the built environment. These experiences differentiate older people according to how annoyed they are by the physical neglect of the neighborhood. When the effects of these experiences are negative, they threaten older people's sense of mastery over their environment and contribute to their anxiety and emotional discomfort. Older people's reputation or status can also be threatened as a result of living in a neighborhood that is less attractive than expected or preferred. However, such outcomes are probably less extreme than those resulting from crime experiences.

Factor 5 contains a set of experiences differentiating old people according to how much difficulty they have in carrying out transactions in the physical environment. Restrictions may result if places are considered beyond walking distance or if transportation services or seating facilities are believed hard to obtain or unavailable. Old people experiencing such barriers are likely to feel anxious, fatigued, and helpless.

Factor 6 documents a very different dimension of old people's experiential environment. Included are experiences describing their likelihood of having a good time in the physical environment and of feeling good about doing different things. When the effects of these experiences are positive, they contribute to the old person's emotional comforts and leisure needs and also to their intrinsic needs for variety, novelty, freedom, and spontaneity.

Factor 7 gathers responses to the urbanized environment (see also factor 4) that differentiate old people according to how likely they are to be bothered or annoyed by noises, sounds, and the dirt of urban living. The negative effects of these experiences are probably less extreme than those resulting from the fear of crime. Nevertheless, they contribute to the old person's physical discomfort, anxiety, and helplessness. Also, if old people closely associate these negative effects with the status of their neighborhood, their self-esteem and personal reputation can be threatened.

Factor 8 isolates another set of physical environment experiences differentiating old people according to their likelihood of having good memories of their neighborhood and their personal possessions. Good memories will result in favorable feelings about objects and events not necessarily because of their present attributes, but because of qualities associated with their past. Such positive experiences will contribute to the old person's emotional comfort, sense of belonging, individuality, identity, and recallings of past achievements and successes.

Factor 9 includes a very different set of experiences consisting of the outcomes of old people's transactions with their natural environment. The first two experiences differentiate old people according to how likely they are to be bothered by the snow and cold of winter or to have postponed their plans because of inclement conditions. Confronted by the effects of these experiences, old people will experience anxiety, physical discomfort, and even helplessness if their activities are severely restricted. The inclusion of the third experience in this category suggests that old people who are bothered and restricted by weather conditions also experience fatigue just getting to places within their community.

The two experiences included in factor 10 involve responses to the personal social environment. Old people who felt lonely also felt bored in their dwelling. The more frequently loneliness or boredom is experienced by older people, the more probable that their current social relationships are inadequate. Possible consequences include isolation, severe emotional discomfort, and feelings of rejection.

Factor 11 includes a set of experiences differentiating old people according to how confined they are to their dwellings. Old people are distinguished who have food or drug items delivered to their home, who are nervous walking in heavy traffic areas, and who experience fatigue getting to places in their community. Old people reporting such constraining experiences also tend to evaluate their dwellings as more attractive (see chapter 7).

Factor 12 includes a pair of social and physical experiences that might appear to have little connection. A grocery store identified as being nearby is associated with the more frequent enjoyment of talking with storekeepers and clerks. This suggests that old people's rewarding social contacts may occur in the public places where they carry out their everyday transactions.

Factor 13 includes experiences involving transactions with the environment inside the dwelling. These experiences differentiate old people according to how they feel about their home's temperature, physical appearance, and appliances. Old people who experience physical discomforts in their dwellings also report difficulty in carrying out transactions outside of their dwellings, as evidenced by concurrent reports of walking problems due to poor sidewalk conditions.

Factor 14 includes two social experiences involving transactions with the personal environment. These experiences differentiate old people according to how available they feel significant others are to provide them with certain critical instrumental supports (e.g., grocery shopping, home help) and expressive supports (e.g., someone with whom to talk over problems or share good feelings). The presence of such supportive experiences can result in considerable peace of mind and contribute to old people's sense of physical independence and emotional security.

Factor 15 includes two experiences involving transactions inside the dwelling. As in factor 12, a social experience and a physical experience are grouped together. Feelings about the lack of privacy in the dwelling are associated with feelings that the dwelling is too small. The negative effects of these experiences, in addition to feelings of crowdedness and lack of privacy, include feelings of anxiety, restriction, helplessness, and a sense of not being in control.

Discussion and Conclusions

The factor analysis solution produced 15 interpretable dimensions by which to differentiate the environmental experiences of Evanston's elderly population.

The findings suggest that both the content and dynamic properties of experiences influence the observed structure. Although factors sometimes consisted of environmental transactions with similar objects or events (i.e., content) they also consisted of dissimilar objects and events that had similar meanings or outcomes (i.e., dynamic properties). Finally, certain experience groupings probably resulted in part from measurement effects. It is likely, for example, that the identical seven-point scale measurement of the "satisfaction" items contributed to their statistical grouping in factor one.

The complexity of the experiential environment is revealed by the substantial number of independent dimensions or categories of experiences required to adequately describe its diverse content and dynamic properties. However, although 15 such dimensions were identified, the factor solution itself still explained less than 50 percent of the total variation displayed by the correlation matrix of experiences. The presence of this unique statistical variation indicates an even more complex experiential environment structure than presented here. For this reason alone, the findings from this particular analysis should be viewed as more exploratory than conclusive.

Chapter 5

Conceptual Model of Individual Differences Underlying Environmental Experiences

It is accepted that individuals do not similarly interpret or evaluate the quality of their everyday environment or its impact on their well-being. However, no consensus exists as to the factors that lead to the very different experiential outcomes reported by a population. More is at issue than the strengths or completeness of one variable set relative to another. Fundamental disagreement exists over the epistemological assumptions underlying the variable selection process. A central and dividing issue is whether environmental or individual factors are more relevant and powerful determinants of the behavior and experiences of persons. Although researchers and writers often choose to ignore or evade this issue, any study that searches for the influences of human behavior (broadly defined) almost always emphasizes one position over another.

The epistemological and theoretical approach adopted in the following chapters emphasizes the importance of individual characteristics as antecedents of the variable impact that an environment has on a population. The study seeks to answer questions such as the following:

Are all old people equally susceptible to the vagaries of their environment?

Why are certain old people more likely than others to experience negative or unpleasant personal outcomes or consequences as a result of their everyday environmental transactions?

What factors peculiar to late life are most likely to influence the types and meaningfulness of an old individual's experiences?

Is the differential impact of a residential setting on the well-being of elderly persons a result of individual variability in the rate of aging or a consequence of diverse social, economic, and personality statuses typically found in any age group?

This chapter outlines a conceptual framework of individual differences to partially account[1] for the dissimilar environmental experiences reported by old people. Two following chapters consider in detail the major components of this framework.

Individual Differences in Old Age: Broad Issues

Much research has documented that old age is marked by the increased probability of certain social, psychological, and biological changes in the individual. For instance, the personal disruptions that result from physical impairments, although obviously afflicting persons at any stage of life, are more likely to occur in old age. Reminiscing about a past life is often a cognitive activity of old age (Lieberman and Falk 1971). Certain diseases of the body more frequently manifest themselves in old age, and the acuity and quickness of certain sensory and perceptual skills often display age-related declines. The older body is also more prone to physiological changes that reduce the quickness and agility of locomotion. Although agreement exists on the greater likelihood of these and various other personal events in old age, much controversy exists in the literature on aging regarding what constitutes normal aging and what individual and socioenvironmental processes are most influential.

A sense of the scientific debate is illustrated by the polarized opinions of gerontologists regarding the validity of the disengagement theory of aging. One side held that the aging individual's often observed decline in social role activity and ego involvement with the outside world could be characterized as voluntary and a result of the natural course of human development. Opponents contended that there was nothing voluntary or intrinsic about role loss, psychological withdrawal, and activity decline. Rather, it was argued that these events were often unwillingly imposed upon the aging individual by severe physiological impairments, chronic illnesses, human-made environmental barriers, social stereotyping, and constraining social institutions (Cath 1975; Rosow 1974:10).

There was also disagreement about whether the differences observed among middle-aged persons, the "young-old," and the "old-old" elderly were age-related or rooted in cohort and period effects (Maddox and Wiley 1976). It was argued that the sometimes documented age-related or developmental differences between middle-aged and elderly populations were a result of these groups being exposed to different historical events, environmental situations, and societal expectations of normative behavior. For example, the present generation of elderly people has less education and drives automobiles less frequently than middle-aged persons. Both differences are primarily a function of the different opportunities and expectations present in the two sociohistorical periods when these population groups were young adults.

Several scholars of aging have emphasized the impact of society's age-graded or age-status system on a population's pattern of aging (Neugarten and Hagestad 1976). As summarized elsewhere:

> Age as a social characteristic provides society with a basis for defining preferred or expected behavior; for allocating and differentiating social roles; for regulating the relationships between its members; for ascribing status; for distributing valued resources, rights, responsibilities, power, and prestige; for regulating participation in social institutions; for facilitating an individual's biological and psychological capacities; for regulating the timing and ordering of life's events; and for influencing an individual's self-perceptions. (Golant 1979b:8–9)

However, there is considerable disagreement about just how pervasive the influence of the age-grade system is and whether it leads to a more beneficial or harmful quality of life for the American elderly population. One scholar stressed the ambiguous and negative impact of these influences and how they discriminated against persons in the late stage of life:

> The transition to old age differs significantly from earlier status successions. Its occurrence tends to be vague, amorphous, and unregulated, as the scarcity of its *rites de passage* effectively reflects. . . . Society attaches little importance to the older person's functions and thereby accords him less than a pro rata share in the distribution of the rewards. (Rosow 1974:24, 27)

Other critics pointed to the deleterious effects of a material culture created by a society unsympathetic to the needs of old people. They argued, for instance, that the physical or human-made attributes of residential settings occupied by old persons often were not conducive to their autonomy or independence. As an illustration, they pointed to the architectural barriers in the housing of old persons that restricted or endangered their freedom of activity (Lawton 1975).

This negative portrayal of society is not uniformly agreed upon by all social scientists, but even those in agreement usually concede that its influences are not similarly felt by all old people. To suggest otherwise would be to erroneously depict an elderly population with homogeneous needs and resources. A promising theoretical basis for predicting the role of individual differences emerges from a set of arguments by Mischel (1973:276). He questioned "when situations are most likely to exert powerful effects and conversely, when person variables are likely to be influential." He suggested that situations have weaker effects when they ". . . do not generate uniform expectancies concerning the desired behavior, do not offer sufficient incentives for its performance, or fail to provide the learning conditions required for successful construction of the behavior" (p. 276). This proposition takes on special importance if Rosow (1974) is correct in his belief that society's old age *rites de passage* are "vague, amorphous, and unregulated," offering as they do ambiguous role and behavior models for the successful transition from middle age to old age. Then by Mischel's reasoning individual variables are probably stronger determinants of behavior in old age; that is, "variance from individual differences will be greater" (1973:276).

In summary, old people who occupy the same sociocultural system and transact with its people, institutions, and material culture will have several dimensions of their behavior and experiences influenced in a predictable fashion. However, the sociocultural system does not have the same beneficial or deleterious consequences for all old persons, nor has it likely exerted similar quality of life influences on individuals at any stage of their development. In a parallel sense, all elderly persons age to some extent in a predictable fashion independently of the sociocultural system of which they are a part, because they share common structures and functions as complex, concrete living systems (Miller 1978). However, it is inaccurate to speak of the normality of aging as if it were an invariable process. Although aging leads to certain predictable changes in individuals, the tempo and patterning of physiological, motivational, and behavioral responses to the aging process display much variability.

Epistemological and Theoretical Orientations

The differential emphasis placed on environmental (situational) and individual factors as influences of the well-being and successful aging of old people reflects fundamentally different epistemological positions.

On the one hand, a situationist approach argues that an individual's behavior and well-being can be accounted for by an observable, objectively, separately defined environment. This position is represented by the Skinnerian school (1953) of psychology and can be characterized as follows:

> Situationism presupposes the distinction between stimulus and response, and explains the latter in terms of the former. If a re-

sponse is not accounted for in terms of a stimulus (either evoking or reinforcing), then we have implicitly abandoned any claim
to an objective account of behavior. (Bowers 1973:316–317)

Carried to its extreme, situationism argues that behavior is ultimately accounted for or controlled by the objective environment.
An alternative epistemological position is embodied in the interactionist or biocognitive view (Endler and Magnusson 1976). It also
acknowledges that a "person's behavior is a function of the situation," but argues forcefully that "situations are as much a function of the person" (Bowers 1973:327), expressed symbolically as
$E = f(I)$. Proposing that individual characteristics influence the types
and meaningfulness of environmental experiences can be seen as
a conceptual and methodological articulation of this $E = f(I)$ position. An elaboration of this functional relationship follows.

Environment as a Function of the Individual

The conceptualization of an experiential environment is in itself an expression of the interactionist position because the environment is described in subjective or personal terms. However,
the adoption of an interactionist position is more than merely a
recognition of an individually defined empirical reality. It also
embodies critical assumptions regarding the causality or origins
of that reality, and it is here that it diverges most from the situationist viewpoint. A discussion of the dual ways in which the environment can be considered a function of the individual should
help elucidate the distinctiveness of the interactionist position.

The first sense in which situations are a function of the person
can be contrasted with a stimulus-response psychological perspective. Interactionists argue that an objectively defined stimulus cannot be accepted as a sufficient cause of a response, because
the properties and consequences of the stimulus are themselves a
function of the individual's cognitive and perceptual processes. The
interactionist, in short, does not "presuppose the separateness of
stimulus and response" (Bowers 1973:328). As a result: "Interac-

tionism's reliance upon thought and inference to establish the objective state of affairs stands in stark contrast to situationism's preference for naive physicalism, which regards inference and abstraction as a retreat from the objectivity of hard facts" (Bowers 1973:331).

Several simple examples illustrate how the reality of the environment is in large part the reality of the "knower." When two different people are asked to *describe* a clearly designated building on a street, their portrayals will inevitably differ. Their different responses will be due, in part, to their different cognitive representations of the building. For example, one person may distinguish attributes (color, shapes, slopes, etc.) ignored or missed by another individual. Similarly, a building's tenant will *evaluate* its attractiveness differently than its architect who had his own idiosyncratic design intentions and purposes. The different evaluations of the building may also be due to the very unlike residential histories of two individuals. The newcomer to a city might view the building merely as a landmark serving to guide his navigations about the city, whereas the longtime resident might recall symbolic and sentimental memories concerning the building's construction, because it marked the advent of a new architectural style. Alternatively, the evaluations may differ because the building's second floor is only accessible by stairs, thus preventing its use by the newcomer who has ambulatory difficulties. And, as a final example, when asked about the benefits and costs of tearing the building down, an art historian might loudly proclaim its loss as a historical monument to the city's past, whereas the land developer would detail the economic gains ultimately to be realized from its removal.

It is important to emphasize that many situationists recognize the existence of an individual's cognitive and perceptual processes and inner mental states. However, it is argued that these are merely *responses* to a lifetime of exposure to external events with the result that "cognitive and phenomenological explanations are incomplete . . . until their situational determinants are uncovered; then they are obsolete." Thus, "cognition is viewed primarily as a response mediating the causal impact of external stimuli" (Bowers 1973:316). Earlier, Mischel clearly elaborated:

> Sometimes mental traits and states are invoked as if they were the causes of behavior while their own antecedents are ignored or forgotten. Unfinished causal sequences are found whenever mental states (cognitions, affects, motives, etc.) are employed as explanations of behavior while the determinants of the mental states themselves are omitted from the analysis. (1968:95)

Situations can be considered a function of the person in a second important sense. It can be demonstrated that individuals create, select, and maintain environments with objects and events (physical and social) that are consistent with their own cognitive, motivational, and behavioral states. As a consequence, the environment possesses qualities that are congruent in some respect to the individual's purposes and intentions. A relevant theoretical construct—Barker's (1968) "behavioral setting"—portrays these reciprocal processes and the resulting behavior-environment congruence. Behavior settings are distinguished by the predictable and uniform (standing) patterns of behavior of their occupants and by the predictable and uniform attributes of their nonpsychological (physical) objects. From Barker's perspective, people's behavior conforms to the designated behavior and attributes of the setting for at least two reasons: first, people have actively selected such settings because of an affinity between their own mental and behavioral states (for example, their goals, abilities, values, etc.) and those supported by the behavioral setting; and second, because of their vested interest in insuring that the settings continue to function in predictable ways, they are motivated to maintain the behavior of the setting by the "deviation countering" or "vetoeing" (Barker 1968:181) of any inappropriate actions of other participating or invading persons. Alternatively, if confronted with an incompatible setting, the occupants can exit themselves.

Other evidence indicates that social or interpersonal environments are created by individuals who are motivated to engender behaviors in other people that are consistent with their own (Bowers 1973:329). For example, Wachtel (1973) suggests that the consistent interpersonal behavior of some individuals results, in part, from their creating consistent and predictable social environments. For instance, people with dominant personalities will select social situations in which the other actors have less dominant personalities.

The creation of an environment that conforms to people's changing needs and resources is further illustrated by the "drift hypothesis" (Faris and Dunham 1939). The hypothesis implies that individuals, because of a decline in their physical, social, economic, or mental competence, move from their present residential settings to others having attributes (such as type and cost of housing) that are more consistent or supportive of their weakened state and new behaviors.

The literature offers other less extreme illustrations of this purposive behavior. For example, Gans (1967) reported that the changed life-styles of former central city residents following their moves to a new low-density suburb (Levittown, New Jersey) were anticipated by them. They had deliberately relocated so as to engage in a life-style associated with the suburban environment. Fischer and Jackson (1976) have similarly stressed the importance of this self-selection process for understanding the population characteristics of the suburbs. A somewhat different illustration is provided by members of a community who do not socially accept a new resident. To cope with this antagonistic response, migrants must educate their environment (that is, its occupants) as to their backgrounds and credentials (Cumming and Cumming 1963).

An Appropriate Model of Man

The conceptualization of an environment that is a function of the individual requires certain accompanying assumptions about the human organism. These are largely encompassed in Altman's (1975) social-systems, ecological model of man. The human must be conceived as not only engaged in subjective psychological processes, but also in overt behavior, the properties and outcomes of which are dependent upon and reciprocally related to an environmental context. Echoing the interactionist position, Altman calls for an ecological model in which "not only does the environment act on people, but they act on environments" (p. 205). The specification of three further assumptions clarifies this study's model of human functioning. These depict persons as boundedly rational, complex living systems, who behave purposively and adaptively.

The Purposively Behaving Individual

The assumption of a purposively behaving or goal-oriented individual implies the presence of the following three conditions:

> (a) a desire, whether actually felt or not, for some [goal, that is,] object, event, or state of affairs, as yet future;
> (b) the belief, whether tacit or explicit, that a given behavior sequence will be efficacious as a means to the realization of that object, event, or state of affairs; and
> (c) the behavior pattern in question. (Taylor 1968:240)

Many psychologists recognize the conception of purposively behaving individuals who actively initiate transactions with their environment in a way that is consistent with their cognitive and motivational contexts. For example, Cantril in his discussion of the genesis of aspirations emphasized: "People do not react *to* their environments in any mechanistic way, but transact *with* an environment in which they themselves are active agents" (1965:15). Central to Fiske and Maddi's theoretical framework for understanding the functions of varied experience is the portrayal of a neuropsychologically active organism . . .

> in continuous interaction with its internal and external environments. . . . [who is] more than simply reactive: it behaves in such a way that it receives stimulation with impact appropriate for

the level of activation required by the particular situation demanded or by its own organic functions. (1961:17)

Similarly, Leff, after reviewing the works of various modern cognitive theorists, concluded:

> Human information processing is *active*. Our conscious experience, whether it derives mainly from perceptual environmental input, from memories, or from imagination, seems frequently to involve complex processes of concept formation, hypothesis testing, abstracting, problem solving, the activation and interlinking of frames of reference, and other active mental operations. . . . the overall nature of human information processing . . . suggests that we should be able to exert considerable self-direction over the quality and content of our experience by performing appropriate cognitive operations. (1978:86)

A further illustration is provided by Wapner, Kaplan, and Cohen's organismic-developmental perspective for understanding man-environment transactions, which conceives of the human being as a "historical, social, goal-oriented organism":

> One does not come into a new environment as an inert passive entity. One goes to a new environment with certain purposes in mind, whether these are vaguely formulated (e.g., getting a new experience) or precisely formulated (e.g., finding a house for one to live in), and with a certain projected schema of what the new environment will be like. (1973:259)

The Adaptively and Optimizing Behaving Individual

Purposively behaving individuals are not merely goal-oriented, however; they are also goal-directed (Buckley 1967:53), that is, adaptively-behaving. Purposeful behavior is initiated in response to positive feedback from earlier environmental transactions. That is, "the results of one's own action are included in the new information by which subsequent behavior is modified. Thus, by responding to what he observes of his own activity a person makes necessary corrections" (Shibutani 1968:333). Such corrections may

involve physiological, cognitive, affective, and behavioral responses to earlier unfavorable transaction outcomes. Thus, individuals attempt to adjust to existing environmental conditions, and
"ideally strive to achieve 'optimal environments,' or those that
maximize the fulfillment of their needs and the accomplishments
of their goals and plans" (Stokols 1978:259). Experientially, this
implies an individual who . . . "in a given situation . . . will generate the response pattern which [he] expects is most likely to lead
to the most subjectively valuable outcomes (consequences) in that
situation" (Mischel 1973:270); and who is propelled . . . "to learn
and to devise new ways of behaving that will enable [him] both
to extend the range and heighten the quality of value satisfactions
and to insure the repeatability of those value satisfactions already
experienced" (Cantril 1965:10).

The Boundedly Rational Behaving Individual

It also is assumed that humans behave rationally. However, as
Simon (1957:198) emphasized, this rationality is bounded by an
individual's world view that inevitably is simplified, limited, and
erroneous. Unlike the scientific observer who is often assumed to
be detached and rational, people neither have complete or accurate information about their environments nor are they likely to
process their available information in the most efficient or advan-
tageous way. As Stokols (1978:258) also observed, "people are often
forced by situational constraints to accept undesirable environmental conditions, or at best to 'satisfice' (Simon 1957)." Moreover, while striving to act adaptively and optimally, individuals
seldom resolve or have under control all or even most of their
sources of stress, unsolved problems, or needs (Howard and Scott
1965).

A Conceptualization of Individual Differences

Two major categories of individual differences are proposed in
this study as antecedents of the variable environmental experi-

ences of elderly persons. First, individuals are conceptualized as knowers of their environment and are differentiated according to how they perceive, interpret, structure, and evaluate information from their environment. This category is a translation of the first interactionist sense in which the environment is viewed as a function of the individual. Second, individuals are conceptualized as having behavioral relationships with their environment and are differentiated according to their environmental occupancy and utilization patterns. This category is a translation of the second interactionist sense in which the environment is interpreted as a function of the individual (figure 5.1).

Individuals As Knowers of Their Environment

To summarize the various ways individuals differently know their environment, they are described by seven mental and behavioral states. These differentiate old persons according to (a) their environmental cognitions; (b) their environmental needs or demands; (c) the benefits or harms they associate with satisfying (or not satisfying) these demands; (d) their anticipation of realizing or fulfilling these demands; (e) their abilities or competencies to satisfy these demands; (f) how well adapted they are to their environment; and (g) how motivated they are to recall memories of the past.

Several individual variables are proposed from which to infer the presence of these states. These measures typify a variety of current approaches used to conceptualize individual differences for the purpose of explaining people's variable evaluative and affective responses to their environment (Wohlwill 1976:75–76). These included measurements of old people's personality traits, environmental dispositions, social and demographic characteristics, and individual "constructs that have specific reference to the processing of environmental stimulation" (Wohlwill 1976:75) such as adaptation level, competence levels, and health status.[2]

Some of these variables predict the evaluative and affective responses of individuals in specific environments or situations. That is, individuals are differentiated along dimensions that are relat-

Figure 5.1. Model of Individual Differences Proposed As Antecedents of Environmental Experiences

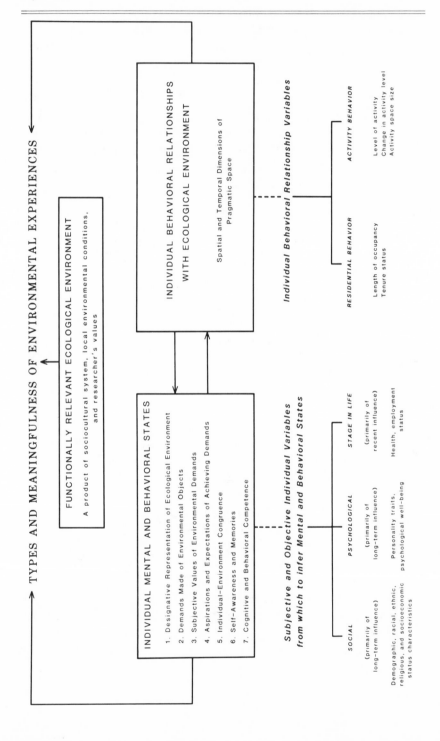

able to commensurate dimensions of objective indicators (for example, according to how favorably (or unfavorably) disposed they are to an urban way of life). Other individual variables are not directly relatable to particular dimensions of environmental attributes. These predict how people will dissimilarly process and interpret information from a wide range of environmental transactions. For instance, old individuals in poor health (from which low competence can be inferred) are predicted to perceive more environmental barriers in their communities than old individuals in good health. A full discussion of these proposed mental and behavioral states and individual variable measures are reported in the following chapter.

The Behavioral Relationships of Individuals With Their Environment

Individuals not only differ as to how they know their everyday environment, but also as to how they actually occupy and utilize its contents. Two distinctive categories of behaviors are proposed as antecedents of old people's variable environmental experiences: residential and activity behaviors. The former differentiates old persons according to the length of time they have lived in a place, and whether they own or rent their dwellings. The latter category differentiates old persons according to the frequency with which they leave their dwellings to temporarily occupy, utilize, and manipulate distinguishable parts and properties of their environment and according to the locational or spatial context of these actions or pursuits. These behavioral relationships influence the content and consequences of old people's experiences in two ways. First, they result in old people carrying out their environmental transactions in different spatial and temporal contexts with different contents and unequal opportunities for satisfying (or not satisfying) their needs and goals. Second, these behaviors, because they are overt expressions of diverse motives, constraints, beliefs, and values, result in environmental transactions having dissimilar social and psychological significance to old people.

These individual variables differ in an important way from those describing the individual *qua* knower. They do not describe something *about* individuals (like their demographic characteristics and environmental processing abilities) or *in* individuals (like their dispositions). Rather, they describe observable tangible relationships *between* persons and their objective environment. In this sense, these individual behaviors more correctly denote individual-environmental differences since they explicitly incorporate concrete environmental referents. For instance, one moves to *someplace*, remains *somewhere*, or travels to some *location*. It is for this reason that activity and residential behaviors are labeled behavioral *relationships*. They literally have no meaning independent of the objective environment to which they are spatially and temporally linked.

The formulation of these variables is predicated on the belief that individuals can be profitably dimensionalized by variables that are functionally relatable to concrete aspects of the environment. The behavioral relationships proposed here as antecedents of old people's environmental experiences constitute such functional measures and serve two obvious purposes (Stokols 1978). First, they provide indicators of how salient environments are to individuals, given the assumption that environmental use and occupancy are evidence of personally significant environmental transactions. Second, they facilitate judgments about the external validity of environment-behavior research findings, which ideally require assessments of not only the representativeness of populations and environments, but also of the representativeness of the transactions occurring between them.

The proposing of activity and residential behaviors as influences of environmental experiences constitutes a major departure from prior research. The literature has treated these behaviors as output or performance variables, as something to be explained, rather than something to do the explaining. Past studies have investigated why attitudes and personality traits lead to certain behaviors; how perceived environmental barriers (for example, large distances, poor transportation facilities) restrict travel behavior; and how social, psychological, and economic factors influence people's moves from their residences. Environment-behavior analyses of the elderly population in particular have failed to evaluate the impact of these behavioral relationships. Although researchers have studied the moving, transportation, and activity patterns of the elderly (Lawton and Nahemow 1973; Golant 1979a) and have noted their potential effects on environmental interactions (Lawton 1977a:280–281), these behaviors have not been formally integrated as *explanatory* factors in current theoretical models (see Parr 1980; Windley and Scheidt 1980; and Howell 1980). A full discussion of these behavioral relationships and their variable measures are reported in chapter 7.

Chapter Six

Elderly Individuals as Knowers of Their Environment

The model's differentiation of individuals as "knowers" was influenced by Mischel's (1973) "cognitive social learning approach to personality." Mischel argued that "a viable psychology of personality demands attention to person variables that are the products of the individual's total history and that in turn mediate the manner in which new experiences affect him" (p. 265). He proposed shifting "the unit of study from global traits inferred from behavioral signs to the individual's cognitive activities and behavior patterns, studied in relation to the specific conditions that evoke, maintain, and modify them and which they, in turn, change" (p. 265). Emphasizing that "a social behavior approach to persons does not imply an empty organism" (p. 265), he proposed a set of cognitive social learning person variables drawn from the cognitive and behavioral psychology literature that "suggest useful ways of conceptualizing and studying specifically how persons mediate the impact of stimuli and generate distinctive complex molar behavior patterns" (p. 265).

Leaving aside the question of whether Mischel considers his "person variables" as antecedents of human behavior—rather than merely "responses" that mediate—his variable conceptualization offers a language for articulating the mental and behavioral states underlying an individual's experiences. For this reason, several of his categorical distinctions are incorporated in the present conceptual framework. However, other of his categories have been reformulated, plus person categories not systematically addressed by Mischel have been added. Consequently, the following proposed set of seven individual states should be judged on its own merits.

An Individual's Mental and Behavioral States

Designative Representation of the Environment

The types and meaningfulness of an individual's experiences most immediately depend on the sources, the amount, and the completeness of the information he has about objects and events in present and past environments; the attributes or properties of objects and events to which he attends; the perceived structure of the attributes associated with these objects and events; the identification of these objects and events as representative of larger categories of environmental phenomena; and the interpretation of this information as serving certain functions.

The individual's designative representation of his environment is one obvious manifestation of his bounded rationality. Either through ignorance or by deliberate acts, the individual attends wholly to certain objects and events (and their attributes) in his environment, filters out the information emitted by others, and is entirely unaware of information potentially available from other sources. One basis for discerning the content boundaries of an individual's environmental transactions is to identify those parts and attributes of the environment he is more aware of than others. For the individual, this selective attention to certain parts and attributes of the environment at the expense of others serves an important adaptive function. It enables the processing of environmental information that is more central to his needs and goals and thereby reduces the possibility of information overload (Milgram 1970).

The individual's representation of his environment depends also on how the attributes associated with particular objects or events are structured, that is, their degree of differentiation, complexity, unity, or organization (Zajonc 1960). For example, an architect's representation of a building, comprising detailed and diverse sets of distinguishing attributes is usually far more structurally complex than a layman's representation.

Environmental objects are assigned membership in general categories on the basis of their denotative attributes. Such categorization often facilitates the identification of similar sets of objects. Certain categories of attributes specifically distinguish the temporal and spatial qualities of objects and events. Examples of the former include the differentiation of objects or events according to their frequency, tempo, promptness, and regularity. Spatial qualities include locational attributes such as distance, direction (north, east, etc.), and density (Golledge and Rushton 1976). Designations of a community as being more urban than rural or as being oriented to families rather than singles are examples of other comparable categorical representations. In a seminal work, Lynch (1960) concluded that an individual's image of the city consisted of five major categories of elements: paths, edges, districts, nodes, and landmarks. These and other object categorizations can directly influence environmental assessments or use, as, for example, when a service facility is designated by middle-class elderly as "catering only to the poor or indigent." Undoubtedly, the most studied and understood categorization with comparable effects is the assignment of individuals to population groups stereotyped according to racial, religious, or ethnic criteria. Thus, the white elderly person's identification of another elderly person as "black" may discourage the initiation of social transactions.

The information received from the environment is represented in different ways according to its functions for the individual. Bruner (1966), for example, distinguished between enactive, iconic, and symbolic representations to characterize the way in which an individual translates or encodes information. Some information is interpreted according to its ability to facilitate behavioral actions or operations—the enactive mode; for example, objects such as landmarks may be identified for their navigation or orientation functions. Iconically represented information is encoded as images, that is, in terms of its overall perceptual qualities, such as the description of a neighborhood as a slum. Finally, information can be encoded into words or language that refer to environmental information as symbols or abstractions, resulting in an interpretation that transcends an object's concrete properties. The singling out of a neighborhood because of its historical significance is an example.

The variability of individuals' designative representations of the environment will contribute most directly to differences in the content of their experiential environments. The result is that certain parts or properties of an environment will not have the same potential of exerting their effects on all individuals. For instance, the senior center that is outside an individual's awareness space cannot be interpreted as having harmful or beneficial effects. However, unknowingly to the individual, it can impose some very high opportunity costs (using the terminology of economists). That is, a lack of awareness can lead to various undesirable experiences such as incomplete information about needed environmental resources (as advertised in a senior center), loneliness (because of "lost" senior center friendships), and so on. Somewhat paradoxically, an "ignorance" of environmental properties may also contribute to more positive experiences. For instance, not being aware of a nearby neighborhood with high crime rates may prevent feelings of anxiety. Similarly, not being aware of other old people who live nearby in better quality dwellings may relieve old respondents from making housing comparisons that could lead them to evaluate their own residential situations less favorably.

There is a danger of assigning too much importance to the individual's designative representation of his environment as a predictor of his environmental experiences. The individual's conception of his world is continually changing in response to new goals and needs. Consequently, an individual's representation of his environment can quickly change as new demands require it. In this sense, new environmental representations and experiences can be acquired simultaneously. For example, the older person requiring services from a new medical center may quickly enlarge his cognitive map of the community to encompass this facility.

Demands Made of Environment

Consistent with the model of man as a purposively behaving being, individuals differ in the demands they make of their environment, a reflection of their variable intrinsically and extrinsically motivated needs, goals, and plans (Hunt 1963). Various examples of such need- and goal-oriented demands were already introduced (figure 4.3) in the review of the alternative consequences of individual-environment transactions. Both the needs (or demands) the individual seeks to satisfy by his environmental transactions and the subjectively interpreted outcomes or effects (meanings) of his environmental transactions may be described by common terminology or considered along commensurate dimensions. As an adaptively behaving organism, the individual strives for environmental transactions that yield positive outcomes, such as enjoyment, companionship, mobility, excitement, self-esteem, and security, and attempts to avoid transactions yielding negative outcomes, such as displeasure, restriction, anxiety, loneliness, conflict, and stress.

Because of individual and societal influences, the fulfillment of certain needs, goals, or plans is of greater importance than the fulfillment of others; not all of an individual's environmental transactions are of equal significance or salience. Consequently, individuals differ not only in the types of demands they make of their environment but also in how these demands are ranked in priority.

Like an individual's designative representation of his environment, the types and salience of an individual's environmental demands can change a great deal during a lifetime. Such change is a reflection of the individual's prior learning experiences and adaptive behaviors. That is, an individual's current environmental demands are in part a measure of his having learned that earlier demands were unreachable, unimportant, or unrewarding and then adapting to these facts. In this sense, the change in the demands that the individual makes of his environment reflects his goal-*directed* behavior, that is, behavior initiated in response to environmental feedback. From this perspective, the environment or situation can be considered as "making demands" of an individual. An obvious inquiry is whether any individual demands, except those motivated by primary drives, are in the final analysis anything but goal-directed. This argument is central to the situationist's position. Its importance largely depends on how far back the investigator wishes to telescope the origins of an individual's experiences.

Interindividual variability in the types and salience of needs and demands will influence the likelihood of experiential outcomes in two fundamental ways. First, the selective seeking or avoidance of particular environmental transactions influences, in turn, the range of possible experienced outcomes. For instance, elderly persons may only initiate environmental transactions for which they anticipate favorable outcomes. This would help explain, for example, why some old people respond they have no needs that must be satisfied after dark; that is, nighttime transactions are associated with criminal activity, something to be avoided. Second, some individuals are more likely than others to satisfy their demands because the environment will not have the same potential of fulfilling or realizing equally the needs or demands of all individuals. For instance, in a given community, old people seeking friendships with persons having the same religious preferences may find it more difficult to satisfy their social needs than old people who are indifferent to the religious preferences of their friends.

Subjective Values of Environmental Demands (the individual's comparison or adaptation level)

For each of the demands the individual makes of his environment, he associates a perceived or subjective value to its expected outcome (Mischel 1973:272). Individuals commonly differ as to the *amount* of benefits or harms they associate with the fulfillment or unfulfillment of their environmental demands (Rosenberg 1956)— that is, *how much* fear, pleasure, satisfaction, excitement, restriction, or fatigue. In extreme instances, individuals differ as to the *direction* of the consequences or outcomes they associate with their environmental demands, that is, whether subjective values are negative or positive. For example, whereas the prospect of meeting new neighbors can be a source of anxiety and displeasure for some old persons, it can be a source of pleasure for others.

Several theorists have proposed that the subjective value of such outcomes depends on the totality of an individual's previous transactions with the relevant objects. As a result of such transactions, an "adaptation level" is established (Helson 1964), referring to a "person's point of subjective neutrality for making judgments along a given dimension" (Leff 1978:121). Similarly, Thibaut and Kelley (1959:81) specified a "comparison level" (CL), that is, a standard against which individuals evaluate the attractiveness of a relationship. Although Thibaut and Kelley were primarily concerned with interpersonal relationships, their specification of the comparison level appears to be an appropriate basis by which to speculate about the value associated with any relational outcome. As Shaw and Constanzo summarize:

> The CL can be represented as the neutral point on a continuum ranging from dissatisfaction to satisfaction. If the outcomes of a given relationship exceed this hypothetical neutral point, the relationship will probably be regarded as attractive and satisfactory. If these outcomes fall below this neutral point, the relationship will probably be considered to be unsatisfactory and unattractive. (1970:93)

Assume, for example, that a city is judged along a dimension ranging from quiet to noisy by two individuals, one migrating from a rural place and the other migrating from another city. Because the city dweller is more likely to be accustomed to loud noises, his adaptation or comparison level would be higher (nearer to the noisy end of the quiet-noisy dimension) than that of the former rural resident. Predictably, the new city would be judged as noisier by the rural resident than by the former city dweller (for such an empirical example, see Wohlwill and Kohn 1976). Consistent with the notion that an individual's adaptation level shifts upward or downward over time in response to new environmental transactions and their salience, it can be predicted that over time the former rural resident's adaptation or comparison level will shift upward, with the result that he will judge the city as being less and less noisy over the long run.

Aspirations and Expectations of Achieving Demands

The likelihood that an individual will experience a certain outcome not only depends on the nature of his demands and the values or amounts of satisfaction or dissatisfaction associated with them. The interpretation of an environmental transaction also depends on whether its outcomes (as assessed by the individual) are *consistent* with those anticipated or hoped for (Fishbein and Ajzen 1975). This anticipation also has an important temporal aspect. Individuals will anticipate not only *if* an outcome will occur, but will anticipate about its imminence, that is, when it will occur (Lazarus 1966:111).

These interpretations depend on what standards the individual employs to measure consistency. Although several standards can be identified, two appear most relevant (Campbell, Converse, and Rodgers 1976:14). One of these is the individual's aspiration level, which refers to the "situation that a person hopes eventually to attain"; the other is his expectation level, which involves the "situation he feels he is likely to attain in the fairly immediate future" (Campbell, Converse, and Rodgers 1976:14). Thus, the interpretation given to a transaction's outcome depends on the extent to which goal outcomes, their associated rewards or harms, and their timing are consistent with the individual's expectations or aspirations.

Two propositions are available that suggest the form of these relationships. First, Campbell, Converse, and Rodgers have focused on the implications of a discrepancy between expected and realized rewards: "satisfaction is presumed to decline the greater the gap between relevant aspirations and the individual's assessment of the actual current situation" (1976:172). Second, Neugarten has been concerned with outcomes whose timing is unexpected:

it is not the occurrence of the life event itself which precipitates an adaptational crisis, for such events are anticipated and rehearsed and the transition accomplished without shattering the sense of continuity of the life cycle. Instead, it is when such events occur "off-time" rather than "on-time," for example, when grandparenthood, retirement, major illness, or widowhood occur earlier in life than expected, that crisis is experienced. (1977:639)

As discussions by Kahana, Liang, and Felton (1980) and Kemper (1978) suggest, these proposed relationships oversimplify the psychological mechanisms involved. The interpretation of a discrepancy depends also on whether the individual has overestimated or underestimated his experiential outcomes. For instance, an environmental transaction expected to yield low satisfaction that in actuality yields high satisfaction probably produces different discrepancy effects than an environmental transaction expected to yield high satisfaction that in actuality yields low satisfaction. The discrepancy effects also will differ depending on whether positive or negative outcomes are involved. The confidence with which the individual holds the expectation or aspiration is a further complicating factor (Kemper 1978). These additional considerations reduce the likelihood of simple propositional relationships. However, as Kemper reasonably proposes, the interactions between anticipation and actual outcomes will not "produce the main effects" but merely amplify or suppress the outcomes that would have been experienced independently of the discrepancies involved (p. 79).

The basis by which individuals establish outcome expectations and aspirations depends on many cognitive and learning processes, not the least important of which is the individual's earlier environmental successes and failures, or his familiarity with the outcomes experienced by respected social reference groups. In this regard, the establishment of expectation and aspiration levels may constitute a form of adaptational response. That is, the individual may lower his expectation and aspiration levels so as to avoid the dissonance likely to result from unmet goals and wishes.

Individual-Environment Congruence

Congruence refers to an affective or cognitive state whereby the individual feels or thinks that he is in harmony with himself and his environment. Implied in the term congruence are an individual's feelings of success or failure that have emerged as a consequence of the totality of his past life's transactions. Measures of inner-inner congruence have indicated the extent that the individual feels his beliefs, values, needs, and goals are consistent with each other or with his actual achievements and status. Measures of inner-outer congruence have indicated the extent that the individual's demands and competence are consistent or have a fittingness with the resources and barriers in his environment. The psychological end-states, self-esteem, morale, and life satisfaction, are often employed as summary indicators of an individual's inner-inner and outer-outer congruence. These variously measure the success with which the individual has adapted to or come to terms with his life and environment (Lieberman 1975; Nydegger 1977).

It is unusual to find a measure of congruence proposed as a factor influencing an individual's responses to his environment. Congruence is usually a state to be explained rather than a state that provides an explanation. Its being proposed here as an influence of the types and meaningfulness of an older person's experiences emphasizes that an individual does not newly come to terms with his environment at every stage of his development. Throughout life, the individual is continually interacting with his environment, with the result that "goodness of fits" are always being established, and reestablished. One's feelings of accord with the lived-in environment are seldom a result of momentary relationships.

When individuals are studied at an arbitrary point in time, they are in varying states of equilibrium or disequilibrium with respect to their environments. It is necessary to consider the impact of this congruence because the outcomes of an individual's environmental transactions in the present are unlikely to be independent of those experienced in the past. They will be interpreted in light of the successes and failures, good and bad relationships, and successful and unsuccessful adjustments that have occurred throughout life.

It is proposed that the individual who feels he has not successfully adapted to life (low psychological well-being) will transfer that maladjustment to all other environmental transactions; that individual's affective and evaluative responses to objects and events in the environment will be dominated by negative tones. On the other hand, the responses to the environment by the individual who feels successfully adapted to life (high psychological well-being) will be dominated by positive tones.

The pioneer of American psychology, William James, suggested the influential role of happiness when he discussed its impact on other individual states and environmental relationships:

> In the first place, happiness, like every other emotional state, has blindness and insensitivity to opposing fact given it as its instinctive weapon against disturbance. When happiness is actually in possession, the thought of evil can no more acquire the feeling of reality than the thought of good can gain reality when melancholy rules. To the man actively happy, for whatever reason, evil simply cannot be there and then believed in. He must ignore it, and to the bystander may then seem perversely to shut his eyes to it and hush it up. (1902:88)

Later, Erich Fromm was to voice a similar argument:

> Happiness and unhappiness are so much a state of our total personality that bodily reactions are frequently more expressive of them than our conscious feeling . . . Likewise, the functioning of our mental and emotional capacities is influenced by our happiness or unhappiness. . . . Unhappiness weakens or even paralyzes all our psychic functions. Happiness increases them. (1947:182)

Theoretical arguments for this role of congruence are found in Kemper's social interaction theory of emotions. He proposed that an individual's interpersonal relationships over his lifetime accumulate to provide a basis for his "subjective estimates of probable success or failure in any new interaction episode. The residue of the relational past is summed up as *optimism* or *pessimism*" (1978:72). This is consistent with Stotland's view (cited in Kemper) that "the effects of successes and failures early in life seem to show that they have lifelong effects, so that a person is consistently optimistic and successful or pessimistic and failing" (1969:75). It is not a large conceptual leap to propose that an individual's optimism or pessimism will influence not only his interpersonal relationships but also various other categories of his environmental transactions. Thus, the individual whose past experiences have been judged successful—leading to optimism—is more likely to exhibit positive future environmental responses; however, an individual with unsuccessful past experiences—leading to pessimism—is more likely to exhibit negative future environmental responses.

Self-Awareness and Memories

Humans are distinguished from other complex living systems in their ability to acquire a personal history or self (John 1976). Such a history includes accumulated memories of past environmental experiences. Moreover, they have the capacity to activate these stored memories in the absence of any external stimulation and to represent them in an abstract or symbolic fashion. This cognitive "ability to manipulate, recombine, and reorganize the accumulated store of memories" (John 1976:6) is one characteristic of an individual's self-awareness that enables him to evoke, reinforce, modify, or deny his previous environmental experiences.

Consequently, the environmental experiences reported by an individual may bear little relationship to the content and dynamic properties of his present environment. Rather these experiences may have their origins in earlier environmental transactions, or at least in environmental transactions as reconstructed by the remembering person. These may often have occurred in a very different environment and at a different stage in life (Rowles 1978).

Individuals differ in the extent to which they have accumulated and retained memories of past environmental experiences, in the types of meanings of memories they have retained, in their ability to retrieve or recall these memories, and in the way they manipulate, recombine, or reorganize them.

Cognitive and Behavioral Competence

Lastly, it is proposed that the individual's competence level underlies the types and meaningfulness of his experiences. Competence, as conceptualized here, refers to both the cognitive and behavioral abilities of the person (Mischel 1973). On the one hand, it can refer to the accuracy with which environmental information is interpreted, the ease with which information is assimilated, the quickness and acuity of perceptual-cognitive skills, the ability to discriminate among environmental cues (Lawton and Nahemow 1973), the understanding of "social rules and conventions that guide conduct" (Mischel 1973:266), the ability to utilize existing information, or the individual's mental age or I.Q. On the other hand, it can refer to the individual's motor skills (e.g., the operation of large motor limbs) and the extent to which they enable him to manipulate or access certain physical and social objects in his environment, as, for example, his ability to walk, or his ability to "generate adaptive, skillful (social) behaviors that will have beneficial consequences for him" (Mischel 1973:267). Competence also involves the ability of the individual to judge accurately his own cognitive and behavioral competence, as when the individual assesses the limitations of his own physical health or the accuracy of his memory.

Very consistent with this perspective is Lawton's (1972) conception of individual competence as a behavioral variable to be evaluated in reference to normative and teleological standards. Lawton hierarchically classifies competence behaviors into seven increasingly complex or higher orders of performance tasks: life-maintenance, functional health, perception-cognition, physical self-maintenance, instrumental self-maintenance, effectance, and social role performance. Before the individual can achieve lifestage normative levels of maximum competence at the highest levels of behavioral functioning, it is assumed that his performance at lower behavioral levels is unimpaired.

Lawton and Nahemow have identified competence as a critical component of an ecological theory of aging. Level of competence is equated with the degree of vulnerability of older people—that is, "in terms of their behavior being controlled by environmental rather than intrapersonal forces" (Lawton and Nahemow 1973:658). The proposition that the environment has a more negative impact on individuals with lower competence is central to this theory. Specifically, the "environmental docility hypothesis" argues: "The more competent the organism—in terms of health, intelligence, ego strength, social role performance, or cultural evolution—the less will be the proportion of variance in behavior attributable to physical objects or conditions around him" (Lawton and Simon 1968:108).

This lower competence or lack of control influences the individual's environmental experiences in two distinctive ways. First, it reduces the individual's ability to engage in environmental transactions that achieve his goals or demands satisfactorily, effectively, or optimally (White 1974; Lawton and Nahemow 1973). Second, it is interpreted by the individual as an indicator of his inability to cope effectively with more stressful, challenging, or complex environmental or life situations—especially those that are unplanned and uninitiated. This will increase the likelihood that a greater number and variety of environmental transactions are interpreted as unrewarding, threatening, or harmful (Lazarus 1966).

Summary of Mental and Behavioral States

The seven mental and behavioral states underlying the different ways old people perceive, interpret, and evaluate information from their environment included: (1) the designative representation of the environment by which the individual selectively encodes and interprets descriptive information about the existence and nature of environmental objects, events, and their attributes; (2) the individual's needs, goals, and plans, which differ in their salience according to their priority for being fulfilled, and that are manifested in the individual's demands of his environment; (3) the benefits or harms that the individual associates with the outcomes of these demands, theorized as being a manifestation of the individual's comparison or adaptation levels; (4) the aspirations or expectations the individual has for achieving his environmental demands and their associated outcomes; (5) the individual's degree of perceptual or cognitive congruence with his environment, reflecting how successful or unsuccessful he has judged the totality of his past environmental transactions; (6) the types of environmental experiences stored, recalled, and reinterpreted from an individual's memories; and (7) the cognitive and behavioral competencies of the individual, indicating his ability to satisfy his demands and goals and to cope effectively with environmental transactions.

Although these states are conceptualized as distinct entities, they are likely to be functionally related to each other. For instance, at times these states will act in concert with one another to produce unambiguous and consistent interpretations of environmental transactions, but at other times the individual will be confronted with contradictory and confusing influences; and certain states more than others will influence the individual's processing and interpretation of his environmental information. A set of conceptual or mathematical rules is lacking that specify how these states systemically influence an individual's environmental experiences. It is possible, therefore, to speculate only on relatively simple relationships and to identify partial interdependencies.

It is interesting also to consider the diverse and complex psychological, social, physiological, and situational antecedents of these individual states. Obviously, an area of concern is how old people identify certain needs and goals as more salient than others, why they value the outcomes of certain demands more than others, or why their expectations for achieving them differ. However, such questions are largely outside of the present analytical concerns.

Individual Variables Underlying Types and Meaningfulness of Experiences

Three major concerns guided the conceptualization of individual variables proposed in this chapter as underlying old people's experiences. First, these variables had to allow inferences about one or more of the mental and behavioral states described above. Second, these variables had to enable speculation as to whether these mental and behavioral states had a recent impact on old people's environmental experiences, or rather had been influential throughout most of their adult lives. Third, these variables had to describe individuals both from the perspective of their own self-assessments and on the basis of objective or behavioral criteria.

Inferred Mental and Behavioral States

Making inferences about an individual's mental and behavioral states from a set of proposed individual variables can present difficulties. In instances where the variables are measured along some distinguishable psychological or behavioral dimension, the task is more straightforward. However, in other instances, where an inference about a mental state is required from a sociological or demographic variable, the danger of misspecification or misinterpretation exists. It also is possible that a proposed variable can attempt to measure too complex an individual state. For instance, one variable might be proposed to measure an individual's competence, but the very multidimensional nature of *competence* actually requires several variable measures. At least two possibilities exist: first, the individual state may be incompletely or inappropriately measured; and second, an observed influence of an individual variable may be given more than one interpretation.

Temporal Origins of Mental and Behavioral States

In the previous chapter, it was questioned whether factors peculiar to late life were most responsible for the environmental ex-

periences reported by old people. This inquiry now can be re-
phrased in more formal terms, such as: Are the demands the elderly
person makes of his environment (for example, physical security,
safety, sense of belongingness) relatively recent in origin or are they
longstanding expressed needs and goals? Have certain needs become more salient or more valued in late life? Are the attributes
the old person associates with the built or natural environment
(for example, the steep slopes of the sidewalks or the unpredict-
ability of the weather) longtime held environmental representations or are they a manifestation of recent physical functional impairments or declines in sensory processing skills? Are the elderly
individual's low expectations for fulfilling his environmental demands lifelong in origin and existence or a relatively recent state
of affairs?

Unfortunately, simple answers are not forthcoming, mainly because past researchers have not carefully articulated these questions. It is certain, however, that individuals differ as to the temporal origins and existence of their mental and behavioral states.
In turn, the environmental experiences of old people will be influenced by personal factors that have been both long-term in existence and recent manifestations of old age.

To enable speculation about these differential effects, individual variables having long-term influences on a person's environmental experiences were distinguished from those having primarily recent or short-term influences. Two sets of long-term social
and psychological influences were proposed, along with one set of
stage-in-life influences.

The first set of long-term *social* variables depicts the heterogeneity of a population typically found in any modernized, urbanized society, composed of groups with varying demographic, racial, ethnic, religious, and socioeconomic characteristics. The old
person's membership in such social groups is assumed to have remained relatively constant throughout his lifetime. Thus, if the
present old population were to be described at an earlier stage in
life, one would expect its members to be distributed similarly at
both points in time. For example, the distribution of blacks and
whites among the present old population would be very similar
to the racial distribution of this population at middle age.

The second set of long-term individual variables describes old people's psychological characteristics, such as personality makeup or psychological well-being. Again, it is assumed that if the present old population were to be described at an earlier stage in life, its members' psychological characteristics would be similarly distributed. This is a less certain proposition. Considerable debate exists in the field of aging as to the stability of personality as the individual progresses from middle age to old age (Neugarten 1977).

The set of short-term individual variables depicts that heterogeneity of an elderly population primarily due to its stage in life. Old persons are predicted to differ in terms of their health status or employment status. To be sure, an old population's present health and employment status distributions are in part due to events occurring earlier in their lives. However, it is argued that certain personal attributes are more likely than others to be present or absent as a result of old age.

Objective and Subjective Individual Variables

Individual variables describing the old population can be derived from either objective or subjective criteria. Objectively measured variables require observations of an individual's status by a detached scientific observer or, alternatively, reports by the individual that require relatively little subjective assessment (for example, the report of an individual's actual household income). In contrast, subjectively measured variables require self-rated assessments by the individual (for example, "Do you have enough money to engage in leisure activities?"). There are several reasons to expect a lack of correspondence between comparable variables describing the *objective person* and the *subjective person* (terms suggested by French, Rodgers, and Cobb 1974:316). At least two types of effects contribute to this lack of correspondence. The first consists of well-documented survey research methodological factors leading to several sources of response bias. For example, response error arises as a result of the respondent's anxiety about the social desirability of his answers or because he has not given previous thought to the questions posed (see Bradburn and Caplovitz 1965). The second effect results from the variability generated by any human judgment approach. For instance, a measure of an individual's subjective health status (self-evaluated or self-rated) usually deviates from the individual's objective health status as measured by behavioral criteria or physician's ratings.

The Operationalizing of Individual Variables

For the empirical analyses, the three sets of social, psychological, and stage-in-life individual variables were subdivided into five categories: (1) personality traits and dispositions; (2) demographic, racial, ethnic, and religious characteristics; (3) socioeconomic status; (4) stage in life; and (5) psychological well-being. These grouping assignments were guided by population distinctions conventionally made in the social and behavioral sciences. The remaining sections of this chapter identify the variable measures constructed for the study's empirical analyses (table 6.1 and figure 6.1), and briefly present illustrations of the mental and behavioral states that can be inferred from them.

Personality Traits and Dispositions

The six variables in this category differentiate individuals according to their relatively stable, enduring, or habitual interpersonal behaviors or physical environment dispositions. These measure an individual's dominance and affiliation traits, perceived locus of control, and urbanism, stimulus-seeking, and antiquarianism dispositions. These measures are derived from old people's reports about their actual or expected behavior in various social and physical situations.

It is expected that individuals identified as having dominant personalities are more likely to attend to social situations and personal environments that accommodate their strong, forceful traits and their organization and leadership behaviors. These persons associate greater satisfaction with environmental transac-

Table 6.1. Variables Differentiating Individuals as Knowers of Their Environment

Independent Variables	Sample Size and Percentage Distribution	Measurement Properties	Interpretation
Personality Traits and Dispositions			
Leary dominance-submission personality	n = 395	interval variable; score range, −32.4 to 41.8; mean = 6.7 SD = 12.1	high score indicates dominance traits
Leary affiliative-hostile personality	n = 395	interval variable; score range −39.5 to 76.7; mean = 3.7 SD = 11.9	high score indicates affiliative traits
Urbanism environment disposition	n = 400	interval variable; score range 17.0 to 40.0; mean = 29.3 SD = 4.5	high score indicates urbanism orientation
Stimulus-seeking environment disposition	n = 400	interval variable; score range 10.0 to 39.0; mean = 22.1 SD = 5.2	high score indicates stimulus-seeking orientation
Antiquarianism environment disposition	n = 400	interval variable; score range 17.0 to 45.0; mean = 30.8 SD = 4.4	high score indicates antiquarianism orientation
Perceived locus of control	n = 400	interval variable; score range 6.0 to 20.0; mean = 13.3 SD = 2.2	high score indicates perceived internal control
Demographic, Racial, Ethnic, and Religious Characteristics			
Sex	n = 400	dummy variable;	"female" is
Male	35	male = 1	reference category
Female	65	female = 0	
Race	n = 400	dummy variable;	"nonwhite" is
White	82	white = 1	reference category
Nonwhite	18	nonwhite = 0	
Marital Status	n = 400	dummy variables;	"married" is
Married	45	yes = 1 no = 0	reference category
Separated-divorced	6	yes = 1 no = 0	
Widowed	42	yes = 1 no = 0	
Never married	8	yes = 1 no = 0	
Total Household Size	n = 399	interval variable;	high score indicates
1 person	38	score range 1 to 3;	a larger household
2 persons	43	mean = 1.8 SD = 0.73	
3+ persons	19		
Ethnic Status	n = 390	interval variable;	high score indicates
Foreign born	12	score range 1 to 3;	third (or more)
Second generation	28	mean = 2.5 SD = 0.70	generation
Third (or more) generation	60		
Religious Preference	n = 400	dummy variables;	"Protestant" is
Protestant	68	yes = 1 no = 0	reference category
Catholic	19	yes = 1 no = 0	
Jewish	6	yes = 1 no = 0	
Other	4	yes = 1 no = 0	
None	3	yes = 1 no = 0	

Table 6.1. (continued)

Independent Variables	Sample Size and Percentage Distribution	Measurement Properties	Interpretation
		Socioeconomic Status	
Total Household Income[a]	n = 380	interval variable;	high score indicates
Under $5,000	18	score range 1 to 11;	higher income
$5,000 to $9,999	21	mean = 6.5 SD = 2.8	
$10,000 to $14,999	21		
$15,000 to $19,999	17		
$20,000 to $24,999	8		
$25,000 or more	16		
Level of Education[b]	n = 400	interval variable;	high score indicates
0 to 4	2	score range 1 to 8;	higher education
5 to 8	13	mean = 5.1 SD = 2.1	
9 to 12	33		
College (13–16)	36		
Post-Graduate	16		
Duncan socioeconomic status	n = 372	interval variable; score range 3 to 96; mean = 52.4 SD = 24.3	high score indicates higher status
Siegal occupational prestige	n = 372	interval variable; score range 9 to 82; mean = 45.7 SD = 15.8	high score indicates greater prestige
Self-Rated Social Class	n = 391	interval variable;	high score indicates
Upper class	9	score range 2 to 5;	higher class
Middle class	68	mean = 3.8 SD = 0.58	
Working class	22		
Lower class	1		
Impact of Housing Expense	n = 390	interval variable;	high score indicates
Many times	16	score range 1 to 4;	greater burden of
A few times	17	mean = 1.9 SD = 1.2	housing expense
Only once or twice	10		
Never	58		
Concern About Enough Money	n = 395	interval variable; score range 1 to 4;	high score indicates greater concern
Most of the time	17	mean = 1.8 SD = 1.2	
Some of the time	12		
Only occasionally	8		
Never	63		
Money Situation Compared with 2 Years Ago	n = 396	interval variable; score range 1 to 5;	high score indicates worse income situation
Much better	6	mean = 3.1 SD = 0.94	
A little better	18		
About the same	49		
A little worse	21		
Much worse	7		
Money Situation Compared with 10 Years Ago	n = 395	interval variable; score range 1 to 5;	high score indicates worse income situation
Much better	26	mean = 2.7 SD = 1.4	
A little better	21		
About the same	25		
A little worse	15		
Much worse	13		
Enough Money for Things	n = 396	interval variable; score range 25 to 100; mean 94.1 SD = 11.4	high score indicates usually have enough money

Table 6.1. *(continued)*

Independent Variables	Sample Size and Percentage Distribution	Measurement Properties	Interpretation
	Stage in Life		
Self-Rated Health	n = 400	interval variable;	high score indicates
Very good	32	score range 1 to 5;	very poor health
Good	44	mean = 2.0 SD = 0.89	
Sometimes good, sometimes not	19		
Poor	4		
Very poor	2		
Self-Rated Hearing	n = 400	interval variable;	high score indicates
No difficulty	72	score range 1 to 3;	greater difficulty
A little difficulty	23	mean = 1.3 SD = 0.57	hearing
A lot of difficulty	5		
Self-Rated Seeing	n = 400	interval variable;	high score indicates
No difficulty	75	score range 1 to 3;	greater difficulty
A little difficulty	18	mean = 1.3 SD = 0.61	seeing
A lot of difficulty	8		
Functional Health	n = 400	interval variable; score range 25.0 to 77.1; mean = 28.2 SD = 6.1	high score indicates lower functional health
Self-Rated Change in Functional Health	n = 398	interval variable; score range 0 to 12; mean = 0.77 SD = 1.7	high score indicates more things were more difficult
Had serious illness	n = 400	dummy variable;	"no" is reference
Yes	16	yes = 1	category
No	84	no = 0	
Had minor illness	n = 400	dummy variable;	"no" is reference
Yes	42	yes = 1	category
No	58	no = 0	
Stopped Activity	n = 400	dummy variable;	"no" is reference
Yes	27	yes = 1	category
No	74	no = 0	
Voluntary retirement	n = 395	dummy variable;	"no" is reference
Yes	4	yes = 1	category
No	96	no = 0	
Forced retirement	n = 397	dummy variable;	"no" is reference
Yes	4	yes = 1	category
No	96	no = 0	
Employment Status	n = 399	dummy variable;	"nonemployed" is
Employed	33	employed = 1	reference category
Nonemployed	67	nonemployed = 0	
	Psychological Well-Being		
How Happy Are You These Days	n = 400	interval variable; score range 1 to 3; mean = 2.3 SD = 0.63	high score indicates greater happiness
Very happy	42		
Pretty happy	49		
Not too happy	9		
Life Satisfaction	n = 400	interval variable; score range 1 to 20; mean = 13.6 SD = 3.6	high score indicates greater life satisfaction

NOTE: Sample sizes of less than 400 reflect missing values (nonresponses) for particular variables.
[a]Variable in empirical analysis had 11 categories.
[b]Variable in empirical analysis had 8 categories.

Figure 6.1. Additional Descriptions of Variables Differentiating Individuals as Knowers of their Environment

Personality Traits and Dispositions

Leary Dominance-Submission Personality. Dimension of interpersonal behavior found in personality model developed by Leary (1957) and then modified and retested by Edelhart (1966) and Rosner (1968). Individuals with dominant personalities describe themselves as strong and forceful, as leaders, and as persons who win respect, approbation, and deference from others. They act in a strong, arrogant manner. Individuals with submissive personalities describe themselves as weak, inferior, easily embarrassed, and shy (see appendix B).

Leary Affiliative-Hostile Personality. Same source as above. Individuals with affiliative personalities strive to be liked and accepted by others. They describe themselves as friendly, affectionate, and understanding in their interrelationships. Individuals with hostile personalities describe themselves as cold, tough, and unfeeling who can be critical, short-tempered, and impatient (see appendix B).

Urbanism Environment Disposition.[a] Summated scale of nine items (see appendix B) which was shortened from a 20-item scale constructed by McKechnie to measure differences in the ways persons habitually interact with their everyday physical environment. Item-scale correlations were significant at the .000 level. The "urbanism-oriented" individual is characterized as follows: "Enjoyment of high density living; appreciation of unusual and varied stimulus patterns of the city; interest in cultural life; enjoyment of interpersonal richness and diversity" (McKechnie 1977:258).

Stimulus-Seeking Environment Disposition.[a] Summated scale of nine items (see appendix B) which was shortened from a 22-item scale constructed by McKechnie to measure differences in the ways persons habitually interact with their everyday physical environment. Item-scale correlations were significant at the .000 level. The "stimulus-seeking" individual is characterized as follows: "Interest in travel and exploration of unusual places; enjoyment of complex and intense physical sensations; breadth of interests" (McKechnie 1977:258).

Antiquarianism Environment Disposition.[a] Summated scale of nine items (see appendix B) which was shortened from 20-item scale constructed by McKechnie to measure differences in the ways persons habitually interact with their everyday physical environment. Item-scale correlations were significant at the .000 level. The "antiquarianism" individual is characterized as follows: "Enjoyment of antiques and historical places; preference for traditional vs. modern design; aesthetic sensitivity to man-made environments and to landscape; appreciation of cultural artifacts of earlier eras; tendency to collect objects for their emotional significance" (McKechnie 1977:258).

Locus of Control. Summated scale of five items (all expressed in first person) constructed by Pearlin and Schooler (1978:5) to measure mastery. It distinguished between persons with perceived internal and external locus of control, that is, "the extent to which one regards one's life-chances as being under one's own control in contrast to being fatalistically ruled." Item-scale correlations were significant at the .000 level (see appendix B).

Socioeconomic Status

Total Household Income. Based on following question: "Approximately what was your household income last year, 1976, before you paid taxes? Please look at this card and tell me the letter that appears next to the approximate amount." Respondents selected from 11 categories ranging from less than $1,000 to $30,000 and more. Income categories were estimated for some nonrespondents by procedures outlined by Cohen and Cohen (1975).

Level of Education. Based on following question: "What is highest grade or year in school that you have completed?"

Duncan Socioeconomic Status. Respondents and, if currently married, their spouses were assigned U.S. Census occupational codes that were then converted into socioeconomic status scores developed by Duncan (1961). The scores reflect a linear combination of an individual's income and educational levels and are hierarchically arranged according to these criteria. When two scores were available from the same household (i.e., husband and wife), the highest socioeconomic score was assigned to the respondent. Therefore, the socioeconomic status score denotes the status of the household as the incumbent of its "highest" occupational role.

Siegel Occupational Prestige. Respondents and, if currently married, their spouses were assigned U.S. Census occupational codes that were then converted into Siegel prestige scores, which reflect the U.S. population's ratings of the social standings of occupational roles (Siegel 1971; and Hodge, Siegel, and Rossi 1964). The household's highest score was assigned to the respondent.

Self-Rated Social Class. Based on following question: "If you were asked to use one of four names to describe your social class, would you say you belonged in the upper class, middle class, working class, or lower class?"

Impact of Housing Expense. Based on following question: "In the past 12 months, after paying the rent or mortgage, property taxes, and heating bills, have you or other household members had to draw on your savings or cut back on what you spend on other things?"

Concern about Having Enough Money. Based on following question: "During the past year were you ever concerned about having enough money?"

Money Situation Compared to 2 Years Ago. Based on following question: "How would you compare your money situation today with the way it was about two years ago?"

Money Situation Compared to 10 Years Ago. Based on following question: "How would you compare your money situation today with the way it was about ten years ago?"

Enough Money for Things. Summated scale of three items constructed from following three questions: "How often do you (and your spouse/other household members) have enough money for (1) your food needs, (2) the medical care you need, and (3) the fun things you want to do?" Each item had four response categories: all the time, most of the time, some of the time, or almost never. The summated scale score was expressed as a percentage of the largest possible score for a respondent with enough money all the time. Item-scale correlations were significant at the .000 level.

Stage in Life

Self-Rated Health. Based on following question: "Thinking about your health would you say it is very good, good, sometimes good and sometimes not, poor, or very poor?"

Self-Rated Hearing Difficulties. Based on following question: "Do you have a lot of difficulty, a little difficulty, or no difficulty at all hearing?"

Self-Rated Seeing Difficulties. Based on following question: "Do you have a lot of difficulty, a little difficulty, or no difficulty at all seeing?"

Figure 6.1. *(continued)*

Functional Health. Summated scale of twelve activity items from instruments described in Rosow and Breslau (1966), Katz el al. (1970), and Lawton (1972) to measure functional health, which refers to "the degree to which older people claim they can manage adequately or are restricted in their activities because of their physical condition or capacity" (Rosow and Breslau 1966:566). For each activity respondent was asked: "Please tell me whether you can do it yourself easily, do it yourself but it is not easy, do it only with help?" A fourth category response was recorded when a respondent indicated that he could not do the activity *even with help.* Summated scale score was expressed as a percentage of the largest possible score for a respondent with the lowest functional health possible. Item-scale correlations were significant at .000 level (see appendix B).

Self-Rated Change in Functional Health. Based on following question: "Compared with a year ago, how many of these things (referring to above 12 functional health items) do you now have more difficulty doing?"

Had Serious Illness. Based on following question: "In the past year, have you had a serious illness or injury?"

Had Minor Illness. Based on following question: "During the past year, did you have a minor illness or injury that required a doctor's attention but not hospitalization?"

Stopped Activity. Based on following question: "During the past year, did you stop doing any activity that was important to you?"

Voluntary Retirement. Included respondents who described themselves as retired or retired but still working *and* who last worked full-time for pay more than two years previously and who did not report forced retirement.

Forced Retirement. Based on following question: "During the past year, were you fired, forced to retire, or given a job demotion?"

Employment Status. Respondents who described themselves as working full- or part-time for pay or as retired but still working were categorized as employed. All other respondents identifying themselves as retired, including housewives and the unemployed or disabled, were categorized as nonemployed.

Psychological Well-Being

How Happy Are You These Days. Based on following question originally from a study by Gurin, Veroff, and Feld (1960): "Taking all things together, how would you say things are these days—would you say you are very happy, pretty happy, or not too happy?"

Life Satisfaction. Based on 20-item Life Satisfaction Index A (LSIA) instrument developed by Neugarten, Havighurst, and Tobin (1961). These investigators theorized that psychological well-being or morale of older people consists of five major components: zest for life as opposed to apathy; resolution and fortitude as opposed to resignation; congruence between desired and achieved goals; high physical, psychological, and social self-concept; and a happy, optimistic mood tone. Item-scale correlations were all statistically significant at .000 level.

---

[a]The original number of items found in each of the three McKechnie environment disposition scales were reduced because relatively brief survey instruments were required when interviewing older people. Items excluded were judged less relevant to elderly persons.

tions evoking or reinforcing such consequences. Similarly, old persons who are disposed toward urban environments are predicted to seek out and expect greater satisfaction from environmental transactions involving objects and events with urban attributes. Individuals identified as having stimulus-seeking personalities are expected to seek out and value more highly environmental transactions that accommodate their exploratory and novelty-seeking demands. Individuals identified as having a perceived internal locus of control are expected to have the ability to control or influence more effectively their environmental transactions. In addition to such competence inferences, the locus of control measure allows inferences about the individual's feelings of congruence with his environment, the reasoning being that an individual's judgment of how much control he presently has over his life and environment reflects the successes and failures of earlier environmental transactions.

In general, this category of individual variables is assumed to have primarily long-term influences on the old person's experiences. However, reservations expressed earlier about the constancy of personality traits as a person ages prevent the uncritical acceptance of this assumption.

Demographic, Racial, Ethnic, and Religious Characteristics

The variables in this category differentiate individuals according to their sex, race, marital status, household size, ethnicity, and religious preferences. The danger of misinterpretation looms large when inferring the mental and behavioral states from these individual variables because the literature does not offer unequivocal evidence for making predictions.[1] However, examples of possible conceptual linkages are suggested below.

These variables enable inferences about an individual's environmental demands and the associated subjective values of their outcomes. For example, foreign-born elderly are more likely than native-born elderly to associate greater benefits with environmental transactions in their immediate neighborhood; the widowed are more likely than the married elderly to consider as a salient need their living in proximity to friends and neighbors (Michelson 1970); widowed elderly are more likely also than married elderly to consider good accessibility to community facilities as a more salient need, and females are more likely than men to demand a physically secure housing environment.

The individual variables in this category also allow inferences about old people's expectations of achieving their demands. Particularly in this generation of elderly, old blacks are more likely than old whites to have lower expectations of fulfilling their environmental needs, largely because of life histories in which demands have often been left unsatisfied.

Membership in certain of these groups is likely to have left its members with inferior social or intellectual skills because of deficient learning opportunities. It is expected that elderly women and blacks have weaker business or organizational skills (for example, to deal effectively with the complexities of urban living) than elderly men or whites. The behavioral competencies of individuals also are predictable from their group membership. For example, women are more likely than men to feel physically vulnerable to crime, and to have less strength and endurance to do physical chores in their dwellings.

The variables in this social group have in common their primarily long-term influences on an old person's experiences. However, the marital status and household size characteristics offer certain ambiguities concerning their temporal origins.[2]

Socioeconomic Status

The variables in this category include both objective and subjective measures of an individual's money situation, education, social class and status.

Traditionally, socioeconomic status has been interpreted as a measure of life-style (Zablocki and Kanter 1976), distinguishing subgroups of individuals according to their consumption patterns (see also Bell 1958), which in turn are viewed as a reflection of shared values and tastes. Three such economically determined life-styles have been defined (Zablocki and Kanter 1976:272): prop-erty-dominated, occupation-dominated, and income- or poverty-dominated. The first is more appropriately addressed in a discus-sion of housing tenure (see next chapter); the latter two are rele-vant here. They allow inferences concerning the objects and events older people attend to in their environments, the types of de-mands they make of them, and the amount of satisfaction or dis-satisfaction they expect from transactions with them. For exam-ple, higher income old people, when evaluating their homes will focus on different dwelling unit design attributes than lower in-come old people and will identify different features of their neigh-borhoods as more important sources of satisfaction (Michelson 1970; Birch et al. 1973).

Also, sufficient justification exists to interpret an individual's socioeconomic status as a measure of his cognitive or behavioral competence. An elderly individual's occupational and educational status is closely associated with his past achievements, standing in his community, power, authority, and informational aware-ness. Along with income level, such indicators of status should al-low inferences about the old person's ability to satisfy his needs or goals, carry out complex environmental transactions, access resources found in his environment, and cope successfully with stressful situations.

In addition, socioeconomic status enables inferences about a person's anticipation of future successes and failures. Higher sta-tus individuals, for example, are identified as having loftier goals and higher aspirations and expectations (Campbell, Converse, and Rodgers 1976; Wilkening and McGranahan 1978).

The variables measuring education or occupational status have had long-term influences on an individual's environmental expe-riences. The temporal effects of an individual's economic status are less clear. An individual's income status may fall sharply after retirement or the death of a spouse. Consequently, its influence on an individual's experiences can be recent in origin. On the other hand, a shift in these *income* sources may not substantially affect the individual's *economic* status, that is, his net financial worth as reflected by his life's savings and material assets (for example, an owned home) (Moon 1974). In either instance, additional and more current insights are offered by variables describing a person's subjective estimates of his income or economic status.

Stage in Life

The variables in this category differentiate individuals according to their health and employment status. Other than chronological age, these are the most frequently used indicators of an individual's entry into old age (Neugarten 1974; Lawton 1972). A caveat is in order, however: the nonemployed status of the elderly woman may only indicate a longtime housewife status rather than any recent employment role changes.

Both health and employment status allow inferences about the old person's cognitive and behavioral competence. Functional health status, in particular, enables inferences about an individual's ability to carry out day-to-day tasks and to gain access to various types of environmental resources. Employment status is closely associated with an individual's social prestige, social status, and social participation and thus allows inferences about his capability of accessing and using various types of information from his environment. Employment and health status are also indicators of an individual's style of living (Bell 1958). Inferences are thus possible concerning the work-related and nonwork-related demands the individual makes of his environment.

The variable measures in this category describe both the objective and subjective health status of the old individual. The evidence suggests that an old person's perceived health is generally more positive than established by either physician's ratings or behavioral (functional) indicators (Rosencranz and Pihlblad 1970:129).

Psychological Well-Being

The two variables in this category differentiate individuals according to their psychological well-being, measuring the life satisfaction and level of happiness of elderly persons. Both these measures of psychological well-being, varying along a continuum of high to low, are interpreted as indicators of congruence—of how successfully old people have adapted to their lives and their environments. Some persons have tolerated and coped successfully with the demands and stresses from their environment and have resolved the inconsistencies between their actual achievements and their expected goals; others have not.

The treatment of these two individual variables as antecedents of environmental experiences departs sharply from convention. Usually such measures of psychological well-being are conceptualized as outcomes of an individual's personal life or environmental relationships (Kasl 1977; Hinkle 1977).

As conceived here, these psychological well-being variables are static measures. They depict the individual at a particular point in time in some state of equilibrium or disequilibrium. However, it is understood that over the lifetime of the individual, many different states of well-being and of equilibrium are experienced.

The variables in this category describe the subjective person. Measures of life satisfaction and happiness depict an individual's internal frame of reference. Whereas one individual's basis for successful adaptation or fittingness with his environment may require the initiation of innovative and change-seeking behaviors, another individual may view habitual and conservative behaviors as the status quo. More generally, the equilibrium the individual strives for and reaches is not necessarily normal from some objective standpoint and, in fact, may be pathological (Hartmann 1958:38). Positive psychological well-being and successful adaptation do not correspond to any unique or fixed objective state (Sawrey and Telford 1967). Nonetheless, it is possible to discern a set of culture-specific meanings that dominate interpretations. The identification of such meanings is consistent with ego psychologist Hartmann's contention that "mental health cannot be considered a product of chance. One of its premises is preparedness for *average expectable environmental situations and for average expectable internal conflicts*" (1958:55). In this regard, one finds repeated reference to positive psychological well-being and successful adaptation embodying such elements as high competence and effectiveness, coping mastery, and positive subjective experiences (Lieberman 1975; White 1974).

Chronological Age as an Individual Difference

Studies of the patterns and processes of aging frequently differentiate members of their population or sample by chronological age. Therefore, the reasons why it is not specified as an individual variable in this study's conceptual model deserve some comment.

Chronological age is often used as an indicator of the rate at which the individual has aged socially, biologically, or psychologically. But these are very broad and complex categories of individual functioning. What inferences should or can be made from a relationship that is discovered between chronological age (as an antecedent condition) and another variable? The statistical correlations of chronological age with the individual variables proposed in this chapter (table 6.2) make clear that simple interpretations are not possible.[3] Statistically significant relationships are present (at .05 level or less) in each of the five variable groupings. Specifically, chronologically older people in the Evanston community have stronger affiliative interpersonal dispositions, weaker stimulus-seeking environmental dispositions, are more likely to be widowed, but less likely to be separated or divorced, live in smaller households, are less likely to be Jewish, have lower educational and income levels, report greater hearing and seeing difficulties and poorer functional health, are more likely to be nonemployed, and are less satisfied with their lives.

These associations highlight the interpretative ambiguity of chronological age as a measure of aging. Chronological age is clearly a multidimensional output indicator of a variety of biological, psychological, and social processes. If it is proposed as a factor underlying the experiences of old people, its interpretation requires the disentangling of the common variance it shares with personality, health, marital status, and employment attributes. This ambiguity makes it a questionable variable to distinguish how individuals differ in old age.

Table 6.2. Correlations Between Chronological Age (60+) and Variables Describing Individuals as Knowers

Individual Differences	Pearson r Coefficients
Personality Traits	
Leary Dominance Personality	−.030
Leary Affiliation Personality	.118**
Urbanism environment disposition	−.004
Stimulus-seeking environment disposition	−.129**
Antiquarianism environment disposition	.067
Perceived locus of control	−.070
Demographic, Racial, Ethnic, & Religious Characteristics	
Male (Yes = 1, No = 0)	−.042
White (Yes = 1, No = 0)	.066
Separated-divorced (Yes = 1, No = 0)	−.160***
Widowed (Yes = 1, No = 0)	.376***
Never married (Yes = 1, No = 0)	.003
Total household size	−.267***
Ethnic status	−.057
Catholic religion (Yes = 1, No = 0)	−.068
Jewish religion (Yes = 1, No = 0)	−.149***
Other religion (Yes = 1, No = 0)	.051
No religion (Yes = 1, No = 0)	.023
Socioeconomic Status	
Total household income	−.269***
Level of education	−.157***
Duncan Socioeconomic Status	−.081
Siegel Occupational Prestige	−.066
Self-rated social class	.061
Impact of housing expense	−.023
Concern about enough money	−.042
Money situation compared to 2 years ago	.061
Money situation compared to 10 years ago	.134**
Enough money for things	.070
Stage in Life	
Self-rated health	.055
Self-rated hearing difficulties	.262***
Self-rated seeing difficulties	.252***
Functional health	.231***
Self-rated change in functional health	.189***
Had serious illness (Yes = 1, No = 0)	−.040
Had minor illness (Yes = 1, No = 0)	−.061
Stopped activity (Yes = 1, No = 0)	−.026
Voluntary retirement (Yes = 1, No = 0)	−.074
Forced retirement (Yes = 1, No = 0)	−.067
Employed (Yes = 1, No = 0)	−.418***
Psychological Well-Being	
How happy are you these days?	−.043
Life satisfaction	−.086*

***p < .001 **p < .01 *p < .05.

Chronological age is also unsuitable as an explanatory variable because it can be a measure of both lifetime and historical age (Neugarten and Datan 1973). Although the health variable's relationship with chronological age probably indicates a decline in health as people become older, other relationships will not be interpreted so easily. For instance, the relationship between educational level and chronological age simply indicates period and cohort effects; that is, the old-old grew up in an earlier historical period than the young-old at the time when lower educational attainment was the status quo. There will often be such competing explanations (lifetime events versus cohort or historical events) for the relationships that chronological age has with other individual and experiential variables.

In summary, to identify manifestations of the individual aging process requires a multiple measure approach—as attempted by the broad cross-section of individual variables proposed in this chapter. Catch-all indicators such as chronological age are acceptable only when alternative variable formulations are unavailable.

Chapter Seven

The Behavioral Relationships of Elderly Individuals with Their Environment

The attention now shifts to the second sense in which the environment is a function of the individual. The focus is on the two sets of behavioral relationships—residential and activity behaviors—theorized as antecedents of old people's variable environmental experiences (figure 5.1). The chapter begins with brief discussions of the definitions and properties of these two sets of individual differences. The next sections identify in abstract terms the processes by which these individual behaviors influence the environmental experiences of elderly people. The remainder of the chapter is divided into two parts. The first part examines the theoretical and empirical evidence for expecting residential behaviors to influence the content and consequences of old people's environmental experiences. It also considers the evidence for conceptualizing residential behavior as a consequence—a coping response of unpleasant environmental experiences. The second part of the chapter presents a comparable analysis of the influence of activity on old people's environmental experiences.

The Concept and Measures of Residential Behavior

Variable Measures

Three aspects of an individual's residential behavior can be distinguished: (1) the length of time the individual has occupied the dwelling *(duration in residence);* (2) the length of time the individual has occupied the community[1] *(duration in community);* and (3) the individual's occupancy of the dwelling as either an owner or renter *(tenure status).* A description of these variables and their measurement properties are found in figure 7.1.

Temporal Properties

Along a temporal scale of human behavior, individual acts of residential relocation are initiated infrequently, over years and decades, rather than over weeks or months. This is especially true of old people's mobility behavior. In 1970 almost 60 percent of elderly-headed households had lived in their present dwelling ten or more years. Residential moves also occur irregularly; constant or fixed intervals of time seldom separate a person's moves. However, a relationship is observed between a person's present and subsequent residential behavior. Generally, length of residential occupancy is inversely related to the likelihood of moving again. The propensity of the individual to move again is particularly strong shortly after a residential relocation (Toney 1976). Demographers have referred to this relationship as the "axiom of cumulative inertia" (McGinnis 1968; Land 1969). As expressed by Morrison: "For a given interval of time and within specific age-groups, the probability of an individual migrating diminishes as his duration of status increases" (1967:555). Independent of the effects of length of residence on subsequent moving behavior, it is also found that homeowners—especially when they are old—are less likely than renters to contemplate or engage in a future residential relocation (Morrison 1972; Pickvance 1973; Simmons 1968;

Figure 7.1. Residential Behavior Variables Proposed as Influencing Types and Meaningfulness of Environmental Experiences

Variable Description	Measurement Properties
Duration in Residence (Dwelling)	
This variable was constructed from the responses to the open-ended question: "How many years have you lived at this address?" Responses were categorized as follows: 1–5 years (including less than one year); 6–10 years; 11–15 years; 16–20 years; more than 20 years. A high score indicates long length of residence.	interval variable; score range 1 to 5; mean = 3.4 SD = 1.6 n = 399
Duration in Community	
This variable was statistically derived from three other variables: the above (but uncategorized) duration of residence variable; a variable describing whether the respondent lived in or outside of Evanston *prior* to occupying the present dwelling and a variable describing the number of years the respondent lived in the previous place of residence. For respondents whose prior dwelling was in Evanston, the number of years previously lived in Evanston was added to number of years lived in the present dwelling. This provided an exact measure of the total years lived in the Evanston community. For all other respondents previously occupying dwellings outside of Evanston, the number of years lived in present dwelling was the same as the number of years lived in the Evanston community. Responses were categorized into the same class intervals as the "duration of residence" variable. A high score indicates long length of community occupancy.	interval variable; score range 1 to 5; mean = 3.9 SD = 1.4 n = 368
Tenure Status	
This variable was constructed from responses to the question: "Do you own or rent this house/apartment?" Respondents were categorized as either owners or renters.[a]	dummy variable; own = 1 rent = 0; "rent" is reference category; n = 400

[a] One respondent who reported "living with renter" was categorized as a renter; nine unmarried respondents who reported "living with the owner" were also categorized as renters.

Speare 1970; Butler and Kaiser 1971; Duncan and Newman 1976; Golant 1977).

Purposes

A change in environment (dwelling, neighborhood, community, or region, for example) is the most manifest goal of an individual's relocation. However, moves and tenure shifts are motivated by a vast array of personal needs and demands (Golant 1976a; Wiseman 1980). The residential behavior of old people in particular is often associated with purposes such as retirement migration or institutional relocations. No agreed upon categories presently exist to classify the purposes of an individual's or population's residential behavior, and such a differentiation is not made here.

Units of Behavior

Residential behavior is treated here primarily as a final act. However, if viewed also as a decision-making process, residential behavior can include various stages or units of behavior. For example, it is possible to consider residential behavior actually beginning when the conscious *decision* is made to move. The search for a moving company and the negotiations with a realtor are examples of legitimate units of residential behavior conceived in this way. Brown and Moore (1970) have considered such stages or alternative units of residential behavior.

Locational Context

Studies of residential behavior have not consistently defined the geographic area over which relocations take place. Thus, the literature speaks of the length of occupancy in the dwelling unit, the community, the county, the region, and so on. These different boundary referents lead to very different measures of an individual's or population's residential behavior. The present conceptualization distinguishes between duration of occupancy in the dwelling or residence and duration of occupancy in the community (Evanston).

Simple Residential Behavior Patterns of Evanston's Elderly

About 63 percent of Evanston's elderly owned their residence. Table 7.1 shows that 38 percent of Evanston's elderly population

Table 7.1. Number of Years in Present Residence by Number of Years in Evanston Community

Number of Years in Present Residence	Number of Years in Community							Percentage Distribution
	1–5	6–10	11–15	16–20	20+	Total	N	
1–5	54%	13	14	4	15	100%	78	20%
6–10	0%	52	13	6	30	100%	54	14
11–15	0%	0	60	4	36	100%	50	13
16–20	0%	0	0	48	52	100%	60	15
20+	0%	0	0	0	100	100%	146	38
Total	11%	10	12	10	58	100%	368	100%

occupied the same dwelling for more than 20 years, but 58 percent lived in the community for this length of time. At the other extreme, 20 percent of the elderly occupied their dwelling less than five years, whereas only 11 percent occupied their community (Evanston) for this short length of time. The importance of distinguishing duration in residence from duration in community is evidenced by the percentages of old people who lived only a relatively short time in their present dwelling, but who lived a considerable length of time in their community. Nonetheless, length of dwelling residence is strongly correlated with length of community occupancy (Pearson $r = .77$; Eta $= .77$).

The Concept and Measures of Activity Behavior

Variable Measures

Activity behavior refers to the everyday actions or pursuits of individuals by which they temporarily occupy, utilize, and manipulate distinguishable parts and properties of their environment in order to attain their needs and goals. The designation of activity as *behavior* emphasizes that to engage in such concrete or direct environmental transactions requires the individual to *select* locations or places with appropriate contents. This necessarily implies that individuals either remain in some currently occupied location or alternatively travel elsewhere (that is, initiate locomotor behavior). (What constitutes a "location" or "place" will vary from study to study depending on how these constructs are operationalized by the researcher.) Three specific aspects of this activity behavior are differentiated: (1) the frequency with which individuals leave their permanent dwelling (e.g., house or apartment) to engage in outside environmental transactions *(level of activity)*, (2) the recent change in the frequency of this individual activity *(change in activity)*, and (3) the usual spatial or locational context of the behavior *(activity space size)*. A description of these variables and their measurement properties are found in figure 7.2.

Temporal Properties

Along a temporal scale of human behavior, an individual's everyday activity behavior contrasts in several ways with his residential behavior. It is initiated relatively frequently, often daily, with the beginning and end of the behavior usually occurring over a relatively short period, involving intervals of minutes or hours rather than years. Activity behavior is also more likely to occur with greater regularity and is usually routinized and habitual in terms of the time of day it takes place, its duration, and its purpose.

Purposes

A considerable amount of the individual's activity behavior serves life-maintenance and sustaining purposes such as shopping, working, medical treatment, and eating. To distinguish these purposes, at least one academic planner attempted to array the individual's activity behavior along a continuum ranging from "obligatory to discretionary forms of activity." Activities are thereby distinguished according to how postponable they are and to whether the individual has more or less latitude for choice (Chapin 1974:37). In practice, however, the distinction between obligatory and discretionary activities in a modern western soci-

Figure 7.2. Activity Behavior Variables Proposed as Influencing Types and Meaningfulness of Environmental Experiences

Variable Description	Measurement Properties

Level of Activity

The respondent was asked, "How often in the past month did you go *someplace* in Evanston, City of Chicago, and other Chicago suburbs?" Specification of three destinations ensured that the designative meaning of someplace was the same for all respondents. For each destination, respondent could select from six frequency categories. Each of the three activity items was then coded from 6 (greatest frequency) to 1 (lowest frequency) and was treated as an interval variable (table 7.1). A summated score of the three items was then calculated for each respondent. Item-scale correlations were all significant at .000 level. A high score indicates high level of activity.

interval variable;
score range 3 to 17;
mean = 9.7 SD = 3.1
n = 400

Activity Space Size

For each of 13 different activities the respondent was asked, "Where do you usually do the following things?" The respondent chose from four possible location categories: in your house/apartment; in your neighborhood, but not in your house/apartment; outside your neighborhood, but in Evanston; or outside of Evanston (table 7.2). Each activity item was scored from 1 to 4, respectively. The items were treated as interval variables and a summated score was calculated for each respondent's set of activities. These scores were then standardized, because every old person did not engage in the same set of activities. For example, all 400 respondents engaged in "free time" activities, but only 125 respondents engaged in "at work" activities (table 7.3). A maximum score was determined for each respondent by computing the score he would have received if all his reported activities had taken place outside of Evanston. Then, his actual summated score was expressed as a percentage of this maximum score. Item-scale correlations were all significant at .000 level. A high score indicates large activity space.

interval variable;
score range 36.1 to 97.5;
mean = 64.5 SD = 10.2
n = 400

Change in Activity

The respondent was asked, "Compared with five years ago, do you now go to places outside your home more frequently, or less frequently?" On initiation of respondent, interviewers accepted the response, "about the same." A high score indicates an increase in activity.

interval variable;
score range 1 to 3;
mean = 1.6 SD = 0.70
n = 396

ety is difficult to make. This is especially true for certain groups like the elderly for whom activities such as recreation and leisure can be viewed as obligatory even though they serve higher order needs, for example, effectance behaviors and social role performance (Lawton 1972). In general, few rigorously defined guidelines exist by which to classify activities according to their purpose. In practice, such decisions are often dictated by the specific goals of the research.[2] There is also little consensus as to whether activities for certain purposes are more satisfying than others to old people. For example, it is reasonable to expect that both very active employed persons and very active leisure-oriented persons may be similarly achieving their personal needs. Havighurst has expressed such a viewpoint in his "principal of the *equivalence of work and play:* to a considerable extent people can get the same satisfactions from leisure as from work" (1961:320). Because of the above difficulties and ambiguities, activity behaviors were not classified by their purposes in this study's conceptualization.[3]

Units of Behavior

An individual's behavior is variously referred to as a "continuous flowing activity" (Stern 1938:78) and an "orderly, continuous whole" (Dewey 1891:161). A basic task of both the theoretician and the empiricist is the conceptualization of the action units or building blocks making up this "stream of behavior" (Barker 1978:6–7).[4] The selection of this unit inevitably involves a decision as to the most appropriate intervals of time over which to analyze the flow of activity. Usually, as the unit of behavior becomes more structurally detailed, the interval of time for it to be completed becomes smaller.

In his analysis of behavior settings, Barker (1968) constructed a very detailed behavior unit, the behavior episode, a goal-directed, uniform, molar unit of behavior completed in seconds or minutes.[5] A longer to complete and less structurally detailed unit of behavior was proposed by Perin in her attempt to understand the personal and environmental resources required by individuals when they engage in various activities. She referred to her fundamental unit of behavior as the behavior circuit, "the round of behaviors people engage in order to accomplish each of their purposes from start to finish" (1970:78). Chapin analyzed an even "coarser" unit of behavior. Consistent with the data needs of an urban and regional planner, he was concerned with "examining interrelationships between activity systems and the spatial organization of the city—its land use systems, its community facilities, and its service systems" (1974:21). Chapin's activity system referred to the "patterned ways in which individuals, households, institutions, and firms pursue their day-in and day-out affairs in a metropolitan community and interact with one another in time and space" (p. 23). For this purpose, the behavior unit selected was the activity, that is, "classifiable acts or behavior of persons or households which, used as building blocks, permit us to study the living patterns or lifeways of socially cohesive segments of metropolitan area society" (p. 21).

Chapin's designation of the "out of home" activity is close to its empirical interpretation in this study. As operationalized here, a unit of action or behavior is completed only after the individual leaves one place or location and arrives at another. A principal concern is to assess the extent to which individuals are integrated with the concrete or material world outside their dwellings. Notably, this conceptualization omits from special consideration the more structurally and temporally detailed units of behavior, such as *episodes* or *circuits*.

Behavior Mechanisms of Activity Unit

The structural complexity of an activity also depends on the behavior mechanisms that are conceptualized as part of its relevant functioning. For example, in Barker's (1968) analysis of individual behavior, five major behavior mechanisms are considered, all of which have in common their ability to be overtly observed: affective behavior (overt emotions); gross motor activity (involvement of large limbs, muscles, and trunk of body); manipulation (involvement of hands); talking; and thinking (overt displays of problem solving and decision making). In this context, a behavior episode may include applauding, talking, or playing a game of cricket. The depiction of behavior mechanisms in Perin's (1970) schema is somewhat equivocal; however, the emphasis is primarily on behavior mechanisms involving gross motor activity. Such locomotor behavior mechanisms are central to Chapin's examination of activity systems.

Although this study does not attempt to distinguish activity behavior along this dimension, its interpretation here is similar to Perin's and Chapin's.

Locational Context of Activity

Studies investigating the locational context of an individual's activity system commonly identify the permanently occupied dwelling of the individual as his spatial and temporal reference point or space-time origin. In large part, this recognizes the dwelling *qua* "home" (see chapter 8) at which the average day's activities both begin and end. The locational context of an individual's activity is often expressed with reference to the dwelling as the focal point, by way of geometric concepts such as travel distance (in units such as miles) and direction or sectoral bias (in units such as angle degrees) (Nystuen 1963; J. S. Adams 1969). A related concept is the "home range" of the individual: a familiar area surrounding the dwelling unit in which the individual relatively frequently and consistently carries out his daily transactions (Stea 1970; Gelwicks 1970; and Buttimer 1972).[6] As conceptualized in this study, the locational context of activity behavior is referred to as the individual's activity space.

Simple Activity Behavior Patterns of Evanston's Elderly

Table 7.2 reveals that the majority of old people leave their dwelling to go someplace in the Evanston community at least

Table 7.2. Frequency of Travel in Evanston, City of Chicago, and Suburbs

Place	Daily	Several times a week	Once a week	2–3 times a month	Once a month	Never	Total	N	Mean
	6	5	4	3	2	1			
In Evanston	27%	37	20	5	5	7	100%	400	4.57
In City of Chicago	6%	10	8	14	19	43	100%	400	2.39
In Other Suburbs	2%	16	16	22	18	27	100%	400	2.82

several times a week, while trips to Chicago and the other sub-urbs are undertaken much less frequently. Still, there is a sizable percentage of old people (at least 12 percent) who rarely (once a month or less) go anywhere—even within their own community.

Table 7.3 confirms that certain activities are more likely than others to be performed in the dwelling and neighborhood, rather than in locations outside the neighborhood. The size of the old person's overall activity space depends, in part, on the specific set of activities in which he chooses to engage. For example, on the average, old people still in the labor force have a larger overall activity space simply because the work location is more likely to be outside the community.

The majority of old people (55 percent) reported a decline in their activity levels compared with five years earlier, while only 12 percent indicated they go to places outside their homes more frequently than in the past. Thirty-three percent of the elderly reported no change in their activity levels.

The correlation relationships (Pearson r's) among the activity behavior variables were all statistically significant (at .01 level or less) and in the predictable directions. Elderly people who had lower levels of activity also had smaller activity spaces (.39) and reported a recent decline in their activity (.27). Old people with a smaller activity space also reported a recent decline in their activity (.22). Although related to each other, these three variables share a sufficiently small amount of variation to suggest they are measuring different aspects of old people's activity behavior.

Table 7.3. Locational Context of Activities

Activity[a]	In your (house/apt.)	In your neighborhood (not in house/apt.)	Outside neighborhood but in Evanston	Outside Evanston	Total	Mean	SD	N[b]
See family or relatives	53%	8	8	32	100%	2.18	1.36	389
See close friends	39%	23	22	17	100%	2.16	1.12	377
See neighbors	31%	64	4	1	100%	1.74	0.55	383
Have fun	41%	15	19	25	100%	2.28	1.23	395
Spend your free time	68%	8	14	10	100%	1.67	1.05	400
Attend a club or social group	1%	18	56	24	100%	3.03	0.41	280
Eat in a restaurant	0%	12	45	43	100%	3.31	0.68	386
Attend or view religious services	2%	30	55	13	100%	2.80	0.69	324
Obtain groceries	4%	45	42	9	100%	2.56	0.71	397
Do other shopping	3%	14	53	31	100%	3.11	0.73	397
Do your banking	0%	14	69	17	100%	3.02	0.56	393
See a doctor	0%	8	65	28	100%	3.19	0.57	393
Are at your job	7%	14	35	43	100%	3.14	0.92	125

[a]Respondents were asked, "Where do you usually do the following things?"
[b]Distributions only include respondents who reported that they actually engaged in activity (64% of respondents engaged in 12 to 13 activities; 31% in 10 to 11 activities; 4% in 8 to 9 activities; and 1% in 6 activities).

Mechanisms by which Behavioral Relationships Influence Elderly People's Environmental Experiences

The following sections discuss in abstract terms the mechanisms by which residential and activity behaviors influence an older population's environmental experiences.

Direct, Concrete, Tangible Contact of Individuals with their Environment

It can be shown that old people display variable residential and activity behaviors. For example, many elderly people have lived almost all their lives in the same community; others have lived in the same place for only a short time. Some elderly people regularly and frequently travel to numerous locations in their city to satisfy their entertainment needs; others seldom leave their dwellings. Some elderly people frequently shop in nearby stores; others regularly shop in more distant regional centers. The important result is that elderly people differ as to the spatial and temporal contexts in which they conduct their everyday environmental transactions. This implies that residents living in the *same* environment do not similarly occupy or utilize its contents nor initiate environmental transactions having the same potential consequences. In more abstract terms, elderly individuals are not availing themselves directly of the same sensory information about their environment's objects and events.

Elderly individuals are thereby being exposed to some parts and properties of their environment, and not others. They are engaging in behavioral relationships that are observably and tangibly linking them—both spatially and temporally—to only *selective* aspects of their environment (Norberg-Schulz 1971; Wheatley 1976). This selective environmental integration is important because not all parts and places of the environment have the same informational exchange potentials. That is, they offer individuals different opportunities to satisfy (or not to satisfy) their purposes, needs, and goals (Bloom 1964; Ittelson 1973). For example, some sections of the city offer a greater potential for the individual to have new, different, and novel experiences; other sections of the city offer a greater potential for the elderly individual to have anxious, stressful, or unpleasant experiences; and yet other sections are more likely to reinforce the elderly individual's prior—and status quo— environmental experiences.

As an extreme example, consider those elderly individuals who never leave their dwellings, who literally close off contact with all of their outside world. They deny, ignore, or forget large portions of an outside material reality, and in turn eliminate the possibility of a wide range of environmental experiences. Instead, these old persons turn their emotional energies inward, freeing themselves from material linkages to recall, reminisce, and fantasize about their remembered pasts. Engaged in efforts to order and systematize these remembered experiences, elderly individuals regard current or new information as a disruption of the stability and unity imposed on an earlier remembered experiential world (Cooley 1902).

Cognitive and Motivational Strategies Associated with the Elderly Person's Residential and Activity Behaviors

These behavioral relationships do not only reveal differences in elderly people's tangible or concrete linkages with their environment; they also are an overt expression of the differing attempts by elderly individuals to satisfy their everyday demands and needs—*purposively, rationally,* and *adaptively.* The result is that residential and activity behaviors are initiated by elderly individuals who are operating by variable cognitive and motivational strategies. This implies that elderly people's behaviors, even when conducted in identical spatial and temporal contexts, may produce very different experiences if they are motivated for different reasons and the environmental information generated by the behaviors is processed and interpreted in different ways.

For example, the residential and activity behaviors of some elderly persons will be intended to maintain status quo environmental experiences; the same behaviors carried out by other elderly persons will be intended to create novel, different experiences. For some elderly persons their long duration in the same dwelling is a reflection of their financial inability to move and their dwelling may be associated with constraining experiences; for others who voluntarily seek and welcome residential stability, the dwelling may be linked to feelings of mastery or control.

The Influence of Residential Behavior on Environmental Experiences

So far the chapter has treated in abstract terms the influence that behavioral relationships have on a population's environmental experiences. More concrete and factual evidence is now presented that links regularities in the properties of residential and activity behaviors to the content and consequences of old people's environmental experiences. The chapter first focuses on the effects of residential behavior.

The Influence of Length of Occupancy on Environmental Experiences

Six sections follow that examine the theorized impact of length of residential occupancy. Although these sections contain some overlapping arguments, they are organized according to issues currently differentiated in the literature, and impose order on what are now fragmented insights. These sections are followed by a theoretical examination of how housing tenure (owner-renter) status, the second major aspect of residential behavior, influences old people's environmental experiences.

Amount of Continuous Environmental Exposure

The length of time an elderly individual has occupied his dwelling or community provides a revealing glimpse of the "latest segment of his residential history" (Taeuber 1961:116). It is one of the few data items that, although collected at a single point in time, link the spatial and temporal dimensions of an individual's environmental relationships. Indicating the amount of time a particular environment (or some part of it) has been continuously occupied can suggest the likely amount of exposure the individual has had with its objects and events. Thus, "length of occupancy" gives insight to the temporal origins and existence of an old person's experiential world.

In contrast to old persons who have relocated one or more times in the recent past, old people who have lived a long time in the same dwelling or community are more likely to have been exposed to an environment that has changed more gradually and less dramatically over time. Obviously, exceptions to this generalization exist, as when neighborhoods undergo rapid and major changes in their land uses and population composition.

Certain experiential outcomes are more likely than others as a result of the longtime, continuous exposure to the same environment. It is probable that the longtime resident has more stable, continuous, and predictable experiences than does the person who moves more frequently. The very constancy of the environment should make its reinforcement potential stronger (Bloom 1964). It is reasonable to expect that such environmental stability facilitates the recalling of long-term memories of pleasant environmental transactions. Zajonc, reviewing his own and others experimental research, also finds that the "mere repeated exposure" (1980:160) to objects leads to individuals' expressing increasing preference for them.

However, there is reason to be uncertain as to whether the longtime exposure to a relatively unchanged environment actually produces good as opposed to bad environmental experiences for the old person. On the one hand, unchanged environmental experiences may be interpreted in positive terms because of their predictability, certainty, unambiguity, and order. Such general outcomes may enable elderly persons to maintain strong continuity with their pasts. Their own sense of competence and control may be enhanced because of environmental transactions that result in such outcomes. In a society that often appears to be changing rapidly and unsympathetically, objects and events to which such constant, long-term meanings are associated can be of considerable comfort to elderly people (Cantril 1965). Together, such continuity and feelings of control contribute to the environment being perceived as more harmonious with the old person's needs and goals. In turn, a more positive self-image may result. On the other hand, the very constancy and certainty of the environmental experiences that accompany long-term occupancy may yield undesirable outcomes. They may contribute to the individual's feelings of boredom, monotony, and apathy because they deprive the individual of needed environmental variation or diversity (Wohlwill 1976). A constant environment may be inappropriate also if it is interpreted by the old person as an indicator of an inflexible or insensitive environment. This may result if the individual's needs or competence have changed such that the resources of the present environment are perceived as inadequate. Such circumstances may apply to the longtime elderly dweller of the auto-oriented suburb who is no longer able to drive and requires nonexistent public transportation.

Adaptation-level or comparison-level theory (Helson 1964; Thibaut and Kelley 1959) also suggests certain consequences of longtime occupancy in a relatively unchanging environment. An increasing number of environmental transactions should generate affectively neutral responses from the individual. However great the interpreted environmental diversity is on initial residential occupancy, over time the elderly person is likely to adapt or accommodate to its earlier effects. Consequently, for the longtime elderly resident, it is less likely that environmental transactions result in either extremely positive or extremely negative feelings.

In total, the evidence suggests that old people who have lived longer in their place of residence and who have weaker dispositions toward novel environments—and whose competence has not declined—are more likely than other old people to have favorable and satisfying environmental experiences.

Adjustment Problems of the Recent Occupant

Evidence is available that old persons who have recently moved are more likely than longtime elderly residents to have unpleasant experiences resulting from their attempts to adjust to a new and different environment (Schooler 1976). The nature of these experiences can be better understood by examining their possible antecedents.

First, recent occupants may have moved initially for reasons that would predispose them to certain types of environmental adjustment problems. For example, moves by old people are sometimes initiated because of poor health, lowered income, or recent social role losses. Thus, these old people enter a new environment in a somewhat weakened state and with less ability to satisfy demands and cope with the consequences of unfavorable environmental transactions (Pastalan n.d.). Second, the stress generated by the physical relocation itself may contribute to old people's negative evaluations of their new environment (Schulz and Brenner 1977; Lawton 1977a; Kasl 1972). For example, such events as dealing with the movers, packing possessions, paying out large relocation expenses, saying goodbye to friends and neighbors, and traveling to the new place of residence all are potential sources of physical and emotional stress. Such vulnerabilities can be aggravated by a move that was imposed on the old person and resulted in "a loss of decisional control" (Schulz and Brenner 1977:329). The mere *anticipation* of these and related moving events may be another basis for stress (Tobin and Lieberman 1976). Third, the old person may have left a familiar and predictable environment that generated a lifetime of positive experiences to enter a new environment devoid of such memories and certainty. Consequently, all new environmental transactions may be tempered with negative emotions. Fourth, the information used to select the new environment may have been erroneous or incomplete. The old person may be confronted with unexpected unpleasant experiences (Pastalan n.d.). Fifth, however desirable the interpreted attributes of the new environment might be, negative experiential outcomes can arise for elderly people who find that the differences between their old and new environments are not easily reconciled. On the one hand, the new residence may be perceived as having features that are less attractive than those found in the previous residence (for example, smaller and fewer rooms in dwelling, less friendly neighbors). Alternatively, confronted with an environment perceived overall as more attractive than the previous residence, the old person may not easily adjust to the "new" (and unfamiliar) kitchen appliances, the large shopping centers (in contrast to the corner grocery store of the previous location), or the modern building (in contrast to the "ancient charm" of the previous one). Sixth, the failure of some old people to adjust successfully to a new environment may be due to their inability to disassociate now inappropriate meanings that were attributed to objects in their past environment (Mischel 1973). This "living in the past" may prevent individuals from dealing effectively with the realities of their new situation (Cumming and Cumming 1963). Seventh, the new resident oftentimes must adjust to his "stranger" status, which can involve reestablishing a personal identity so as to gain people's recognition and acceptance. The migrant's "temporary disruption of organization" has been considered by Cumming and Cumming:

> His concept of himself no longer receives automatic reinforcement from those who know such things as to whom he is kin, where he went to school, and the occupation of his wife's father. He must be overt, occasionally to the point of embarrassment, in setting forth his achievements, his avocations, his values, and his beliefs. In displaying them, he may for the first time examine their meaning himself. He finds himself in a minor crisis. (1963:48–49)

Strength of Community Social Bonds

A considerable sociological literature documents a strong positive relationship between the length of residence of individuals and the strength of their community social bonds (Zimmer 1955; Speare, 1970; Lansing and Mueller 1967:143–144; Taylor and Townsend 1976). It is theorized that as length of residence increases a greater likelihood exists that persons become assimilated into the social fabric of the community. Thus extensive friendship and kinship bonds and widespread associational ties are more likely to occur in the absence of residential mobility of a place's occupants. More positive social experiences follow that in turn lead to more favorable overall community experiences (Kasarda and Janowitz 1974).

Empirical evidence comes from a study of Great Britain communities in which 2,199 adults were interviewed. Kasarda and Janowitz (1974) examined the relationship between length of residence and several measures of social bonds. They found that as individuals' length of residence increased, a higher percentage of their acquaintances were within their community, a greater number of their relatives lived nearby, and a larger proportion of their friends and relatives resided in the local area. Further, they reported that as length of residence increased, so did the individual's sense of community. These relationships persisted even when controlling for other possible sources of explanation, such as the community's population size and density and its occupants' socioeconomic status and stage-in-life characteristics. Thus, they concluded that "length of residence is the key exogenous factor influencing local community attachment" (cited in Berry and Kasarda 1977:65).

The relationship between length of occupancy and community social bonds, although relevant in all stages of a person's life, may have special salience to old people (Windley and Scheidt 1982). To the extent that social ties are more likely to be disrupted in old age because of the death of friends, loss of employment, and loss of contact with friends and relatives, the importance of maintaining permanent, stable community social bonds should increase.

A social climate (Moos 1976) in the community (for example, the age-segregated status of the population) can potentially weaken this proposed relationship if it is evaluated as incompatible with an elderly occupant's life-style. Similarly, community social bonds may be weakened if the population composition changes, due to racial change, gentrification, and so on.

Development of Psychological Attachment

Evidence exists that length of residence is positively associated with individuals' psychological attachment to a place, that is, their strong affective involvement with and sense of belonging to their longtime residence (Taylor and Townsend 1976).

Literature produced primarily by psychologists specifically considered the meanings of attachment behavior. Its major emphasis was on attachments between mother and infant and how these subsequently influence attachment to peers and nonfamily persons in early childhood (Hartup and Lempers 1973). More recently, however, literature emphasizing a life-span approach to old age interprets the concept of attachment more broadly (Lerner and Ryff 1978; Antonucci 1976). Kalish and Knudtson (1976), for example, proposed an attachment model in which types of attachment included not only people and social groups but also "things and places." In this framework, a person's attachment, of whatever type, is distinguished by its "strong affective involvement with the attachment object" (Kalish and Knudtson 1976:172) and its "self-produced feedback" (that is, some form of sensory, affective, or cognitive stimulus received from the attachment object). Such attachment (and resulting feedback) serves two functions, according to Kalish and Knudtson (p. 173). First, it contributes to the sense of mastery felt by individuals because their relationships with the attachment object are anticipated and predictable. Second, it increases the feelings of security of individuals and thereby enables them to explore other aspects of their environment with greater creativity and abandonment.

There is reason to predict that such feelings achieved through attachment behavior become especially important in old age. Because of developmental and cohort effects, old persons may perform less competently—physically or socially—than younger persons in several domains of their life, and they may feel less in control or less independent. Consequently, there is a theoretical basis for the prediction that attachment behaviors toward the dwelling, neighborhood, or community and their concomitant experiential outcomes (e.g., the feeling of security) are likely to be of greater significance to older than younger people. This will be especially true when earlier objects of old people's attachment— a career, a spouse, or a longtime friend—no longer exist.

Degree of Familiarity With Environment

Various studies report that people living longer in the same place are more familiar with their environment. Representative of the elderly literature, Lawton, Kleban, and Carlson's study suggested that older people's "preference for the familiar (knowledge of how to get about, or which routes to take when going to visit, or which shops to patronize)" may underlie the motivation of longtime older occupants to remain in a neighborhood that is otherwise very unattractive because of physical deterioration and decline (1973:447). In a very different setting, Rowles (1979) argued that older people, when they first enter a nursing home, experience adjustment problems because the new environment offers little in the way of familiar objects or spatial cues. Thus these older people find themselves in a state of geographical disorientation.

Langford (1962) suggested a very different interpretation of the consequences of familiarity with a longtime residence. She proposed that the duration of residence or the degree of familiarity with a neighborhood influences older people's attitudes toward living in an age-integrated residential situation (see also Golant 1980). She observed:

> In a familiar environment with the security and satisfactions of their home and with neighbors who are known, the aged appear to be relatively indifferent to the age composition of the neighborhood or to the age of new people moving in. In contrast, when an aged person moves into a new community, the absence of people his own age may be a deterrent in his making social contacts, and he may desire some degree of insulation from the noise and activities of younger families and their children. (1962:8)

In their national survey of the U.S. population, Campbell, Converse, and Rodgers similarly pointed to the significance of the longtime occupied residential setting to old people. In their words, "the new learning required to achieve a comparable familiarization with another environment may appear particularly forbidding to the elderly, long past the period when exploration of the new is an intriguing challenge" (1976:164).

The positive relationship between length of residence and environmental familiarity is supported by analyses of the psychological or cognitive representations that individuals have of their city (Milgram 1970; Moore 1979). Golledge (1978:81) argued that greater familiarity with a city's physical environment contributes to an individual's having a more coherent and cohesive cognitive representation of its nodes, paths, and areas. A greater likelihood exists that the individual has learned (through direct, instructional, and observational processes) to discriminate efficiently an environment's physical objects that are personally more salient (Golledge and Zannaras 1973). Such a cognitively represented environment should contribute to environmental transactions that more predictably and effortlessly yield positive outcomes for the individual. However, Downs and Stea (1973:25) suggested that over time or with individual maturation people forget some of the information that once was included in their cognitive representations. Milgram (1970) argued that such diminution is adaptive and enables the resident to cope with the information overload of everyday life and to focus selectively on the most important environmental information.

Amount of Residential Satisfaction

A persistently positive relationship is reported between place (dwelling, neighborhood, or community) satisfaction and a population's length of occupancy. Findings from a national study (Campbell et al. 1976:163) indicated that, for a short period immediately following occupancy in a new environment, reported satisfaction levels are much higher than in later periods. It is suggested that because individuals make a major emotional and financial commitment to a new place—often with the anticipation of long-term occupancy—they initially block out or repress any negative evaluations of their new residences. In effect, this denial by individuals may be essential in the beginning (the first year) when they are confronted with a variety of adjustment problems and must assure themselves that they have made a correct choice. After this initial "momentary phase of dissonance reduction" and period of self-congratulation and pleasure, individuals once more become rational observers and evaluate the faults of their residences less emotionally. After about five years, however, satisfaction levels of individuals increase, in part because of their progressive accommodation to their situation and in part because of a "decline in the salience of competing alternatives" (p. 164). It is argued that this accommodation is a result of individuals maintaining or lowering their aspiration levels after occupying their new residences such that alternative residential environments are either not considered or viewed less favorably than the individual's present residence. Another interpretation is offered by Taylor and Townsend (1976), who argued that longtime residents lack the motivation or ability to "evaluate or conceptualize features of attraction or rejection" in their community.

For a relatively small percentage of elderly, however, their continued longtime residential occupancy will be accompanied by a decline in satisfaction levels in response to a variety of dwelling and neighborhood problems (Newman and Duncan 1979; Varady 1980). Declines in health, income, and other personal resources may "lead to a mismatch between the elderly householder's housing needs and his housing situation" (Varady 1980:307).

The Influence of Tenure Status on Environmental Experiences

An Experiential Perspective on Tenure Status

Historically, textbooks on jurisprudence defined an *owner* as: "A person who has the totality of rights, powers, privileges, and immunities which constitute complete property in a thing is the 'owner' of the 'thing'" (American Law Institute 1936:25). The legal and financial reality by which the individual possesses such a totality can be rightfully challenged. For instance, it can be legitimately argued that the existence of many such rights and powers depend not on the tenure status by which the property is occupied but on the occupant's type of building structure. Thus, the greater rights of the owner may apply only when the unit occupied is a single-family structure, but not when it is part of a high-rise, multifamily building. As a result, owner-renter distinctions become blurred when the owned unit is a condominium in a high-rise building or when the rented unit is a single-family dwelling. Such ambiguity may also characterize ownership arrangements in building cooperatives and certain low-interest homeownership programs. The legal and financial complexities of owning a home compared with renting led one careful analyst of the subject to conclude that "relatively trivial differences [exist] in the legal or financial attributes that are inherent in the forms of tenure" (Marcuse 1972:187).

Be that as it may, it is crucial for the student of the environment to distinguish between the objective and experiential realities of housing tenure status. In this regard, a convincing case can be made that the majority of North American residents perceive the legal and financial rights and powers of owners as superior to those of renters. As importantly, the behavior of owners is likely to be consistent with these values and beliefs. When the press reports on the often desperate situation of old renters who are displaced by condominium conversion, from the public's viewpoint it is the renter who suffers the economic, psychological, and social hardships and whose rights are ignored.

Returning to the original definition of *ownership*, it may well be true that, in legal terms, tenure status does not confer an unambiguous set of rights, privileges, powers, and immunities on owners. But such a view must be tempered by a consideration of the beliefs and values held by individuals about their tenure status and whether they behave as if these rights and privileges actually do exist. In short, an objective or societal perspective on tenure status must be carefully distinguished from an experiential perspective. The former emphasizes that "ownership (or tenancy, for that matter) is not a relationship between a person and a thing, but a relationship among persons, subject to rules laid down and enforced by society" (Marcuse 1972:22). The experiential perspective, on the other hand, argues that tenure status *does* constitute a behavioral relationship *between the individual and his dwelling* and that this relationship is different for owners than for renters.

The proposed basis for this differentiation is the owner's identification of his dwelling as a *possession*. The following sections consider the meanings given to the concept of possession and how these underlie the beneficial or unpleasant experiences of the old homeowner.

Benefits of Dwelling Possession

A central and recurring theme is that the possession of an object contributes to an individual's "ability to produce effects in the environment—to experience causal efficacy and control" (Furby 1978:320). In this sense, the psychological function of possession is similar to that of attachment. In both instances, either the possession of or the attachment to an object is associated with an individual's feeling in control. Thus, he is able to effect desired outcomes and to experience the positive feelings and emotions that accompany an individual's sense of mastery over his environment. For the old homeowner, such control is likely to be manifested in various ways that are not usually available to the old renter. Examples include the ability to regulate the dwelling's heat or air conditioning and to freely make alterations and improvements to the dwelling. Such control also gives the homeowner the right to ignore the visible signs of an aging and deteriorated housing unit, to avoid the vigilance of an apartment landlord, and to escape from the numerous restrictions often found in a renter's lease (Marcuse 1972). Fundamental to the control available to the old homeowner, but not to the renter, is the ability to dispose of one's dwelling after death. Deciding to whom to bequeath his property is often the only domain in which the old person can exercise such complete control. Findings by Chen (1973) have emphasized the importance old people place on this right.

The feelings of control associated with homeownership also are a product of the old person's certainty and confidence that his remaining lifetime in a chosen place is guaranteed. By the time owners reach their sixty-fifth birthday, 84 percent of them have paid off their home mortgages (Welfeld and Struyk 1979:27) and do not have to confront the lingering fear of being displaced. This may be particularly important to the present cohort of old people who grew old in a period characterized by rapid societal changes and economically difficult times. In sharp contrast, the continued occupancy status of the older renter is always in doubt, subject to the whims of the landlord who chooses not to renew the lease or to renew it with such an exorbitant increase in rent that relocation is the only alternative. The late 1970s witnessed yet another major source of anxiety for the older renter: the prospect that the long-occupied apartment building would be converted to a condominium, leaving the older person to choose between the formidable cost of ownership or relocation.

The advantage of homeownership over renting is particularly notable for low-income elderly persons. Because the owned unit is a major economic asset, the elderly occupant has the option, however reluctant he may be to exercise it, of selling or refinancing the dwelling to realize its cash value. This option is not available to the renter. Whether it is a viable financial strategy for the old homeowner is relatively unimportant. What matters is that the owner's fear of economic impoverishment and financial dependence is likely to be less than the elderly renter's.

To the extent that old people do experience loss of status in American society (Rosow 1974) (see chapter 5), there is reason to expect that the old homeowner bears the brunt of this loss more successfully than the old renter. Homeownership is perceived by the individual owner and by society as an indicator of social status, achievement, and power. Thus, possession of a dwelling is a conspicuous sign (Veblen 1899) of an individual's life accomplishments and successes and consequently is likely to be a source of considerable pride and satisfaction. Because old age is a period in which a positive self-image may be threatened, homeownership can serve as an indicator of the achieved social status of the old person. Thus a dwelling possession can be viewed as "an extension of the individual [which] helps define individuality" (Furby 1978:317)—dwelling and individual status become inseparable.

Homeownership also requires its occupants to make decisions and carry out tasks involving the care and maintenance of the dwelling. Thus, a possession may represent to the old person the only hard evidence of his capability of maintaining independence, responsibilities, and authority in his life.

There is also good reason to believe that the individual-dwelling relationship influences the old person's attitudes toward his neighborhood and community. Unlike the renter, the homeowner has a considerable financial investment in his dwelling and thus may display greater awareness and concern about the status of his immediate residential environment. This interest may be manifested by his more active participation in its local organizations.

Unpleasant Experiences of Dwelling Possession

The possession of a dwelling may also result in unfavorable environmental experiences from which the old renter is spared. Although homeownership may be accompanied by feelings of competence and control, it also may be the source of physical and economic stresses that can lead to feelings of weakness and dependence.

Elderly homeowners often occupy older buildings with plumbing, heating, or lighting systems that work inefficiently or break down. With building age, the likelihood of physical deterioration increases also, as exemplified by sagging and leaking roofs, rotting foundations, flaking paint, cracked and warped siding, and worn-out floors (Lowry 1970). In the 1970s, the materials and labor required to deal with such problems constituted one of the most rapidly rising components of the consumer price index. More generally, the costs of routinely operating a home, including property taxes, heating, water, and electricity, have also risen at a higher than average rate.

Consequently, dwelling possession may be the basis for various stressful experiences. If considerable funds are required to maintain and upgrade the owned home, the elderly person—especially if poor—may find little comfort in the fact that his home represents a substantial asset. Moreover, when the costs of heating and air conditioning become an economic burden, the ability of the old person to exercise control over temperature conditions is restricted. If house systems begin to break down and structural defects occur, which make the dwelling unsafe or uncomfortable, the old person who lacks either the personal energy or assistance from others (emotional, behavioral, financial) to cope with these problems may clearly feel out of control and a slave to his dwelling. When such breakdowns occur unexpectedly, the owned home only serves to confirm the uncertainty and ambiguities of old age. When the older homeowner finds himself in this compromising and even degrading situation, his perceived social status and self-concept are likely to suffer. Moreover, the recognition that he no longer has the ability to take care of his possession may signal to the older homeowner that he has lost his authority and independence, leading to feelings of incompetence and weakness.

Under such conditions, old people may find that *not* possessing (owning) a dwelling yields a more favorable set of environmental experiences. The renter is spared the responsibilities of homeownership and possibly also the feelings of vulnerability produced by coping failures. Indeed, the old person who has the added restrictions and uncertainties of renter status may be more than compensated by the operating and maintenance assistance provided by the building's landlord or janitor (Audain and Huttman 1973).

Residential Behavior as a Response to the Experiential Environment

Until now, the chapter has focused on the theoretical basis for expecting that residential behavior influences the environmental experiences of old people. However, equally valid arguments can be made that residential behavior and environmental experiences are reciprocally related; that is, each continually and simultaneously acts on the other, as both cause and effect. Thus, residential behavior not only can influence an individual's environmental experiences but also may represent a consequence of an individual's environmental experiences. This latter relationship occurs when residential adjustments are initiated by individuals so as to avoid or eliminate environmental transactions that yield negative outcomes. An actual or anticipated move from one environment to another thereby represents a coping mechanism designed to create a more favorable set of environmental experiences. In short, although environmental experiences are continually shaped and molded as length of residential occupancy increases, the resulting experiential outcomes themselves may underlie the termination of this occupancy.

The following discussion considers the precedents for conceptualizing residential behavior as a consequence of or a coping response to unpleasant environmental experiences. To enable subsequent empirical investigations of this relationship, two variables are constructed that describe the moving anticipations of Evanston's elderly population.

Residential Behavior as an Adjustment Process

The conceptualization of residential mobility as an adjustment or coping response to a stressful or unsatisfactory housing environment is found in an investigation by Rossi (1955). Residential mobility is here considered "a mechanism by which a family's housing is brought into adjustment to its housing needs" (Rossi 1955:122). Rossi emphasized that new housing space needs were generated by life cycle changes, specifically the expanding family as children are born and later the constricting family as children marry and leave the household. He also identified other dwelling qualities, such as dwelling unit design, layout of rooms, and orientation of dwelling to other buildings, that would be more suitable for certain stages of life than others.

Rossi's primarily empirical work was followed by several formal attempts to conceptualize mobility behavior as an adjustment process (Wolpert 1965, 1966; Golant 1971; Brown and Moore 1970; and Speare 1974). Wolpert (1965), for example, proposed that an individual evaluates the place in which he lives and assigns to it a subjective utility, which is then compared with the utilities of alternative residential sites. When existing utility levels are low relative to an individual's aspirations and expectations and when alternatives have higher utilities, a move is more likely to take place. In a more general theoretical formulation that shared similarities with Wolpert's (1965) model, Golant (1971) proposed that residential movement was one of several types of human spatial behavior initiated as a coping response to environmental stress. Speare's (1974:175) model of mobility is similarly formulated, although he speaks of an individual's "dissatisfaction, rather than stress, to avoid the connotation of mental tension."

A small number of studies have attempted to verify the relationship suggested in these models. Noteworthy is a study (Newman and Duncan 1979) of a national sample of U.S. population (all age groups) that found housing and neighborhood problems were unrelated to actual mobility behavior. The authors suggested the following explanation for the apparent discrepancy: "The desire to move among those with serious housing and neighborhood problems is indeed strong, but impediments to searching for and finding suitable housing intervene between the desire and the behavior" (p. 164). This discrepancy was earlier noted in a study by Goldscheider, Van Arsdol, and Sabagh (1966). Focusing on both older and younger populations, these investigators examined the extent to which residential plans, desires, and mobility behavior were consistent with each other. In 1961, they inquired about the following year's moving plans and desires of a probability sample of adult households living in the Los Angeles metropolitan area. One year later, they reinterviewed this sample to ascertain if residential moves were carried out. They found that 34.2 percent of the younger population (under age 50) planned to move, 51.9 percent desired to move, and 31.3 percent actually did move within the one-year period. In contrast, 23.4 percent of the older population (over age 50) planned to move, 31.0 percent desired to move, but only 15.2 percent moved during the one-year period.

Two social psychologists theorized that mobility intentions or anticipations *should* be related to actual mobility behavior (Fishbein and Ajzen 1975:368–383). However, these authors also pointed to several factors that weaken this relationship. In light of the above empirical findings, the most important of these may be "the degree to which carrying out the intention is completely under the person's volitional control" (Fishbein and Ajzen 1975:369).

The above discussion emphasizes the importance of distinguishing between mobility plans, expectations, or preferences, on the one hand, and mobility behavior or behavioral performance, on the other. No matter how unfavorable the environmental experiences are, the critical issue may be whether the individual has sufficient personal resources available to carry out his preferences or intentions. That is, reports of moving anticipations, rather than observed mobility behavior, may serve as a better indicator of stressful environmental experiences. Moving behavior, in the final analysis, may be primarily an indicator of the extent to which people are competent enough to carry out their mobility desires.

Much of the relevant literature on the subject, in fact, has examined how residential dissatisfaction is related to individual reports of moving anticipation rather than behavior. In general, these studies provided empirical support for the theoretical arguments that residential dissatisfaction leads to moving expectations, plans, or preferences (Speare 1974; Bach and Smith 1977; Campbell, Converse, and Rodgers 1976; Lawton, Kleban, and Carlson 1973; Rosow 1967; Nelson and Winter 1975; Neff and Constantine 1979; Duncan and Newman 1976).

Typical are the findings of Lawton, Kleban, and Carlson, who interviewed 115 older residents in an older rundown inner-city neighborhood and found that the following environmental stresses lead to moving plans:

> A substandard dwelling unit; a dwelling unit with too much space, too many steps, or other obstacles; too-great distance from necessary services or amenities; physical insecurity due to crime, traffic, climatic conditions, and so on; necessity for shared living accommodations; absence of socially integrating personal relationships; cost of new housing that exceed available means, particularly after the death of a spouse. (1973:447)

In a study of all population age groups, Speare (1974) also found that residential dissatisfaction strongly influenced the "wish to move." Moreover, once the influence of this "dissatisfaction" was taken into account, the explanation of who wished to move was not improved by considering other individual variables, such as age, education, income, duration of residence, crowding, and the availability of friends and relatives.

Variable Measures of Residential Behavior as Coping Response

Two residential behavior variables measured old people's coping responses to their environmental experiences: moving prefer-

Figure 7.3. Residential Behavior Variables Proposed as Consequences of Environmental Experiences

Variable Description	Measurement Properties
Moving Preferences	
This variable was constructed from responses to the question: "If you really had your choice, would you prefer to stay in this house/apartment or move?" On initiation of the respondents, interviewers accepted a response of "uncertain." A high score indicates stronger preference to move.	interval variable; score range 1 to 3; mean = 1.4 SD = 0.73 n = 400
Moving Expectations	
This variable was constructed from responses to the question: "Within the next two years, do you think you will definitely move, probably move, probably not move, or definitely not move?" On initiation of the respondents, interviewers accepted a response of "uncertain." A high score indicates a greater expectation of moving.	interval variable; score range 1 to 5; mean = 2.0 SD = 1.3 n = 400

ences and moving expectations. A description of these variables and their measurement properties are found in figure 7.3.

The Moving Preferences and Expectations of Evanston's Elderly

The tabulations shown in table 7.4 confirmed that the large majority of Evanston's old persons expected and preferred to remain in their present dwellings. Eighty percent of the old population preferred not to move, and 73 percent reported they definitely or probably will not move within the next two years.

Although moving preferences and moving expectations were highly correlated (Pearson $r = .61$; Eta = .63), there were signifi-

cant percentages of old people whose preferences and expectations did not coincide. For instance, of elderly persons who reported they "definitely expect to move" in the next two years, 18
percent expressed a *preference* "to remain" in their present dwelling. Similarly, of elderly persons reporting they "probably will
move," 44 percent expressed a preference for not relocating. This
lack of correspondence between preferences and expectations was
further illustrated by old people who reported they definitely or
probably will not move in the next two years, but who in fact preferred to move (from 3 percent to 11 percent).

Table 7.4. The Relationship Between Moving Expectations and Moving Preferences

Moving Expectations	Moving Preferences				N	Percentage Distribution
	Stay	Uncertain	Move	Total		
Definitely not move	95%	2	3	100%	229	57%
Probably not move	84%	5	11	100%	63	16
Uncertain	74%	11	16	100%	38	10
Probably move	44%	8	47	100%	36	9
Definitely move	18%	6	77	100%	34	9
Total	80%	4	16	100%	400	100%

At least in part, the conflicting preference and expectation responses emphasize the different connotations of these concepts. A
preference is closely related to an *aspiration*—"what a person wants
and longs for" (Cantril 1965:8) or feels entitled to (Campbell, Converse, and Rodgers 1976:173) if he had "freedom of choice" (Proshansky, Ittelson, and Rivlin 1970:174). Thus, a preference is less
likely to be anchored or adjusted to personal or environmental
realities and refers to a response to an ideal or hypothetical situation (Pocock and Hudson 1978). An *expectation*, on the other hand,
is similar to a *behavioral intention* (Fishbein and Ajzen 1975) and
thus is likely to reflect an individual's self-appraisal of the personal resources he has available to carry out a behavior, the physical and social environmental constraints he might encounter, and
the likelihood the behavior would result in favorable or unfavorable consequences.

Influence of Activity Behavior on Old People's Environmental Experiences

The examination of how activity behavior influences the environmental experiences of old people is more difficult for two reasons.

First, whereas residential behavior is conceptualized and measured fairly uniformly in the literature, this is not the case for activity behavior. The psychologist's concepts of act, action (social), behavior, response, and adaptive behavior share some similarities with activity behavior but also differ substantially in other ways (Wolman 1973). The sociologist's concept of social activity can variously refer to individuals' locomotor activities for social purposes, their interpersonal contacts and relationships, and the content and complexity of their social role set. These inconsistent definitions become an issue when interpreting the research literature. Inevitably, it becomes necessary to draw on theoretical and empirical literature that does not define activity behavior in a desired fashion but nonetheless offers sufficiently important insights and interpretations.

Second, in contrast to the residential behavior literature, there is almost a complete absence of either conceptual or empirical treatments of activity behavior as an antecedent of everyday environmental experiences. What insights are found in the literature are in response to research issues very different from those presented in this chapter. One exception, however, is the theoretical insights found in a literature reviewed by Kelman (1974), who was concerned with how the acts or behaviors of individuals are reciprocally related to their attitudes.[7] (Attitudes represent one type of self-reported response encompassed within the concept of environmental experiences.) In the cognitive dissonance and self-perception literature discussed by Kelman, attitude change is conceptualized as a cognitive adjustment; individuals attribute to themselves and to others an attitude that is more consistent with the particular way they have acted toward an object. Attitude, in this sense, is viewed as a "post hoc adjustment to action" (Kelman 1974:315). However, Kelman argued that attitude change should be interpreted more broadly as "an outcome of various motivational and informational processes that are generated by the action" (p. 317). Similar processes were identified earlier in the chapter as constituting one mechanism by which behavioral relationships influence old people's variable environmental experiences.

The examination of how activity behavior influences the environmental experiences of old people is organized as follows. First, a brief summary is provided of the variable activity behavior patterns of elderly people. The next sections propose how these variable behavioral relationships lead to elderly people differently knowing and perceiving their environmental contents and experiencing different environmental outcomes or consequences. The final sections consider how the different meanings and interpretations that old people ascribe to their activity behavior lead to their having different experiential outcomes.

Patterns of Activity Behavior in Old Age

Various studies confirm that as persons age chronologically, their levels of both interpersonal and noninterpersonal activity are expected to decrease (Maddox 1963; Havighurst, Neugarten, and Tobin 1968; Botwinick 1973; Golant 1972, 1976b).[8] Other research found that the frequency of vehicular trip behavior (that is, all locomotor behavior that involves auto, public transit, or taxis as modes of transportation) is lower for older people (over age 65) than for younger populations (Golant 1972; Markovitz 1971; and Wynn and Levinson 1967). Also, with increased age, such vehicular activity becomes increasingly oriented to nonwork trips and disproportionately occurs during the daytime hours (Golant 1972, 1976b). According to Havighurst the tempo of activity also slows down in old age and "older people fill their time with less action than younger people do" (1961:341).

The locational context of activity behavior also becomes more restricted in old age, with dwelling-centered activities becoming more likely. De Grazia (1961) reported on several national studies indicating that older persons (aged 50+) were more likely than younger persons to spend a greater proportion of their average day engaged in activities in or around, rather than away from, their homes. Gordon and Gaitz, in their report on the leisure activities of older persons, concluded that "external-to-the-home forms of leisure were less frequently engaged in and enjoyed among each successively older age group" (1976:332). They also confirmed that older people were more likely to engage in expressive (for example, leisure-oriented) activities than out-of-the-home instrumental (for example, at work) activities. Chapin and Brail reported that "older individuals spend more time at relaxing, reading, and watching television or listening to radio" (1969:121). Findings from the National Center for Health Statistics (1974) also point to the more limited activity space of older people. Higher percentages of noninstitutionalized older people are housebound, have difficulty getting around, and are disabled more days of the year. The more restricted activity space of old people is also suggested by Niebanck (1965) and Newcomer (1976). They find that facilities intended for use by the elderly should be within certain critical walking distances of their residence; otherwise dissatisfaction is expressed. More generally, Carp (1971) has emphasized the considerable importance of walking as a mode of transportation for elderly people.

The findings of other studies emphasized the need for caution when making the above generalizations. Maddox (1968) and Palmore (1968), reporting on findings from the Duke Longitudinal Study of older people, concluded that a very high proportion of older people (close to 80 percent), although displaying changes in their activity behavior over time, persistently maintained their own characteristically high or low levels of activity as they grew older. Golant (1972), investigating only the vehicular travel behavior of older people in Toronto, found that when only nonwork activity was considered, the average number of vehicular trips per old person (aged 65+) was virtually identical with that of the middle-aged population (aged 55–65). In another study of the vehicular travel behavior of populations in six U.S. cities, the authors concluded "that for nonwork purposes which account for most of his travel, the elderly person can be expected to become more wide-ranging in travel than his younger counterpart" (Ashford and Holloway 1972:15). After considering the importance of automobile availability, the authors also concluded that "older persons who have the means of travel are quite willing to make trips within urban areas as lengthy as trips by younger adults" (p. 47). In these last two studies, interpretations must be tempered by the fact that older people who were homebound or depended on walking as their primary mode of transportation were not studied.

Several of the above studies also concluded that among elderly people there is considerable variation in activity behavior patterns. Moreover, this interindividual diversity is often a product of factors unrelated to chronological age, such as race, sex, education, and income. In short, the basis for elderly people's varied travel patterns has often been established well before old age (Chapin 1974; Golant 1972, 1976b).

Activity Behavior's Influence on the Content
of Elderly People's Environmental Experiences

The best documented evidence of activity behavior's influence on the contents of the environment that is known and perceived by the individual is found in the cognitive or psychological mapping literature (Downs and Stea 1973; Moore 1979). This literature is concerned with describing and understanding people's variable awareness (completeness, schematization, accuracy, and augmentation) of the physical phenomena and properties found in the everyday environment. Geographers have specifically focused on the relative location (attributes) of these phenomena (that is, where they are, how far away, and in what direction). This literature has demonstrated that people's knowledge of their city's contents is at least partially influenced by the extensiveness, organization, and efficiency of their everyday travel behavior. These movements result in individuals' accumulating information about alternative places and routes in their environment and acquiring increasingly complete, accurate, and structurally integrated images of its contents (Golledge and Zannaras 1973). A comparable investigation of these relationships as they specifically apply to old people is represented by Regnier's (1981) research that demonstrated the close relationship between old people's use of neighborhood facilities and resources and the configuration of their cognitive maps.

The conclusions of this literature, along with scattered findings and inferences from a large environment-behavior literature, led to the construction of the following propositions that relate the content of the elderly individual's environmental experiences to his *usual space-time locus of activity behavior. Locus* here refers to the *set* of all points (or locations) in time and space defined by the individual's activity behavior. Thus a *usual* space-time locus of activity refers to an individual's average or customary activity regime, implying the usual frequency with which activities occur and their usual spatial or locational extent. These propositions should be viewed as preliminary formulations that are subject to empirical validation.

1. Environmental transactions purposively initiated by elderly people are more likely to occur within the usual space-time locus of their activity behavior.
2. Environmental transactions purposively avoided by elderly people are more likely to be with objects and events found outside the usual space-time locus of their activity behavior.
3. Elderly people are more aware of and familiar with environmental objects that are found within the usual space-time locus of their activity behavior.
4. The contents of elderly people's environmental experiences are more likely to coincide with the environmental objects and events found within, rather than outside, their usual space-time locus of activity behavior.

Propositions 1 and 2 argue that elderly people are more likely to perceive and interpret information from those parts of the environment that are enclosed within the boundaries of their usual activity regime. It follows that elderly individuals are more aware of and familiar with these parts of the environment (proposition 3), and that the contents of elderly people's environmental experiences are more likely to coincide with its actual objects and events (proposition 4). Together, the four propositions imply that certain parts of an elderly individual's environment have greater functional relevance than others. That is, the properties of the environment contained within the usual space-time locus of an elderly population's activity behavior are more likely to have the potential of influencing (reinforcing, modifying, evoking) its members' environmental experiences than the environmental properties outside of this activity regime.

Situational Proximity versus Activity Behavior as Antecedents of Experiential Content

Propositions 1 to 4 present relationships that together explain why the objective properties attributed to an environment can be very different from those perceived and known by its elderly occupants. This results when the parts of the environment directly or materially transacted with by the elderly individual contain properties that are not consistent with or representative of those typifying the whole environment. (In practice, *whole* and *part* environmental referents will depend entirely on operational decisions made by a particular researcher.) This discrepancy is predicted to increase as the space-time locus of the elderly individual's activity behavior diverges from the boundaries and contents of the whole environment. In the extreme case, the objective attributes of the whole environment will bear no resemblance to the contents of the old person's environment *qua* experienced.

Yet an assumption is often made that the smaller the distances between individuals and parts of their environment, the more likely it is that their behavior and experiences are influenced by its attributes. Thus the individual occupying or living *in* or *near* a particular environment is predicted to have experiences more congruent with its objective attributes than individuals living outside of or farther from such an environment. This assumption can be referred to as the *situational proximity argument*. However, if propositions 1 to 4 are valid, this argument obviously will not be generalizable to all situations. Several examples may help to demonstrate this point. An older woman living in an age-segregated apartment building may carry out most of her socializing with *younger* persons living in a distant suburb. She may rarely see her neighbors if she spends most of her time away from her apartment. A building's homebound elderly residents may never use the grocery store only one block away; neither may elderly residents who do most of their shopping in a distant regional shopping center.

Researchers engaged in situation-behavior analyses may never critically examine this assumption because of the very nature of their research settings. Within a laboratory or a small-scale environment such as a school, a hospital, or an old-age institution, the whole environment is often assumed to be under investigation. To use Barker's terminology, the environment is considered circumjacent to the individual: "it is enclosing, environing, encompassing" (1968:19). The situational proximity argument is not raised as an issue because environmental proximity and environmental utilization are identical referents. This is not the case in a large-scale, natural setting, such as a community located within a larger metropolitan region in which individuals do not live in a temporally or spatially closed system. Here, individuals who live in a particular part of an environment may have little contact with it and be little influenced by its qualities. Nor do large geographic distances between individuals and particular places necessarily imply the absence of environmental transactions or impact.

On the other hand, there are certain conditions under which the elderly individual's behavioral relationships with his environment may be closely associated with his proximity to its objects. For example: if the salient demands of the individual can be satisfied by the proximate environment; if the individual values highly the consequences or rewards expected from these local environmental transactions; if the individual is less aware or incorrectly informed about the rewarding opportunities found in more distant locations; if past transactions in more distant places resulted in unrealized demands or failures; if the individual has sentimental or emotional ties to his local environment; or if the individual lacks the competence or personal resources (for example, money or health) to physically reach more distant places.

In total, this discussion argues for the validity of the following proposition:

>   5. The likelihood of transactions by elderly individuals with objects and events in their environment depends not only on their proximity to them, but, as importantly, on the nature of their activity behavior relationships with them.

The important implication of this proposition is that the properties of the proximate environment (the nearby residential setting, such as the dwelling and neighborhood, and perhaps the small community) will less reliably predict the experiential content of those old people whose activity behaviors occur over a larger locational (environmental) context.

Activity Behavior's Influence on the Consequences of Old People's Environmental Experiences

Although researchers have shown little interest in how activities influence the outcomes of elderly people's experiences, numerous isolated empirical insights can be found in the gerontological literature. For instance, it is noted that bus trips are important for their own sake because they provide some old people with pleasurable, spontaneous, and unplanned personal contacts with other elderly passengers. Similarly, Rowles (1979) points out the importance of the dwelling window as a source of environmental stimulation for inactive old people. However, at present no conceptual tree exists on which to hang these unconnected observations.

The following propositions—deduced in part from propositions 1 to 5—relate the activity behavior patterns of an elderly population to the outcomes of their environmental experiences. These relationships should be treated as preliminary formulations that require empirical verification. Reference to a *smaller* space-time locus of activity implies either less frequent travel outside the dwelling (home) and/or travel that is more restricted to locations near the dwelling.

6. The smaller the space-time locus of activity behavior, the more personally salient are the demands elderly people make of objects and events in their proximate environment.
7. The smaller the space-time locus of activity behavior, the more likely that elderly people's environmental demands and goals are satisfied or rewarded by transactions with objects and events in their proximate environment.
8. The smaller the space-time locus of activity behavior, the more likely that elderly people adapt successfully to less desirable experiential outcomes involving objects and events in their proximate environment.
9. The smaller the space-time locus of activity behavior, the less temporally diverse or variable are the outcomes of elderly people's environmental transactions.
10. The smaller the space-time locus of activity behavior, the more likely that elderly people experience predictable, expected, or customary outcomes from their environmental transactions.
11. The smaller the space-time locus of activity behavior, the more likely that elderly people's environmental experiences derive from memories and fantasies of earlier environmental transactions.

Propositions 6 and 7 argue that elderly people who are less active and whose travel is more spatially restricted are more likely to have their most salient (environmental) needs and demands satisfied from transactions in their nearby residential setting. Concomitantly, the more distant (from the dwelling) parts of the environment will be less relevant to these elderly people's needs and goals and probably less attended to as potential sources of pleasure and rewards. There is no shortage of evidence in the gerontological literature demonstrating that old people assign important material and symbolic significance to their proximate environments—such as their dwellings and neighborhoods (Lawton 1980:38–42); however, the relevant analyses have not controlled for the effects of activity behavior.

Proposition 8 is deduced from propositions 6 and 7. It argues that if the proximate environment is satisfying the most salient or central of elderly people's demands and goals, then these people are strongly motivated to ignore, deny the presence of, or constructively deal with the less desirable outcomes experienced in their proximate environment. Without such coping processes, intolerable stress and anxiety is predicted (Lazarus 1966), given the implicit assumption that an enlarged space-time locus of activity behavior is not a viable coping strategy to counter these unpleasant experiences. Again, there is no shortage of evidence in the gerontological literature indicating that old people often deemphasize the unpleasant aspects of their living quarters—but again the intervening effects of activity behavior are not specified.

Proposition 9 is inspired by methodological insights from the literature on neighborhood racial segregation (Bogue and Bogue 1976). Probabilistically, smaller blocks or neighborhoods are likely to contain homogeneous (that is, segregated) populations. Similarly, when transactions by elderly individuals occur consistently in a small (and probably homogeneous) part (e.g., neighborhood) of their whole (e.g., community) environment, less diverse and variable experiential outcomes are predicted. In turn, it can be deduced that the experiential outcomes of these transactions are probably more predictable or expected (proposition 10). However, it remains unclear whether such status quo outcomes will be interpreted positively (the virtues of certainty) or negatively (the offensiveness of monotony).

Proposition 11 was derived from gerontological findings showing that less active elderly individuals are also more likely to be psychologically disengaged, which in turn is accompanied by a greater probability of introspection and reminiscing (Havighurst and Glasser 1972). The implication is that as individuals reduce their material linkages with the outside world, they become more inner-directed and introspective (see chapter 8).

Variability of Environmental Outcomes among Old Population

Propositions 6 and 7 account for why old persons differ as to the outcomes they experience in the proximate parts of their environment. Old people with small rather than large space-time loci of activity behavior are predicted to evaluate their proximate places as more salient or central to their needs and to consider them a greater source of environmental satisfaction and rewards. Old people who have activity patterns centered around their proximate environment are also predicted to adapt more successfully to any problems they confront in these places (proposition 8).

Propositions 9 and 10 suggest that old people with small rather than large space-time loci of activity behavior will experience more predictable and expected environmental outcomes. Finally, proposition 11 predicts that old people with small rather than large space-time loci of activity behavior will experience outcomes that depend more on the content and consequences of their environmental memories.

Experiences of Old People Inconsistent with the Objective Properties of their Environment

Propositions 6 to 11 provide one explanation for why old people often report high levels of satisfaction even though they occupy physically run-down or deficient dwellings and neighborhoods. Old people whose lives revolve around their proximate environment are predicted to depend heavily on its contents to satisfy their everyday material (shopping, services, and so on) and social needs (friendships, neighbor relationships) (propositions 6 and 7). Furthermore, on the assumption that they do not have easy access to other parts of their community, they are predicted to overlook the deficiencies of their proximate environment (proposition 8). This environment has the added favorable feature (for some elderly) of yielding relatively predictable outcomes (proposition 9 and 10). Beyond this environment's concrete properties, it may also be associated with a lifetime of happy memories (proposition 11).

Experiential Impact of Cognitive and Motivational Strategies Associated with Old People's Activity Behavior

The gerontological literature contains insights into the varied meanings and interpretations that old people assign to their activity behavior. These, in turn, lead to predictions of why old people experience dissimilar environmental outcomes. Generalizations must be made cautiously, however, because the literature offers contradictory evidence. A summary of the relevant evidence follows, which considers whether higher or lower activity levels are believed to be more adaptive to old people and whether old people's activity behavior is voluntarily initiated.

The Theoretical Basis for Causal Linkages

Many insights emerged from the debate in the gerontological literature concerning whether high or low activity contributed to higher morale in old age. These were often discussed in the context of the disengagement and activity theories of aging (Hochschild 1975; Longino and Kart 1982).[9] On the one hand, *higher* activity levels are suggested to be associated with successful aging or adaptation. That is, higher activity levels:

> Are a sign of strength and dominance, consistent with the American ethic of rugged individualism. Therefore, a failure to maintain the activity patterns of middle age or old age is a sign of personal weakness and submissiveness (Kuypers and Bengston 1973; Havighurst and Albrecht 1953).

> Enable old people to ignore or deny the physical frailty of their bodies so as to appear intact or active (Cath 1975).

Enable old people to confirm their own competence and to demonstrate that they have not succumbed to the physical frailties and dependence of old age (Kuhlen 1968).

Confirm that old age is little different from middle age. Achieving such continuity between middle age and old age is a salient goal for many old people.

Enable old people unexpectedly and spontaneously to "find outlets for [their] feelings," uncover "hidden personal resources," or develop "meaningful relationships with others" (Kutner 1956:104).

On the other hand, *lower* activity levels are suggested to be associated with successful aging or adaptation. That is, lower activity levels:

Are consistent with society's values and edicts that condone and support a less active and socially involved aging population and that withholds reinforcements (for example, pleasure, status, or prestige) for the maintenance of many middle-aged roles and activities (Cumming and Henry 1961).

Enable individuals to become more emotionally involved with themselves and less involved with the people and material world around them.[10] Thus older people engage freely and guiltlessly in increased introspection, reminiscing, and fantasizing.

Enable old people whose physical and mental competence has declined to avoid public exposure that would lead to social criticism, ridicule, or embarrassment (Cath 1975).

A second set of insights emerges from a concurrent debate concerning whether the observed activity behavior patterns in old age are voluntarily or involuntarily initiated.

One group of proponents argue that lower activity, smaller activity spaces, and declining activity levels are *voluntarily* initiated. They contend that old people are desirous of decreased environmental involvement, in part due to inner, developmentally

related psychological forces, in part due to a society that con-
dones and welcomes such disengagement (Cumming and Henry
1961). In contrast are those who argue that lower activity, smaller
activity spaces, and declining activity levels are *involuntarily* initiated. They point to the impact of uncontrollable cognitive and
physical impairments suffered by old people and an unsympathetic society that erects and tolerates institutional and environmental constraints and barriers to activity and involvement (Cath
1975; Dowd 1975; Kuhlen 1968; Thomae 1979).

Two Contradictory Sets of Propositions

To represent these opposing perspectives in the gerontological
literature, are the following two sets (12a, 13a, 14a and 12b, 13b,
14b) of propositions:

12a. The smaller the space-time locus of activity behavior, the more likely old people feel they have un-
successfully adapted to old age.

13a. The smaller the space-time locus of activity behavior, the more likely old people's activities are uncontrollable and involuntary.

14a. The smaller the space-time locus of activity behavior, the more likely old people have stressful, unpleasant, or embarrassing environmental experiences.

12b. The smaller the space-time locus of activity behavior, the more likely old people feel they have successfully adapted to old age.

13b. The smaller the space-time locus of activity behavior, the more likely old people's activities are controllable and voluntary.

14b. The smaller the space-time locus of activity behavior, the more likely old people have happy, pleasant, or enjoyable environmental experiences.

The gerontological literature has made clear that high or low
activity levels can be adaptive to elderly people (12a versus 12b)

and that low activity levels may or may not have been voluntarily sought by elderly persons (13a versus 13b). From these opposing interpretations are deduced the alternative propositions 14a and 14b. Proposition 14a implies that those old people who more closely associate their low activity levels with personal meanings such as vulnerability, lifetime discontinuities, constraints, and involuntariness will have the evaluative outcomes of their transactions dominated by negative affects (emotions). In direct contrast, proposition 14b implies that those old people who more closely associate their lower activity levels with personal meanings such as socially acceptable behavior, greater opportunities for introspection and reminiscing, stress avoidance, and greater personal control will have the evaluative outcomes of their transactions dominated by positive affects (emotions).

Although the presenting of these contradictory propositions is scientifically disagreeable, the issues cannot be obfuscated by the arbitrary selection of one position over another. It is very likely that there are different groups of elderly people whose respective activity-experience relationships are indicative of *both* positions. That is, on the one hand, there are old people who are homebound and evaluate their dwelling-restricted life-style and all its environmental referents in very negative terms. On the other hand, there are old people who have voluntarily chosen a home-centered life-style (despite having the competence to do otherwise) and enjoy the sedentary experiences connected with their dwelling. Research attempting to verify which of the activity or disengagement theories of aging was the more valid has demonstrated that various personal factors (e.g., life-style continuity between middle and old age, personality makeup, timing of life events, role losses, mental and physical competence) interact with activity levels to produce both high and low morale levels (Larson 1978). It is therefore reasonable to predict that different mental and behavioral states and societal influences will interact with activity levels to produce both enjoyable and unenjoyable environmental experiences. In this regard, the resolution of the following two issues would increase one's confidence of prediction.

The first concerns the temporal constancy of the proposed relationships. There is the question of how long a period the size of the space-time locus of activity behavior results in environmental experiences with the proposed affect. For instance, from propositions 13a and 14a it is predicted that unpleasant dwelling experiences occur in conjunction with the uncontrollable activity behavior of old people. Left ambiguous, however, is the time period over which this restricted activity continues to lead to unpleasant experiences. A corollary to this proposition may be that over time old people adapt successfully to their changed mobility patterns with the result that restriction ceases to be a factor influencing their environmental experiences. This is obviously a matter for empirical research, although it will not be investigated in this study.

A second and more complex issue is whether propositions 14a and 14b are describing the main or secondary effects of activity behavior. Propositions 6 to 8 earlier predicted that old people with smaller space-time loci of activity behavior will be more satisfied with their dwellings than other old people. To what extent, then, is this relationship weakened if the smaller space-time loci of behavior are involuntary, perhaps due to the old person's physical incompetence? The present view is that the meanings ascribed to activity will, on the average, only *amplify* or *dampen* the evaluative outcomes predicted by propositions 6 to 8. That is to say, the meanings and interpretations ascribed to activity behavior itself constitute the secondary rather than the dominant or primary effects on a population's environmental experiences. They contribute, for example, to old people feeling *somewhat* less satisfied or *somewhat* more satisfied. Unfortunately, it will not be possible to assess the validity of this viewpoint in the Evanston study.

Unaddressed Issues

Various conceptual issues requiring clarification and empirical questions requiring investigation (the majority of the propositions) have been discussed in this chapter, but at least three unaddressed and researchable issues remain. Because these became apparent only after the research design of the Evanston study was in place, they could not be empirically investigated. Nonetheless, it is important to bring them to the attention of other researchers.

The first issue concerns an implicit assumption of the theoretical approach, namely, that the impact of elderly people's activity behavior is independent of the impact of their residential behaviors. There was no consideration of the simultaneous effects of these two sets of behavioral relationships. In fact, it is highly probable that the effects of residential and activity behaviors on elderly people's environmental experiences will either reinforce or counteract each other. For example, longtime residential occupancy and lower levels of activity both are theorized as contributing to old people's having more favorable environmental experiences and to their knowing more accurately the most salient features and properties of their proximate environments. In this unambiguous case, it would be predicted that old persons who have lived a long time in their current residences and whose activity behaviors have revolved around their dwellings and neighborhoods will be subjected to reinforcing forces that lead to similarly perceived environmental content and similarly evaluated consequences. More complicated and ambiguous relationships result when old people display counteracting individual behaviors, such as when they are longtime residents but have high activity levels that usually take them outside of their neighborhoods. Whereas longtime residential occupancy is theorized as producing predictable, status quo experiences, more frequent and locationally extensive activity behavior is theorized as increasing the opportunities for new and different environmental experiences. Lacking is any theoretical or empirical basis for predicting which of these individual behaviors will have the stronger or dominant influence. Along with empirical research to resolve this question, it would be informative to inquire whether old people living different lengths of times in the same place have modified or changed their activity behavior patterns for the purpose of obtaining different types of environmental experiences.

A second issue concerns the inability of this theoretical approach to predict unambiguously the impact of the cognitive and motivational states associated with elderly people's initiation and interpretation of their activity and residential behaviors. Although it was proposed that on the average these states have secondary rather than dominant effects on old people's experiences, this was probably an oversimplified generalization. Clear documentation exists that involuntary behavior patterns, whether residential or activity, can produce very unfavorable emotional and physiological outcomes for old people (Brail, Hughes, and Arthur 1976; Byerts 1975; Cutler 1975; Schulz and Brenner 1977). In these circumstances, the outcomes of most environmental transactions are likely to be dominated by negative feelings and evaluations. A profitable empirical inquiry would be to identify how a representative set of personal states act in conjunction with particular activity and residential behaviors to influence old people's experiential outcomes.

A third unresolved issue concerns the range of values of activity and residential behaviors (that is, length of time, frequency, locational extent) that are most likely to "produce" the theorized outcomes. The convenience of analytical discourse dictated that monotonic relationships be implied between the proposed individual behaviors and environmental experiences. These probably oversimplify the true relationships. It is more reasonable to expect that once a particular threshold of activity frequency or residential occupancy length of time has been surpassed, then the marginal effects of more years or more travel will be small. For example, the impact of a residential occupancy period of ten years may differ little from that of twenty-five years. Empirical research is necessary to establish these threshold levels.

Chapter Eight

The Types and Meaningfulness of Territorial Environment Experiences

This is the first of three chapters devoted to empirical analyses of the types (meanings) and meaningfulness of the experiences reported by the Evanston elderly population. Four questions are pursued in this chapter: why are old people more likely than younger populations to be satisfied with, to be proud of, and to have good memories about their communities, neighborhoods, and dwellings, that is, their territorial environments; to what extent are these territorial environment experiences related to old people's moving expectations and preferences; which of the social and physical experiences are associated with each of these three territorial experiences; and which of the proposed individual differences influence the occurrence of these territorial experiences?

These analyses will be better understood by first discussing the literature's interpretations of the experience consequences, satisfaction, pride, and good memories and of the territorial environments, community, neighborhood, and dwelling.

Territorial Experiences

Brief Theoretical Interpretations of Satisfaction, Pride, and Good Memories

Satisfaction with Environment

The consequences or the meanings of a person's environmental transactions are indicated often by reports of satisfaction. The

University of Michigan's Survey Research Center's quality of life study of persons aged 18 and older in the United States contained the most precise interpretation of the concept. Its authors proposed that satisfaction reflected the degree of congruence between an individual's aspirations and his present reality (Campbell, Converse, and Rodgers 1976). Other conceptual insights were provided earlier by White, who suggested that satisfaction is not a result of a "consummatory climax," but instead lies "in a considerable series of transactions, in a trend of behavior rather than a goal that is achieved" (1970:132). This interpretation is consistent with that of the University of Michigan study, which considered a person's report of satisfaction to be a product of continuous environmental transactions rather than a consequence of one or two environmental episodes. In this process, the likelihood of a change in satisfaction not only depends on the changing objective qualities of environmental transactions but also on the adaptational mechanisms initiated by the individual. The nature of satisfaction is clarified further by comparing it with the meaning of *pride*.

Pride in Environment

The presence of personal pride generally implies a more intense self-feeling than satisfaction. Whereas the opposite of satisfaction is dissatisfaction or the presence of some complaint (Schorr 1970:323), the opposite of pride is *shame*, which, along with guilt, anxiety, and depression, belongs in a category of more severe emotional disorders (Kemper 1978:199).

More so than satisfaction, feelings of pride are closely related to the person's sense of self-worth or self-esteem. Amount of pride appears to depend on the extent to which the individual feels he has given the appearance of acting or performing competently. This implies that his status, actions, or possessions are recognized as accomplishments or achievements. The individual's assessment of this "appearance" depends on what performance standards he believes are held by society or significant others (Kemper 1978). Thus, an individual's pride in an environment derives from having acquired, achieved, or transacted with "something" in a manner deemed competent according to some perceived standard. There results an enhancement of the person's self-concept or self-worth.

Theoretically, it is possible for the individual to feel proud and not to have met his aspired goals (that is, to be dissatisfied) as long as he believes he has acted competently in striving to reach these goals. It is also possible for very accomplished individuals not to feel proud of their environments if their expectations for performance are exceedingly high. As Kemper pointed out: "If one has been socialized to unrealistic standards of performance, that is, where one's capabilities have been evaluated far above their true measure and therefore performance always falls beneath the standard, the likelihood of shame is very strong" (1978:280).

Thus the individual who reports being proud is not only satisfied with his accomplishments but also has obtained "imagined approval" (Cooley 1902) from persons whose opinions he values or has met a perceived standard of behavior. This interpretation was set forth in Coleman's (1978:5) discussion of neighborhood survey findings. Respondents answered that one of their wishes about their neighborhood was that it be "an environment that you can be proud of—a place that meets your class and economic position." Or, in other terms, it should confirm that the occupants' (environmental) achievements or accomplishments are consistent with their class, status, or economic position.

Positive Memories of the Environment

The long-term memories of elderly people are usually investigated as indicators of mental capacity, cognitive functioning, or performance levels and are studied in laboratory situations. In contrast, few investigations focus on why old people differ in their propensity to recall and reconstruct their past everyday environmental experiences. The most useful insights come from research on old people's reminiscing, that is, their strong awareness of and preoccupation with past experiences (Havighurst and Glasser 1972). Although reminiscence is one aspect of memory recall, "it is not

identical with memory" (Havighurst and Glasser 1972:245). Reminiscing apparently involves more frequent memory recall and
emotionally intensive retrospection in which considerable time is
devoted to remembering. It also involves other persons to whom
these memories are communicated (Lewis 1971). However, consensus is lacking on how reminiscence should be defined as a concept (Merriam 1980; LoGerfo 1980–81).

Interpretations of reminiscence have been influenced by the developmental stage theory of Erikson (1963). He proposed that successful adaptation or life adjustment is related to a coming to terms
with one's past life—a task that reminiscence can help accomplish. However, several recent studies, which investigated the relationship between reminiscence and the old person's self-concept, personal adjustment, and life satisfaction (Merriam 1980), did
not report consistent findings.

A more relevant theoretical issue—at least for this study—is how
the recall of good memories or reminiscing is related to the activity behavior patterns of old people. Studies by Havighurst and
Glasser (1972) and Lewis (1971) found that psychologically disengaged (inner-directed) older people (implying infrequent out-of-
dwelling activity) were more likely to reminisce than those who
were psychologically engaged (outer-directed). Much earlier, Cooley
made some especially insightful observations concerning the
"cogitation" of the inner-directed individual:

> Minds of one sort are, so to speak, endogenous or ingrowing in
> their natural bent, while those of another are exogenous or out-
> growing; that is to say those of the former kind have a relatively
> strong turn for working up old material, as compared with that
> for taking in new; cogitation is more pleasant to them than ob-
> servation;
> . . . the tendency of the endogenous or inward activities is to se-
> cure unity and stability of thought and character at the possible
> expense of openness and adaptability; because the energy goes
> chiefly into systematization and in attaining this the mind is
> pretty sure to limit its new impressions to those that do not dis-
> turb too much of that unity and system it loves so well. (1902:200–
> 201)

Theoretical Interpretations
of the Three Territorial Environments

The territorial environments of community, neighborhood, and dwelling can be understood both as boundaries or areas of pragmatic spaces and as *places* or *existential spaces*.

Boundaries or Areas of Pragmatic Space

First of all, community, neighborhood, and dwelling can be considered as concrete, material, or pragmatic spaces with definable boundaries enclosing continuous areas.

A community's boundaries, for instance, are often defined by political or administrative criteria. These enclose a self-governing unit distinguished by its social, economic, and political institutions and organizations. Less frequently, these boundaries are defined by the spatial or locational extent of a population's activity behavior patterns. Community is also sometimes synonymous with the human ecologist's "natural area," a product of competitive and self-selection processes, which result in its occupants' having relatively uniform social, cultural, economic, or ethnic attributes. In contrast to these approaches, *community* often is defined in more traditional, Durkheimian terms. In this sense, community depends on a sociological rather than physical conception of space. It refers to the individual's social context or social space, as indicated by his network of interpersonal human relationships upon which he depends for emotional and material supports. Because this space may not necessarily correspond to the compact, continuous pragmatic space, there can be, in Webber's (1963) terms, a "community without propinquity."

Neighborhood is almost always considered to be a continuous, pragmatic space enclosed by some objectively or perceptually defined boundaries. The classic treatment was Perry's "neighborhood unit plan," which was introduced as a physical planning component in the Regional Plan for New York and the Environs (Perry 1929). Here, the neighborhood's size and boundary characteristics were articulated in a relatively precise way. However, such objective interpretations of neighborhood are more the exception than the rule. Customarily, *neighborhood* is defined in subjective terms, as a pragmatic space enclosed by boundaries perceived or cognitively represented by its residential occupants. Consequently, the "same" neighborhood's boundaries may vary greatly. Nonetheless it is usually agreed that the size and boundaries of a neighborhood encompass an area larger than the dwelling, but smaller than the politically or administratively defined community.

The dwelling encompasses the least designatively ambiguous pragmatic space. Although there may be impreciseness as to where the dwelling space "ends" and the lot or building space "begins," little disagreement usually exists as to its area or boundaries.

Places or Existential Spaces

Communities, neighborhoods, and dwellings have other qualities that are not embodied in their treatment as pragmatic spaces. Additionally, they may be conceived as existential spaces or places. From this perspective, they are imbued with holistic or systemic meanings that transcend the specificity conveyed by their social and physical objects. Philosophers, architects, and geographers have variously addressed the meanings that underlie the organization of the environment into places (for reviews, see Norberg-Schulz 1971; Wheatley 1976). The assignment of distances/separations, directions/continuity, and areas/enclosures— that is, spatial relationships—is fundamental to the identification of a place or existential space. The center of this projection is the individual and the "projected" spatial relationships constitute the individual's assigned place. As Samuels put it:

> The assignment of place is always a reference *to* something *from* someone. The reality (existence) of things-in-their place is confirmed by and contingent upon the reality (existence) of someone's projection. The reference to and from is the link between object and subject, distance and relation. "Place" is always an act of referencing and "places" are nothing more or less than reference points in someone's projection. (1978:30)

Such an assignment of places reflects a combination of influences: the values common to the human species in general, those unique to a particular society or culture, and those that reflect individual idiosyncracies. As Samuels pointed out:

> The assignment of meanings to places and projections of place is never an indulgence in pure subjectivity. Rather, it is always contingent on situations into which men are thrust, over which they may have little control, and about which they may be imperfectly aware, even as they become concerned. (p. 32)

Two relatively common symbolic meanings associated with this assignment of place are those conveyed by its characterization as *home* and *territory*. As a home, the existential space assumes a relative position in concrete and abstract space around which the individual's total existence or sphere of temporally and spatially defined environmental transactions revolve. It is a space from which the individual "leaves" but to which he always "returns." As Norberg-Schulz expressed it:

> The word "home" simply tells us that any man's personal world has a centre. . . . the centre represents to man what is known in contrast to the unknown and somewhat frightening world around. It is the point where he acquires position as a thinking being in space, the point where he "lingers" and "lives" in the space. (1971:19)

As territory, the cognitively and materially defined existential space becomes, to varying degrees, exclusively used, possessed, or personalized by an individual or a population such that it is relevant to distinguish between "us" and "them." Thus there are people who belong to or identify with the territory and those who do not— insiders and outsiders. Regulatory or controlling mechanisms initiated by the insiders to deter invasion by the outsiders are also characteristic of territorial spaces (see Altman 1975).

Empirical Measures of Community, Neighborhood, and Dwelling

Chapter 7 (note 1) confirmed that, with very few exceptions, old people readily identified their community as Evanston. To elicit responses about the dwelling of the old person, it was referred to as "this house" or "this apartment." These labels also did not create any designative ambiguities for the older respondents.

The neighborhood of the old person was measured in subjective terms. Very early in the survey schedule, each elderly respondent was asked two questions: "About how many square blocks would you say your neighborhood includes?" and "What are some other ways of thinking about or describing the size of your neighborhood?" Relatively small percentages of elderly people thought their neighborhood was either very small (less than three square blocks) (17 percent) or very large (more than ten square blocks) (25 percent). About 7 percent of the elderly population were unable to describe the size of their neighborhood in terms of block size. When asked to think about or to describe the size of their neighborhoods in other ways, by far most respondents referred to an area delineated by street boundaries (42 percent). The second set of most frequent responses associated neighborhood size with some locally significant district designation (12 percent). About 17 percent of the old people distinguished their neighborhoods by the physical objects they contained (stores, services, facilities, landmarks, or land use changes). Another 9 percent of the respondents thought the neighborhood area could be expressed with regard to distance from their dwellings ("blocks from dwelling" or "within walking distance"). About 4 percent defined the neighborhood size in terms of its social objects (that is, its people). About 6 percent of the responses could not be classified simply, and 8 percent of the elderly respondents had difficulty articulating a description of their neighborhood size or boundaries.

It can be concluded that neighborhood designations by the elderly display considerable interindividual variability. However, because the territorial environment of neighborhood was introduced early in the survey, there was greater certainty that a respondent would refer to the concept (when answering later survey items) in a consistent fashion.[1]

Interpreting the Territorial Experiences of Evanston's Elderly Population

Likelihood of Positive Experiences

The eight questions eliciting the territorial experiences of Evanston's elderly and their response distributions are shown in table 8.1. (Further details concerning the measurement of residential satisfaction appear in chapter 4.)

The majority of old people reported having had very positive territorial experiences. High percentages of old people were completely or almost completely satisfied with their dwelling, neigh-

Table 8.1. Distribution of Responses to Territorial Environments

Territorial Experience	Satisfaction-Dissatisfaction									
	Completely Dissatisfied 1	2	3	4	5	6	Completely Satisfied 7	Total	Mean	N
Community as place to live in[a]	2%	1	1	7	16	20	55	100%	6.13	400
Neighborhood you live in	2%	1	2	8	14	21	54	100%	6.08	400
Dwelling you live in[b]	2%	1	2	4	10	15	66	100%	6.30	400

	Proud to Live In					
	Strongly Disagree 1	Disagree 2	Agree 3	Strongly Agree 4	Total	Mean	N
This community	2%	4	32	63	100%	3.56	398
This neighborhood	2%	5	38	55	100%	3.47	399
This dwelling	2%	3	32	63	100%	3.56	400

	In Past Few Months, Thought About Good Memories Brought Back by					
	Never 1	Only once or twice 2	A few times 3	Many times 4	Total	Mean	N
This neighborhood	22%	7	22	49	100%	2.98	399
This dwelling	20%	8	18	55	100%	3.08	399

NOTE: Totals may not add to 100% due to rounding errors.
[a] In the interview schedule questions were asked about the *Evanston* community.
[b] In the interview schedule questions were asked about the elderly person's *apartment* or *house.*

borhood, and community as places to live (from 75 to 81 percent). Similarly high percentages of old people strongly agreed that they were proud to live in these places (from 55 to 63 percent). Somewhat smaller, although still large, percentages of elderly persons reported that in the past few months they had thought many times about the good memories associated with their dwellings and neighborhoods (from 49 to 55 percent).

Old people typically report such very positive territorial experiences. Several national and local studies of subjective indicators of housing quality confirmed the very positively skewed response distributions of interviewed old people (see, for example, Lawton 1978). The similarity of this study's satisfaction-dissatisfaction distributions with those found in the University of Michigan study is especially noteworthy. The Michigan study reported that of the population aged 65 and older, 56 percent were completely satisfied with their community, 29 percent were satisfied, and 15 percent were neutral or dissatisfied. The comparable elderly (aged 60 and over) response distributions in Evanston were 55 percent, 36 percent, and 11 percent.[2] The University of Michigan study, along with others, reported another relationship that, although unverifiable in the Evanston study, highlights the positive territorial experiences of old people. The researchers found that older people were more satisfied than younger people with their residential environments.[3] Specifically, 20 percent of the surveyed population aged 18–24, 30 percent of those aged 25–34, 47 percent of those aged 45–64, and 56 percent of those aged 65 and older reported they were completely satisfied with their community (Marans and Rodgers 1975:314).

Several possible explanations for why elderly residents have more positive territorial experiences are considered below.

Explaining the Very Positive Territorial Experiences in Old Age

The quality of the objective environment is fundamental to any explanation of the elderly population's very positive territorial experiences. It is probably true that the better than average quality of Evanston's residential environment contributes to the elderly population's favorable experiences. However, findings as reported in the Evanston community are not unique to middle-class community settings (Struyk and Soldo 1980:168; Lawton 1978:48). High levels of satisfaction are also reported by national samples of elderly persons and by those occupying environments with acknowledged housing deficiencies (for example, Bild and Havighurst 1976).

A second explanation can be derived from a theory of coping behavior outlined by Lazarus (1966). Expressions of satisfaction may reflect the operation of "denial" coping mechanisms designed to avoid, reduce, "or make more tolerable many of the biologically and socially induced deprivations to which older people are exposed" (Lawton 1978:49). Lawton viewed such judgments as "a positively adaptive mechanism to try to persuade oneself and others that a situation that is perceived as unchangeable is, in fact, not so bad after all" (p. 49).

The already noted positive relationship documented in the literature (chapter 7) between length of occupancy and residential satisfaction is the basis for a third explanation. Because old people are more likely than younger populations to be longtime occupants of a particular place, their satisfaction levels should be higher. This relationship is based on the strong probability that older residents have had more time to adapt, adjust, or accommodate their needs and goals to their existing environments. They have had the opportunity to become desensitized to what might have been unpleasant experiences earlier in their residential occupancy. In more positive terms, they have developed stronger social and psychological attachments to their place of residence.

A fourth explanation draws on Campbell, Converse, and Rodger's (1976) proposition that an individual's aspirations and expectations decline with age. Therefore, residential satisfaction should be greater in old age because a smaller gap is predicted between hopes and expectations on the one hand and the evaluated reality on the other. There are at least three reasons to expect that a person's residential expectations are lower in old age. First, it is very likely that many old people selected their present social and physical environments at an earlier stage in life when their occupational status and economic status were at their highest levels. After this career peak the opportunities available to the old person to improve his residential situation may decline, especially if money and health problems accompany old age. Consequently, individual expectations and aspirations for improving an earlier selected housing setting are probably weaker. Second, the lower expectations of old people may be due to a cohort effect. The University of Michigan study found that education levels are positively related to expectation levels. Because older people are members of a cohort that obtained less formal education, their expectation levels are predicted to be lower on the average than younger populations. Third, an older person's environmental expectations are influenced by his perceptions of how long he has to live. If the assumption is correct that the perceived distance to death is shorter as a person grows older (Lieberman and Coplan 1969), then the fixed costs of realizing any increased residential benefits have to be borne over a shorter period of time. As a consequence, the ratio of benefits to costs declines as distance to death becomes shorter, which, in turn, is predicted to dampen an individual's expectations of future environmental improvements.

A fifth explanation for old people having more positive territorial experiences also relies on a life-span perspective on environmental occupancy decisions. As proposed earlier (chapter 7), long-time occupancy in one environment increases the probability of cumulated positive (territorial) memories. Thus, the greater environmental satisfaction expressed by old people is due, in part, to their ability to selectively recall and reconstruct a lifetime of favorable environmental experiences that reinforce their present positive feelings and beliefs about their territorial environments.

A sixth explanation rests on the argument that the residential environment has more salience for people as they become older and thus is a more important source of satisfaction or pride than it is for younger populations. One reason for this salience is the greater likelihood of psychological and social disengagement in old age, which can result in the community, neighborhood, and dwelling acquiring especially strong symbolic meanings as "home."

The old person perceives these places as settings in which most of his life- and self-maintenance needs are satisfied and as sources of emotionally rewarding attachments (Firey 1945). A second basis for this place salience is the personal uncertainty often experienced in old age. Chapter 5 referred to the ambiguous role models that society provides for its older people and to the unexpectedness of poor health, income decline, loss of independence, and so on. In the face of such uncertainty, there is special virtue to those environmental transactions that yield positively valued and predictable experiences. Whereas old people cannot count on their good health, they can be confident about occupying a residential setting that is a source of favorable, rewarding social and physical experiences. In these environmental settings old people may also receive assurance that their behavior is acceptable by *local* standards and that here they are "sheltered" from the hostility and alienation of the larger society.

A seventh explanation revolves around the importance of the older person's overall personal context. Growing old often requires major adjustments to stressful events such as poor health and unplanned retirement. In the absence of an environment marked by extremely negative qualities, these other domains yield more pressing concerns for the old person. Thus, apparent problems arising from territorial environmental transactions may pale in comparison with the problems confronted in other aspects of life. As such, the place of residence is less likely to elicit unpleasant experiences.

In summary, seven types of explanation can be offered for the strongly positive territorial experiences of Evanston's old population: (1) the more favorable quality of life in a middle-class community such as Evanston; (2) the initiation of denial coping mechanisms by the old person; (3) the adaptive behavior patterns of longtime residential occupants; (4) the decline of aspirations and expectations with increased age; (5) the greater likelihood of selective memory recall of long-term positive or pleasant territorial experiences; (6) the greater salience of the residential environment in old age, because of its identity as "home" and its predictable and controllable experiential outcomes; and (7) the interpretation of any environmental stresses or problems as minor relative to other of life's difficulties.

Similarity of Dwelling, Neighborhood, and Community Experiences

The distributions in table 8.1 present equivocal findings as to whether one territorial realm yields more favorable experiences than the others. A higher percentage of old people were satisfied

Table 8.2. Correlations (Pearson r's) Among Territorial Experiences

Territorial Experiences	1	2	3	4	5	6	7
1. Satisfaction with community as place to live	. . .						
2. Satisfaction with neighborhood you live in	51***	. . .					
3. Satisfaction with dwelling you live in	42***	43***	. . .				
4. Proud to live in community	54***	22***	25***	. . .			
5. Proud to live in neighborhood	39***	50***	27***	64***	. . .		
6. Proud to live in dwelling	37***	29***	48***	62***	68***	. . .	
7. Thought about good neighborhood memories	17***	28***	22***	21***	34***	29***	. . .
8. Thought about good dwelling memories	13***	15***	23***	18***	23***	30***	81***

NOTE: Decimal points omitted.
***p<.001   **p<.01   *p<.05

with their dwellings than with either their neighborhood or their community. The dwelling was also more frequently associated with positive memories than was the neighborhood. However, the same percentages of old people agreed that they were proud of both their dwelling and their neighborhood. Also, old people were equally satisfied with their community and their neighborhood; and old people similarly agreed that they were proud to live in both their community and their neighborhood.

Although all the territorial experiences had an overall positive tone, the response distributions were far from perfectly correlated with each other (table 8.2).[4] The strongest correlations usually existed among territorial experiences measuring the likelihood of the same meanings or consequences. For example, community, neighborhood, and dwelling satisfaction were strongly interrelated (Pearson *r*'s ranged from .42 to .51), as were the three territorial pride experiences (Pearson *r*'s ranged from .62 to .68). These findings also reflect the fact that community, neighborhood, and dwelling territories constitute an overlapping or a nested hierarchy of pragmatic spaces. That is, the community contains neighborhoods and dwellings, and the neighborhood, in turn, contains dwellings. Thus responses to a territorial environment often reflect responses to one or more of its component parts.

Weaker associations were observed among territorial experiences measuring different meanings. For example, although community pride and community satisfaction was significantly and positively intercorrelated, as was neighborhood pride and neighborhood satisfaction, their far from perfect associations (Pearson *r*'s were .54 and .50 respectively) indicated their depiction of unequally occurring territorial consequences. Similarly, dwelling pride and satisfaction experiences were significantly and positively correlated with good dwelling memories, but the relatively small correlations indicated that their experiential impacts were largely independent of the other.

Moving Expectations, Preferences, and Territorial Experiences

Simple correlational relationships (Pearson *r*'s) substantiated the earlier predictions (chapter 7) that negative environmental experiences are associated with a greater likelihood of moving expectations and preferences by old people (table 8.3). Old people less satisfied with or proud of their territorial environments, and for whom these environments did not bring back good memories, were more likely to have moving plans and preferences. The best experiential outcome predictors were measures of "satisfaction" followed by "pride" and then by "good memories." While the magnitudes of these correlational relationships were sizable, they were all less than .50, confirming that unfavorable territorial experiences offer only a partial explanation of future moving plans or preferences.

Table 8.3. Correlations (Pearson *r*'s) Between Territorial Experiences and Moving Expectations, Moving Preferences

Territorial Experiences	Moving Expectations	Moving Preferences
Satisfaction with community as place to live	−.31 ***	−.37 ***
Satisfaction with neighborhood you live in	−.20 ***	−.29 ***
Satisfaction with dwelling you live in	−.34 ***	−.47 ***
Proud to live in community	−.26 ***	−.29 ***
Proud to live in neighborhood	−.22 ***	−.27 ***
Proud to live in dwelling	−.28 ***	−.40 ***
Thought about neighborhood good memories	−.11 *	−.19 ***
Thought about dwelling good memories	−.11 *	−.21 ***

***p<.001   **p<.01   *p<.05

Of the three territorial environments, the experiences arising from transactions with the dwelling were the strongest predictors of both the moving expectations and the preferences of Evanston's old population, whereas neighborhood experiences were the weakest. Thus old people who were dissatisfied with their dwelling, were not proud of it, and did not often recall good memories about it were the most likely to express moving preferences and expectations. This implies that neighborhood or community experiences are interpreted as less pressing or salient reasons for moving than dwelling experiences. Alternatively, it may be that older people are better able to adjust to or rationalize the negative consequences of these experiences.

Moving preferences rather than moving expectations were more strongly associated with negative territorial experiences—a predictable finding according to earlier discussions. A statement of preference is an expression of what would be desired or what ought to be if the individual had complete freedom of choice. On the other hand, a statement of expectation is an expression of preference cloaked in the individual's perceptions of what is likely to happen and what the individual is capable of doing. Consequently, there is a stronger relationship between unpleasant residential experiences and moving preferences. That is, many old people who would prefer to move—in light of their unpleasant territorial environments—do not expect to move, because they realistically recognize the constraints.

Meanings Underlying the Territorial Experiences of Evanston's Elderly

It was emphasized above that the characterization of the places, community, neighborhood, and dwelling as home and territory conveyed general meanings—such as territorial control, identity, belongingness—that transcended the specific properties of their physical and social contents. Additionally, these territorial experiences are aligned more closely to the "generality" end of the generality-specificity dimension distinguished by Jessor and Jessor (1973:33) (see chapter 4). That is, they are more pervasive than momentary experiences: reports of satisfaction, pride, and good memories are a result of reinforcing, orderly experiences taking place over a relatively long period, years, not months. Thus, a full understanding of the environmental antecedents of these experiences is probably beyond a cross-sectional research design (that is, a single point-in-time study) such as this. Yet, it should be possible to isolate the meanings or consequences of transactions with specific social and physical objects and events that serve as the "building blocks" of these more pervasive experiences. This was the task of the following empirical investigation.

Methodology

A set of social and physical environmental experiences was hypothesized as being associated with each of the following eight territorial experiences: satisfaction with community, satisfaction with neighborhood, satisfaction with dwelling, pride in community, pride in neighborhood, pride in dwelling, good memories about neighborhood, and good memories about dwelling.

The experiences selected as possible correlates were intended to characterize transactions with objects and events occurring within each of these territorial environments, but not within their nested territorial realms (for example, the community "contains" the neighborhood and dwelling, and the neighborhood "contains" the dwelling). Thus, the analysis attempted to understand the social and physical meanings of the community, the neighborhood, and the dwelling as distinct and independent entities. The making of such clearcut distinctions was not without difficulty. Inevitably, certain experiences elicited by the interview questions were ambiguous with regard to their relevance for understanding community as opposed to neighborhood experiences. For instance, the experience "fear of street crime" could conceivably underlie either community or neighborhood territorial experiences. When such an ambiguity occurred, the specific environmental experience was proposed as a correlate of more than one of the three territorial experiences.

This methodology resulted in the examination of three primarily different sets of social and physical environmental experiences as antecedents of the territorial experiences of Evanston's elderly population. One set was hypothesized as underlying community satisfaction and community pride; a second set as underlying neighborhood satisfaction, neighborhood pride, and neighborhood memories; and a third set as underlying dwelling satisfaction, dwelling pride, and dwelling memories.

The statistical analysis consisted of the following steps. First, zero-order (simple Pearson r's) correlations were calculated between each experience and the territorial experience. Experiences with a statistically significant simple correlational relationship (at or near the .05 level) were then entered in a forward stepwise regression analysis if they had F-levels of greater than 3.83 (that is, very close to the .05 or less level of significance),[5] and if they had a tolerance of .25 or more, that is, if 25 percent or more of their variation was not already explained by the environmental experiences already in the regression equation.

It is evident that this variable selection process depended entirely on statistical criteria. Because there was no theoretical basis to order the experiential variables in any hierarchical fashion or to assign them *a priori* importance as predictors of the three territorial experiences, this approach was considered satisfactory.

Discussion of Findings

The findings are reported in the following order: first the social and physical experiences underlying community satisfaction and community pride are summarized, followed by those underlying neighborhood satisfaction, pride, and good memories, and then by those underlying dwelling satisfaction, pride, and good memories (see table 8.4).

Satisfaction with Community as Place to Live

Fourteen environmental experiences were significantly correlated with community satisfaction—six of which remained statistically significant in the stepwise regression analysis. Old people more satisfied with their community were also more satisfied with its services, its proximity to Chicago, and its stores. They were less likely to feel annoyed by the garbage or litter found on their community's streets or sidewalks, more likely to feel good about doing something different in the community, and less likely to have had their homes robbed[6] in the past year.

The absence of transactions involving social objects is notable in this set of experiences. Although three social experiences were significantly *correlated* with community satisfaction (greater satisfaction with friends, less likely to feel lonely, and more available social support), they did not remain significant in the regression analysis (after controlling for the other experiences). These findings emphasize the importance of the physical meanings of the community when it is considered apart from its nested territorial realms (that is, its neighborhoods and dwellings).

The three most important physical experiences (that is, with the largest beta weights) primarily involved objects that addressed the physical comfort and security of the old person. They consisted of transactions with the built or social welfare environments (figure 4.2)—the outcomes of which depended on the locational availability or accessibility of its objects or events. These provided old people with opportunities to maintain independent households, to acquire material comforts, and to achieve emotional peace of mind.

Table 8.4. Social and Physical Experiences Associated with Territorial Experiences (Pearson correlations and beta values)

Correlates of Community Experiences

Satisfaction with Community	r	b	Proud to Live in Community	r	b
Satisfaction with community services	.394***	.262***	Satisfaction with stores in community	.247***	.195***
Satisfaction with living near Chicago	.242***	.172***	Feeling good about doing something different	.148**	.128**
Satisfaction with stores in community	.304***	.142**	Satisfaction with community services	.148**	.113*
Annoyed by litter on sidewalks	−.190***	−.114*	Had item lost or stolen (Yes = 1, No = 0)	−.106*	−.109*
Feeling good about doing something different	.138***	.102*			
Home robbed (Yes = 1, No = 0)	−.125*	−.095*			
Satisfaction with friends in community	.279***	.089			
	$R^2 = .256$			$R^2 = .101$	
	df = 7/383			df = 4/388	

Correlates of Neighborhood Experiences

Satisfaction with Neighborhood	r	b	Proud to Live in Neighborhood	r	b
Satisfaction with people in neighborhood	.754***	.680***	Satisfaction with people in neighborhood	.426***	.334***
Annoyed because other buildings less attractive	−.350***	−.173***	Frequency food or drug items home-delivered	−.115*	−.110*
Concerned that thief might break into dwelling	−.232***	−.125***	Annoyed because other buildings less attractive	−.211***	−.108*
Satisfaction with living near Chicago	.223***	.066*	Had item lost or stolen (Yes = 1, No = 0)	−.156**	−.099*
Satisfaction with dwelling's nearness to places	.229***	.059	Annoyed by dirt or soot on window	−.183***	−.090
			Enjoyment from visiting with neighbors	.241***	.090
			Enjoyment from neighborhood's social class composition	.177***	.083
	$R^2 = .631$			$R^2 = .256$	
	df = 5/371			df = 7/379	

Good Neighborhood Memories

	r	b
Enjoyment from visiting with neighbors	.244***	.240***
Had good time in own neighborhood	.130**	.138**
Tired just from getting to places in community	.232***	.118***
Satisfaction with people in neighborhood	.328*	.116*

$R^2 = .156$
$df = 4/386$

Correlates of Dwelling Experiences

Satisfaction with Dwelling

	r	b
Felt dwelling too small (Yes=1, No=0)	-.347***	-.314***
Attractiveness of building	-.348***	-.238***
Satisfaction with dwelling's nearness to places	.136**	.142***
Annoyed by dirt or soot on window	-.260***	-.135**
Felt dwelling too cold in winter	-.281***	-.127**
Felt bored in dwelling	-.174***	-.092*
Annoyed by broken down appliances	-.183***	-.078

$R^2 = .312$
$df = 7/389$

Proud to Live in Dwelling

	r	b
Attractiveness of building	-.307***	-.239***
Felt dwelling size too small (Yes=1, No=0)	-.161***	-.133**
Felt bored at home	-.179***	-.131**
Felt dwelling was too cold in winter	-.218	-.130**
Enjoyed company of a pet	.103*	.110*

$R^2 = .158$
$df = 5/387$

Table 8.4. (continued)

	Good Dwelling Memories	
	r	b
Thought about memories of personal things	.427***	.405***
Places beyond walking distance (Yes = 1, No = 0)	.127*	.126**
Felt dwelling was too cold in winter	−.140**	−.114*
Felt bored at home	−.089	−.111*
Bothered by people talking too loudly outside	.148**	.109*
Enjoyed company of pet	.135**	.107*
Felt dwelling size too small (Yes = 1, No = 0)	−.093	−.087
Felt dwelling size too big (Yes = 1, No = 0)	.102*	.083
	R^2 = .262	
	df = 8/383	

Community satisfaction also depends on the qualities of the urbanized environment. It is greater when sidewalks and streets are not littered, thereby enabling the old person to avoid the accompanying annoyances, perceived lack of control, and, possibly, status-threatening feelings (related to a declining community image). Community satisfaction is stronger for households that have not experienced a home robbery and with it the inevitable feelings of fear, helplessness, and anxiety. On a different level, community satisfaction is a function of environmental transactions that involve doing "something different," thereby satisfying individual needs for novelty, change, and impulsiveness.

Together, the six experiences (excluding satisfaction with friends) explained about 25 percent of the variation in community satisfaction.[7]

Proud to Live in Community

Thirteen environmental experiences were significantly correlated with community pride—four of which remained statistically significant in the stepwise regression analysis. Old people proud of living in their community were more satisfied with its stores, felt good about doing something different in their community, were more satisfied with its services, and were less likely to have had a personal item lost or stolen the previous year.

Although fewer experiences remained significant than in the community satisfaction analysis, the similarities between the two were apparent. With a minor exception, the same categories of the physical environment were represented (see figure 4.2), and the same experience meanings could be inferred.

Community pride is influenced by the availability and the accessibility of community facilities and services. It is greater in a place that encourages new or different behaviors and where fear and anxiety are not present due to the theft or the loss of personal items. Although three social experiences were significantly correlated with community pride, as was the case for community satisfaction, none of these experiences remained statistically significant in the stepwise regression analysis. Although the urbanized environment experience, "annoyed by litter or garbage on streets and sidewalks," was significantly correlated with community pride, it did not remain significant in the subsequent regression equation (as it did in the community satisfaction analysis).

Together the four experiences contributed about 10 percent of the variation in reports of community pride by Evanston's old population. These findings begin a pattern of relationships in which specific environmental experiences are able to account for less variation in territorial pride than in territorial satisfaction.

Satisfaction with Neighborhood as a Place to Live

Twenty-seven environmental experiences were significantly correlated with neighborhood satisfaction—only four of which remained statistically significant in the stepwise regression analysis. Old people more satisfied with their neighborhood were also more satisfied with the people in their neighborhood, were less likely to be annoyed by unattractive buildings in their neighborhood, were less likely to be concerned with the possibility of a home break-in, and were more satisfied with their neighborhood's proximity to Chicago.

One social experience clearly dominated the set, namely, "satisfaction with people in the neighborhood." A satisfactory social situation (see figure 4.2) probably contributes to old people's peace of mind and pleasure, feelings of social acceptability, and positive self-concept. Two other social experiences, "satisfaction with friends" and "enjoyment from visiting with neighbors," were also relatively highly correlated (.25 and .28) with neighborhood satisfaction, but did not significantly enter the regression equation (because they shared common variance).[8]

The next two significant experiences indicated the impact on neighborhood satisfaction of an unattractive built environment ("other buildings are less attractive") and an unsafe urbanized environment ("fear of thief breaking into dwelling"). The negative outcomes of these two experiences are likely to include greater emotional discomfort, poorer self-concept (because of a poor neighborhood image), greater anxiety, helplessness, insecurity, and fear.

The significance of the experience "satisfaction with living near Chicago" and the just barely insignificant experience "satisfaction with dwelling's nearness to places" ($F = 3.3$) echo the importance of convenience and accessibility reported earlier as antecedents of community satisfaction.

Together, these five experiences explain more than 63 percent of the variation in neighborhood satisfaction, most of which is due to the effects of a satisfying neighborhood (people) social situation.

Proud to Live in Neighborhood

Twenty-two environmental experiences were significantly correlated with neighborhood pride—four of which remained significant in the stepwise regression analysis. Old people proud to live in their neighborhood were more satisfied with the people in their neighborhood, were less likely to have had food or drug items home-delivered, were less likely to be annoyed because of the unattractiveness of neighborhood buildings, and did not have a personal item recently (in the past year) lost or stolen. Three other experiences fell just short of being statistically significant. Neighborhood pride was positively influenced by reported enjoyment from visiting with neighbors, by the absence of annoyances from window dirt or soot, and from reported enjoyment from being in a neighborhood with the same class of people.

The similarity between this set of experiences and that underlying neighborhood satisfaction is notable. The most important (largest beta weight) experience underlying neighborhood pride again involved a satisfying social situation ("satisfaction with people in neighborhood"), and two other comparable social experiences had significant or near significant effects. Less statistically important influences of neighborhood pride were the attractiveness of the built environment and a safe (urbanized) environment ("had item lost or stolen"). Experiences with comparable meanings had similarly influenced the neighborhood satisfaction of old people.

One new dimension of meaning underlying pride in neighbor-

hood emerged from this analysis. Old people proud of their neighborhood had their food or drug items home-delivered less frequently. Earlier (see table 4.1) it was hypothesized that both
negative consequences (dependency, restriction) and positive consequences (physical comfort, peace of mind, self-maintenance) were
possible effects or outcomes of this behavioral response. However,
the present empirical relationship suggested that old people viewed
home delivery in negative terms. This interpretation is supported
by other findings in this study. Old people in poorer health (according to both objective and subjective indicators) were more
likely to receive the home delivery of food or drugs. Additionally,
it was found that high-income elderly were not more likely than
low-income elderly to receive home food deliveries—that is, home
delivery is not an indicator of wealth or status. If home delivery
is a reflection of the poor health or functional impairments of the
old person, then feelings of dependency, status inferiority, and
feelings of personal helplessness are experiential consequences that
are reducing the likelihood of neighborhood pride.

Together, the seven experiences accounted for about 26 percent
of the variation in reported neighborhood pride expressed by old
people.

Thought about Good Neighborhood Memories

Fourteen environmental experiences were significantly correlated with good neighborhood memories—four of which remained statistically significant in the stepwise regression analysis. Old people who thought about the good memories brought back
by their neighborhood enjoyed visiting with their neighbors, recently had a good time in their neighborhood, became tired while
getting to places in their community, and were more satisfied with
the people in their neighborhood.

Two of the four experiences involved transactions with the social environment, a response pattern consistent with the other
neighborhood territorial experiences. Here, however, positive outcomes derived not only from transactions with a satisfactory social situation ("satisfaction with people in neighborhood") but also

from a satisfying personal environment ("enjoyment from visiting with neighbors") (see figure 4.2).

Two new dimensions of meaning underlying neighborhood experiences were suggested by these findings. First, old people who had good neighborhood memories also reported they "had good times in own neighborhood" in "past few months." This implies that the recalling of good memories is more likely for old people who are enjoying their neighborhood in the present.

Second, the recall of good neighborhood memories was more likely for old people who experienced fatigue when they engaged in activities outside of their neighborhood. This suggests good memories are more likely to occur when the neighborhood is currently a more salient aspect in old people's lives. Subsequent empirical analyses reported on in this study support such inferences. Old people who recalled good memories had smaller activity spaces and experienced a recent decline in their overall activity.

In contrast to the neighborhood satisfaction and neighborhood pride, territorial experiences, the (attractive) built environment, and the (safe) urbanized environment were not associated with the recall of good neighborhood memories.

Together the four significant environmental experiences accounted for about 16 percent of the variation in the reported frequency of good neighborhood memories by Evanston's old population.

Satisfaction with Dwelling as a Place to Live

Fifteen environmental experiences were significantly correlated with dwelling satisfaction—six of which remained statistically significant in the stepwise regression analysis. Old people more satisfied with their dwellings did not (on the average) perceive them as too small, evaluated their buildings (their houses or apartment structures) as more attractive, were more likely to be satisfied with their dwellings' nearness to places, were less likely to be annoyed by dirt or soot on their windows, were less likely to feel that the temperature of their dwellings was too cold in the winter, and were less likely to feel bored in their dwellings.

These findings indicated that the dwelling satisfaction of old people was closely associated with outcomes from transactions with the natural, built, and urbanized objects of the physical environment (figure 4.2). Although three social experiences were significantly correlated with dwelling satisfaction—(not) "feeling lonely," (not) "feeling lack of privacy," and "enjoyment from being home alone"—none of these remained significant in the stepwise regression analysis. Only the social experience, "feeling bored in the dwelling," was significantly related (and only marginally so) to dwelling satisfaction in the final regression equation. However, it can be legitimately argued that "boredom" is a consequence of the quality of the individual's physical environment transactions.

The above physical experiences are likely to increase overall feelings of satisfaction for several reasons. The attractiveness of the building contributes to the old person's sense of personal status or accomplishments if it is construed as a symbol of a successful life; the dwelling that is perceived as adequate in size (that is, not too small) implies that feelings of restriction or crowdedness are not problems. Satisfaction with a dwelling's nearness to places leads to greater emotional and physical security and confidence in one's ability to live independently. The suitably warm temperature of a dwelling in the winter not only contributes to the physical comfort of the old person but also helps avoid feelings such as helplessness and submissiveness in the face of an uncontrollable dwelling environment. Avoiding the annoyance of dirty windows can result in some unexpected positive consequences. Rowles (1979) argued that windows in a dwelling ensure that the old person has visual access to the world outside, with surveillance abilities over a wide range of physical and social objects and events otherwise inaccessible. Thus more than aesthetic reasons alone may explain why clean windows underlie dwelling satisfaction.

Together, the seven experiences accounted for about 31 percent of the variation in reports of dwelling satisfaction by old people.

Proud to Live in Dwelling

Eleven environmental experiences were significantly correlated with pride in dwelling—five of which remained statistically significant in the stepwise regression analysis. Old people proud to live in their dwellings perceived their buildings as more attractive, were less likely to feel that their dwellings were too small or too cold in the winter, were less likely to feel bored in their homes, and were more likely to enjoy the company of a pet.

The similarity of these experiences to those associated with dwelling satisfaction is apparent—four of the five experiences were identical. Two social experiences, although significantly correlated with dwelling pride, did not remain statistically significant in the final regression analysis. Thus, dwelling pride, along with dwelling satisfaction, appears to be most strongly associated with physical environmental experiences.

The "pet" experience is a possible exception. It was categorized earlier as a transaction involving a social object, albeit with an animal rather than a human (table 4.1). This labeling was based on Levinson's (1972) arguments that pets serve various social functions. Most importantly, the pet allows the old person to transfer affection, emotions, and care to an object that offers predictable companionship and friendship. Consequently, pet experiences help the old person avoid "feelings of uselessness" (Levinson 1972:101) and shore up his sense of worth or self-image. By communicating with the pet, the old person also can maintain contact with reality rather than withdraw into a fantasy world (Levinson, 1972:87). One result is that the dwelling apparently becomes a more attractive place to live.

Together, the five environmental experiences contributed about 16 percent of the variation in reports of dwelling pride by old people.

Thought about Good Dwelling Memories

Eleven environmental experiences were significantly correlated with good dwelling memories—six of which remained statistically significant in the stepwise regression analysis. Old people who thought about good memories brought back by their dwellings were more likely to recall memories about the personal things in their homes (photographs, souvenirs, dishes, etc.). They reported that certain places were not visited because they were not within walking distance. They were less likely to feel their dwellings were cold in the winter, less likely to feel bored in their homes, more likely to be bothered by people talking too loudly outside, and more likely to enjoy the company of a pet.

As before, these experiences were dominated by transactions with the physical environment, variously involving its built, natural, and urbanized aspects (figure 4.2). Considerable overlap existed between these experiences and those underlying dwelling satisfaction and dwelling pride. Additionally, several experiences differentiated old people according to whether their life-styles were centered around their home. For instance, old people who recalled good dwelling memories often found their outside environments inaccessible ("places beyond walking distance", were surrounded by memory-laden objects ("memories about personal things"), enjoyed the time spent in their dwellings ("enjoys company of a pet" and "does not feel bored"), were easily annoyed by the noises outside their dwellings—perhaps because they intruded on the remembering of the past—and in general found their dwellings comfortable inside ("dwelling is not too cold in the winter").

Together, the six experiences explained about 25 percent of the variation in old people's reports of good dwelling memories.

Individual Differences Underlying the Meaningfulness of Territorial Experiences of Evanston's Elderly

Attention now turns to the findings of a set of multiple regression analyses that identified those individual variables (chapters 5, 6, and 7) that influenced the occurrence of these eight territorial experiences—in order of discussion: community, neighborhood, and dwelling satisfaction; community, neighborhood, and dwelling pride; and good neighborhood and dwelling memories.

Methodology

Three statistical stages were carried out. First, zero-order correlations (Pearson r coefficients) were computed between a specified dependent variable (an environmental experience) and each of the proposed individual variables. Several variables were immediately dropped from consideration at this stage either because their theoretical relevance was in question or because their statistical relationships were insignificant at the .05 level or less. It is possible that the small size of a correlation coefficient may be due to suppression effects of one or more other intervening variables, but the choice to eliminate such variables can be justified on two grounds. First, multiple measures of the same or similar individual construct were usually considered. It was statistically improbable that these variables would be similarly suppressed. Second, operationally, it was not feasible to partial out or control for the indirect and spurious effects of all possible suppression variables. Each dependent variable analysis required an initial examination of the simple correlational relationships of up to 46 independent (individual) variables (for complete variable list, see Appendix D). The reader can assume that when a variable is not discussed in a particular analysis, either it initially had an insignificant or trivial zero-order relationship with the dependent variable or there was only a weak theoretical basis for the proposed relationship. In practice, the variables eliminated at this stage had zero-order coefficients of less than .08.

In the second statistical stage a series of multiple regression equations were calculated in which the dependent variable was linearly associated with each of the eight different sets of individual variables. The purpose of this stage was to eliminate variables *within* a specified category that offered redundant or spurious information about the elderly individual. Often, individual variables within the same category were highly intercorrelated either because they measured the same construct or because the constructs in reality were strongly related (for example, certain objective and subjective measures of income or measures such as household size and marital status). In each of the stage two regression equations, variables within a category that had significant direct effects on the dependent variable (after controlling for others in the set) were thereby distinguished from those that had only indirect or spurious effects.

In the third statistical stage, a single regression equation was calculated in which each environmental experience was treated as a dependent variable and linearly related to independent variables that had significant direct effects in the stage two regression equations. This analysis identified those individual measures that had significant direct effects on the dependent variable after simultaneously controlling for the direct effects of the others (see appendix C for a discussion of the problem of "overcontrolling" for direct effects and appendix D for the correlation relationships among all individual variables). In practice, variables found statistically insignificant in the stage two analyses were sometimes included in this third stage if they were considered important control variables, or if only one variable remained to represent a particular category of individual variables, considered of theoretical importance.[9]

Because of space limitations, the following sections mainly report on findings from the stage three statistical analyses.[10]

Direct Effects of Individual Variables on Community, Neighborhood, and Dwelling Satisfaction

Findings

Satisfaction with Community. Five individual variables significantly influenced community satisfaction. Old people more satisfied with their community were more happy with their lives, had a stronger urbanism environment disposition, were women, and had a lower household income but were not burdened by housing expenses (table 8.5).[11]

Satisfaction with Neighborhood. Four individual variables significantly influenced neighborhood satisfaction. Old people more satisfied with their neighborhoods were less active, were more sat-

Table 8.5. Multiple Regression Analyses of Individual Variables Underlying Community, Neighborhood, and Dwelling Satisfaction

Independent Variable Categories	Community Satisfaction		Neighborhood Satisfaction		Dwelling Satisfaction	
Personality						
Urbanism environment disposition	.201***		.149**		.080	
Stimulus-seeking environment disposition			−.069		−.100*	
Demographic and Racial						
Males (Yes=1, No=0)	−.157**	(−.420)				
Whites (Yes=1, No=0)			.082	(.275)		
Separated-divorced (Yes=1, No=0)			.056	(.311)	−.038	(−.196)
Widowed (Yes=1, No=0)			.112*	(.291)	−.004	(−.011)
Never married (Yes=1, No=0)			.048	(.234)	−.010	(−.046)
Socioeconomic Status						
Self-rated social class					.055	
Impact of housing expenses	−.116*				−.098	
Level of education	−.106					
Concern about enough money	−.100				−.014	
Total household income	−.149*					
Stage in Life						
Employed (Yes=1, No=0)			−.045	(−.122)		
Experienced minor illness (Yes=1, No=0)	−.062	(−.160)				
Psychological Well-Being						
How happy are you these days	.211**				.242***	
Life satisfaction			.160**			
Activity Behavior						
Level of activity	−.051		−.158**		−.236***	
Duration in Residence					.110*	
Tenure Status (Own=1, Rent=0)					.085	(.216)
R²	.190		.099		.176	
F	9.373***		4.734***		6.489***	
df	9/360		9/390		12/364	

NOTE: Unstandardized partial regression coefficients of dummy variables are shown in parentheses.
***p<.001   **p<.01   *p<.05

isfied with their lives, had a stronger urbanism environment orientation, and were widowed rather than married. Although neighborhood satisfaction was greater for whites than blacks, the race variable was just short of being significant (table 8.5).

Satisfaction with Dwelling. Four individual variables significantly influenced dwelling satisfaction. Old people more satisfied with their dwellings were happier with their lives, were less active, lived longer in their present dwellings, and had a weaker stimulus-seeking environment disposition (table 8.5).[12]

Discussion of Findings

Urbanism Environment Disposition. One would expect from earlier discussions (chapter 5) that old people with stronger urbanism environment dispositions would more likely be aware of, attend to, seek out, and associate greater satisfaction with place attributes that were perceived and interpreted as having stronger urban than nonurban qualities. Possible attributes include a place's good accessibility, variety of activity opportunities, and cultural life. Moreover, one might expect that these old people would be more tolerant of some of the unpleasant aspects of urban living, such as pollution, crime, and noise. In light of these expectations, this individual variable behaved in a predictable fashion. It was most strongly related to community satisfaction (Evanston is more urban than rural), had a weaker but still significant association with neighborhood satisfaction, and had a nonsignificant direct effect on dwelling satisfaction. In all three instances, the sign of the coefficient indicated that a stronger disposition to an urban way of life led to greater satisfaction with community, neighborhood, and dwelling territorial environments.

Stimulus-Seeking Environment Disposition. In contrast to the urbanism environment disposition, a stimulus-seeking environment disposition was most strongly and significantly related to dwelling satisfaction, and it had insignificant effects on community and neighborhood satisfaction. One would expect that old people with stronger stimulus-seeking personalities would more likely be aware of, attend to, seek out, and associate greater satisfaction with environmental transactions that lead to pleasingly novel or unusual consequences. However, the dwelling is an unlikely setting for such variation-producing environmental transactions. For old persons who are less demanding of such experiences, the predictability and tranquility of the dwelling environment are a source of satisfaction. For others who value such experiences positively, the mundane qualities of dwelling occupancy are probably a source of displeasure, especially for old persons unable to satisfy their needs for environmental variation elsewhere. However, old persons who have such environmental alternatives should be less inclined to evaluate their dwelling in these terms. For these persons, dwelling satisfaction is unlikely to be related to their stimulus-seeking dispositions.

Race. Black-white racial differences among old people were insignificantly correlated with either community or dwelling satisfaction.[13] Although race was significantly correlated with neighborhood satisfaction, it fell just short of being significant in the stage three multiple regression analysis. The value of its unstandardized coefficient indicated that whites were, on the average, more satisfied than blacks with their neighborhoods. If based on objective indicators, this would be a predictable finding; however, in light of the lower environmental expectations and aspirations usually attributed to the black elderly, one would have predicted the opposite finding. That is, the quality of the neighborhood environment perceived by black elderly residents should be closer to their aspirations and expectations, leading, in turn, to their greater neighborhood satisfaction. White elderly, on the other hand, should perceive a greater gap between their expectations and perceived realities, leading to their greater dissatisfaction. An alternative explanation is that the expectation and aspiration levels adopted by blacks as a standard by which to evaluate their neighborhoods are influenced "upward" by their proximity to better quality white neighborhoods. The greater neighborhood dissatisfaction of elderly blacks thereby reflects observable discrepancies between these expectation levels and the quality of their own neighborhoods.

Sex. Of the three territorial experiences, only community satisfaction was significantly influenced by the sex of the old person.[14] Women were more satisfied than men with their community. There is no simple explanation as to why a person's sex influences community satisfaction and not neighborhood and dwelling satisfaction, but the following arguments may shed some light.

For several reasons, old women should receive greater rewards or benefits from their community transactions than old men. Elderly women are usually nonemployed and thus are more likely than elderly men to carry out their activities within the community. Other empirical findings in this study confirmed that the activity levels of women are lower and depend more on walking and public transportation than elderly men's activity behavior does. Together, these observations point to the female population as being more dependent on the community's facilities and services—a dependence that has likely existed for a considerable time. In contrast, although many retired old men spend most of their time in the community, this activity pattern usually has a shorter history. Moreover, old men probably do not value community services and facilities as highly because they have greater transportation mobility and because they view the community as merely one of many alternatives to satisfy their demands.

If this interpretation is valid, it helps explain why "duration in residence" did not influence community satisfaction as predicted. Simply, the very different community dependency relationships that old men and women have take precedence over the influences of length of community occupancy. It also helps explain why sex status was unrelated to neighborhood satisfaction. A previous analysis revealed that greater neighborhood satisfaction was a result of a favorably evaluated social situation. This was in contrast to community satisfaction, which was related to the availability and accessibility of services and facilities. Thus, the insignificance of sex status implies that neighborhoods have the potential of satisfying the social needs of both old men and old women equally.

Marital Status. The marital status of old people significantly influenced only their neighborhood satisfaction. Widows were more satisfied than the married elderly with their neighborhood. It is again useful to remember the strong relationship between neighborhood satisfaction and reports of satisfaction with people in the neighborhood. The implication is that old widows are more likely than married elderly to obtain enjoyment from the social composition of their neighborhoods, and that elderly persons living with spouses consider the neighborhood's social situation as less important. For probably similar reasons, separated-divorced old people are more satisfied with their neighborhood than married elderly (as indicated by the variable's sizable unstandardized regression coefficient).

Socioeconomic Status. Socioeconomic status significantly influenced the likelihood of old people's community satisfaction but had weak or nonsignificant effects on neighborhood and dwelling satisfaction.[15] Lower income and less well-educated (although this latter variable was just short of being significant) old people were more satisfied with their community. In direct contrast, old people who perceived housing expense burdens and had greater money concerns (although this latter variable was just short of being significant) were less satisfied with their community. These contradictory findings highlight the importance of distinguishing between objective and subjective individual differences (chapter 6).

Earlier theoretical arguments predicted that lower income and less education would lead to greater community satisfaction because both income and education were positively associated with personal expectations and aspirations. Thus as an individual's aspirations and expectations became higher, the more likely it was that his residential environment would be considered inadequate for his needs. Consequently, it was expected that higher individual expectations and aspiration levels (implying higher incomes and education levels) would depress residential satisfaction levels.

The ways in which the individual variables—impact of housing expenses and money concerns—differ from income and education levels help explain their opposing influences on community satisfaction. First, they represent subjective interpretations of income status and personal competence. That is, they require a judgment from the respondent as to whether present income resources are congruent with his material demands. Second, these subjective measures are present-oriented. In contrast, the individual's educational level is received much earlier in life, and his income level, although it strongly reflects the present, is influenced as much or more by the individual's past earning history.

Earlier arguments concerning how a person's feelings of congruence influenced his environmental experiences are relevant for interpreting the experiential impact of these subjective economic status measures. When the gap between income demands and income resources is large, the old person probably feels pessimistic about the success or viability of future environmental transactions, particularly those involving money. Consequently, the experiential opportunities offered by the community environment may be perceived as more restricted or less accessible and thus result in a less positive evaluation.

The statistically insignificant direct effect of "impact of housing expenses" on dwelling satisfaction appears largely due to statistical overcontrol (see appendix C). Controlling for two statistically related and conceptually similar measures of subjective economic status—"impact of housing expenses" and "concern about having enough money"—reduce the probability of either variable remaining statistically significant. In this instance, if concern about money is not controlled for in the final multiple regression equation, impact of housing expenses remains statistically significant (at the .05 level). That neither an old person's subjective or objective economic status influenced neighborhood satisfaction suggests that assessments of a neighborhood's social situation—fundamental to overall neighborhood satisfaction—are relatively unaffected by a person's financial well-being.

Stage in Life. All three of the territorial experiences had for the most part trivial associations with the proposed stage-in-life variables. Two significant simple direct (regression) effects were initially observed: old people who recently had a minor illness were less satisfied with their community; and nonemployed elderly were more satisfied than employed elderly with their neighborhood.

However, the direct effects of these relationships disappeared when the analysis controlled for other individual variables (table 8.5).

Activity Behavior. Less active old people were more satisfied with both their neighborhood and their dwelling, but their community satisfaction was not significantly influenced.[16] The discussion of the adaptive and maladaptive functions of activity behavior in old age (chapter 7) helps explain what otherwise might appear to be unexpected findings. For less active old people, the dwelling and neighborhood become very salient components of their everyday environment. There is a greater dependence on the proximate environment to satisfy most material and psychological needs. Thus, the dwelling and the neighborhood become the settings for many of the elderly's experiences and are more regular and persistent sources of pleasure and satisfaction. Concomitantly, alternative environments—outside the dwelling or neighborhood—become less central to the old person's life-style and thus are attended to less as standards for comparison. This narrowing experiential world and increasing significance of the proximate environment is in turn likely to result in the old person's greater accommodation to any place problems or deficiencies. Consequently, both real and imagined dwelling and neighborhood problems may be denied, deemphasized, or ignored—a particularly adaptive response when "freedom of [activity] choice" (Proshansky, Ittelson, and Rivlin 1970) and alternative sources of satisfying environmental experiences do not exist.

Duration of Residence and Tenure Status. For reasons already suggested, duration in residence was statistically unrelated to community or neighborhood satisfaction although it significantly and positively influenced dwelling satisfaction. The statistically insignificant effect of tenure status on dwelling satisfaction (table 8.5) appears to be primarily a reflection of statistical overcontrol. If duration of residence is not controlled for in the final regression analysis, tenure status becomes significant,[17] and on the average, owners are more satisfied with their dwellings than renters. The theoretical arguments for expecting both homeownership and longer duration of residence to increase dwelling satisfaction are discussed fully in chapter 7.

Psychological Well-Being. The theoretical prediction of a positive relationship between psychological well-being (happiness and life satisfaction) and territorial satisfaction (chapter 6) was given empirical support. It was proposed that old people who are unhappy or dissatisfied with life will displace the effects of this incongru-

Table 8.6. Activity level, Level of Happiness, and Dwelling Satisfaction (percentage respondents completely satisfied with dwelling unit)

	Activity Level				
Level of Happiness	Lowest Quartile	Second Quartile	Third Quartile	Highest Quartile	Total
Not too happy	54	33	33	25	40
	(13)	(6)	(12)	(4)	(35)
Pretty happy	69	69	56	45	60
	(42)	(55)	(48)	(51)	(196)
Very happy	88	88	76	70	79
	(33)	(34)	(45)	(57)	(169)
Total	74	74	62	57	66
	(88)	(95)	(105)	(112)	(400)

NOTE: Numbers in parentheses represent case base upon which percentages are calculated.

ence or maladjustment to all of their environmental transactions. Consequently, their affective and evaluative responses are accentuated or dominated by negative tones.[18] The findings supported this proposition: old people more unhappy or dissatisfied with their lives were also more dissatisfied with their community, neighborhood, and dwelling environments.

Activity Behavior and Psychological Well-Being. The effects of psychological well-being and activity behavior on territorial satisfaction may be demonstrated in another way. Table 8.6 displays how old people categorized simultaneously by happiness and activity levels differed in their degree of dwelling satisfaction. The totals confirmed that "very happy" old people were almost twice as likely as "not too happy" people (79 percent versus 40 percent) to be *completely* satisfied with their dwelling; also the least active elderly (74 percent) were far more likely than the most active elderly people (57 percent) to be completely satisfied with their dwelling. However, the tabulations also confirmed that at *any level of happiness*, low activity led to greater dwelling satisfaction; similarly, at *any activity level*, greater happiness led to greater dwelling satisfaction.

Consequently, the old people who were the most completely satisfied with their dwelling (88 percent) were very happy, but had very low activity levels. Similarly, old people who were the most completely dissatisfied (25 percent) were very unhappy and had very high activity levels.

Direct Effects of Individual Variables on Pride in Community, Neighborhood, and Dwelling

Findings

Pride in Community. Seven individual variables significantly influenced reported pride in community. Old people who were proud of their community as a place to live were more happy with their lives, were widowed, separated, or divorced rather than married, had a stronger urban environment disposition, lived longer in their community, were less active, and had a stronger antiquarianism environment disposition (that is, were more favorably disposed toward old and historical things). A finding just short of being significant was that old people forced to retire recently were less likely to have community pride (table 8.7).

Pride in Neighborhood. Six individual variables significantly influenced reported pride in neighborhood. Old people proud of their neighborhood as a place to live were more happy with their lives, had a stronger urban environment disposition, were owners rather than renters, were widowed rather than married, were less active, and had more frequent hearing difficulties (table 8.7).

Table 8.7. Multiple Regression Analyses of Individual Variables Underlying Pride in Community, Neighborhood, and Dwelling

Independent Variable Categories	Beta Values		
	Pride in Community	Pride in Neighborhood	Pride in Dwelling
Personality			
Stimulus-seeking environment disposition			−.052
Leary Dominance Personality	.069		
Antiquarianism environment disposition	.099*		
Urbanism environment disposition	.142**	.163**	.099*
Demographic			
Separated-divorced (Yes=1, No=0)	.128* (.357)	.071 (.206)	−.012 (−.030)
Widowed (Yes=1, No=0)	.177** (.228)	.140* (.192)	.174** (.220)
Never married (Yes=1, No=0)	.062 (.150)	.003 (.007)	.050 (.115)
Total household size	.110	.085	.146**
Socioeconomic Status			
Money situation compared to 2 years ago			−.099*
Self-rated social class			.093
Stage in Life			
Self-rated hearing difficulties		.118*	
Forced to retire (Yes=1, No=0)	−.093 (−.323)		−.095 (−.316)
Psychological Well-Being			
How happy are you these days	.205***	.170***	.151**
Activity Behavior			
Level of activity		−.137*	
Activity space size	−.102*		
Duration in Community	.113*		
Duration in Residence		.090	.097*
Tenure Status (Own=1, Rent=0)	.071 (.093)	.141* (.197)	.188*** (.243)
R²	.157	.128	.177
F	5.669***	5.613***	6.657***
df	12/366	10/381	13/372

NOTE: Unstandardized partial regression coefficients of dummy variables are shown in parentheses.
***p<.001   **p<.01   *p<.05

Pride in Dwelling. Seven individual variables significantly influenced reported pride in the dwelling. Old people proud of their dwellings were owners rather than renters, were widowed rather than married, were more happy with their lives, were members of larger households, had a stronger urbanism environment disposition, perceived their present money situation as better than that of two years earlier, and occupied their dwellings longer. A finding just short of being significant was that old people forced to retire recently were less likely to have pride in their dwellings (table 8.7).

Discussion of Findings

The following discussion focuses on those individual variables that were not interpreted in the previous analyses or that behaved somewhat differently or unpredictably.

Urbanism Environment Disposition. A stronger urbanism environment disposition led to a greater likelihood of community, neighborhood, and dwelling pride. Although this individual variable had similar effects on community, neighborhood, and dwelling satisfaction, a different interpretation may be in order. One can infer that urban-oriented individuals feel more competent in an urban environment and are more confident about satisfying their needs and goals. Such certainty of accomplishment should lead, in turn, to a greater sense of environmental pride.

Race. Race was insignificantly correlated with all three of the territorial pride experiences. Thus black old people on the average are just as proud of their territorial context as white elderly. This implies that both groups are equally likely to perceive a fittingness between their environmental accomplishments (the quality of their residential setting) and what they perceive as their performance expectations.

Marital Status and Household Size. The sex of old people was unrelated (in second stage regression analyses) to any of the three territorial pride experiences; however, marital status differences were important predictors. Old widows were more likely than elderly married persons to be proud of their community, neighborhood, and dwelling, whereas separated-divorced elderly were more likely than married elderly to be proud of their community and neighborhood. These results did not differ substantially from those observed in the previous satisfaction analyses, in which elderly women were more satisfied with their community, and widowed and separated-divorced elderly were more satisfied with their neighborhood. Notably, 81 percent of the widowed elderly and 70 percent of the separated-divorced elderly were women. For this reason, the explanations given earlier for elderly women's greater community satisfaction and the widowed elderly's greater neighborhood satisfaction are also relevant here.

Additionally, the general meanings specifically associated with territorial pride (as opposed to territorial satisfaction) may help account for the significant direct effects of an old person's marital status. At any age, and certainly in late life, loss of a spouse usually puts the surviving partner in a disadvantaged psychological, social, and economic position compared with married persons. One coping response made by widowed elderly is to assign greater salience to other persons and certain material objects as sources of gratification and pride in their lives. Consequently, the places these old persons permanently occupy—communities, neighborhoods, and dwellings—may become more valued and salient environmental components and serve as important symbols of achievement, success, and status. They may remain as the most important tangible expression of an individual's past life and career accomplishments and, especially for the elderly widow, they are continuous reminders of rewarding family memories. These places or existential spaces become an important basis for the old person's self-worth and their continued occupancy ensures a positive and respectable self-image that, in turn, commands approval and status recognition from neighbors, friends, and relatives. Without such a territorial context and the accomplishments and respect they signify, the elderly widow is stripped of the important symbolic trappings that reinforce the pride she feels in herself and her environment. This line of reasoning may also explain the greater territorial pride of divorced-separated elderly women.

It might appear contradictory that both larger households and a person's widowed and divorced status, which implies a small household, can positively influence community and dwelling pride. However, there were 47 widows (28 percent of all elderly widows) and nine separated-divorced persons (30 percent of all separated-divorced elderly) who occupied two- or three-person households. Further empirical analyses of these data confirmed that widowed elderly in larger households and married elderly in three or more person households were more likely to be proud of their community and dwelling. However, irrespective of household size, elderly widows were more likely than married elderly to be proud of their community, neighborhood, and dwelling.

Socioeconomic Status. The likelihood of being proud of the dwelling, neighborhood, and community as places to live was largely independent of old people's objective or subjective socioeconomic status. However, a present money situation worse than that of two years earlier and a lower self-rated class status did lead to a reduced likelihood of dwelling pride. These results contrasted with the stronger effects that socioeconomic status had on community satisfaction. They support the contention that pride depends less on some absolute standard of economic competence than on whether the old person perceives his status as consistent with his own or others' standards. More generally, these findings suggest that the old person may be proud of where he lives regardless of the amount of his wealth or level of poverty.

Stage in Life. Stage-in-life individual variables also had generally weak effects on territorial pride. Only "hearing difficulties" significantly influenced neighborhood pride, but in an unexpected direction. Greater hearing difficulties led to a greater likelihood of neighborhood pride. A possible explanation is that environmental transactions outside the neighborhood made the old person feel less secure or comfortable because of greater demands on his auditory skills, unlike the familiar "communications" environment of the neighborhood. Thus the neighborhood is identified as a setting in which the hearing impaired old person feels more competent to carry out his everyday activities, leading to its more favorable evaluation.

It was predictable—given the earlier interpretation of pride—
that old people recently forced to retire would not be as proud to
live in their communities or dwellings (table 8.7).[19] Such an involuntary loss of a social role is probably accompanied, at least
temporarily, by a loss of self-esteem. Predictably, there is also an
increase in the amount of time spent in the dwelling, neighborhood, and community environments. But time spent in such an
"empty" way is contrary to the life-style needs of a once employed person. Consequently, the majority of residential environmental transactions, especially in the dwelling, will be evaluated
unfavorably because they symbolize the old person's "failure."

Activity Behavior. The explanation for why old people's higher activity levels and larger activity spaces led to their feeling less proud
of their community and neighborhoods is identical to that given
for activity behavior's influence on neighborhood and dwelling
satisfaction.

Less easily explained is the lack of a significant inverse relationship between activity behavior and dwelling pride.[20] One
interpretation is that low activity is considered a sign of normatively *unacceptable* social withdrawal by many older people. Although they find the dwelling to be highly salient and rewarding
for many of their needs, the excessive amount of time spent in it
deflates their feelings of self-worth. Thus the dwelling to some extent becomes symbolic of a "prison" and inactivity generates feelings of uselessness and incompetence. These counteracting interpretations of activity behavior's effects—leading to both satisfaction
and uselessness—may account for the insignificant relationship.

Length of Occupancy and Tenure Status. The relationship between
residential behavior and territorial pride was stronger than that
between residential behavior and territorial satisfaction. One explanation is that the sense of greater competence and predictability generated by longer residential occupancy and homeownership impinges more on personal pride than on personal satisfaction.

Psychological Well-Being. Old people with higher levels of happiness were more likely to be proud of their community, neighbor-

hoods, and dwellings. These findings are consistent with and can be interpreted similarly as those reported in the analysis of territorial satisfaction.[21]

Direct Effects of Individual Variables on Having Good Neighborhood and Dwelling Memories

Findings

Good Memories about Neighborhood. Five individual variables significantly influenced the likelihood of good neighborhood memories. Old people reporting good neighborhood memories lived longer in their present dwelling, were likely to report a recent decline in their activity level, had a current money situation better than that of ten years earlier, were more favorably disposed toward old and historical things (antiquarianism environment disposition), and were more likely to have had a serious illness in the previous year. A finding just short of being significant was that separated-divorced old people were less likely than married old people to have good neighborhood memories (table 8.8).

Good Memories about Dwelling. Four individual variables influenced the likelihood of good dwelling memories. Old people reporting good memories about their dwellings occupied them longer, were generally more satisfied with their lives, were more likely to have experienced a recent decline in their level of activity, and reported having a serious illness in the previous year. Two findings were just short of being statistically significant. Separated-divorced old people were less likely than married old people and Jewish old people were less likely than Protestant old people to have thought about good dwelling memories (table 8.8).

Discussion of Findings

Antiquarianism Environment Disposition. Of the set of personality and disposition differences proposed as underlying good neigh-

Table 8.8 Multiple Regression Analyses of Individual Variables Underlying Good Memories about Neighborhood and Dwelling

Independent Variable Categories	Beta Values			
	Good Memories About Neighborhoods		Good Memories About Dwelling	
Personality				
Stimulus-seeking environment disposition	−.043			
Antiquarianism environment disposition	.122*			
Demographic and Religious				
Catholic religion (Yes = 1, No = 0)			−.063	(−.190)
Jewish religion (Yes = 1, No = 0)			−.083	(−.404)
Other religion (Yes = 1, No = 0)			−.018	(−.118)
No religion (Yes = 1, No = 0)			.022	(.011)
Separated-divorced (Yes = 1, No = 0)	−.092	(−.474)	−.078	(−.397)
Widowed (Yes = 1, No = 0)	.033	(.081)	.006	(.137)
Never married (Yes = 1, No = 0)	.028	(.124)	.024	(.107)
Socioeconomic Status				
Money situation compared to 10 years ago	−.164***		−.055	
Stage in Life				
Had serious illness (Yes = 1, No = 0)	.109*	(.362)	.120*	(.392)
Psychological Well-Being				
Life satisfaction			.155**	
Activity Behavior				
Activity space size	−.038			
Change in activity	−.177***		−.139**	
Duration in Residence	.266***		.303***	
Tenure Status (Own = 1, Rent = 0)	.054	(.135)	.069	(.168)
R^2	.193		.194	
F	8.093***		6.854***	
df	11/373		13/370	

NOTE: Unstandardized partial regression coefficients of dummy variables are shown in parentheses.
***$p < .001$ **$p < .01$ *$p < .05$

borhood and dwelling memories, only one significant direct relationship was observed. An antiquarianism environment disposition increased the likelihood of good neighborhood memories. One would expect that old people with antiquarianism personalities would be more attentive to the past and would value more highly the older and more historically significant parts of their environment. Predictably, they should enjoy recalling memories about their long-occupied neighborhoods. However, the failure of this individual variable to influence good dwelling memories is not explained away easily. Possibly, the dwelling and its artifacts were not cognitively associated as "old" by the elderly resident.

Demographic and Religious. The likelihood of good neighborhood or dwelling memories was not simply correlated with sex, racial status, or household size. Also, marital status and religious preferences did not have significant direct effects (in the third-stage multiple regression analysis). However, the instances in which these latter variables fell just short of being significant deserve comment.

There is a good theoretical basis for finding that one's separated-divorced status should decrease the likelihood of good dwelling or neighborhood memories. The past may be associated with the painful disruption of an earlier marriage—hardly the subject for good memories. Other empirical analyses also revealed that divorced-separated old people were more likely than married people to have lived a shorter time in their present dwelling, a factor proposed earlier as being unconducive to the recall of environmental memories (chapter 7). However, it is more difficult to explain why Jewish elderly were less likely than Protestant elderly to have thought about good dwelling memories. The close-knit family life of Jewish persons should increase the likelihood of their having good dwelling memories. A partial explanation can be found in other observed relationships between Jewish religious preferences and activity behavior: Jewish elderly have higher activity levels and larger activity spaces than the Protestant elderly. These stronger and more frequent linkages to the environment outside the dwelling would be predicted to decrease the likelihood of recalled memories about the proximate environment.

Socioeconomic Status. Consistent with its weak influence on territorial satisfaction and pride, only one individual variable in this category had significant effects on territorial memories. Old people who perceived their money situation going from worse to better during the past ten years were more likely to have thought about good neighborhood memories. An opposite finding might have been predicted; that is, memories would be recalled because of their associations with better economic times in the past. Instead, old people who presently felt more competent economically were more likely to recall good neighborhood memories. One interpretation is that old people who perceived improvement in their financial status were able to look back on their past lives with a more comfortable feeling. They felt good about their economic achievement over their lifetime and its material manifestations such as their neighborhoods. Thus the likelihood of good neighborhood memories was influenced by lifelong trends that heightened the old person's feelings of competence and success.

The recall of dwelling memories was likewise significantly correlated with an improved money situation. However, after controlling for other individual differences in the final regression equation, this measure of subjective economic status lost its significance.

Stage in Life. Two individual variables initially had significant simple correlational relationships with dwelling and neighborhood memories: "self-rated health" and "a recent serious illness." Memories were more likely to be recalled by old people who perceived their health as poorer or who had a recent (in past year) serious illness. In the stage three multiple regression analysis, only "a recent serious illness" remained statistically significant.

It can be theorized that old people who recently had a very serious illness have seriously contemplated their own death and as a consequence have been more attentive to the amount of time remaining until their death. If this interpretation is valid, then the psychological changes in the dying person should also occur (albeit to a lesser degree) in the person who is seriously ill (Lieberman and Coplan 1969). The most fundamental of these is disengagement, whereby the individual turns psychologically inward and focuses his energies on recalling, organizing, and reminiscing about about past events in his life (Kalish 1976). When comparing old and young people's responses to the prospects of dying in six months, investigators found that "three times as many older persons as younger would spend their time in prayer, reading, contemplation, or other activities that reflect inner life, spiritual needs, or withdrawal" (Kalish 1976:487). Another prediction is that the "coming of death" strips most future activities of their meaning, "because whatever is attempted will be transient or unfinished, a situation that renders a person helpless to achieve what he feels is important" (Kalish 1976:487).

There is another, perhaps simpler, explanation for the relationship between serious illness and memories. Old people with a serious illness are more likely to have been disabled for a substantial period and will have spent more time in their dwellings and neighborhoods. This unexpected amount of free time would increase the opportunities for reminiscing.

Activity Behavior. An explanation for why a decline in activity leads to a greater likelihood of both dwelling and neighborhood memories is found in an earlier discussion of psychological and social disengagement. In brief, the old person who reduces his level of activity is interpreted as weakening his pragmatic or material linkages with the world outside his dwelling or neighborhood. In turn, greater self-awareness and introspection is substituted for these weaker linkages resulting in an old person who is more likely to cogitate about past environmental transactions. In that the old person is likely to spend more time in the dwelling and neighborhood as his overall activity declines, this proximate environment is a logical focus of his reminiscing and memories.

Duration in Residence and Tenure Status. The likelihood of good dwelling and neighborhood memories increased as the length of occupancy in the present dwelling increased. The theoretical basis for this relationship can be briefly reviewed (chapter 7). It is more likely that the longtime resident is exposed to a continuous, stable, and only slowly changing dwelling and neighborhood environment. Such longtime exposure contributes to a very familiar, satisfying, and affectively rewarding environment with strong reinforcement potentials because of its constancy. Environmental memories of a place in which a substantial part of a person's life has been lived are a predictable consequence.

Tenure status was also strongly correlated with good dwelling and neighborhood memories. On the average, owners were more likely than renters to recall good memories. However, this residential behavior variable became insignificant after controlling for "duration in residence." This is another possible illustration of statistical overcontrol. Without controlling for "duration in residence" in the final regression equations (explaining dwelling memories and neighborhood memories), "tenure status" remains statistically significant.

Life Satisfaction. Although greater life satisfaction increased the likelihood of dwelling memories, it did not significantly influence the likelihood of good neighborhood memories.[22] One possible explanation is that the affective and evaluative responses to the dwelling environment more closely reflect the old person's self-identity and self-concept than the neighborhood does. The dwelling is the more tangible expression of the individual's status and self-worth, a manifestation of the individual's historical past, and a symbol of the goals that he has or has not achieved. Thus, memories recalled about the dwelling are closely tied to the individual's personal life. Consequently, old people who feel satisfied and optimistic about their lives are also likely to have more positive memories about the dwelling environments in which they have spent their earlier years.

Chapter Nine

The Types and Meaningfulness of Physical Environment Experiences

Nine categories of the elderly population's structured (factored) experiential environment involved transactions with physical objects or events (chapter 4). A representative set of these was selected for investigation in this chapter. The experiences involved transactions with objects and events in all four categories of the physical environment (see figure 4.2) and depicted a broad array of positive and negative outcomes. In all, seven major groups of physical experiences containing 45 items were considered.[1]

The empirical analyses had three goals: to ascertain the likelihood that old people in Evanston had particular physical environment experiences involving certain outcomes or consequences; to assess how the proposed individual variables influenced the likelihood of these experiences; and to ascertain which of them were related to old people's moving expectations and preferences.

Everyday Annoying Problems of Urban Living

Residents, young and old alike, who live in an older community such as Evanston must inevitably confront the "normal" or usual nuisances of urban living. Except when they are extreme in their effects, these are unlikely to seriously threaten the physical or mental well-being of the urban resident. However, they are potential sources of minor stress and anxiety especially if several of them are present at one time. Noise, pollution, and the physical unattractiveness of a neighborhood's buildings and properties are the most typical problems (see Struyk 1977).

By almost any objective standards, these urban ills are quite real. However, it is unlikely that their properties or attributes are perceived similarly by all urban residents and even if so, they are unlikely to produce the same distress or anxiety.

Seven experiences involving transactions with the neighborhood built environment and the urbanized environment are summarized in table 9.1. Old people were asked how often in the past few months they had each of these experiences. In the earlier factor analysis (table 4.1), these experiences were identified as members of two dimensions or clusters, "annoyed at neighbor's care of property" (factor 4) and "bothered by noise and dirt" (factor 9).

Simple Empirical Patterns

It is immediately apparent that the large majority of old people (from 65 to 87 percent) were not bothered by these urban nuisances (table 9.1). However, a very small percentage of old people (from 3 to 9 percent) did find them a frequent source of annoyance. Another somewhat larger group (from 6 to 13 percent) although not frequently annoyed, still found these urban problems more than an incidental source of irritation (in that they were bothered by them more than once or twice in the past few months). The response distributions show also that some of the unpleasant experiences were more likely to occur than others. These involved the noise of traffic, airplanes, and televisions, the neglect of property by neighbors, the garbage and litter found on the streets or sidewalks, and the polluted air.

Individual Variables Underlying Annoyance with the Neglect of Property by Neighbors

That the explanation for why old people do not similarly experience their environment can be complex is illustrated by the

Table 9.1. Likelihood of Unpleasant Experiences in the Built and Urbanized
Environments

Experiences	Never 1	Only once or twice 2	A few times 3	Many times 4	Total	Mean	N
Annoyed because neighbors neglect property	69%	11	12	8	100%	1.59	399
Annoyed because other neighborhood buildings less attractive	87%	4	6	3	100%	1.24	399
Annoyed because streets or sidewalks have litter	75%	10	8	8	100%	1.48	399
Annoyed by polluted air	74%	10	11	6	100%	1.48	399
Annoyed by dirt and soot on windows	77%	10	7	6	100%	1.42	400
Bothered by people talking loudly outside dwelling	76%	13	8	4	100%	1.40	400
Bothered by traffic and airplane noises, loud TVs	65%	14	13	9	100%	1.67	400

findings of the following analysis, which sought to explain why
old people were not similarly annoyed with their neighbors' neglect of their property.

Most obviously, the major cause may be the varying physical
conditions found in different neighborhoods. By most objective
standards, some neighbors inevitably are more likely than others
to neglect their properties. However, a strong individual basis exists for the observed variations. First, *neglect* itself is something
that must be perceived or recognized, and old people differ according to whether they label buildings as "neglected." Second,
even with agreement on the presence of neglect, old people differ
as to their likelihood of feeling annoyed as a consequence.

As in the previous chapter, three-stage statistical analyses assessed which of the proposed individual differences influenced reports of annoyance by the elderly. After the stage three multiple
regression analysis, five individual variables had significant direct effects (table 9.2). Old people more likely to be annoyed had
a weaker urban environment disposition, rated their health more
poorly, reported fewer hearing difficulties, and had lived longer

Table 9.2. Multiple Regression Analysis of Individual Variables
Underlying Feelings Toward Neighbors' Care of Their Properties

Independent Variable Categories	Annoyed Because Neighbors Neglect Properties (beta values)	
Personality		
Urbanism environment disposition	−.171***	
Demographic		
Separated-divorced (Yes = 1, No = 0)	− .035	(−.145)
Widowed (Yes = 1, No = 0)	−.141**	(−.284)
Never married (Yes = 1, No = 0)	.074	(.268)
Socioeconomic Status		
Total household income	.051	
Stage in Life		
Self-rated health	.104*	
Self-rated hearing difficulties	−.105*	
Duration in Residence	.126*	
Tenure Status (Own = 1, Rent = 0)	.047	(.096)
R^2	.106	
F	4.856***	
df	9/368	

NOTE: Unstandardized partial regression coefficients of dummy variables are shown in parentheses.
***$p < .001$ **$p < .01$ *$p < .05$

in their present dwelling. Widowed elderly were less likely than married elderly to be annoyed. Unexpectedly, several individual variables did not influence the likelihood of annoyance reports: race, socioeconomic status, activity behavior, tenure status, and psychological well-being.

A possible explanation for the insignificance of race illustrates the interweaving of objective and perceptual antecedents of environmental experience. Blacks, as confirmed earlier (chapter 3), were more likely to live in Evanston neighborhoods that had objectively poorer housing. From a situationist perspective, one would expect elderly blacks to be more annoyed with their neighbors' housing neglect than elderly whites living in better quality neighborhoods. The sign of the race-annoyance simple correlational relationship (not shown here) supports this contention, but the coefficient is small and insignificant. However, there is also a rationale for predicting that black elderly would be less likely than white elderly to identify their neighbors' properties as "neglected." On the average, blacks in contrast with whites are predicted to have lower housing quality expectations, less stringent standards of comparison, and to have adapted more fully to housing deficiencies. Consequently, black elderly might be less likely in the first place to associate neglect with their neighborhood housing, and, if they do, feelings of annoyance may be less likely.

The individual variables *with* significant effects were consistent only in part with our theoretical expectations. It was predictable that a stronger urban environment disposition would be less likely to lead to annoyance. Old people oriented to urban living are less likely to judge a building as neglected for the same reasons given to explain the comparable designations of black elderly. That is, urban dwellers are more likely to expect, tolerate, and adapt to poorer quality housing. Even if a judgment of neglect is made, an urban-oriented individual may not be as easily annoyed as a person less positively disposed toward urban living.

The finding that widows were less annoyed than married people may be explained by the fact that a physically more attractive urbanized environment is probably a less salient need for widows. Rather, the consequences of their social environmental transactions have greater importance. One manifestation may be that widows pay less attention to the quality of their neighborhood housing and therefore are less likely to identify it as being neglected.

It was predictable that persons who rated their health as poorer should be more annoyed. The relationship suggests that personal vulnerability and incompetence makes an old person more susceptible to unpleasant environmental outcomes. For elderly persons in poor health, who already feel less in control of their lives, the perceived neglect of nearby housing serves as a further reminder of a material world that is beyond their control. Thus, the perceived ills of urban living merely reinforce an already existing personal malaise.

In direct contrast, persons with hearing difficulties were annoyed less frequently, but for no obvious reason. It was also unexpected that longer residential occupancy would lead to more frequent annoyance, given the usually positive relationship between length of occupancy and residential satisfaction (see chapter 7). These reports of annoyance may be due to longtime elderly occupants having a greater pride in, attachment to, and future concern for the buildings in their neighborhoods. Because of this greater emotional and material investment, longtime residents may be more attentive to and vigilant of violations of what are believed to be accepted standards of neighborhood quality.[2]

Uncomfortable or Unpleasant Dwelling Experiences

The unpleasant or uncomfortable experiences of daily living may have little to do with the occupancy of an urban setting. Instead, the source of old people's discomforts may emanate from transactions within their own dwellings. Both academic researchers and planning professionals have expressed concern over the potentially dangerous, stressful, or nonfacilitative aspects of an old person's dwelling environment. Various design recommendations have been suggested to reduce the likelihood of these consequences (see Lawton 1975; Kassabaum 1962a, 1962b, 1962c; Musson and Heusinkveld 1963; and Madge 1963). Some of these are highlighted below in order to illustrate the potential impact that the dwelling's physical environment has on an older person's well-being.

Many of the design recommendations attempted to compensate for the sensory, perceptual, and mobility impairments that accompany old age (Pastalan 1977). High on the list of priorities were design changes that improved the dwelling's physical safety so as to reduce the probability of home accidents. For example, the risk of danger from falls can be reduced by avoiding the installation of slippery materials and finishes, especially in stairway areas, and by providing railings and grab bars in locations such as bathrooms where falls are likely to occur. The risk of danger from scalds or burns can be minimized by improved kitchen design. Injuries from fire and smoke can be lessened if units are constructed with fire-resistant materials, automatic sprinkler systems, and effective alarm systems.

Other design recommendations were intended to improve the comfort of the dwelling. Because old persons are particularly sensitive to overheating and underheating and to drafts, they should be able to personally regulate the temperature controls in all their rooms. The decline of vision in old age, particularly the reduction of light admitted to the eye, may be compensated for by careful placement of the dwelling's windows. Window location also influences the capability of old persons to observe outside street activities, which is particularly important if they are homebound. Although elderly persons generally require a smaller amount of living space than larger, younger families, the size of the dwelling unit ideally should not constitute a radical departure from earlier occupied environments. The unit should be sufficiently large to entertain friends, to display and store valued possessions and furniture, and perhaps even to accommodate visits from children.

Some design recommendations were meant to facilitate old people's usual activities in the home. Byerts and Conway identified three major types of architectural barriers to be eliminated: "those which prevent the old person from passing easily from one (dwelling) area to another, those that keep him from orienting himself to his surroundings, and those that prevent him from using the equipment in his dwelling safely and easily" (1972:22). For example, doors in the dwelling should be wide enough to accommodate wheelchairs; control devices should be easily identifiable, reachable, and easy to manipulate; doors and windows should open easily, without necessitating considerable physical strength; and the number of right-angle turns in a dwelling unit should be minimized because the need to change directions when walking makes some old persons more susceptible to falls.

Although recommendations such as the above represent thoughtful proposals, few studies have systematically investigated how different dwelling (noninstitutional) design features influence the experiences of old people. Carp's findings in a San Antonio public housing project showed how the best of design intentions can fail:

> Low clothes rods (to reduce stretching) drooped clothes on the floor. High refrigerators (to eliminate stooping) were difficult to see into and messy to defrost. Back control panel stoves seemed less safe for old people (than children's safety) because of their poor vision and unsteadiness. (1965:153)

Other recommendations to improve the quality of dwelling experiences focused on nondesign solutions. Often, everyday physical discomforts can be alleviated by the presence of knowledgeable and sympathetic staff. In this regard, a Canadian study (Audain and Huttman 1973) reported that elderly persons more positively evaluated their public housing projects if they perceived their building managerial personnel as helpful.

In this study, several experiences involving transactions with the dwelling's built and natural environment were identified as items in the statistical dimension, "discomforts in dwelling" (factor 13), in the factor analyzed experiential environment (table 4.1). Six other analyzed experiences differentiated between the dwelling transactions of owners and renters (table 9.3).

Simple Empirical Patterns

Only a very small percentage of old people experienced unpleasant or stressful outcomes as a result of their transactions (of the past few months) with the built and natural aspects of their dwellings (table 9.3). About 8 percent of the elderly felt bothered relatively frequently because of their household appliances breaking down; as many as 15 percent of the elderly found that at least some of the time their dwelling's temperature was too hot in summer or too cold in the winter or autumn; and 9 percent of the elderly reported that the buildings they occupied appeared unattractive from the outside. The question yielding the most frequent negative responses concerned the appropriateness of the present

Table 9.3. Likelihood of Uncomfortable or Unpleasant Experiences in the Dwelling Environment

	Never 1	Only once or twice 2	A few times 3	Many times 4	Total	Mean	N
Annoyed because appliances have broken down	79%	14	6	2	100%	1.30	400

	Never 1	Only Occasionally 2	Some of the time 3	Most of the time 4	Total	Mean	N
Felt dwelling was too hot in summer	70%	16	11	4	100%	1.48	399
Felt dwelling was too cold in winter or autumn	78%	10	9	3	100%	1.37	399

	Very attractive 1	Somewhat attractive 2	Somewhat unattractive 3	Very unattractive 4	Total	Mean	N
Attractiveness of building	54%	38	8	1	100%	1.54	399

	Too big 1	Just about right 2	Too small 3		Total	Mean	N
Perceived dwelling size[a]	16%	78	6		100%	1.89	400

	Only Occasionally 1	Some of the time 2	Most of the time 3	All the time 4	Total	Mean	N
How clean, good repair is building[b]	4%	7	10	79	100%	1.36	162
Helpfulness of janitor[b]	7%	6	15	72	100%	3.51	163

	Never 1	Only once or twice 2	A few times 3	Many times 4	Total	Mean	N
Bothered by insects or rodents[b]	75%	10	9	6	100%	1.46	164
Caring for home too expensive[c]	47%	15	21	18	100%	2.10	231
Caring for home too much time[c]	69%	7	13	10	100%	1.65	231
Caring for home too tiring[c]	59%	7	20	14	100%	1.89	231

[a] In empirical analysis, "perceived dwelling size" was measured by two dummy variables with "just about right" as reference category.
[b] Responses from renters only.
[c] Responses from owners only.

dwelling unit size. Almost one-quarter of the elderly believed their dwelling units were either too large (16 percent) or too small (8 percent). Old people who reported that their dwellings were too big had also occupied them for a longer time (Pearson $r = .17$). These findings were consistent with other evidence that old people often do not leave the houses or larger apartments they moved into earlier in their lives when their families were larger and their space needs greater.

A consideration of whether homeowners or renters would be more likely to have the above experiences produced some predictable findings. Homeowners were more likely to report that their houses were too big; renters more likely to report that their dwellings were too small. Homeowners were considerably more likely to perceive their buildings (houses) as attractive from the outside. Homeowners were also less likely to find their dwellings too cold in the winter. Homeowners were not significantly more likely to be annoyed about broken down appliances.

Elderly homeowner and renter groups were each asked a different set of questions pertaining to their specific tenure arrangements. Those asked of renters did not indicate a high incidence of unpleasant or dissatisfying outcomes. Only 11 percent of the elderly renters believed that their apartment buildings were not kept clean or in good repair most or all of the time; 15 percent of the renters were bothered by insects or rodents at least a few times in the previous months; and 13 percent felt that the janitor of their building was *not* personally helpful most or all of the time.[3]

Relatively small percentages of elderly homeowners had unpleasant dwelling experiences. During the previous year, 18 percent very frequently felt that caring for their home was too expensive; 10 percent very frequently felt that caring for their home took too much time; and 14 percent very frequently felt that caring for their home was too tiring. However, these percentages may underestimate the occurrence of negative outcomes. The respective percentages of homeowners who reported having these problems more than incidentally (that is, more than once or twice in the past year) were 39, 23, and 34 percent.

As might be expected, these latter three experiences did not occur independently of each other. Old homeowners who felt that caring for their homes was too expensive also were likely to feel that caring for their homes took too much time (Pearson $r = .36$) and was too tiring (Pearson $r = .36$). Old homeowners who found caring for their dwellings took too much time also were very likely to find it a fatiguing experience (Pearson $r = .60$). Further insight into the origins of these experiences was provided by an open-ended question about the problems or difficulties encountered when taking care of a home. The four most frequently mentioned problems included heavy chores, home financial difficulties, doing routine cleaning, and difficulty finding professional workers. Less frequently mentioned problems included the great expense of hired help, house maintenance, and difficulty in using the house (e.g., climbing stairs, opening windows).

Environmental Experiences Associated with Stressful Homeownership Experiences

It appears reasonable to expect that old homeowners who report having overall difficulties caring for their dwellings also would have other types of unpleasant experiences. To examine this question, a selected set of natural, built, urbanized, and social welfare experiences were correlated with each of the three homeownership experiences (table 9.4, bottom).

Those elderly people who were more likely to feel that caring for their homes was too tiring also were more likely to be annoyed by dirt and soot on their windows and by their appliances breaking down; they were more likely to feel their houses were too hot in the summer and too cold in the winter or autumn; and they felt their houses were too big. The fatigue from caring for their houses was also manifested in their out-of-dwelling experiences: they were more likely to get tired going to places; they had difficulty getting transportation to places in their community; they were less likely to go to places that were not within walking distance; they were more dissatisfied with how near their dwellings were to community services; they were more likely to need the

Table 9.4. Selected Individual Variables and Environmental Experiences Associated with Stressful Homeownership Experiences (Pearson r's)

| | Caring for Home | | |
Individual Differences	Too expensive	Too much time	Too tiring
Socioeconomic Status			
Total household income	−.250***	.067	−.185**
Level of education	−.057	.159**	−.008
Impact of housing expense	.424***	.112*	.234***
Concern about enough money	.253***	.089	.064
Money situation compared to 2 years ago	.278***	.128*	.176**
Money situation compared to 10 years ago	.174**	.102	.133*
Enough money for things	−.273***	−.050	−.076
Stage in Life			
Self-rated health	.215***	.158**	.253***
Self-rated hearing difficulties	−.067	.005	.031
Self-rated seeing difficulties	.132*	.161**	.121*
Functional health	.139*	.108	.140*
Self-rated change in functional health	.124*	.104	.160**
Had serious illness (Yes = 1, No = 0)	.047	.141*	.155**
Had minor illness (Yes = 1, No = 0)	.013	.013	.022
Employed (Yes = 1, No = 0)	.106*	.043	−.025
Force to retire (Yes = 1, No = 0)	.019	.009	.149*
Environmental Experiences			
Annoyed by dirt and soot on windows	.207***	.131*	.221***
Annoyed because appliances have broken down	.111*	.146*	.129*
Felt dwelling was too hot in summer	.103	.224***	.169**
Felt dwelling was too cold in winter or autumn	.250***	.203***	.170**
Attractiveness of building	.178**	.051	.049
Felt dwelling size too small	.089	−.061	−.058
Felt dwelling size too big	.121*	.297***	.256***
Tired just getting to places in community	.152*	.244***	.266***
Difficulty getting transportation to places	.150*	.165**	.121*
Didn't go places not within walking distance	.136*	.260***	.251***
Satisfaction with dwelling's nearness to community places	−.131*	−.172**	−.134*
Number of basic services needed now	.167**	.067	.125*
Frequency food or drug items home-delivered	.104	.113*	.082
Had good time in community	−.059	−.069	−.117*
Satisfaction with dwelling you live in	−.201***	−.177**	−.097
Proud to live in dwelling	−.132*	−.019	.031
Thought about good dwelling memories	−.120*	.001	.047

***p < .001   **p < .01   *p < .05

most basic of human services (an issue addressed below); and they were less likely to have a good time in their community. The two other stressful homeownership experiences were similarly associated with unfavorable environmental transactions. From this simple analysis, the homeownership experience emerges as a mirror reflection of a large and diverse set of everyday environmental experiences. When maintaining a home is reported to be expensive, tiresome, and time consuming, it is also more likely that an old person's overall experiential environment is dominated by transactions yielding disagreeable outcomes or effects.

An analysis also ascertained the relationship of these stressful homeownership experiences to old people's territorial experiences—dwelling satisfaction, pride, and good memories (table 9.4, bottom). Only the burdensome financial expense of home care was persistently associated with the reduced likelihood of satisfaction, pride, and good memories. In contrast, the fatiguing experience of homeownership was unrelated to all three territorial experiences, and the time-consuming nature of homeownership was significantly related only to dwelling dissatisfaction. Apparently the fatiguing and time-consuming aspects of homeownership are not by themselves sufficient to negatively influence the more deep-seated feeling of dwelling pride or the recalling of good dwelling memories. Although the house must be taken care of at a slower pace, the overall experience of homeownership is not severely dampened. However, it becomes more difficult for old people to feel as satisfied with their dwellings when they become too expensive to care for. Because such financial difficulties may be linked to their own incompetence, dwelling pride also suffers. Finally, when suffering from this financial burden, old people are apparently less motivated to recall good dwelling experiences.

Individual Variables Underlying Stressful Homeownership Experiences

It is expected that individual variables that indicate low competence levels in old people would be the most strongly related to

stressful homeownership experiences. To examine this relationship, each of the proposed individual variables were correlated with
each of the three homeownership experiences.

None of the personality traits were significantly related, with
one exception. Old people feeling in greater control of their lives
(perceived internal locus of control) were less likely to report that
caring for their homes was too tiring. A consideration of demographic, racial, ethnic, and religious individual variables revealed
that only race had significant associations. Whites were less likely
than blacks to feel that caring for their homes was either too expensive or too time consuming. Activity and residential behavior
patterns were not related to any of the three homeownership experiences.

The individual variables most strongly related to the three
homeownership experiences were those in the socioeconomic and
stage-in-life categories (table 9.4). When selected variables in these
two categories, along with the individual variables, perceived locus of control and race, were simultaneously controlled for in a
multiple regression analysis, the latter two variables lost their
statistical significance. However, the relatively strong and significant effects of the socioeconomic and stage-in-life individual
variables persisted. Lower income and education levels, perceived money problems, and poor functional and self-rated health—
all indicative of lower levels of competence—were associated with
all three of the stressful homeownership experiences. More specifically, *subjective* individual variables such as self-rated health and
a sufficient money supply often had stronger associations than *objective* individual variables such as functional health and reported
income.

The conclusion that poor health can contribute to the financial
stress of homeownership deserves elaboration. It can be suggested that poor health prevents old people from personally taking care of their dwellings, resulting in greater dependence on paid
personnel. Thus the threat or reality of increased housing costs
becomes a consequence of reduced physical competence (Struyk
and Soldo 1980:75–94). Similar reasoning suggests that caring for

a home is likely to be more tiring for old people who cannot afford to hire help.

Although it may be spurious, one statistical relationship in table 9.4 must be interpreted differently from the others. People who felt that caring for their homes took too much time were also better educated, possibly because they valued their time differently than less educated elderly. That is, they were more likely to feel that taking care of their homes deprived them of time to engage in other more rewarding activities.

Satisfaction with a Community's Built and Social Welfare Environment

The routinized life-style of most old people regularly involves them in transactions with many different community facilities (stores, shops, banks, and restaurants) and municipal and social services. These address a wide ranging set of goals and needs, but infrequently have a dramatic impact on old people's physical and emotional well-being. Exceptions do exist, however, such as when a utility company turns off a dwelling's heat supply because the elderly occupant's bill is in arrears or when a restaurant conveniently located and regularly patronized by old people closes down.

The positive impact of these facilities and services may derive less from the benefits obtained from their actual use than from old people's knowledge that they are available and locationally and economically accessible in time of need. Peace of mind and a sense of security can result if old people have confidence that a service or store is available, even if they have no immediate plans to use it. Sometimes the perceived availability of these services and stores change not because of their own changing properties, but because the attributes and behaviors of old people change. For example, the sudden inability to drive a car and the resulting reliance on walking or transit as primary modes of transportation may make a once accessible facility difficult to reach.

Only a few experiences constructed for this study fell into this category, the responses to which are summarized in table 9.5. The

Table 9.5. Likelihood of Positive Experiences in the Community Built and Social Welfare Environment

	Completely Dissatisfied						Completely Satisfied			
	1	2	3	4	5	6	7	Total	Mean	N
Community services	1%	2	2	12	14	19	50	100%	5.91	399
Stores and shopping	3%	2	5	11	21	21	38	100%	5.58	400
Dwelling's nearness to community places	2%	1	2	11	11	20	54	100%	6.02	400

	Never	Only once or twice	A few times	Many times	Total	Mean	N
	1	2	3	4			
Annoyed because of higher grocery costs where shop	63%	9	10	19	100%	1.85	400
Annoyed because no place to rest while shopping	84%	4	4	8	100%	1.37	400

first three experiences clustered in the first dimension of the factor analyzed experiential environment (table 4.1).

Simple Empirical Patterns

The majority of old people were completely satisfied with the services in their community and their dwelling's nearness to the community places they wished to visit. Old people were somewhat less satisfied with the stores and shopping facilities found in the community. Almost 20 percent of Evanston's elderly population were frequently annoyed (in past few months) because they thought the prices were higher where they shopped; and 8 percent of the elderly were frequently annoyed (in past few months) because there was no place to rest while shopping.

Individual Variables Underlying Satisfaction with Stores and Shopping in Community

A three-stage statistical analysis (see chapter 8) investigated which individual variables influenced old people's satisfaction with their community's stores and shopping. Very few of the proposed individual variables were significantly related. In the final multiple regression solution, only four individual variables had significant direct effects (at .05 level or less). Old people more satisfied with the stores and shopping in their community had a stronger urbanism environment disposition, a lower household income, a smaller activity space, and a higher level of lifesatisfaction.

An entirely adequate explanation is not available for the positive effect a stronger urban environment disposition had on store satisfaction. Urban-oriented old people are perhaps more accepting of or accommodating to the uneven quality of goods and services, crowds, and higher noise and traffic levels found in many urban shopping districts.

Earlier interpretations of why higher income levels led to lower satisfaction levels should also apply here (chapters 6 and 8). In brief, old people with higher incomes may be less likely to consider the local community's shopping opportunities as central to their shopping needs and they may not associate as many benefits or rewards with local shopping. Because their higher incomes give them greater ability (in terms of both transportation flexibility and purchasing power) to shop elsewhere, they are *more* likely to compare the community's facilities unfavorably with those found *outside* the community. More generally, the (shopping and store) expectations of the higher income elderly are greater, increasing the probability that the actual benefits of community shopping will fall short of their expectations. The finding that old people with smaller activity spaces are more satisfied with their community's stores and facilities supports this interpretation. This implies that old people with more restricted activity spaces depend more heavily on local environmental opportunities—including shopping and stores—and that these represent a source of predictable benefits. On the other hand, old people with larger activity spaces simply have more shopping alternatives; they can afford to be more critical of shopping facilities in their immediate community because they confront relatively few constraints in utilizing alternatives located farther away.

The relationship observed between life satisfaction and store satisfaction is also consistent with earlier theorizing (see chapter 6). The old person more satisfied with his life, who feels a sense of congruence with his environment, is likely to look more favorably on his everyday routinized community transactions.[4]

The findings provide little evidence that the stage-in-life characteristics of old people influence their store satisfaction. Neither health nor employment status was significantly related to store satisfaction. Only the significant effects of an individual's activity space size may be a function of stage in life to the extent that a smaller activity space reflects psychological disengagement or functional impairment.

The Concern and Worry about Crime

There is no shortage of documentation of old people's fear of crime and its identification as an important problem (Louis Harris and Associates 1975).[5] However, the accuracy of the data that describe the actual victimization rates is frequently called into question. The victimization rates of elderly people are usually higher when they are based on household surveys rather than on police reports. Irrespective of the data source, the victimization rates of the U.S. elderly population are lower than for younger groups. However, for certain types of crimes such as personal larceny and robbery which involve bodily contact as in purse or wallet snatching, the victimization rate of the old is similar to or somewhat higher than that of younger populations. These national findings may disagree sharply with those from local analyses that often report much higher elderly victimization rates.

These data differences are accounted for in various ways. Elderly victimization rates are higher in the inner city or in larger communities where crime rates are generally higher (Malinchak and Wright 1978; Smith 1979; Goldsmith and Goldsmith 1976). Certain local areas are occupied by elderly persons who are greater crime risks because of their greater real or perceived vulnerability. Various studies have considered the characteristics of old people that make them more vulnerable as crime victims. A Kan-

sas City study (Midwest Research Institute 1977) found that elderly victims are more likely to be widows living alone and to be
black rather than white. Other studies confirmed that elderly victims are more likely to be physically vulnerable, poor, black, and
female (Conklin 1972; Brostoff, Brown, and Butler 1972). Some
police departments underestimate crime against the elderly because their reports do not include the age of the victim or because
the elderly victims do not report the crimes (Malinchak and Wright
1978). An important reason for the often lower than expected rate
of crime against the elderly is frequently missed. Because old people have lower activity levels than the young, they are on the average less exposed to street crimes.[6] The greater likelihood of old
people being victimized in or near their homes (Smith 1979; Antunes et al. 1977) may similarly reflect their usually smaller activity spaces.

What is not in debate is that both the threat and the reality of
criminal victimization create serious physical and emotional
stresses for many old people. Those who have such fears may experience considerable anxiety even when routinely carrying out
their neighborhood and community activities. Moreover, other
findings from the Evanston study indicate that such fear may lead
to less frequent and more locationally restricted activity behavior, especially after dark.

Old people who are victims of crime often experience multiple
difficulties. Their money losses are often small in absolute terms,
but large relative to their limited personal finances. Even more
devastating may be the damage inflicted on their physical and
psychological well-being. Old people are more likely than younger
persons to sustain serious physical injuries and to be left with an
increased sense of vulnerability, a painful reminder of their advanced age.

In this study, old people were asked to report several affective
and behavioral outcomes of their crime experiences (table 9.6). The
first three of these experiences originally grouped together in the
third dimension of the factor analyzed experiential environment
described in chapter 4. These indicated how often old people experienced restriction, fear, anxiety, and a sense of helplessness as

Table 9.6. Likelihood of Fear, Restriction, and Insecurity from "Crime" Experiences in Urbanized Environment

	Never 1	Some of the time 2	Most of the time 3	All the time 4	Total	Mean	N
Afraid to go out at night because of crime	39%	17	11	33	100%	2.38	400

	Never 1	Only occasionally 2	Some of the time 3	Most of the time 4	Total	Mean	N
Worry about being attacked, robbed while walking	54%	16	12	18	100%	1.95	399

	Never 1	Only once or twice 2	A few times 3	Many times 4	Total	Mean	N
Concerned that thief might break into home	50%	16	16	19	100%	2.03	400

	No 0	Yes 1	Total	Mean	N
Attacked while walking past year	98%	2	100%	0.02	400
Dwelling burglarized or vandalized	91%	9	100%	0.09	400
Lost or stolen item past year	90%	10	100%	0.10	400

a result of crime. The last three experiences, comprising behavioral responses, indicated whether old people were actually crime victims.

Simple Empirical Patterns

Even a full acquaintance with other investigations was not sufficient preparation for the relatively high percentages of Evanston's elderly population who felt threatened by the prospects of being crime victims. About 61 percent admitted that they were afraid to go out at night at least some of the time because of the threat of crime; 30 percent were worried at least some of the time about being attacked or robbed while walking; and 35 percent reported that in the past few months they had been relatively frequently concerned that a thief might break into their home. Simple correlational analyses also confirmed the substantial associations among these experiences. That is, old people who feared going out at night because of crime also worried more frequently about being attacked and robbed while walking at any time.

The behavioral response distributions confirm the large gap that exists between the threat and the actuality of crime experiences. Only 2 percent of Evanston's elderly population were attacked while walking in the previous year; only 9 percent had their home robbed; and 10 percent had an item lost or stolen.

The small number of elderly persons actually victimized prevented any definitive conclusions about the relationship between affective and behavioral responses to crime. However, simple correlational and contingency table analyses showed that greater fear and worry about crime were significantly associated with actual crime episodes.

Individual Variables Underlying the Fear of Crime

Although the likelihood of being afraid of crime is an obvious reflection of environmental conditions and one's actual behavioral encounters with crime, it also is influenced by how crime is interpreted or perceived by old people. The fact that individual variation does exist is supported by Clemente and Kleiman's (1976) findings that fear of crime was greater among aged women than aged men, greater among elderly blacks than elderly whites, and greater among the poor than wealthy aged.

The following statistical relationships were found when a comparable set of individual variables were correlated with each of the three affective crime experiences (table 9.7).

Old people more likely to be afraid of going out at night felt less in control of their lives, were women, had lower income and educational levels, presently had poorer functional health, had recent declines in their functional health, and were not employed.

Table 9.7. Simple Individual Correlates of Fear of Crime (Pearson r's)

	Afraid to go out at night, crime	Worry about attack while walking	Concern about home break-in
Urbanism environment disposition	−.025	−.080	−.139**
Locus of control	−.122**	−.104*	−.077
Males (Yes = 1, No = 0)	−.303***	−.087*	.084
White (Yes = 1, No = 0)	−.030	−.103*	−.175***
Separated-divorced (Yes = 1, No = 0)	−.105*	−.034	−.006
Widowed (Yes = 1, No = 0)	.221***	.015	−.167***
Never married (Yes = 1, No = 0)	.034	−.016	.001
Total household income	−.233***	−.107*	.021
Level of education	−.187***	−.217***	−.061
Impact of housing expenses	.093	.172***	.128**
Concern about enough money	.039	.185***	.217***
Self-rated health	.089	.149***	.103*
Functional health	.085*	−.012	.026
Self-rated change in functional health	.174***	−.021	−.015
Employed (Yes = 1, No = 0)	−.230***	−.062	.103*

***p<.001   **p<.01   *p<.05

Widows were more likely than married elderly to be afraid to go out, but separated-divorced old people were less afraid than married people.[7] The individual variables not significantly correlated (at .05 level), but having coefficients with signs in the predictable direction were also revealing. Fear was more likely to be experienced by old people who were black, had a weaker urbanism environment disposition, lower subjective economic status, and a lower subjective health status.

Old people more likely to be worried about being attacked while walking felt less in control of their lives, were women, were black, had lower income and education levels, had to draw on their savings or cut expenses (impact of housing expenses), had money concerns, and rated their health as poorer.

Old people more concerned about their home being broken into had a weaker urban environment disposition, were black, had to draw on their savings or cut expenses, had money concerns, rated their health as poorer, and were employed. Widowed elderly were less likely than married elderly to be concerned about a home break-in.

Two general conclusions follow from these findings. First, crime is considered a source of stress or a barrier to activity by old people who are physically, socially, or psychologically more vulnerable, insecure, or incompetent. The elderly residents more concerned about being attacked while walking or about having their home broken into were financially poorer, perceived themselves as having money difficulties, and rated their health as poorer. The elderly residents who feared going out at night because of crime believed they had less control over their lives and they had less education and lower incomes.

Second, most of the individual variables were significantly related to only one or two of the crime experiences, but in no instances to all three. For example, whites were less likely than blacks to worry about being attacked while walking or to fear a home break-in, but whites and blacks did not differ significantly as to their fear about going out at night. Sometimes the individual variable relationships were not even in the same direction. For example, nonemployed elderly were more likely than employed elderly to be afraid of going out at night, but less likely to be concerned about a home break-in.

One explanation for these latter findings is that each of the crime experiences, while generating fear, also has consequences that impinged differently on old persons, depending on their distinctive needs. The consequences of the first experience—afraid to go out at night—included restrictions on old people who wanted to pursue (but could not) out-of-dwelling activities; the second experience—worry about being attacked while walking—resulted in stress and anxiety for old people who depended on walking as their primary mode of transportation; and the third experience—concern about home break-in—resulted in a possible violation of old people's feelings of territorial control or integrity and a threat to their belief that their homes are defensible against criminal invasions (Newman 1973).

The fact that different interpretations can be given for the effects of the same individual variable is well illustrated by the finding that widows were more likely than married elderly to be afraid of going out at night because of crime, but less fearful than married elderly of a home break-in. The widowed elderly population's greater fear of going out at night may be explained by the high proportion of widows who are women. They are more likely than elderly men to feel physically vulnerable to street crimes, especially when it is dark. Women, moreover, are more dependent on walking, which, although reasonably safe during the day, is virtually ruled out as a form of transportation at night. However, a different interpretation is required for the widowed elderly population's weaker concern about a home break-in. Widowed elderly are, in fact, more likely than married elderly to live alone, and although they are apparently more vulnerable, they also need concern themselves only about their own safety and not the safety of their spouses. In old age, the dependency of one spouse on the other and the salience of their interpersonal relationships are sufficiently strong so as to make each feel particularly threatened over the prospect of the other's loss or injury. By this reasoning, the possibility of a home invasion is particularly ominous to a married person. This explanation, however speculative, does emphasize the need to recognize the varied consequences old people may attribute to crime experiences and the possibility that very different types of individual influences are responsible.

Studies that investigated the individual correlates of crime experiences have often focused on simple correlational relationships. The danger always exists that ensuing generalizations are based on spurious relationships. To help reduce this possibility, multiple regression analyses assessed how the correlated individual variables simultaneously influenced each of the three affective experiences of crime. The findings from the analysis of the experience "fear of going out at night" is reported below.

Three individual variables had statistically significant direct effects (table 9.9). Women rather than men, the nonemployed rather than the employed, and the less educated were more likely to be afraid of going out at night because of crime. Separated-divorced old people were less likely and widowed elderly were more likely than married old people to be afraid. (These latter two individual variables were just short of being significant, but had relatively large unstandardized regression coefficients.) The previously correlated individual variables, perceived locus of control, household income, and change in functional health, lost their significance in the multivariate analysis.

The greater fear of elderly women (and widows) is usually interpreted as evidence of their self-perceptions (whether or not correct) as physically more frail and vulnerable or of their belief that criminals perceive them in this way. In combination with their previously mentioned transportation disadvantages, sex thereby differentiates elderly persons according to their feelings of competence.

It is not entirely clear why less educated elderly had a greater fear of crime. The possibility cannot be ruled out that less educated elderly live in lower income neighborhoods that by most objective standards are higher crime-risk environments. Alternatively, irrespective of present residence, the fears of the less educated old person may be based on memories of residential experiences in places that were not secure from crime. Consequently, however free from crime the present residence might be, these old persons are unable to erase a lifetime of fearful memories. Other possible interpretations emerged when examining the individual variables that lost their significance while controlling for education level in the multiple regression analysis. Specifically, the less educated elderly felt less in control of their lives (Pearson $r = .24$) and were likely to have smaller incomes (Pearson $r = .24$). These relationships suggest that feelings of psychological and economic vulnerability may also underlie the less educated person's fear of crime.

A similar interpretation may explain why employed old people were less afraid to go out at night. They may feel more competent because they are active members of society (their labor force status). Alternatively, their life-styles are more likely to involve activities at night (as indicated by other empirical analyses of this study) to fulfill demands that a daytime work schedule prevent. Engaged in such nighttime activity throughout their adult lives, the employed elderly have adapted or have become desensitized to the threat of crime at night long ago. Thus they are less likely to associate fear or danger with nighttime environmental transactions because these have always been an essential part of their usual activity regime.

It is more difficult to explain why separated-divorced old people were less fearful than married persons. In fact, other empirical findings of this study indicated that separated-divorced elderly persons were less competent in several ways. They were less likely than married old persons to feel in control of their lives; they had lower incomes and greater concerns about money; and they were more likely to have lived a short time in their dwellings. In light of their apparently greater vulnerability, their less frequently reported fear of going out at night ran counter to theoretical expectations. One can only speculate that the divorced or separated elderly persons were accustomed to living more autonomously since the breakup of their marriages. Thus these persons were instilled with a "survivor's" spirit that dulled their fear of many environmental threats, including nighttime crime.

With one exception the four individual variables significantly influencing fear of crime were not a function of a person's stage in life. An individual's sex, marital (separated-divorced) status, and education level are characteristics that have exerted their influences throughout much of the person's adult life. Only an employed status, which necessitates a nighttime-oriented activity behavior pattern, is possibly stage in life related. However, even this interpretation must be qualified (as suggested earlier) in that the nonemployed status of women is usually a product not of old age but of an earlier chosen life-style.

Constraining Experiences in the Natural, Built, and Urbanized Environments

The everyday environment is often portrayed as insensitive to the needs of individuals who have grown old because it has the potential to restrict their behavior and life-styles. Harsh weather, inadequate transportation, difficult-to-cross traffic arteries, and multiple flights of stairs exemplify features that can discourage, impede, or constrain the elderly's environmental transactions

(Yeates 1979). Such objects and events are often referred to as *environmental barriers* and have a similar though somewhat broader connotation than the concept architectural barriers, introduced earlier to describe the restrictive aspects of the dwelling environment.

The depiction of an urban environment as constraining is reinforced by a parallel conception of old age as a period of decline— in human strength, agility, ambulatory abilities, and acuity and rapidity of perceptual and motor skills. In the face of such impairments, the old person's environmental transactions are more sensitive to potential obstacles or barriers. It will be recalled that the activity theorists maintained that the declining activity of old people was due in part to such external factors.

It is obviously incorrect to assume that all old people equally suffer from such bodily declines. However, it is just as erroneous to assume that environmental barriers uniformly exert their negative consequences on all old people, and that consensus exists as to which environmental properties are interpreted as constraining.

To examine these issues, old people were asked how frequently in the past few months they had experienced constraining consequences from their transactions with the natural, built, and urbanized objects or events in their residential environment (table 9.8). Most of these experiences were variously clustered in factors 3, 5, 9, and 11 of the factor analyzed experiential environment (table 4.1). The crime experience "afraid to go out at night because of crime" is also considered to be in this group.

These experiences differ from each other not only because they involve transactions with different categories of environmental objects and events but also because they have potentially different consequences. The consequences may be direct or immediate as in the postponement, prevention, or restriction of activity; alternatively, they may merely make the execution of environmental transactions emotionally or physically disagreeable. Such consequences may not actually prevent activities but they can discourage their likelihood (frequency) if only because they consume so much of an old person's physical or psychic energy. Feel-

Table 9.8. Likelihood of Constraining Experiences in the Urbanized, Built, and Natural Environments

	Never 1	Only Occasionally 2	Some of the time 3	Most of the time 4	Total	Mean	N
Trouble walking, sidewalks in bad condition	55%	14	21	11	100%	1.87	400
Tired just getting to places in community	72%	12	10	6	100%	1.49	398
Postpone plans because of bad weather	33%	27	22	18	100%	2.25	399
Bothered by snow and cold weather	29%	20	25	26	100%	2.47	400

	Never 1	Only once or twice 2	A few times 3	Many times 4	Total	Mean	N
Difficulty getting transportation to places in community	87%	3	6	5	100%	1.29	400
Nervous walking because of heavy traffic	94%	1	3	2	100%	1.14	400
Poor street lighting discourages activity	74%	3	7	16	100%	1.65	399

	No 0	Yes 1	Total	Mean	N
Didn't go places because not within walking distance	88%	12	100%	0.12	400

	Walking 1	Public transit, taxi, auto passenger 2	Auto Driver 3	Total	Mean	N
Type of transportation most frequently used	8%	43	50	100%	2.42	400

ings of fatigue, nervousness, or fear are examples of such consequences.

Another experience in this group is the "type of transportation most frequently used." Its consequences are assumed to be aligned along a "flexible-inflexible" behavior dimension. Automobile drivers are considered to have the most flexible and least constraining mode of transportation. A car is more fully under the person's control and unfavorable environmental conditions are less likely to impede destination access. In direct contrast, old people who depend on walking as their principal mode of transportation are limited by their own temporary or permanent frailties and by numerous environmental conditions (most obviously, distance) that can impede destination access. In between these two polar groups are old people who depend on others (transit drivers, other car drivers, taxis) to provide them with transportation. These modes usually provide more flexible and less constraining transportation mobility than walking, but in contrast to auto drivers old people who rely on them usually have less consistent control over their means of reaching their destinations.

Simple Empirical Patterns

Some of the experiences were more constraining than others. Notably, bad weather had a strong impact on community activities and resulted in 40 percent of the elderly population postponing their plans at least some of the time. Poor street lighting also more than incidentally discouraged the nighttime activity of 23 percent of the elderly population. Twelve percent of the elderly population had not recently gone someplace because the walking distance was too great. After or while completing certain environmental transactions, sizable percentages of elderly persons experienced difficulties. Thirty-three percent of the elderly population had trouble walking on sidewalks in bad condition at least some of the time; 18 percent experienced fatigue at least some of the time as a result of getting to places in their community; 51 percent were bothered by snow and cold weather at least some of the time; and 11 percent had relatively frequent difficulty getting transportation to places in their community. In contrast, only a very small percentage of elderly persons (5 percent) reported that heavy traffic conditions made them nervous at least more than incidentally when they walked. This small percentage was due, in considerable part, to the small percentage of old people (8 percent) who depended on walking as their principal mode of transportation to reach places in their community. About 50 percent of the elderly population used automobiles as their principal mode of transportation; the remainder of the elderly population (about 43 percent) were usually passengers in taxis, transit, or other autos.

Individual Variables Underlying Constraining Experiences

Three-stage statistical analyses (see chapter 8) assessed which individual characteristics influenced the likelihood of three of these constraining experiences (in addition to the already discussed "afraid to go out at night because of crime"). Two of the three experiences involved energy-consuming transactions with the built environment—"trouble walking because of bad sidewalks" and "tired just getting to places in community"—and the third involved transactions restricted by the natural environment—"postpone plans because of bad weather." The findings of the final multiple regression solutions are summarized in table 9.9.

Old people more likely to postpone their plans because of bad weather were less likely to be employed, felt less in control of their lives (perceived external locus of control), were more likely to report seeing difficulties and declining functional health.

Old people more likely to be tired just getting to places in their community reported that they felt in poorer health, had seeing difficulties, and declining functional health.

Old people more likely to have trouble walking because of bad sidewalks were more likely to be women, had to draw on their savings or cut back on other things (impact of housing expenses), and reported seeing difficulties.

Discussion of Findings

Personality. The observed relationship between an individual's perceived external locus of control and the postponement of plans

Table 9.9. Multiple Regression Analysis of Individual Variables Underlying Constraining Environmental Experiences

Independent Variable Categories	Beta Values			
	Afraid to go out at night, crime	Postpone plans, bad weather	Tired getting to places	Trouble walking, bad sidewalks
Personality				
Urbanism environment disposition		−.060		
Locus of control	−.063	−.111*	.042	−.087
Demographic				
Males (Yes=1, No=0)	−.240*** (−.648)		−.085 (−.151)	−.140** (−.317)
Separated-divorced (Yes=1, No=0)	−.095 (−.526)		−.044 (−.157)	
Widowed (Yes=1, No=0)	.078 (.207)		.050 (.087)	
Never married (Yes=1, No=0)	.027 (.129)		.083 (.259)	
Socioeconomic Status				
Level of education	−.111*			
Total household income	−.088	−.068	−.076	
Impact of housing expenses				.109*
Stage in Life				
Employed (Yes=1, No=0)	−.140** (−.380)	−.159** (−.362)		
Self-rated health		.078	.146**	
Self-rated seeing difficulties		.104*	.237***	.132**
Self-rated change in functional health	.022	.126*	.264***	.062
Psychological Well-Being				
Life satisfaction		−.006	−.030	−.064
How happy are you these days		−.061		
R²	.183	.163	.286	.102
F	9.137***	9.026***	14.635***	7.222***
df	9/368	9/368	10/366	6/381

NOTE: Unstandardized partial regression coefficients of dummy variables are shown in parentheses.
***p<.001 **p<.01 *p<.05

because of bad weather demonstrates the effects of psychological vulnerability or incompetence. The old person who feels in control of life is probably less sensitive to the vagaries of the environment and more confident of his own capabilities. For such a person, environmental or external influences are less likely to act as barriers. Old people who presently feel in control of their lives probably have been so disposed throughout most of their adult lives. On the other hand, it is possible that the persistent feeling of not being in control is recent in origin, acquired as a result of a series of age-related unsuccessful environmental transactions.

The locus of control measure was also significantly correlated with "trouble walking because of bad sidewalks," although it lost (just barely) its significance when the other individual variables were controlled for in the multiple regression analysis. (Old people with a perceived external locus of control had lower socioeconomic status and poorer health.)

Demographic, Racial, Ethnic, and Religious Characteristics. Most of the variables in this category were statistically unrelated to the three constraining experiences. However, women were more likely than men to have trouble walking on bad sidewalks. Other findings confirm that women are more likely than men to use walking as their major mode of transportation in the community. Because walking is a more salient need for old women, they are probably more likely to attend to, be aware of, and physically confront poor walking environments. Sex status and marital (widowed) status were also significantly correlated with "tired just getting to places in community," but they lost their significance after the other individual variables were controlled for in the multiple regression analysis. The greater fatique experienced by female elderly "getting to places" is also consistent with the above explanation.

Socioeconomic Status. Relatively strong and statistically significant simple correlational relationships existed between the socioeconomic status individual variables and each of the three constraining experiences. Although lower socioeconomic status increased the likelihood of constraining experiences, its influences largely disappeared after the other individual variables were controlled for in the multiple regression analysis. In this third statistical stage, only the likelihood of walking problems was significantly influenced by the subjective measure of socioeconomic status, "impact of housing expenses." The explanation of this relationship is similar to that given for the effects of sex status. Old people with greater money difficulties are more dependent on walking to reach their destinations or their transit vehicles. As more frequent users of sidewalks, low-income old people are more aware of and more likely to negotiate poor walking environments.

Stage in Life. Predictably, poor health status increased the likelihood of all three constraining experiences. The most influential variables described the old person's functional health or behavioral impairments rather than his perceptions or self-ratings of his health status. Thus it is what the old person can or cannot competently do rather than how he feels about his health that most influences his interpretation of environmental barriers.

Very different inferences were drawn from the finding that nonemployed elderly persons were more likely than employed elderly persons to postpone plans because of bad weather. The employed old person will not have as much free time as the nonemployed old person to accomplish his nonwork-related needs or as much flexibility as to when that free time is available. Confronted with this more scarce resource—time—the employed old person can less afford the luxury of postponing an activity because of bad weather, because needs will remain unsatisfied indefinitely. In contrast, the comparable nonwork-related needs of the nonemployed old person may be more readily shifted to another available time slot. This interpretation, if correct, illustrates how the salience and rewards associated with the timing of environmental transactions can contribute to their completion, even in the presence of objectively defined barriers, such as bad weather.

Psychological Well-Being. The decision to evaluate psychological well-being as an individual state underlying these constraining experiences is especially likely to invite criticism. After all, how does psychological well-being or morale influence fatigue, walking difficulties, and postponed plans? In response it can be argued that the old person who is unhappy or dissatisfied with his life will seek to prevent additional psychological or social assaults on his self. Environmental transactions that are expected to reinforce existing unhappiness or add new sources of grief are thereby avoided. Thus the old person may postpone plans identified with unpleasant consequences, may interpret many potential activities as "efforts" whose positive returns are insufficient in light of the energy that must be expended to carry them out, and may find fault with environments as a way to rationalize his less frequent transactions with them.

Relatively strong statistically significant simple correlational relationships (in the predicted directions) were found between the psychological well-being variables and all three constraining experiences. However, after controlling for the other individual variables in the multiple regression analyses, their direct effects disappeared.[8] Thus the proposed influence of psychological well-being was not verified empirically.

Residential Behavior and Activity Behavior. There is no theoretical basis for expecting that either length of residential occupancy or tenure status should influence the likelihood of these three constraining experiences. The activity behavior variables were found to be significantly correlated with these experiences. However, it was theorized that lower activity levels and smaller activity spaces were consequences rather than antecedents of environmental barriers.

Dependence on the Social Welfare Environment

Old people frequently identify independent living arrangements as a salient need or goal. As Carp emphasized:

> The most dreadful possibility to an old person is that of becoming a burden on others; the most desired personal attribute is

independence. Therefore, every environmental support to the capacity of independent living is directly fulfilling of the basic need
for autonomy. For example, bathroom handholds guard not only
against physical injury but also against dependence. (1976a:37)

Similarly, Cantor concluded:

Adulthood presumes the ability, skills, and competence to effectively control environment and determine the course of one's own
existence. The degree to which this is possible determines to a
considerable extent the individual's mental health and integrity
of personality. A sense of powerlessness is anathema to successful adulthood in industrialized societies. (1976:41)

These observations make clear that the maintenance of independent living arrangements is closely tied to the satisfaction of
needs such as autonomy, mastery, internal control, and individuality. The possibility that independent living arrangements will
have to be given up threatens to reverse a long period of continuous personal growth. Ever since infancy, the individual has
steadily acquired independence, responsibility, and competence.
Thus, to surrender independent living arrangements or to lose
control over an accustomed residential life-style is inconsistent with
lifelong patterns of need satisfaction.

Despite the tenacity with which old people cling to this independence, there may come a time when personal and family resources are insufficient to satisfy physical health and self-maintenance needs (Lawton 1970). Consequently, the continuation of
independent living arrangements is jeopardized unless some form
of outside support, resources, or assistance is supplied. The presence of such a weakened individual condition cannot always be
predicted by objective or behavioral indicators of need. The seeking out or acceptance of environmental resources from the organized social welfare environment is very much a personal decision. Although some degree of functional impairment is usually a
necessary condition, it is not sufficient to predict service needs.
Brody's observation, albeit in reference to institutional needs, rings
true:"Given similar physical, mental, and environmental situa-

tions, a fiercely independent individual may continue to live in the community well beyond the point at which institutional care is sought by his dependent, fearful neighbor" (1977:102–103).

In short, the admission of "dependence," except in extreme instances of individual vulnerability, depends not only on objectively verifiable cognitive and behavioral incompetencies but also on the old person's own assessment that "out of the ordinary" community services are required to cope successfully with present impairments. This admission necessarily depends on how the individual interprets the acceptance of assistance. Social services

Table 9.10. Percentage of Elderly Persons Responding They Now Need Basic Services (N = 400)

Special food service to bring hot meal to home	3
Emergency financial help to pay gas, electric bills	7
Counseling services to talk about personal problems	7
Special door-to-door transportation services	15
Home service for cleaning home, cooking meals	6
Groups that have persons visit at home for company	4

	Respondents Reporting									
	0	1	2	3	4	5	6	Total	Mean	N
Total number of basic services needed now	74%	16	7	1	2	—[a]	0	100%	0.42	400

[a] Less than .05%

from either government or religious organizations may be associated with the indigent and misfits of society. Use of such services may symbolize a loss of dignity or self-respect or a loss of autonomy, independence, and control (Blenckner, Bloom, and Nielsen 1971). In the final analysis, admission or acceptance of need will depend on the old person's willingness to trade off some perceived loss of status and autonomy so as to receive the resource supports of others and to realize an extended occupancy in relatively independent residential arrangements.

To measure old people's experiential dependency on the social welfare environment (see figure 4.2), they were questioned about their present needs for six different services that were available in the Evanston community (table 9.10).[9] These services were ear-

lier classified as addressing the needs of the moderately dependent elderly and defined as "alternatives" without which the
maintenance of relatively independent residential arrangements
would be more difficult and the threat of premature institutionalization would be greater (Golant and McCaslin 1979a, 1979b).

Simple Empirical Patterns and Individual Variables Underlying Service Need

Only a small percentage of Evanston's old population expressed
a need for services (table 9.10), a finding substantiated by many
other studies of relatively independent elderly populations. The
most frequently needed of the six services was special door-to-door
transportation (15 percent); the least frequently needed service was
home-delivered hot meals (3 percent).

A three-stage statistical analysis (see chapter 8) assessed which
individual characteristics influenced the number of services reported as needed. Initially, many of the proposed individual variables were significantly correlated with service need; however,
several lost their significance in the second- and third-stage multiple regression analyses. The correlational relationships of these
variables had revealed that a greater number of services were
needed by old people who felt less in control of their lives (perceived external locus of control), had poorer functional health, had
a decline in their functional health, had a major illness in the past
year, were recently forced to retire, were not employed, were less
satisfied or happy with their lives, and had lower activity levels.

In the final multiple regression analysis, only five individual
variables remained statistically significant (see table 9.11). Old
people reporting a greater need for services were black, drew on
their savings or cut expenses to pay for their housing (impact of
housing expenses), felt they did not have enough money, rated their
health as poorer, and had a smaller activity space.

A comparison of the correlation and regression findings led to
the following observations. First, after all variables were simultaneously controlled for, subjective rather than objective individ-

Table 9.11. Multiple Regression Analysis of Individual
Variables Underlying Present Need for Basic Services

Independent Variable Categories	Number of Basic Services Needed Now (beta values)
Personality	
Locus of control	−.080
Racial	
Whites (Yes = 1, No = 0)	−.179*** (−.406)
Socioeconomic Status	
Total household income	.001
Impact of housing expenses	.140**
Enough money for things	−.136**
Stage in Life	
Self-rated health	.160**
Self-rated seeing difficulties	.040
Psychological Well-Being	
Life satisfaction	.039
Activity Behavior	
Activity space size	−.124*
Level of activity	−.009
R^2	.226
F	10.856***
df	10/363

NOTE: Unstandardized partial regression coefficients of dummy variables are shown in parentheses.
***$p < .001$ **$p < .01$ *$p < .05$

ual variables (see chapter 5 and 6) usually influenced service need. For instance, self-rated health rather than functional health and subjective economic status (such as enough money for things) rather than actual income levels (total household income) were more likely to have significant and nonspurious direct effects. Second, the loss of significance of the perceived locus of control individual measure was due primarily to its sharing considerable variance with the socioeconomic status variables. Perceived internal locus of control was greater for elderly persons with higher socioeconomic status. Third, the loss of significance of the psychological well-being variables was due primarily to their sharing considerable variance with the health and socioeconomic status individual variables.

A consideration of the individual variables found to significantly influence service need leads to the following four conclusions.

First, and most obviously, physical incompetence (primarily poor health) underlies greater service needs. Second, the admission of service need is more likely among old people who feel economically less competent. This may reflect a belief held by the poor elderly that if they wish to satisfy their basic needs, they have little choice but to turn to government or publicly funded social services. Third, older people with smaller activity spaces due to functional impairments or environmental constraints probably have less capability to access those ordinary community resources necessary to satisfy present needs. Their dependency on a proximate environment that does not adequately address their needs leads them to seek service alternatives provided and delivered by the organized social welfare environment. Alternatively, if old people's smaller activity spaces are due to voluntarily initiated psychological disengagement, they may lack the motivation to seek assistance. Less able or willing to personally resolve their own problems, these people may increasingly depend on formal social welfare support systems to satisfy their unfulfilled needs. The significant effect of race is consistent with other studies. The fact that elderly blacks are more likely than whites to require services from the organized social welfare environment probably reflects their greater real or perceived needs for such services and their association of these with greater benefits or satisfactions. An alternative interpretation is that old blacks may be less apt to view negatively the admission of service need or the acceptance of help from social welfare organizations.

Good Time Experiences in the Community and Neighborhood

It is perhaps not surprising (see chapter 2) that few researchers of the aging process investigate why old people are not equally likely to have fun or good times as a result of their environmental transactions. Like other social scientists, gerontologists predominantly emphasize an environment's negative impact on well-being. Preoccupation is with strain, deviance, pathology, and unhappiness.

This deemphasis of pleasure and enjoyment is somewhat paradoxical given that the pursuit of leisure and recreation is presumably a normatively acceptable life-style in old age and retirement. In contrast to employment activity that is likely to have "as its

Table 9.12. Likelihood of Good Time Experiences in Community and Neighborhood

	Never 1	Only once or twice 2	A few times 3	Many times 4	Total	Mean	N
Had good time in community	16%	10	32	43	100%	3.01	400
Had good time in neighborhood	29%	17	29	26	100%	2.52	400
Had good time in community or neighborhood	13%	9	31	48	100%	3.14	400
Felt good about doing something different in community	37%	17	28	18	100%	2.27	400

	Completely Dissatisfied 1	2	3	4	5	6	Completely Satisfied 7	Total	Mean	N
Places to have fun, relax in community	4%	2	3	22	18	19	32	100%	5.31	399

aim achievement of one or more goals or objectives and their attendant future gratifications," leisure activity involves "primary rewards and gratification intrinsic to itself, immediately in its doing" (Gordon and Gaitz 1976:310).

This study examined the likelihood of old people having several fun, good time, or leisure-satisfying experiences (table 9.12). These (with one exception) were identified earlier as clustering in factor 6, labeled as "good time from activity" in the factor analyzed experiential environment (chapter 4).

The first two experiences measured how often in the previous few months old people had a good time in their community and a good time in their neighborhood. From these responses, a new "good time" experience was constructed that described the likelihood (how often in the past few months) of old people having a good time in *either* their community *or* their neighborhood. To measure the likelihood that old people experienced the positive consequences of varied or complex environmental transactions, they were asked how often in the past few months they had done something different in the Evanston community that made them feel particularly good. Finally, they were asked how completely satisfied or dissatisfied they were with the places in their community to have fun or to relax.

Simple Empirical Patterns

Forty-three percent of the old population reported having a good time in their community many times in the past few months; an additional 32 percent of elderly persons more than incidentally (that is, at least "a few times") had such experiences. A smaller, but still substantial percentage of Evanston's elderly frequently had a good time within their neighborhood (26 percent). Almost half of the elderly reported frequent good time experiences in *either* their community or their neighborhood. Despite the majority of positive responses, a sizable percentage of elderly persons (13 percent) reported not recently having a good time in either their community or neighborhood.[10] Only a relatively small percentage of elderly persons very frequently had felt good in the past few months because of their doing something different (18 percent), and 37 percent of the elderly never had this type of experience. Although the majority of old people (69 percent) were satisfied with the places to have fun or to relax in their community, a substantial number (31 percent) were either dissatisfied or did not have strong feelings either way.

Individual Variables Underlying Good Time Experiences in Community or Neighborhood

A three-stage statistical analysis (see chapter 8) evaluated which individual variables influenced the likelihood of old people hav-

Table 9.13. Multiple Regression Analysis of
Individual Variables Underlying Having a Good
Time in Community or Neighborhood

Independent Variable Categories	Having a Good Time (beta values)
Personality	
Locus of control	−.090
Urbanism environment disposition	.028
Socioeconomic Status	
Level of education	.070
Enough money for things	.045
Stage in Life	
Functional health	−.095
Self-rated health	−.172**
Psychological Well-Being	
Life satisfaction	.223***
Activity Behavior	
Level of activity	.140**
Duration in Community	.055
R²	.218
F	11.681***
df	9/377

***p<.001   **p<.01   *p<.05

ing good time experiences in either their community or their
neighborhood. The final multiple regression analysis (stage three)
showed that only three individual variables had significant direct
effects. Old people more likely to have good times perceived
themselves as more healthy, were more satisfied with their lives,
and had higher activity levels (table 9.13).

Simple correlations (stage one) had initially indicated that none
of the demographic, racial, ethnic, or religious individual variables were significantly influencing the likelihood of good time
experiences. Although two personality variables had significant
simple effects, these disappeared after the other proposed individual variables were controlled for. Their simple correlations had
indicated that old people who felt more in control of their lives

and had stronger urban environment dispositions reported good time experiences. Both objective and subjective individual measures of socioeconomic status also were positively and strongly correlated with the likelihood of good time experiences; however, they, too, became insignificant after the other individual variables were controlled for. None of the residential behavior variables had significant direct effects on the likelihood of good time experiences.

Consideration of the individual variables significantly influencing good time experiences in the final multiple regression analysis (table 9.13) leads to the following three sets of generalizations.

Poor health self-ratings impinge upon a person's good time experiences in two ways. First, if such evaluations are a direct manifestation of functional or pathological impairments, then good time experiences are less likely because the old person's curtailed locomotor behavior will prevent the occurrence of potentially enjoyable environmental transactions. Second, perceptions of poor health may be accompanied by negative mood tones, pain, fatigue, or depression that can reduce the likelihood of benefits and satisfactions being associated with any environmental transactions. Importantly, such effects may operate independently of how intact the old person's health status is deemed by objective or behavioral standards.

The positive effects of higher activity levels on good time experiences were predicted by several of the arguments presented earlier (chapter 7). One interpretation of high activity portrayed it as a strategy by which persons successfully adapt to old age. Given that it is voluntarily initiated and interpreted in positive terms, high activity will tend to increase the old person's opportunities for favorable transactions and, in turn, the likelihood of good time experiences.

The relatively strong relationship observed between life satisfaction and good time experiences is not surprising. At issue, however, is its interpretation. As conceptualized here, life satisfaction is proposed to be an antecedent rather than a consequence of good time experiences. Therefore, the likelihood of good time experiences should be greater for an old individual who feels in harmony with his environment and who has successfully adapted to old age. If it is correct to assume that current levels of life satisfaction are not primarily stage-in-life related, then one can also conclude that its effects were operating prior to old age.

Although life satisfaction is treated here as an influence of good time experiences, it is likely to be reciprocally related—greater life satisfaction leads to the greater likelihood of good times, which, in turn, leads to greater life satisfaction. However, it remains unanswered as to whether it is empirically possible to isolate the one-way effects of this relationship without doing an injustice to its feedback processes.

Moving Expectations, Preferences, and Physical Experiences

It is expected that old people who are having disagreeable physical environment experiences would be more likely to plan or prefer a move from their present residential situation. To consider these relationships, the seven major groupings of physical experiences examined in this chapter were correlated with the elderly population's moving expectations and preferences (table 9.14).

The majority of physical environment experiences did not have statistically significant relationships with either moving expectations or preferences. The significant correlation coefficients, moreover, were often small. Certain of the seven groups of experiences, however, contained items with persistently higher correlations with moving expectations and preferences.

With few exceptions, the experiential consequences of "crime," "constraints," "dependency" (number of needed services), and "good times" were insignificantly correlated with moving expectations or preferences. Of the crime experiences, only a greater concern about a home break-in led to the increased likelihood of moving expectations and preferences. Of the constraining experiences, old people bothered by snow and cold weather and those who had more flexible transportation modes available to them were more likely to expect and to prefer to move. Of the good time experiences, old people who did not have a good time in *either* their

Table 9.14. Correlations (Pearson r's) Between Physical Environment Experiences and Moving Expectations, Moving Preferences

Physical Environment Experiences	Moving Expectations	Moving Preferences
Built and Urbanized Environments		
Annoyed because neighbors neglect properties	.090*	.047
Annoyed because other neighborhood buildings less attractive	.075	.041
Annoyed because streets or sidewalks have litter	.057	−.007
Annoyed by polluted air	.102*	.031
Annoyed by dirt and soot on windows	.210***	.154***
Bothered by people talking loudly outside dwelling	.143**	.106*
Bothered by traffic and airplane noises, loud T.V.s	.041	.057
Dwelling Environment		
Annoyed because appliances have broken down	.145**	.094*
Felt dwelling was too hot in summer	.076	−.073
Felt dwelling was too cold in winter or autumn	.188***	.147**
Attractiveness of building	.149***	.193***
Felt dwelling size too small	.155**	.168***
Felt dwelling size too big	.154**	.186***
How clean, good repair is building	−.219***	−.212***
Helpfulness of janitor	−.254***	−.264***
Bothered by insects and rodents	.254***	.264***
Caring for home too expensive	.122*	.147*
Caring for home too much time	.288***	.265***
Caring for home too tiring	.239***	.212***
Community Built and Social Welfare Environment		
Satisfaction with community services	−.102*	−.123**
Satisfaction with stores and shopping	−.081*	−.092*
Satisfaction with dwelling's nearness to community places	−.070	−.079
Annoyed because of higher grocery costs where shop	.032	.033
Annoyed because no place to rest while shopping	.071	.016
Crime in Urbanized Environment		
Afraid to go out at night because of crime	−.053	−.050
Worry about being attacked while walking	.032	.026
Concerned that thief might break into home	.119*	.085*
Attacked while walking, past year	−.008	−.027
Home robbed, past year	.069	.043
Lost or stolen item, past year	.048	.043
Constraints in Natural, Built and Urbanized Environments		
Trouble walking, sidewalks in bad condition	.079	.054
Tired just getting to places in community	−.054	−.048
Postpone plans because of bad weather	.058	.009
Bothered by snow and cold weather	.167***	.027
Difficulty getting transportation to places in community	.000	−.011

Table 9.14. (continued)

Physical Environment Experiences	Moving Expectations	Moving Preferences
Nervous walking because of heavy traffic	.052	−.046
Poor street lighting discourages activity	.049	.016
Didn't go places because not within walking distance	.046	−.025
Type of transportation most frequently used	.104*	.013
Social Welfare Environment		
Number of basic services needed now	.029	.007
Good Times in Environment		
Had good time in community	−.007	−.062
Had good time in neighborhood	−.042	−.074
Had good time in community or neighborhood	−.010	−.090*
Felt good about doing something different in community	−.056	−.071
Satisfied with places to have fun, relax in community	−.090*	−.089*

***p<.001   **p<.01   *p<.05

community or their neighborhood preferred to move, and those elderly more dissatisfied with the places to have fun or to relax in their community were more likely to expect and to prefer to move.

Somewhat stronger correlates were found in the group of community built and social welfare environment experiences. Old people more dissatisfied with a community's services and its stores and shopping were more likely both to expect and to prefer to move.

Moving expectations and preferences were most consistently correlated with the everyday problems of urban living and with uncomfortable or unpleasant dwelling experiences. Several annoyances associated with the urbanized environment—neglected properties of neighbors, polluted air, dirt and soot on windows, and loud noises made by people outside of the dwelling—were significantly correlated with moving expectations and preferences (although less consistently with preferences). The strongest moving correlates were the dwelling experiences. Old people who expected and preferred to move were annoyed about their dwelling's appliances breaking down, felt their dwelling was too cold in the winter or autumn, perceived their dwelling (building) as unattractive, and felt their dwelling was either too big or too small.

Renters expected or preferred to move when they thought that their building was not kept clean or in good repair, when the janitor was not usually helpful, and when they were more frequently bothered by insects or rodents. Homeowners expected or preferred to move when caring for their home was too expensive, took too much time, or was too tiring.

As a group the physical experiences were weaker predictors of moving expectations and preferences than were the territorial experiences (chapter 8). This is not too surprising because major residential relocations are less likely to be contemplated or planned in response to any specific environmental experience. Whereas a territorial experience reflects a broad spectrum of positive or negative reinforcing experiential outcomes, a particular physical environment experience is likely to impinge on only a narrow segment of a person's residential goals or well-being. Moreover, only a few of the physical experiences considered in this chapter have the potential, by themselves, to create great environmental hardship for the old person. In any case, most persons are able to tolerate a certain level of stress from their living conditions. It is only when stressful consequences accumulate beyond an individually determined threshold level that a response such as moving is contemplated or preferred (Golant 1971; Howard and Scott 1965; and Wolpert 1966). Unfortunately, these data do not enable such analytical distinctions.

In one important way, these findings are consistent with those of the last chapter. It was reported that of the territorial experiences, dwelling satisfaction and pride were the most strongly correlated with moving preferences and expectations. Here, the physical experiences involving transactions with the dwelling environment were also the most persistently and strongly related to moving plans and preferences. Moreover, several other significantly correlated experiences involving transactions with the urbanized environment at the same time involved transactions with the dwelling built environment, notably those concerned with dirt and soot on the dwelling's windows, loud talking perceived outside the dwelling, and fear of a home break-in.

The last chapter argued that because unpleasant dwelling territorial experiences impinged upon more salient needs or goals of old people, they were more likely to lead to future moving plans or preferences than were unpleasant community and neighborhood territorial experiences. Another equally valid interpretation is suggested by the above findings. It depends on the argument that moving expectations and preferences result not only from stressful or unpleasant experiences in the present residential environment but also from the individual's belief that he will not have these negative experiences in a new residential location. Therefore, unfavorable dwelling experiences become stronger determinants of future moving behavior because the dwelling environment is perceived as more easily and effectively changed, manipulated, or controlled as a result of a residential relocation. In contrast, moves may not be contemplated in response to neighborhood or community problems because there is little guarantee that a new neighborhood or community will be free of comparable problems or will not develop them at a later period. For instance, constraining or crime experiences may not lead to moving plans because little certainty exists that similarly negative experiential outcomes can be avoided in another community. This is especially true if the old person believes that his present negative experiences are mostly caused by his own mental or behavioral incompetence or inflexible life-style rather than by the actual qualities of his residential environment.

Chapter Ten

The Types and Meaningfulness
of Social Environment Experiences

By research design, only a few of the study's constructed experiences involved transactions with objects and events in the social environment. The social experiences investigated in this chapter were identified earlier as items in five different dimensions of the Evanston elderly population's factor analyzed experiential environment (chapter 4). These involved transactions with two categories of social objects: the social situation and the personal environment (figure 4.2). Additionally, this chapter briefly describes experiences involving a third category of social events referred to earlier as stressful life events.

The empirical analyses in this chapter had three goals: to ascertain the likelihood that old people had social experiences involving particular outcomes or consequences; to assess how the proposed individual variables influenced the likelihood of certain of these social experiences; and to ascertain which of the social experiences were related to old people's moving expectations and preferences.

Social Activity Behavior of Old People

Background

It is important for two reasons to examine the activity behavior of old people that is specifically initiated for social purposes. First, the frequency and quality of old people's social activities are empirically linked to various aspects of their interpersonal relationships and their well-being. Second, social activity has certain properties that provide another perspective on old people's concrete or tangible linkages with the environment outside their dwellings.

Many studies have documented the outcomes of old people's social activity patterns. These have been linked to their patterns of social engagement or disengagement; the incidence, intensity, and quality of their interpersonal relationships; their levels of participation in various social organizations; the complexity of their social role sets; their degree of social isolation; and the likelihood of their having various social experiences, particularly loneliness.[1] A review of this vast literature is beyond the purview of this chapter. However, one pervasive myth put to rest by research was that the majority of old people are isolated from their families and see them infrequently (Shanas 1979). Interpretations of family network linkages had initially emphasized the small and declining percentages of old people who lived together in the same household with their grown children. However, this research failed to recognize that highly efficient transportation and communication technologies facilitated the exchange of goods and information between geographically separated households. Instead, spatial (i.e., geographical) distances between family members were mistakenly thought to be barriers to social interaction. As scholars of different backgrounds later observed, there may be "community without propinquity" (Webber 1963) and "intimacy at a distance" (Rosenmayr and Kockeis 1965). In summary, although the contemporary family of spouses, children, grandparents, and siblings often is not housed under the same roof, it remains important as a systemically functioning unit in North American society (Shanas et al. 1968).

A focus on activity behavior for social purposes is useful for a second reason. It facilitates a broader interpretation of what constitutes environmental contact. Level of activity referred to the frequency with which old people occupied and utilized the environment outside their dwellings. Its conceptualization and measurement were designed to assess old people's concrete linkages with their *outside* environment. So too, social activity behavior is conceptualized and measured in order to assess old people's linkages with the social properties of their outside environment. However, to focus only on social activity that requires locomotor behavior results in an incomplete and inaccurate portrayal of these linkages.

This is due primarily to the fundamental way in which physical and social objects differ from each other. With the exception of the relatively small portion of the physical environment that is inside of or circumjacent to the dwelling, most physical and natural objects are anchored relatively permanently in spatial or environmental positions outside the dwelling. Consequently, locomotor behavior represents the prime mechanism by which concrete contacts occur. Contacts with the social environment, however, can be accomplished by at least two other mechanisms.

First, outside social objects and events may temporarily enter the individual's dwelling environment because they contain their own mobilizing energies and, unlike physical objects, are not spatially or environmentally anchored. Thus individuals may be strongly linked with their outside social environment without ever leaving their dwellings. It would be difficult to argue cogently and logically that old people who have many friends and relatives visiting them in their homes daily are any less socially engaged than old people who visit daily at the homes of friends and relatives. Nor would it be reasonable to argue that these inside contacts are any less salient or potentially beneficial in their impact.

Individuals may be tangibly linked to their social environment via a second mechanism that does not apply to the physical environment. Objects in the social environment are complex living organisms that are capable of sending and receiving (by mail or telephone) firsthand, unfiltered, private communications and material goods. Consequently, old people may be linked to people in their social environment without their being any face-to-face contact. Again, little basis exists to indicate that such communication linkages are any less tangible or salient (Graney and Graney 1974).

In summary, estimates of the strength of old people's linkages with their social environment must consider transactions regardless of whether they occur inside or outside their dwellings. Ideally, such linkages should also encompass telephone and mail communications.

Social Activity Behavior of Evanston's Elderly

Family Activity Behavior

About 26 percent of the elderly population had no living children and 10 percent had no close relatives. Those old people with

Table 10.1. Frequency of Seeing Children, Close Relatives, and Close Friends

Frequency		Child	Relative	Friend[a]
At least once a week	6	56%	29%	57%
At least once a month	5	17	20	25
Several times a year	4	12	13	6
About once or twice a year	3	12	20	4
Less than once a year	2	2	14	2
Never	1	1	4	6
Total		100%	100%	100%
Mean		5.09	4.18	5.14
N		295	355	397

[a]The "never" category refers to old people who have no close friends (6%).

family saw them relatively frequently (table 10.1). Seventy-three percent of the elderly saw a child and almost 50 percent saw a relative at least once a month. Old people who did not see a child or a relative on a fairly regular basis constituted a small minority. More than half of the elderly population (53 percent) reported that their social activities with family or relatives usually took place in their own house or apartment, whereas 16 percent of the elderly usually saw their family elsewhere in the community and 32 percent usually visited with their family in locations outside the Evanston community (table 7.3). These percentages confirmed the importance of the elderly's proximate environment as a setting for family social activity.

The most often seen child or relative was usually located within a relatively short travel time of the elderly respondents. About 57 percent of the visited children lived within 30 minutes driving time, and another 10 percent were within an hour's drive away. Relatives tended to be somewhat farther away with about 44 percent located within 30 minutes driving time and 10 percent within an hour's drive away.

Friend and Neighbor Activity Behavior

The large majority of Evanston's elderly population (80 percent) reported having four or more friends; however, about 6 percent of the elderly population reported having no friends. Fifty-seven percent of the elderly population saw at least one of their friends once a week or more, another 25 percent saw a friend at least once a month, whereas 6 percent saw their friends only about once or twice a year (table 10.1). In contrast to the locational context of family activity, friends were less likely to visit in the old person's dwelling. Although 39 percent of the elderly population (with at least one friend) usually visited with friends in their own homes, the remainder usually saw their friends about equally in their neighborhoods, elsewhere in the community, or outside the community (table 7.3). Predictably, the majority of the elderly (83 percent) lived within 30 minutes travel time of their friends.

Neighborhood social activity also occurred with considerable frequency. More than half the elderly (51 percent) reported visiting or chatting with their neighbors at least once a week. On the other hand, about 20 percent of the elderly saw their neighbors only one to three times a month, and the remainder (29 percent) less often than that (table 10.2).[2] Predictably, virtually all neighboring is neighborhood-based (table 7.3).[3]

The Social Situation Experiences of the Elderly Population

Background

Many of the old person's social experiences do not result from transactions with individuals such as family members, friends, or neighbors, but rather from transactions with the population en masse occupying the neighborhood or community. The large majority of individuals in these groups are never met, talked to, or even seen, and they are responded to only as defining members of a larger social collectivity. This population may be designated by only one or two distinctive compositional attributes such as race, class, status, age, or ethnicity. These alone, however, may be the basis for stereotypic labelling from which tenaciously held attitudes are formed. Little effort may be expended to confirm or deny whether these associations accurately apply to individual mem-

Table 10.2. Frequency of Get Together with Neighbors

Frequency		Percentage
Daily	6	7
Several times a week	5	22
Once a week	4	22
Two or three times a month	3	11
About once a month	2	9
Less often than that	1	8
Never	0	21
Total		100
Mean		3.01
N		391

bers. Consequently, the types and meaningfulness of these social situation experiences derive primarily from feelings and beliefs about the neighborhood population as a whole.

Evaluations of the social situation often depend on whether old people perceive their neighborhood population as similar or dissimilar to themselves. Such similarities or differences may connote favorable or unfavorable consequences, depending on old people's attitudes toward living in a neighborhood with a homogeneous rather than a heterogeneous population composition.

Outcomes of social situation experiences are also influenced by the opinions of "reference" persons who are respected and listened to as knowledgeable observers. These reference persons may include community and organization leaders, friends, relatives, and neighbors. Such assessments may carry particular weight if they are believed to mirror the outsiders' beliefs about the old residents themselves. Thus, if a neighborhood social situation is evaluated as having a low social status or the appearance of an age-segregated geriatric ghetto, the old residents may, in turn, believe that comparable attitudes are held about their own social status, achievements, and competence.

Gerontological investigations of old people's neighborhood or building social (population) situation have focused primarily on its chronological age composition. Theoretical arguments are available to explain why either (old) age-homogeneous (segregated) or age-heterogeneous (integrated) social situations should be positively experienced by old people (Rosow 1967; Golant 1980). The empirical studies by gerontologists have persistently found that age-homogeneous social situations yield positive experiences for their old residents. Conclusions must be made cautiously, however, because most findings are based on investigations of planned or quasi-planned age-homogeneous settings such as public housing and retirement housing. The results lack generality if only because these settings were purposively selected by old people who wanted or who were willing to occupy age-segregated residences. The emphasis in the gerontological literature on the age composition of a population must also be placed in perspective. It is probable that social situation experiences of old people depend just as much or more on the similarity of a population's racial and social class attributes (Michelson 1970). Evidence on this question is not available.

Old people may interpret unfavorable social situation experiences as a threat to their personal safety or security, as evidence of the social hostility and incompatibility of their neighbors, and, in general, as a source of emotional discomfort. Because the status of a neighborhood's population may be the basis by which the neighborhood's overall quality is evaluated, unfavorable social situation experiences can result in fears that the neighborhood has acquired a bad reputation or is about to fall victim to rapid, unfavorable population and land use changes.

Although the origins and consequences of social situation ex-

periences may differ substantially from those of old people's interpersonal experiences (to be shortly discussed), some parallels
are likely. Old people who occupy a neighborhood with favorable
social situation experiences are predicted to have more rewarding
personal experiences with its individual members, and these relationships should persist even as the population composition
changes for the worse. On the other hand, it is less likely that old
people will establish rewarding personal relationships with residents identified with a population group toward which they hold
strongly negative attitudes.

Social Situation Experiences of Evanston's Elderly

To describe the social situation experiences of Evanston's elderly population required the identification of the compositional
attributes they cognitively associated with their neighborhood's
population. They were asked whether a good many of the residents in their neighborhood were about the same age as they,
whether most of the people in their neighborhood were the same
social class as they (see chapter 6); and whether the people in their
neighborhood were all or mostly white (or black) or about half
white and half black.

About 35 percent of the elderly population believed they lived
in a neighborhood in which a good many people were the same
age as they (age-homogeneous), whereas 51 percent believed they
occupied a neighborhood in which a good many people were not
the same age as they (age-integrated) and 14 percent were uncertain. This assessment was statistically unrelated (at .05 level or
less) to the chronological age of the elderly respondent. Eighty-
one percent of the elderly population believed they lived in a
neighborhood with people of the same class as they, whereas only
10 percent believed they lived in a class-heterogeneous neighborhood and 10 percent were uncertain. Although this assessment did
not vary systematically with the class of the respondent, upper-
class elderly were the most likely to identify the other neighborhood residents as having a different social class as they. About 87
percent of the elderly population believed they occupied a neigh-

borhood of the same race (white or black) as they. Responses categorized by the race of the respondent indicated that 89 percent of the white elderly perceived their neighborhood as all or mostly white, whereas 79 percent of the black elderly perceived their neighborhood as all or mostly black. Thus the black elderly were more likely than the white elderly to consider their neighborhood population as racially mixed.

Old people were then asked if, as a result of these compositional attributes, they enjoyed living in their neighborhood more or less, and how satisfied they were with the people in their neighborhood. Their overall satisfaction was relatively high (more than 50 percent of the population were completely satisfied), and the majority of old people also believed they obtained more enjoyment from living in their neighborhood because of its age, class, and racial composition. Of the three compositional attributes, it was the neighborhood's present social class composition that led to the greatest likelihood of enjoyment (table 10.3). Statistically, however, the differences were very small.

To assess the effects of population homogeneity on enjoyment,

Table 10.3. Enjoyment or Satisfaction from Population Composition of Neighborhood

Responses		Enjoyment from Population's		
		Age	Class	Race
Much less enjoyment	1	2%	1%	3%
A little less enjoyment	2	4	3	5
Neither more nor less	3	34	28	36
A little more enjoyment	4	18	20	17
Much more enjoyment	5	42	48	40
Total		100%	100%	100%
Mean		3.94	4.12	3.87
N		343	352	398

	Completely Dissatisfied						Completely Satisfied			
	1	2	3	4	5	6	7	Total	Mean	N
People who live in neighborhood	2%	1	2	9	13	23	51	100%	6.03	400

NOTE: Respondents excluded were uncertain about age or class composition of their neighborhoods or were uncertain as to their own class.

Table 10.4. Age and Class Homogeneity of Neighborhood as Source of Enjoyment[a]

	Neighborhood Perceived as:	
Responses	Age-homogeneous	Age-integrated
Much less enjoyment	2%	1%
A little less enjoyment	6	4
Neither more nor less	31	37
A little more enjoyment	23	15
Much more enjoyment	39	44
Total	100%	100%
N	141	202
	Neighborhood Perceived as:	
Responses	Class-homogeneous	Class-integrated
Much less enjoyment	0%	3%
A little less enjoyment	1	20
Neither more nor less	27	46
A little more enjoyment	21	17
Much more enjoyment	52	14
Total	100%	100%
N	317	35

[a] Respondents were excluded who were uncertain about age or class composition of their neighborhoods or uncertain as to their own class.

old people were categorized according to whether by their own designations they occupied age, class, and racially homogeneous neighborhoods. Elderly persons occupying age-heterogeneous (integrated) neighborhoods were about equally as likely to enjoy their neighborhoods as elderly persons occupying age-homogeneous (segregated) neighborhoods. Statistically (.05 level or less), the two distributions were not significantly different (table 10.4). A comparison of the enjoyment levels of elderly people living in class-homogeneous and class-heterogeneous (integrated) neighborhoods produced a very different finding. The two enjoyment distributions were significantly different (at .05 level) from each other: old people living in class-homogeneous social situations obtained more enjoyment from their neighborhoods than old people living in class-integrated social situations. Finally, it was found that old people living in racially homogeneous neighborhoods also obtained more enjoyment from their social situation than elderly persons occupying racially integrated neighborhoods, although the statistical difference was not large.

Personal Environment Experiences of the Elderly Population

Background

Unlike social situation experiences, personal environment experiences involve transactions with individuals rather than population collectivities. Elderly persons do not attend to the compositional attributes of a population group, but rather to the social and psychological attributes of individuals who are described and evaluated as friends, strangers, relatives, acquaintances, rivals, neighbors, professionals, and so on. The positive outcomes of these personal relationships are well understood and documented and include companionship, emotional security, respect, affection, advice, knowledge, understanding, material supports, and so forth.

Although the consequences of family and friendship relationships are well-known, other personal relationships yield less frequently identified benefits. For example, the everyday casual contacts with business persons such as mailmen, salesclerks, repairmen, bus drivers, and so on can result in considerable intrinsic satisfaction because they are spontaneous, immediate, informal, and unplanned. Such social encounters, although they may appear superficial, are valued highly by some old people. So too are the personal relationships with neighbors, which can yield a very diverse set of experiential consequences, depending on the qualities old people associate with desirable neighbors. As Keller (1968) observed, a "good neighbor" may not only be helpful, but may be someone who minds his own business. Thus, positive experiences may derive from transactions with neighbors who are good friends and reliable lenders, but also with neighbors who only regularly and politely nod their heads every morning.

Less obvious social transactions can also be the source of rewarding personal experiences. A good example is the house pet (see chapter 8) that enables the old person to give affection and care and to receive friendship and companionship in return. In addition to helping the old person avoid feelings of uselessness, the pet may serve as a means for the old person to maintain contact with reality rather than withdraw into a fantasy world (Levinson 1972:87). The pet may also help the old person to cope more successfully with the stressful events of old age. As Brickel argued: "An animal companion provides solace in bereavement, attenuates the pain of social isolation and depression, and actively serves a role in preventing social withdrawal and alienation" (1980:122).

A focus on old people as primarily receivers of emotional and material supports from their individual relationships also provides only a partial portrayal of their personal experiences. Several studies emphasize the emotional and material assistance old people provide to others, especially to family members. Examples include babysitting, gardening, shopping assistance, financial gifts, advice, and so on (Bengston and Cutler 1976). These "helping" transactions result in a variety of potentially rewarding consequences for old people, including feelings of emotional well-being, achievement, control, and competence.

Satisfying personal experiences may occur in a perhaps paradoxical social climate, where the old person is free from the observation of and contact with other persons (Westin 1967) and is able to avoid receiving and processing other people's verbal and nonverbal communications. The absence of such transactions leads to the experience referred to here as *aloneness* and to what others have referred to as *privacy* or *solitude* (Westin 1967; Altman 1975; Chermayeff and Alexander 1963).[4] There is a good theoretical basis to expect that such aloneness experiences are emotionally and functionally beneficial to old people and represent a highly effective adaptation to the events of old age. Not surprisingly, such arguments parallel those presented by proponents who identify social and psychological disengagement as contributing to successful aging. Necessarily, there is a disagreement as to "how much" or "how often" aloneness is desirable for an old person's well-being and to what extent aloneness experiences are purposively and voluntarily sought rather than passively and involuntarily accepted.

On the positive side, aloneness can be linked to the fulfillment of at least three sets of human needs. First, aloneness experiences provide moments during which the old person can temporarily avoid many of the stressful, embarrassing, or otherwise unpleasant transactions of everyday life. Second, the aloneness experience allows the old person to engage in introspection, reminiscing, and fantasizing. It is a time to evaluate and resolve the good and bad of life's experiences, to become more aware of one's accomplishments and failures, and to anticipate and plan for future activities. Third, aloneness may be considered an experience during which the individual exhibits independence and autonomy and exerts "selective control" (Altman and Chemers 1980:77) over his personal environment transactions. It is a time when old people can experience their individuality and "avoid being manipulated or dominated wholly by others" (Pastalan 1970:90; Altman and Chemers 1980). The individual may freely express his behavior and emotions in this "offstage" state (Pastalan 1970).

Although the aloneness of old people can be interpreted as a positive experience, it is more frequently viewed in negative terms, whereupon it is more appropriately denoted as *loneliness*. Basically, loneliness is an unwelcome and unsatisfying aloneness that results from transactions with a personal environment that is perceived as inadequate or deficient in some way. There is considerable consensus as to the impact of loneliness on young and old people alike. Sullivan, for example, referred to loneliness as the "inadequate discharge of the need for human intimacy" (1953:290). Weiss, reviewing the literature on loneliness, depicted it as "gnawing discomfort" (1973:14), "chronic distress without redeeming features" (p. 15), and "emotional isolation" (p. 18). Loneliness is characterized by "unwanted individuation" (p. 15), implying "the absence of some particular relational provision" (p. 17), involving other individuals, the community, or the society. Individuals who report being lonely are therefore apt to describe their world as "desolate, barren, devoid of others" (p. 18) and to feel "empty, dead, or hollow" (p. 21).

A state of loneliness is also distinguished by its absence of stimulation, variety, excitement, and challenges. One possible consequence is *boredom*, or what White (1970) referred to as unpleasant monotony. Boredom may also result from an individual's inability to share the joys or frustrations of environmental experiences with another person or to obtain confirmation as to the acceptability or desirability of one's transactions. As Weiss elaborated:

> Boredom seems to come about as the tasks that make up one's daily routines, because they are inaccessible to the affirmation of others, lose their meaning and begin to be simply busy work. The day's duties then are a burdensome ritual which one can hardly persuade oneself to observe. Again, there is restlessness and difficulty in concentration, preventing the individual from becoming engaged in a distraction such as a book or television. (1973:22)

The last set of personal experiences to be considered in this section consists of old people's assessment of whether there are individuals available who can provide them with a variety of social and psychological supports. The consequences of these experiences depend on how certain old people are about being able to activate future personal relationships. These relationships may satisfy expressive or emotional needs, such as a person available to share one's happiness or grief. Alternatively, the needs may be more practical, task-oriented, or instrumental in character, such as the help required from other persons to do household chores or grocery shopping in time of sickness. Old people who are confident that persons are available to satisfy these two categories of needs predictably experience greater peace of mind, which, in turn, leads to greater self-confidence and self-dignity. Even if elderly persons never require such assistance, its perceived availability can reduce feelings of isolation, aloneness, and helplessness. In particular, old people's feelings of autonomy and competence are likely to be strengthened because of their greater certainty that future emotional and material crises can be handled effectively without severe disruption to their highly valued independent living arrangements and life-styles.

Personal Environmental Experiences of Evanston's Elderly

Enjoyment and Satisfaction from Family, Friends, Neighbors, Acquaintances, Pets

The majority of elderly persons (68 percent) were satisfied with how near they lived to their family and relatives, but a sizable proportion (32 percent) expressed either indifference or dissatisfaction with their present accessibility relationships (table 10.5). Predictably, the more satisfied old people visited more frequently with their children (Pearson $r = .37$) and relatives (Pearson $r = .26$). Also, the more satisfied elderly persons lived shorter travel-time distances from their children (Pearson $r = -.43$) and relatives (Pearson $r = -.34$).

A high percentage of old people were completely satisfied with their friends in the Evanston community (64 percent). The majority of old people (52 percent) also derived very frequent enjoyment from just chatting or visiting with their neighbors. Nonetheless, a substantial minority of old people (25 percent) had a minimal amount of enjoyable social transactions with their neighbors. Assessments of old people's relationships with pets produced strong polar responses. Elderly persons either very frequently (21 percent) or very infrequently (77 percent) enjoyed the company of a pet. The majority of old people obtained frequent enjoyment from transactions in which they gave some form of assistance. Seventy-six percent of the elderly relatively frequently enjoyed helping another person with a chore or a problem. Old people also enjoyed the casual, informal, unplanned social contacts that result from carrying out everyday transactions. About 67 percent of the elderly relatively frequently obtained such enjoyment from talking with storekeepers, salespersons, clerks, and so on.

Table 10.5. Likelihood of Positive Personal Environment Experiences

Experiences	Completely Dissatisfied 1	2	3	4	5	6	Completely Satisfied 7	Total	Mean	N
Nearness of dwelling to family, relatives	13%	4	4	12	13	13	42	100%	5.14	399
Friends you have in community	1%	1	2	7	11	15	64	100%	6.25	400

	Never 1	Only once or twice 2	A few times 3	Many times 4	Total	Mean	N
Enjoyment from visiting with neighbors	13%	12	24	52	100%	3.13	396
Enjoyed company of pet	77%	0	2	21	100%	1.66	399
Enjoyed helping someone with chore or problem	12%	11	32	44	100%	3.09	400
Enjoyed talking with storekeepers or clerks	20%	14	30	37	100%	2.83	400
Enjoyed being home alone	10%	5	20	65	100%	3.40	399
Felt lack of privacy in dwelling	94%	2	2	2	100%	1.13	400
Felt lonely	65%	13	13	9	100%	1.67	400
Felt bored in dwelling	74%	9	13	6	100%	1.50	400

NOTE: Respondents were asked about the occurrence of the above eight experiences "in the past few months."

Individual and Experiential Correlates of Enjoyment from Visiting with Neighbors

Predictably, old people who visited more often with their neighbors also were more likely to obtain enjoyment from them, but the association was far from perfect (Pearson $r = .45$) (table 10.6). Thus frequency of social contact with neighbors was, by itself, insufficient to predict the likelihood of positive neighboring experiences. This finding is consistent with earlier observations that enjoyable neighbor relationships may take different forms. An even weaker relationship existed between enjoyable neighbor visits and the frequency with which friends were seen, which is not surprising given that friendship is only one of many potential roles played by a neighbor, and friends often will live outside the neighborhood. The proposition that enjoyable neighbor contacts might serve as a substitute for weakened or infrequent family relationships was given no support by the correlational analyses (table 10.6).

However, the conclusion that old people who enjoyed their neighbors had other similarly beneficial interpersonal relationships is supported by the statistical significance of three correlated experiences. Old people who enjoyed their neighbors were more satisfied with the friends they had in their neighborhood, more frequently enjoyed talking with storekeepers and salesclerks, and more frequently enjoyed helping another person with a chore or problem. On the other hand, the frequency of enjoyable neighbor experiences was totally unrelated to old people's confidence that dependable persons were available to provide salient emotional or material support (experiences discussed below). Nor was more frequent enjoyment from neighbor relationships in any sense an experience substituted for such stressful losses as the recent death of a spouse or a close relative. However, old people who more frequently enjoyed being with their neighbors were less likely to feel lonely or bored in their dwellings; at the same time they were still more likely to enjoy the time spent alone at home.

Enjoyable neighbor visits were especially likely when old people were satisfied with their neighborhood's social situation, especially with its age and social class composition. In particular,

Table 10.6. Individual and Experiential Correlates of Enjoyment from
Visiting with Neighbors (Pearson r's)

Frequency child seen	−.011
Frequency relative seen	−.014
Frequency neighbors visited with	.454***
Frequency close friend seen	.225***
Enjoyment from age composition of neighborhood	.224***
Enjoyment from social class composition of neighborhood	.277***
Enjoyment from racial composition of neighborhood	.061
Neighbors' age perceived same as respondent	.062
Neighbors' class perceived same as respondent	.097*
Neighbors' race perceived same as respondent	.103*
Satisfaction with people in neighborhood	.306***
Satisfaction dwelling's nearness to family, relatives	.066
Satisfaction with friends in community	.242***
Enjoyed helping someone with chore or problem	.096*
Enjoyed talking with storekeepers or clerks	.306***
Enjoyed being home alone	.161***
Felt lonely	−.085*
Felt bored in dwelling	−.140**
Availability of sociopsychological supports	.011
Availability of instrumental supports	−.026
Availability of expressive supports	.038
Spouse's death in past year	−.014
Close relative's death in past year	.039
Jewish religion	−.136**
Catholic religion	−.010
Other religion	−.105*
Separated-divorced	−.098*
Forced to retire	−.101*
Life satisfaction	.090*
Employed	−.002
Duration of residence	.131*
Activity space size	−.153**
Change in activity	−.081

***p<.001   **p<.01   *p<.05

enjoyable neighbor visits were more likely when neighbors were
perceived as having the same class and race as the elderly respondent. The age of neighbors was a less important consideration. The diversity in ages of the neighbors visited by old people
was confirmed by responses to another question. Elderly respondents indicated that about 8 percent of their neighbors were older
than they, 27 percent were about the same age, 40 percent were

younger, and 24 percent thought that the ages of their neighbors were evenly mixed, that is, "half older and half younger."

Very few of the proposed individual variables statistically influenced the likelihood of enjoyable neighbor visits (table 10.6). This is not surprising because a person selects a neighborhood that has social characteristics consistent with his own needs and resources. Thus, old people with very different personal characteristics and living in very different neighborhoods can be equally likely to enjoy their neighbor relationships.

This generalization is less likely to apply to elderly residents who, by reason of their sex, race, marital status, or other personal characteristics, are minorities in their neighborhoods. These old persons are expected to have a more difficult time finding neighbors who have needs and personal resources compatible with their own. Consequently, it is more likely that their neighbor relationships do not yield beneficial or rewarding experiences. This reasoning appears to explain the significant correlational and regression relationships of three individual variables.

The Jewish elderly were less likely than other elderly persons, particularly Protestants, to enjoy their neighbors. This seems to reflect the general inability of elderly Jews to satisfy their social needs within the Evanston community. Although the elderly are a minority population in Evanston, large residential concentrations of Jewish persons are located in nearby suburban communities and in Chicago. Consequently, greater opportunities for enjoyable social relationships with persons of the same religious preference exist outside the community.

The divorce-separated elderly were less likely to enjoy their neighbor relationships than other elderly persons, particularly the married elderly. This may similarly reflect their inability to acquire satisfactory social contacts with married neighbors. In support of this interpretation, the study's findings indicated that the divorced-separated elderly had a larger activity space than other elderly persons.

Old people who were forced to retire recently (in the previous year) were less likely to have enjoyable neighbor experiences. Possibly, these elderly persons were uncomfortable or unfamiliar with

their new nonemployed status and found it more difficult to initiate or maintain neighbor contacts. Alternatively, they may have
felt that their newly acquired life-style was inconsistent with that
of their neighbors, most of whom were employed.

Three other individual variables significantly influenced the
likelihood of enjoyable neighbor visits. Enjoyment was greater for
old people who had smaller activity spaces, who lived longer in
their dwellings, and who were more satisfied with their lives. The
theoretical bases for these relationships were discussed in earlier
chapters.

Aloneness, Loneliness, Boredom, and Privacy

The majority of old people (65 percent) frequently experienced
enjoyment from simply being at home alone (table 10.5); however, a sizable minority of old people (15 percent) rarely or never
enjoyed such solitude. Simple correlational analyses confirmed that
the likelihood of this enjoyment was unrelated to the incidence of
either loneliness or boredom. Whether or not old people enjoyed
being home alone was also unrelated to their family and friendship activity behavior patterns. Together, these relationships suggest that aloneness is a positive experience that is voluntarily and
purposively initiated for its own intrinsic satisfaction.

Only a small percentage of old people (less than 20 percent) often
felt lonely or bored. However, boredom and loneliness were experiences that often occurred hand in hand (Pearson $r = .38$). Predictably, loneliness was associated with several other social experiences. Simple correlational analyses showed that lonely old
people were more dissatisfied with their dwelling's nearness to
family and relatives, were less satisfied with their friends in the
community, were less likely to enjoy visiting with neighbors, were
more likely to have lost their spouses in the previous year, and
were less confident about the availability of other persons to provide them with emotional and material supports in time of need.

The likelihood of loneliness, perhaps surprisingly, was not significantly related to how frequently old people saw their children,
their close relatives, or their neighbors. On the other hand, old

people who saw their friends more frequently were less likely to feel lonely. A caveat is in order here. The correlational relationship between loneliness and child visits was first examined only for old people who reported having at least one child. However, an adjusted "frequency seen child" variable was constructed that included old people not having a living child in its "never" category. When this alternative variable was correlated with loneliness, it was statistically significant. That is, old people who saw a child infrequently or who had no children were more likely to feel lonely.

It was rare for old people to feel they did not have enough privacy.

Individual Factors Underlying Loneliness

A three-stage statistical analysis (see chapter 8) assessed the influences of the proposed individual variables on the occurrence of loneliness. The findings of the final (third stage) multiple regression analysis are displayed in table 10.7. Old people who felt lonely more frequently had less affiliative (or more hostile) personalities and felt less in control of their lives (perceived external locus of control). Widowed elderly persons were, on the average, more likely to feel lonely than married elderly persons. The never-married elderly were also, on the average, more likely to feel lonely than married elderly, although this latter relationship was just short of being statistically significant (at the .05 level). Catholic elderly persons were less likely than Protestant elderly to feel lonely. Old people who felt lonely more frequently perceived their health as poorer, generally felt unhappy or dissatisfied with their lives, and lived a shorter time in their present community. Neither subjective nor objective measures of socioeconomic status significantly influenced the likelihood of loneliness, although *simple* correlational analyses indicated that lower incomes and perceived money problems were associated with greater loneliness. None of the activity behavior measures significantly influenced loneliness; however, simple correlational analysis initially revealed that lonely old people had lower activity levels.

Table 10.7. Multiple Regression Analysis of Individual Variables Underlying Feeling Lonely

Independent Variable Categories	Feeling Lonely (beta values)	
Personality		
Leary Affiliation Personality	−.107*	
Leary Dominance Personality	−.030	
Locus of control	−.183***	
Demographic and Religious		
Separated-divorced (Yes = 1, No = 0)	−.013	(−.058)
Widowed (Yes = 1, No = 0)	.138**	(.286)
Never married (Yes = 1, No = 0)	.081	(.316)
Catholic religion (Yes = 1, No = 0)	−.128**	(−.330)
Jewish religion (Yes = 1, No = 0)	−.021	(−.089)
Other religion (Yes = 1, No = 0)	−.063	(−.353)
No religion (Yes = 1, No = 0)	−.024	(−.138)
Socioeconomic Status		
Impact of housing expense	−.013	
Stage in Life		
Self-rated health	.110*	
Self-rated seeing difficulties	.065	
Functional health	.084	
Psychological Well-Being		
Life satisfaction	−.215***	
Activity Behavior		
Level of activity	−.029	
Duration in Community	−.106*	
Tenure Status (Own = 1, Rent = 0)	−.015	(−.031)
R^2	.307	
F	8.709***	
df	18/354	

NOTE: Unstandardized partial regression coefficients of dummy variables are shown in parentheses.
***$p < .001$ **$p < .01$ *$p < .05$

The loneliness of old people with less affiliative (or more hostile) personalities is predictable. It is less likely that these individuals strive to be liked and accepted by others or are considerate of or lenient with others. They are less likely to establish harmonious and amicable relationships. Thus their psychological or social demands limit their ability to have emotionally rewarding or satisfying interpersonal experiences, and their susceptibility to feelings of loneliness is greater.

A very different explanation can be suggested for the finding that old people who feel less in control of their lives feel lonely more often. These persons are expected to be more accepting of unsatisfactory changes in their interpersonal relationships, believing that little can be done to control or ameliorate their negative effects. They are more likely to accept passively the consequences of social role losses (caused by changed family and employment lifestyles, and lost friendships due to death, relocation, or changing personal interests). Thus, loneliness results when an old person feels it is futile to try to change his unsatisfactory personal environment.

The greater likelihood that widowed, never-married, and Protestant elderly experience loneliness is probably due to these groups perceiving fewer opportunities (relatives, friends, children, and so on) in their personal environments to satisfy their social needs. Additionally, elderly widows may have especially high expectations regarding how their social experiences "ought" to be, because of memories of an intact (husband–wife) family and its rewarding and satisfying social experiences. Consequently, interpersonal experiences that fall short of these standards are judged as unsatisfactory—a basis for the widow's feelings of loneliness.

Although several of the stage-in-life health measures displayed sizable simple correlations with loneliness, only perceived health remained statistically significant in the final multiple regression analysis. (The functional health measure fell just short of being statistically significant at the .05 level.) It is expected that old people who do not feel in good health because of functional impairments, illness, or chronic ailments have less physical and emotional energy to initiate, improve, or maintain satisfying interpersonal relationships. This reduced competence increases the likelihood of loneliness.

The significant antecedent role of life satisfaction is consistent with earlier theorizing. Old people who feel down about their lives are expected to find it emotionally more difficult to initiate or maintain rewarding or satisfying personal relationships. Their pessimism about life leads them to assess negatively their family and friendship relationships. Loneliness is a predictable consequence.

In anticipation that other researchers will not fully accept the reasons given for life satisfaction's influence on loneliness, the final multiple regression analysis was repeated without controlling for its effects. However, the findings did not change in any substantive way. The beta weights of the two personality variables (affiliation and locus of control), the Catholic and never-married dummy variables, and all three of the health measures were of a larger magnitude and in some instances statistically significant at a higher level.

In light of earlier arguments (chapter 7), it was predictable that loneliness was less likely for old people who lived a longer time in their communities. Long-time elderly occupants are more likely to have established stronger community bonds and attachments. If the personal environment contains a greater number of more stable and dependable social contacts, loneliness becomes a less likely consequence.

A fuller theoretical understanding of the effects these individual variables have on loneliness requires that one recognize how the impact of social environmental transactions can differ from those of physical environmental transactions. An individual's transactions with the physical environment usually involve inanimate objects, whereas transactions with the personal (social) environment involve other adaptively behaving, boundedly rational, goal-seeking individuals. Thus the old person's personal environment itself can initiate, interpret, and act on social transactions. For example, one can ask how an income level influences the individual's evaluation of his dwelling, but not how the dwelling evaluates the income level of the person.[5] In contrast, not only does the poor health of an old person influence his ability to maintain a friendship with another person, but also the "other person'" assesses whether to remain friends with someone in poor health. More generally, the proposed individual variables not only allow inferences to be made about an old person's mental and behavioral states, but also permit inferences about how *other* people interpret the old person's mental and behavioral states. Several of the relationships just discussed can be reinterpreted from this perspective. Specifically, it can be argued that potentially satisfying interpersonal experiences are less likely to occur if old people are judged by others as hostile, widowed, never married, in poor health, or having low morale. For instance, poor health makes certain old people unattractive as friends or companions (Blau 1973). Similarly, persons may avoid relationships with old people who are morose about their lives, because inevitably all social transactions with such persons become tainted with unpleasant or bad feelings.

The findings also offer insights to whether loneliness is primarily a product of old age or of lifelong influences. It is likely that personality and religion have exerted their effects over a long period. On the other hand, the effects of widowhood (assuming its relatively recent occurrence) and health are probably stage-in-life related. The effects of life satisfaction and duration lived in community have probably been more pronounced in old age, but have been influential throughout the old person's adult life.

Sociopsychological Support Experiences of Evanston's Elderly

Old people were asked whether someone was available all of the time, most of the time, only some of the time, or none of the time to satisfy five potential needs. Satisfaction of two of the needs required the availability of someone with whom to communicate about personal problems and to share moments of happiness. Satisfaction of three of the needs required the availability of someone to help with chores around the house, to assist the old person if bedridden due to sickness, and to obtain grocery items. Persons available to satisfy the first set of emotional needs were referred to as expressive sociopsychological supports, and those available to satisfy the second set of material and maintenance

Table 10.8. Likelihood of Expressive and Instrumental Sociopsychological Supports

	Availability of Person						
	All of the time 4	Most of the time 3	Some of the time 2	Never 1	Total	Mean	N
Expressive Support Items							
Availability of person to talk to about personal problem	75%	12	5	9	100%	3.53	399
Availability of person to share happiness with when feeling good about something	82%	12	3	3	100%	3.74	400
Instrumental Support Items							
Availability of person to depend on for help when there are chores around the house	61%	18	8	14	100%	3.26	400
Availability of person to depend on if in bed because of sickness	68%	16	6	10	100%	3.42	398
Availability of person to depend on if something is needed from grocery store	76%	15	3	6	100%	3.61	398

needs were referred to as instrumental sociopsychological supports.[6]

The majority of old people felt that they had someone available all the time to satisfy each of these needs (table 10.8). Nonetheless, small percentages of elderly persons (from 3 percent to 14 percent) believed that such persons were never available. On the whole, old people were more confident about the availability of persons to supply expressive rather than instrumental needs. Old people were least confident about having someone to depend on if they needed help doing chores around the house, if they required assistance when sick in bed, or if they needed someone to talk to regarding a personal problem.

The greater unavailability of the first two instrumental supports (table 10.8) probably reflects the nature of the potential needs to be satisfied. A considerable investment of another person's time and energy is required to help with chores around the house or to satisfy the everyday needs of the bed-confined old person. In contrast, relatively little effort is required to supply an old person with items needed from a grocery store.

Persons providing expressive supports are probably perceived as more available because their physical presence in the old person's dwelling is unnecessary. For example, the giving of advice, the sharing of emotions, and the working out of personal problems may be effectively accomplished by telephone or letter. This is not true of the instrumental supports, which require the actual presence of the "helping" person. Thus the availability of persons providing expressive supports is largely independent of where older people live and how transportation accessible are their homes.

Simple correlational findings further help to elucidate these responses. Old people who were more confident about the availability of persons to satisfy both their instrumental and expressive needs tended to live in larger households, usually saw their family and relatives in their own dwellings, saw their children more frequently, and were more satisfied with the nearness of their dwelling to family and relatives. However, of the two sets of supports, the perceived availability of instrumental supports was more strongly correlated with the above variables, thereby suggesting the greater importance of locationally accessible people.

Personal Relationship of Helping Persons

Old people were asked who they thought of as the first, second, and third most important persons when they described the availability of someone to provide them with these instrumental and expressive supports. All but one percent of the elderly population could name at least one person on whom they could depend at least some of the time. Six percent of the elderly could not name a second person, and an additional 11 percent could not name a third person.

Just over a third (37 percent) of the elderly named their spouses as the most important (first) persons; 25 percent of the elderly depended most on a child; 14 percent depended on another relative;

and 21 percent depended on a friend. Four percent of the elderly population depended most on "other persons" such as boarders, professional workers, and hired help.

Further clarification is achieved when elderly persons are categorized by their marital status and sex. Married old people predominantly depended on their spouses (81 percent) and to a much lesser extent on their children (11 percent). The widowed elderly depended most on their children (43 percent) and primarily on their daughters (30 percent); however, a sizable percentage depended on their friends (34 percent), who were also primarily women (27 percent). The separated-divorced elderly depended about equally on their children (32 percent), other relatives (28 percent), and their friends (37 percent). The never-married elderly depended most on other relatives (50 percent), who were primarily women (43 percent), and on friends (40 percent), who were primarily women (37 percent). One percent of the married, 6 percent of the widowed, 10 percent of the never-married, and 5 percent of the separated-divorced elderly populations depended most on "other persons" such as boarders, professional workers, and hired help. The comparable response distributions categorized according to the sex of the elderly persons strongly reflect the high proportion of elderly who are both female and widowed. The male elderly (69 percent of whom were married) predominantly depended on their wives (61 percent) for their sociopsychological supports and to a lesser degree (16 percent) on their children (about equally on sons and daughters). Female elderly (32 percent of whom were married) depended on their husbands (24 percent), their daughters (21 percent), their female relatives (12 percent), and their female friends (24 percent). About 8 percent of the female elderly depended most on their sons.

It is expected that the availability of helping persons is influenced by the relationship between these individuals and the old person. That is, certain relationships more than others are likely to generate greater trust, confidence, reliability, and so on. To evaluate this question, elderly people were classified into three categories according to whether they had very high, high, or low expressive and instrumental support availability scores. Elderly

Table 10.9. Availability of Expressive and Instrumental Sociopsychological Supports by Relationship of Helping Person to Old Individual

Relationship of First Helping Person	Availability of Expressive Supports				
	Very High	High	Low	Total	N
Spouse	81%	13	6	100%	145
Other kin	73%	15	12	100%	149
Friends	56%	27	17	100%	86
Other[a]	53%	20	27	100%	15
Total	72%	17	11	100%	395

Eta = .23; Chi Square = 22.595, p = .001.

Relationship of First Helping Person	Availability of Instrumental Supports				
	Very High	High	Low	Total	N
Spouse	75%	21	3	100%	145
Other kin	63%	29	8	100%	148
Friends	38%	42	20	100%	84
Other[a]	27%	53	20	100%	15
Total	61%	30	9	100%	392

Eta = .33; Chi Square = 43.205, p = .000.
[a]Includes boarders, professional workers, and hired help.

people were simultaneously classified according to which of four categories of helping persons they relied most on (see table 10.9). The results of simple cross-tabulation analyses showed clearly that the perceived availability of persons to satisfy either expressive or instrumental needs was strongest for old persons who relied most on their spouses and other kin, and weakest for old persons who depended most on their friends and other persons.

Recent Stressful Events

The third category of social experiences reported by the old person involved the occurrence of recent stressful events. These events are usually perceived as having undesirable consequences and their occurrence is largely independent of the perceptions or interpretations of old people.[7] However, the experiential conse-

Table 10.10. Occurrence of Stressful Life
Events in Past Year

Stressful Event	Percentage Responding Yes
Child divorced	7
Spouse's death	4
Close relative's death	24
Relative's serious illness	24
Friend's death	21
Friend moved away	25
Child or relative moved away	12

quences of these events vary along two distinctive dimensions: the amount of distress or upset they cause the old person (Paykel, Prusoff, and Uhlenhuth 1971); and the amount, duration, and intensity of change they create in the old person's accustomed style of living (Holmes and Rahe 1967).[8]

An investigation of these consequences was not carried out in this study; however, the percentages of old people who experienced six relatively common stressful events of old age are displayed in table 10.10.

Social Activity Behavior, Social Experiences, and Moving Expectations and Preferences of Evanston's Elderly

Like the observed effects of unfavorable territorial and physical environment experiences, it is expected that certain social experiences increase the likelihood of moving plans and preferences of Evanston's elderly population. Simple correlational analyses revealed the following relationships (table 10.11).

Old people who saw their children less frequently were more likely to expect and prefer to move. However, other measures of social activity were unrelated. Old people's dissatisfaction with the nearness of their dwelling to their family or relatives also was associated with stronger moving expectations, but not with greater moving preferences. This perhaps implies that dissatisfying fam-

Table 10.11. Correlations (Pearson r's) between Social Activity Behavior and Experiences and Moving Expectations, Moving Preferences

Social Activity and Social Experiences	Moving Expectations	Moving Preferences
Frequency child seen	−.125*	−.120*
Frequency close relative seen	−.039	−.043
Frequency close friend seen	.046	.013
Frequency neighbors visited	−.023	−.046
Enjoyment from age composition of neighborhood	−.182***	−.170***
Enjoyment from social class composition of neighborhood	−.151***	−.159***
Enjoyment from racial composition of neighborhood	−.109*	−.117**
Satisfaction with people in neighborhood	−.143*	−.239***
Neighbors' age perceived same as respondent	−.004	.035
Neighbors' class perceived same as respondent	−.099*	−.088*
Neighbors' race perceived same as respondent	−.096*	−.063
Satisfaction with dwelling's nearness to family, relatives	−.125**	−.070
Satisfaction with friends in community	−.061	−.095*
Enjoyment from visiting with neighbors	−.082*	−.149*
Enjoyed company of pet	−.040	−.037
Enjoyed helping someone with chore or problem	.014	.010
Enjoyed talking with storekeepers or clerks	.003	−.043
Enjoyed being home alone	−.027	−.053
Felt lack of privacy in dwelling	.154***	.117**
Felt lonely	.108*	.104*
Felt bored in dwelling	.143**	.138**
Availability of sociopsychological supports	−.073	−.019
Availability of expressive social supports	−.054	−.033
Availability of instrumental social supports	−.068	−.008
Child divorced in past year (Yes = 1, No = 0)	.002	.022
Spouse's death in past year (Yes = 1, No = 0)	.007	.050
Close relative's death in past year (Yes = 1, No = 0)	.005	.010
Relative's serious illness in past year (Yes = 1, No = 0)	−.022	−.040
Friend's death in past year (Yes = 1, No = 0)	−.007	.043
Friend moved away in past year (Yes = 1, No = 0)	−.012	−.027
Child or relative moved away in past year (Yes = 1, No = 0)	−.006	.018

***p < .001 **p < .01 *p < .05

ily experiences are cause for some old people to plan a move, but, if given a choice, some would prefer not to. In contrast, dissatisfaction with friends was associated with moving preferences, but not with moving expectations. This perhaps implies that some old people would prefer to move in order to improve their friendship experiences, but that these unsatisfactory relationships are not of sufficient urgency for them to plan or expect a future move.

The social situation experiences were among the strongest and most consistent correlates. Dissatisfaction with people in the neighborhood and less enjoyment from a neighborhood due to its population's age, class, and racial composition were associated with stronger moving expectations and preferences. Neighbors who were perceived as being of a different class or race (but not age) were at least part of the reason for these moving responses. Old people who expected and preferred to move also had enjoyable neighbor visits less frequently.

Experiences involving the social environment of the dwelling also proved to be relatively strong correlates. Lack of privacy and the greater incidence of both loneliness and boredom were significantly associated with moving plans and preferences. In contrast, the perceived unavailability of sociopsychological supports and the recent occurrence of stressful life events were statistically unrelated to either moving plans or preferences.

Chapter Eleven

Conclusions

The preceding chapters have described and explained in both theoretical and empirical terms the variable impact that the everyday residential environment has on a relatively healthy, independent elderly population in an urban middle-class community. The length and complexity of the material covered preclude a detailed summary. However, this chapter summarizes the major lessons derived from the empirical research, identifies the strengths and weaknesses of the conceptual efforts, and discusses the relevance of the findings to planners and policy makers.

Lessons from the Empirical Analyses

The data collected from structured interviews of a random sample of Evanston's aged 60 and older population facilitated two distinctive sets of empirical analyses. The first set, which was primarily descriptive, ascertained the likelihood that elderly people would experience particular outcomes or consequences from their environmental transactions. The second set, primarily explanatory, determined which individual characteristics influenced the occurrence of these environmental experiences. Some general insights and impressions that emerged from these analyses are summarized below.

Descriptive Analyses

The empirical findings underscored the difficulty of comprehensively summarizing the impact of the everyday residential environment on an elderly population. The 15 categories of environmental experiences distinguished by the factor analysis (chapter 4) only partially encompassed the varied ways in which the environment can impinge on its elderly residents. Given that a research effort such as this can hope to record only a small portion of a setting's empirical reality, the task of thoroughly documenting old people's experiential worlds is imposing. Nonetheless, the findings of this study demonstrated the numerous ways in which the environment of the old person may be a source of positive and negative experiences. Some of the positive outcomes were more predictable and less remarkable than others: the comfort and pride of occupying a safe, controllable, trouble-free, and manageable dwelling, the enjoyment derived from having compatible neighbors, friends, and relatives living nearby, the good times had from activities in the community, and the peace of mind from knowing that there is a person to rely on in time of need. Other positive outcomes, because they have been less often documented by social scientists, were more interesting: the rewards and pleasures of having a pet in one's house, the enjoyment derived from doing something for someone else, the spontaneous, unplanned, casual, and enjoyable exchanges with storekeepers, clerks, and other working people, the novelty and variation experienced by doing something different in one's community, and the assurance derived from having a helpful janitor in one's apartment building.

The types of environmental transactions yielding negative outcomes were also varied. Some environmental features were sources of anxiety and frustration because they prevented or constrained the activities of old people; others simply made activities physically or emotionally more troublesome to complete such as bad weather or poor walking conditions. Some environmental qualities did not directly impinge on old people's activities, but their occurrence resulted in emotional stress and anxiety: the fear of a home break-in, the grief from losing loved ones, the persistent discomfort from a dwelling too warm in the summer or too cold in the winter. Other environmental aspects appeared to be less stressful but still constituted important nuisances: the loud noises outside the house or apartment, and the polluted air.

In total these findings provide an important lesson. Social scientists should be wary of making oversimplified generalizations about the consequences old people experience in the course of living in a place. The environment impinges on an elderly population's well-being through its positive *and* negative aspects, its minor *and* major stimulations or assaults, its habitual *and* spontaneous events, its social *and* physical qualities, through its more specific, detailed parts *and* its larger, system components (e.g., its existential spaces—chapter 8), and through its effects on overt *and* covert behaviors. A full appreciation of an environment's impact on old people requires an understanding of its multidimensional fabric.

Despite this diversity and complexity, an orderliness exists. Similar types of experiences are shared by groups of old people— some old persons more than others feel fear, anxiety, or fatigue as a result of transacting with very different aspects of their residential setting. For example, old people who have difficulty dealing with their inside-dwelling problems also have more difficulty negotiating with parts of their out-of-dwelling environment; old people who look with favor on the population composition of their neighborhood are also more likely to have satisfying neighborhood friendships.

The descriptive empirical analyses also made it possible to assess the extent of an environment's impact on a population of elderly residents. The findings echoed those of other research investigations (e.g., Lawton 1978). Most old people were satisfied with, were proud of, and had good memories about their community, neighborhoods, and dwellings. The majority of the elderly population experienced pleasurable outcomes from the physical aspects (natural, built, urbanized, and social welfare) of their residential settings. For example, most elderly people were not bothered by the usual nuisances of urban living (e.g., noise, pollution). They felt their houses and apartments had qualities that yielded comfortable experiences (e.g., size, temperature, attractiveness); they were satisfied with the availability and accessibility of their community services; they were able to accomplish their everyday needs in the community without experiencing physical or emotional stress; they did not feel the need for social welfare services; and they experienced "good times" in their community or neighborhoods. The majority of elderly people also enjoyed good experiences from their social environments. For example, they were satisfied with their neighborhood social situations (distinguished by their homogeneity of inhabitants' race, class, and age); they enjoyed visiting with their neighbors and were satisfied with their friends; they obtained enjoyment from helping other people with chores; they did not feel lonely or bored; and they felt they knew at least one reliable person to satisfy their emotional and material needs.

The social scientist seeking generalizations might be tempted to end the discussion here. However, to do so would obscure another important lesson conveyed by the response distributions. Sizable minorities of elderly persons, although occupying a relatively desirable middle-class community, reported they often had unfavorable, unpleasant, and stressful environmental experiences. For instance, some 8 percent of the elderly were frequently annoyed because their neighbors neglected their properties and because their streets or sidewalks were strewn with litter; some 9 percent were bothered by noises outside their dwellings; 16 percent of the elderly felt their houses were too big; 4 percent often felt fatigued as a result of caring for their homes; 8 percent frequently felt annoyed about having no place to rest while doing their shopping; 33 percent persistently felt frightened about going out at night because of crime; 18 percent persistently worried about being attacked or robbed while walking and 19 percent worried that a thief might break into their home; 26 percent were frequently bothered by cold weather and snow and 18 percent persistently postponed their plans because of bad weather; 16 percent often were discouraged from going out at night because of poor street lighting; 12 percent did not go places in their community because they were not within walking distance; 9 percent frequently felt lonely; 13

percent were dissatisfied with how far they lived from their family and relatives; and 14 percent felt they could not count on someone to help them with chores around their house.

The environment's impact was also measured by identifying environmental experiences that were significantly correlated with old people's moving expectations and preferences. Unpleasant dwelling (house or apartment) experiences most persistently contributed to old people's preferring or expecting to move. Two explanations were offered. First, it was argued that the dwelling constituted the most salient of the territorial contexts occupied and used by elderly people and thus dwelling-linked outcomes would have considerable personal impact. Outcomes were less likely to be ignored or dismissed as unimportant because they impinged on needs essential to the emotional and material well-being of elderly people. Moreover, whereas elderly persons could shut out the stressful aspects of the community and neighborhood, such avoidance strategies in response to dwelling experiences would be less successful.

The second explanation shifted attention to the relative effectiveness of alternative environmental (relocation) coping strategies (Lazarus 1966). If an elderly person who seeks an improved dwelling environment carefully selects and maintains a new dwelling, he can be fairly confident that it will not be afflicted with the same ills as the previous one. In contrast, this is a far less effective coping strategy for old people wishing to alleviate their current neighborhood or community problems. There would be few guarantees that the same problems could be avoided in a new residential location, and unlike dwelling deficiencies they would be perceived as being outside of one's personal control. Because of such uncertainties, stressful community and neighborhood problems are not as likely to lead to anticipated relocations.

Explanatory Analyses

A consideration of the empirical analyses that assessed which individual variables influenced the likelihood of environmental experiences leaves the researcher with at least two impressions. First, the amount of variation explained by the individual variables was not large; and second, these variables influenced the environmental experiences of elderly people in very diverse and complex ways.

The individual variables usually explained from 10 to 25 percent of the total variation in any given dependent variable (the occurrence of an environmental experience). This level of explanation is similar to, if not higher than, past studies with comparable analytical goals. The presentation of these figures, however, belies the intent of the investigation, which was *not* to construct statistical or predictive models, but to identify those individual variables most likely to influence the variable impact of the everyday residential environment. Nevertheless, because some readers will judge the utility of these analyses on this basis, it is important to account for the relatively small amount of variation explained by the individual variables.

Probably the most important reason is that individuals are complex living systems and the time and cost limitations of a research project make it prohibitive to measure but a small number of attributes that are likely to influence a person's environmental cognitions and perceptions. Furthermore, any one individual variable is likely to account in only a small way for people's variable perceptions and interpretations of their world. Second, despite the lack of very extreme environmental contrasts in the Evanston community, considerable differences were observed (chapter 3) in the qualities of the territorial, physical, and social environments occupied by the elderly. These variable objective conditions undoubtedly constituted another source of unmeasured influences on old people's environmental experiences. A third reason is more complex and less often identified. Many of the environmental experiences being explained are relatively less pervasive and enduring than the individual variables providing the explanation (see ref. Jessor and Jessor 1973, chapter 4). Environmental experiences, even if constant over a period of several months or a few years, often are more temporally specific than many of the individual characteristics, including those identified with a particular stage in life. Thus, there is often an attempt to explain relatively transitory environmental perceptions and evaluations by relatively long-term individual processes. On the other hand, explaining the more temporally enduring experiences is also complicated because to a considerable extent they do not reflect an old person's currently perceived reality, but rather a mixture of past and present recollections. Thus the individual variables are really explaining not just the environmental experiences of old people, but those of younger persons now grown old. Accounting for the variability of experiences of unknown origin and existence is obviously a more difficult task.

The variables found to have statistically significant direct effects demonstrated the multiple individual processes that influence old people's interpretations and evaluations of their residential setting. The following examples illustrate the diversity of the reported relationships.

Satisfaction with both the community and neighborhood settings was greater for old people who were more strongly disposed to an urban way of life. Such a disposition implied that their environmental needs were more likely to be satisfied in an urban-oriented community, that they associated greater benefits with urban living, and that they were more likely to have accommodated to the problems and stresses of urban living. In contrast, the dwelling dissatisfaction of old people with stimulus-seeking dispositions implied their inability to satisfy their needs for novelty, variation, and excitement in their dwellings. The finding that widows were more proud of their dwellings than married people was given a very different interpretation. It was inferred that widowed elderly persons considered the dwelling to be a more salient and valued part of their environment, viewing it as an important material symbol of their past lives, a reminder of a formerly happy family life, and an indicator of past achievements and successes. In contrast, it was inferred that separated-divorced elderly had unpleasant reminders of their past lives and this explained why they were less likely than married elderly to recall good memories about their homes. Another type of explanation was given for why higher income elderly persons were less satisfied with their community than lower income elderly. It was inferred that higher income elderly had higher expectations and aspirations than lower income elderly. This resulted in their evaluations of their community's quality of life falling short of their expectations, a gap that manifested itself in expressions of dissatisfaction. Other individual characteristics were also interpreted as reducing the likelihood of demands being satisfied. For instance, it was inferred that elderly who were divorced-separated, Jewish, or recently forced to retire had less in common with their neighbors and that this minority status led to their less frequently enjoying visits with their neighbors. Experiential outcomes that depended on the elderly person's physical ability to perform particular tasks were more likely to be influenced by individual variables from which competence levels could be inferred. For example, old people who found that taking care of their homes was too tiring or who had trouble walking because of bad sidewalks were also likely to rate their health as poorer and to have more functional impairments. Similarly, old people who were more dependent on social welfare services were more likely to rate their health as poorer. It was also found that old people who felt less in control of their lives (perceived external locus of control) were more likely to postpone plans because of bad weather. Certain types of emotional discomforts or anxieties—such as produced by one's fear of crime—were also more likely to be experienced by old people, who, psychologically, financially, and physically, were more vulnerable or weaker. The finding that the employed elderly were less likely than the nonemployed elderly to fear going out at night because of crime was interpreted very differently. It was inferred that the employed elderly, because they were busy working during the day, placed greater importance on and were more accustomed to satisfying their needs after dark.

Certain individual variables statistically influenced the environmental experiences of old people more consistently than others. This was true of the individual variables measuring psychological well-being. It was theorized that old people who had not successfully adapted to life (low psychological well-being) would transfer this maladjustment to all their environmental transactions, resulting in affective and evaluative environmental responses dominated by negative tones. This proposition was supported by findings demonstrating that old people dissatisfied with their lives were more likely to evaluate their residential settings and their social relationships less favorably. Old people's activity behaviors were also found to influence often the occurrence of environmental experiences. For example, old people who were less active or who displayed locationally restricted travel patterns (small activity spaces) evaluated the proximate parts of their environment (such as their dwellings and neighborhoods) more positively. These findings suggested that old people whose lives revolved around their most immediate residential setting regarded it as especially salient for their happiness (Golant 1983).

The findings emphasized the need to distinguish between objective and subjective individual differences as determinants of environmental experiences. For instance, reported household income sometimes did not influence environmental outcomes in the same way as perceived money needs. One explanation for the discrepancy was the different mental and behavioral states associated with these individual differences. Higher income levels were linked with people's higher environmental expectation levels—a personal state that increased the probability of environmental dissatisfaction. On the other hand, an absence of perceived money difficulties suggested that persons felt more economically competent and thus were better able to achieve their needs—a condition that increased the probability of environmental satisfaction.

The findings also showed that the outcomes of environmental experiences often do not depend on a population's stage in life. Rather, they reflect individual differences found among populations of any age that are due to attributes such as sex, race, socioeconomic status and personality dispositions. It would be predicted, for example, that females of all ages are more fearful than males of the threat of being a crime victim.

Two factors contributed to the ambiguous interpretation of individual influences. First, there was the possibility that individual characteristics revealed less about individuals *qua* individuals than about the objective qualities of the environment they occupied. For example, the finding that elderly blacks were more likely than elderly whites to experience certain environmental outcomes may not reflect their different needs or levels of competence as much as it reflects the systematic differences in their residential environments. Thus elderly blacks' greater concern that their homes might be burglarized probably reflects not only their greater vulnerability but also their occupying neighborhoods with higher crime rates (although this was not investigated).

Second, there was the possibility that individual characteristics indicated less about how old people differently perceived and interpreted their environment than about how "other persons" differently perceived and interpreted the characteristics of elderly people. This ambiguity was especially apparent when interpreting how the individual variables influenced the social experiences, but also occurred when interpreting the individual antecedents of physical experiences. For example, it may be inferred that elderly persons in poor health are less able to initiate or keep friendships because they are physically unable to visit or go out with other persons. Feelings of loneliness are a predictable result. Alternatively, the poor health of elderly persons may increase the probability that other people view them as less attractive friends, because they feel uncomfortable being with sick people. Again, feelings of loneliness are the result, but the empirical analyses do not reveal which interpretation is more correct.

Theoretical Approach: Lessons and Directions

Conceptualization and Measurement of Environmental Impact/Experiences

Early chapters in this book revealed the numerous decisions that are made by the researcher who seeks to describe the subjectively defined impact of the everyday environment on old people. The conceptual and methodological boundaries of the research inquiry were shown to depend on the selection of the research site's sociocultural and local settlement qualities; the selection of the parts and components of the environment (e.g., houses, services, people, sidewalks, weather, crime, transportation); the designation of their attributes or properties (e.g., homogeneity, physical condition, complexity, temperature); and the specification of potential consequences of individual-environment transactions. These decisions give the researcher considerable control over the character of the investigated environment. It is critical to understand the implications of this "control," because the researcher's personal and scientific views of people and their environments influence greatly the findings and conclusions of any investigation. In this study these research decisions produced what was identified as the "scholar's dilemma" (chapter 2).

This research effort attempted to portray the residential environment as comprehensively and holistically as possible, encompassing the qualities of a place with which old people typically transact in the course of their everyday lives. This was not easy given the complex form and functioning of the nonlaboratory, unplanned setting. To accomplish breadth of analysis, it became necessary to sacrifice some of the specificity demanded by scientific analysis. For example, many aspects of the Evanston environment were designated by only one or two physical or social properties. As a result, respondents were presented with a comprehensive set of people, things, and events to evaluate, but these were depicted as relatively simple entities. Thus there was danger that respondents evaluated their environments on the basis of attributes that were not the most significant to them. To address the limitations of this approach, another common research strategy was initiated, but it also suffered from inherent weaknesses. Old people were asked to evaluate environmental parts and components that were not delineated by any specific properties or attributes. For instance, respondents were asked about their satisfaction with their dwellings or neighborhoods. But this also results in uncertainty as to which attributes or properties the respondents have in mind when they evaluate their dwellings and neighborhoods as satisfactory. Moreover, the possibility exists that these places are being evaluated on the basis of entirely different sets of attributes.

To achieve breadth of analysis, the study also broadly conceptualized the alternative subjective outcomes that can arise from occupying and utilizing the everyday residential environment. Again, such a research design results in an undesirable "thinness" of empirical coverage and the risk that the most relevant outcomes of particular transactions are not being measured. This study's comprehensive depiction of environmental impact is also susceptible to the criticism that subjective outcomes were not measured consistently or systematically across all environmental events and objects. That is, many of the measured potential outcomes were specific to particular environmental transactions and contents. For example, fear was measured as a consequence of crime, and fatigue was measured as a consequence of walking. This eclectic approach had the advantage of translating environmental impact into terms that were part of the respondent's everyday language. On the other hand, it was a less rigorous and replicable approach than that of Mehrabian and Russell (1974) (see chapter 4), who summarized all environmental outcomes as a function of three primary emotional responses.

There is no simple resolution of the above issues. However, an awareness of the strengths and weaknesses of a study's strategies may be helpful to other researchers.

Environmental Impact: How New?

A reader of this book commented on its static quality, stating that little was learnt about actual mobility patterns; what happens to those old people who prefer or intend to move; and how environments just recently selected by old people impinge on their well-being. Although legitimate areas of concern, their investigation would have required a very different research design. However, there is a more subtle way in which this research can be accused of being static. This is in its failure to explore systematically the effects of the elderly person's life history (Rowles 1978).

The introduction to this book made an obvious observation: life does not begin at age 60 or 65. In likewise fashion an old person's environmental experiences do not begin at some arbitrary chronological age. An environment is seldom making its first impressions on a person at age 60 or 65. Most old people have lived a substantial period of time in their current houses, apartments, and communities. Moreover, over half of Evanston's elderly population had frequently thought about the good memories brought back by their dwellings and neighborhoods. Thus although interviewers may ask respondents about their current environmental reality, their replies in considerable part reflect environmental judgments and attitudes formed earlier in their lives. This observation is probably less true for elderly who are relative newcomers to a place. However, even the current environmental responses of this group will reflect earlier acquired housing tastes and preferences and prior accommodations to earlier experienced environmental deficiencies.

Although these are relatively unremarkable observations, few students of environmental impact are careful to point them out. Researchers often make references to the "consequences of living in a place" as if they are describing a uniquely current relationship. Many popular articles along with scientific reports describe the housing deficiencies or the noxious neighborhoods of elderly persons as if these outcomes or consequences are now only being experienced for the first time in old age. More likely, for many of these elderly, these very same problems existed in their younger years. It is in the inability of this research to trace and assess the impact of these environmental pasts that makes it vulnerable to the criticism of being static.

Environmental Impact: How Important?

People who become old in the United States today typically confront numerous sources of stress and grief. They suddenly have to fill what may appear as excessive amounts of free time due to retirement, adjust to living alone without a spouse, accept the loss of valued relatives and lifelong friends, deal with the limitations imposed by health and body changes, cope calmly and wisely with the recognition that they cannot relive or change their past lives, and deal constructively with the realization that they have a limited number of years to live. On the other hand, old age may bring with it many new rewarding challenges and opportunities. Old people may thrive on the large amounts of free time available to engage in leisure and recreation activities, embark enthusiastically on a second career earlier considered too risky or inappropriate, and contemplate meaningfully about their religious, spiritual, or inner selves. The frequency old people confront both these tribulations and joys and how well they cope with their consequences are undoubtedly important factors to be fitted into any equation designed to understand how successfully they grow old.

In light of this complex matrix of events and activities, it is reasonable to inquire about the relative impact of the residential situation—the place called home—on old people's well-being. To what extent do the environmental experiences examined in this book impinge on the overall aging experience?

What can be said with certainty is that where one lives produces—in the minds and bodies of old people—some very real consequences, whether these be the fears and locomotion restrictions due to crime and the annoyance of an unattractive neighborhood, or the excitement and exhilaration of engaging in novel or different community activities and the pride of living in a place. It is also clear that some of these residential experiences are sufficiently unpleasant in their impact to prompt old people to make moving plans or express strong moving preferences.

These are the certainties; but we are still left in doubt as to the degree to which positive and negative environmental outcomes influence the overall aging experience. The findings offer no basis by which to assign some relative weight or magnitude to the observed environmental effects. For example, it is impossible to determine the extent to which the misery resulting from a severe illness or loss of ambulatory ability is *compensated for* by an attractive, secure, clean, intact, viable neighborhood, good friends, and responsive social welfare organizations. It is impossible to know the extent to which a loving and supportive spouse and a life judged as successful can *compensate for* the anxieties created by architectural barriers, a run-down neighborhood, and poor transportation services.

Even the relative impact of specific environmental experiences is less than perfectly clear because the findings leave unresolved two important issues. First, it is not possible to ascertain the extent to which the consequences of different environmental experiences counteract or reinforce one another. For instance, do the consequences of equally good and equally bad experiences cancel each other out? Do the consequences of several positive (or negative) experiences produce an impact greater than the sum of their separate effects? Is it possible that what were referred to earlier as minor disturbances of urban living may in the aggregate produce an outcome much more stressful than the most stressful life event (Holmes and Rahe 1967)? Second, although we can document the frequency with which an old person experiences fear, anxiety, or other emotional discomforts, the findings do not reveal how elderly individuals differently handle or cope with these stresses. Some old people will undoubtedly deal with their discomforts, fears, and failures better than others. Thus it is very likely that the same perceived environmental consequences will impinge differently on the overall well-being of old people.

Studies of relatively large samples of population (old or young) have not as yet provided answers to these difficult questions. However, their resolution will be necessary to obtain a full understanding of the impact of the everyday environment on the overall aging experience—an important agenda for future research.

Model of Individual Differences

The model of individual differences proposed in this book distinguished itself in two general ways. First, in recognition of the complex and systemic functioning of the individual, elderly persons were simultaneously distinguished by several categories of personal attributes. This contrasted with the more limited perspectives of other studies. These focused only on one or two individual constructs to explain the variable impact of the environment on old people—such as expectation and aspiration levels (Campbell, Converse, and Rodgers 1976), adaptation level and information processing abilities (Wohlwill 1976), competence levels (Lawton and Nahemow 1973), locus of control (Parr 1980), and psychoenvironmental history (Howell 1980; Rowles 1978).

Second, several of the individual characteristics in this study were analyzed as antecedents of elderly people's variable environmental experiences even though they were examined in past research as consequences. This was in response to both theoretical and empirical evidence suggesting that these earlier stereotypic causal relationships were unnecessarily limiting. The antecedent roles theorized for the individual variables, psychological well-being (life satisfaction and level of happiness) and activity behavior (activity levels, activity space size, and change in level of activity), illustrated this study's departure from past practices. Importantly, the conceptualization of these variables as antecedents of an elderly person's environmental experiences did not rule out their conceptualization as consequences also. For instance, it was probable that higher morale levels led to old people's favorable evaluations of their residential settings and that, in turn, these positive subjective outcomes contributed to old people's higher morale levels. One issue that cannot be addressed in this book is whether it is ever possible to isolate—theoretically or operationally—the components of such reciprocal relationships without "destroying the subject we are setting out to study" (Ittelson et al. 1976:192).

After the model was tested in Evanston, it became apparent that certain conceptual and operational refinements were needed. First, the model should specify more carefully the mental and behavioral states being measured by the individual variables. For example, sometimes more than one mental or behavioral state could be inferred from the same individual variable as when female status was interpreted as an indicator of an old person's style of living and of an old person's physical vulnerability in the face of a hostile environment. These are both acceptable interpretations that have been reported many times in the literature; however, scientific rigor is threatened when an individual variable's effects can be interpreted in several ways. Another related weakness concerns the inadequate measurement of certain personal domains. For example, the variables from which competence level was inferred obviously did not fully depict the different types and levels of mental and behavioral functioning that are embodied in this individual state. These difficulties can be remedied by simple methodological modifications.

The model could be improved in a second way. This would require measuring the interpretations old people give to their residential and activity behaviors. Conceptually, the study identified alternative cognitive and motivational states associated with elderly individuals' initiation of their activity behaviors, but no equivalent empirical measures were constructed. Thus it was not possible, for example, to assess whether old people with involuntarily restricted small activity spaces had environmental experiences that differed from those with voluntarily initiated small activity spaces. This leaves open the possibility that several of the weak or nonexistent statistical relationships found between activity space size and environmental experiences resulted from individuals having opposing motives that statistically canceled out the true effects of their associated behaviors. For instance, small activity spaces may have consistently led to unpleasant environmental experiences only for those old people who were involuntarily confined to their proximate environment, but not for those elderly whose home-centered life-styles were of their own choosing.

A third extension of the model involves the specification of the theoretical linkages between and among the "knowing" and "behavioral relationship" individual variables. For example, it is unclear the extent to which longtime occupancy in the same place lowers or raises an individual's expectations of environmental quality or the extent to which physical incompetence leads to a different set of individual needs. Understanding such linkages would facilitate hypotheses about the reinforcing or contradictory effects that different personal characteristics have on environmental experiences. For example, although various individual states may contribute to an old person feeling secure from the threat of crime, the presence of poor health—and the vulnerability it generates—may be sufficient to override these positive influences. The theoretical arguments for the systemic impact of these individual variables require further development.

A fourth recommendation is to measure the temporal properties of the individual variables. Although the variability of certain individual characteristics (e.g., health status) was judged to be a function of a population's stage in life, this judgment was not based on empirical evidence. Obviously, it would be more desirable to ascertain from interview data (when necessary and appropriate) the actual length of time that a particular individual characteristic has existed. This methodological strategy would help clarify the extent to which old people's environmental experiences are a product of recent or lifelong individual influences.

A final recommendation concerns the need to address a broader, more fundamental research issue. This is to identify the environmental conditions (or situations) in which individual variables tend to be worse or better predictors of human behavior (Mischel 1973). When considered in the context of this book's research, the question can be framed as follows: In what types of environments will old people's mental and behavioral states and behavioral relationships have stronger effects on their environmental experiences? To examine this question requires that environments or places be differentiated by a set of objectively verifiable and generalizable variables. In other work I (1984) identified five place attributes for this purpose: heterogeneity, complexity, predictability, extremeness, and restrictiveness. This earlier paper theorized about how the effects of old people's behavioral relationships would vary in environments differentiated by these attributes. It was proposed that the more heterogeneous, complex, unpredictable, unextreme, and unrestrictive the properties of the environment, the more likely that variation in the content and consequences of environmental experiences would be explained by a population's activity and residential behaviors. It is useful to give some of the reasoning behind this proposed relationship.

When an environment's contents are homogeneous (or uniform) and simple (that is, few components, designated by few properties), people's variable activity behaviors are predicted to make less of an impact on their environmental experiences, because similar opportunities for experiences will exist in almost all spatial and temporal contexts. Additionally, the greater environmental familiarity that is theorized as accompanying longer length of occupancy will have little significance, because accurate and complete cognitive representations of these homogeneous and simple environmental conditions will be achievable in a much shorter time period.

In an environment distinguished by its predictability and certainty, human activities are less likely to have the potential of yielding spontaneous experiences, simply because the relevant opportunities will be fewer. Furthermore, in a predictable environment, the greater environmental familiarity and feelings of security that would be derived from a longer duration in residence would be much less significant.

When an environment has properties consistently aligned along the extreme end of certain dimensions of attributes (for example, extremely noisy, very high crime rate, or very hot temperatures), then an individual's residential and activity behaviors will less effectively modify or change the impact of these qualities. In effect, it is less likely that the activity and residential behaviors of individuals can "create" any satisfactory environmental contents.

Finally, and most obviously, when the qualities of the environment continually restrict activity or residential behaviors, then, by definition, these behaviors cease to become mechanisms by which individuals can select, modify, or change the contents of their environment.

Similar propositional relationships can and should be identified to predict how the effects of the old individual's mental and behavioral states (e.g., competence, morale) will vary among places differentiated by similar properties.

Focus on the Elderly Person: Planning and Policy Implications

Difficulties of Interpreting the Practical Significance of Environmental Experiences

Subjective indicators of environmental quality—such as provided by the measurement of environmental experiences—constitute one basis by which to diagnose a population's problems and formulate recommendations to solve them. Although this book was not written for the purpose of making such planning and policy assessments, some readers will undoubtedly interpret its findings from this perspective. Consequently, it is important to point to some of the strengths and weaknesses of a subjective indicator approach. At the outset it should be emphasized that a full treatment of this topic would require an essay much longer than appropriate for a concluding chapter. Thus, only a few key issues are considered here. For more extensive discussions, readers are referred to Campbell, Converse, and Rodgers (1976) and Johnston (1981).

Most important is the recognition that subjective indicators of environmental quality display a "positivity bias" (Campbell, Converse, and Rodgers 1976). That is, people's subjective evaluations of their environment will lean toward the positive. One social scientist has explained this pattern as a function of three factors: "(1) the basic positive orientation of American culture, (2) the consistent rating of self-happiness higher than happiness of others, and (3) social desirability-conformance with a social norm dictating expressions of satisfaction or happiness, especially evident in personal interview situations" (Smith 1979:19, as quoted in Wilcox 1981:4). This positivity bias may be accentuated in the Evanston study because of two additional factors. First, as discussed in chapter 2, the study of elderly people in a middle-class community probably portrays their well-being more favorably than studies which have focused on more vulnerable elderly populations occupying specialized or noxious settings. Second, as outlined in chapter 8, there are numerous reasons to expect that old people's subjective responses to their residential environment will be more favorable than those of younger people.

The positivity bias of subjective indicators led one critic to charge that survey data generally painted an unrealistically generous portrayal of the quality of life of the American population (Wilcox 1981). In response, one well-known researcher in the field of subjective indicators argued:

> On the contrary, given all the ways people change their lives and/or their criteria of judgment in order to enhance their sense of well-being, it would be surprising if large proportions of Americans were fundamentally dissatisfied with most of the common and basic life concerns . . . This assertion does not imply that life is heavenly for most people—surely it is not. However, there is an important psychological need to experience at least some positive elements in aspects of life that are closely linked to oneself, and it appears that most people achieve this for themselves most of the time. One way of achieving it is to make changes in the objective circumstances of one's life, take a part-time job, move to a warmer climate, and so on. Another way is to adjust the criteria by which well-being is judged, for example, to decide that the way one presently spends one's days is good or to conclude that snow is fun or pretty. Both of these ways of coping with potential dissatisfactions are common, and achievement of an improved sense of well-being by either means is real and important. If people then report substantial levels of satisfaction—as most people do—this seems likely to be a reflection of what they actually experience. (Andrews 1981:27–28)

This response echoes the essence of the interactionist model. Subjective assessments of a residential setting are based not only on objective criteria but also on the states and behaviors of highly complex human beings, or *whole persons.* In large part old people's reports of how they feel about their homes and communities reflect how satisfied they are with their overall lives, how they view their life styles, how important it is for them to fulfill their needs and preferences, how competent they feel, what things they are willing to overlook, what their residences say about their status and position in the community, where they usually perform their activities, and so on. The result is that old people's positive or negative environmental experiences may have only weak connections with the objective properties (whether good or bad) of their residences. For example, old people's satisfaction with their dwellings was related to their morale, activity patterns, environmental dispositions, perceived economic status, and length of residence. When these individual variables are carefully scrutinized, it becomes clear that they have highly tentative and unpredictable environmental referents (Golant 1982).

An acknowledgement that subjective indicators have a positivity bias and reflect "whole persons" cautions against using them alone to diagnose environmental needs (Golant 1982). Without an understanding of their idiosyncratic origins, subjective indicators of environmental quality may yield findings that are highly ambiguous, difficult to interpret, and even misleading. Taken together these observations should give pause to those who interpret the book's findings to imply that housing, neighborhood, and community problems of the elderly are not of sufficient severity to merit current levels of program funding or government support.

On the other hand, it is just as true that a society's standards—by which objective indicators of environmental well-being are derived and interpreted—are inadequate by themselves as guidelines for making policy-planning evaluations. Inevitably, these standards will be derived from a characterization of an "average" elderly person who is aging in a "typical" way. Despite the best of intentions, it is entirely unclear that the imposition of these general standards of environmental well-being will be sensitive to or detect those old people who are most in need of assistance. Indeed, interventions based on these objective and detached standards may be more damaging or injurious to individual well-being than any inaction—as early demonstrated by various sociological studies of urban life (e.g., Firey 1945; Fried and Gleicher 1961). One must confront some complex ethical issues if one is going to inform elderly people that they should *not* be satisfied or happy with their residential settings because they have been judged inadequate by objective criteria. Old people, however much they are molded by the expectations and pressures of society, will still act to a considerable degree *qua* individuals with the result that their idiosyncratic preferences, evaluations, feelings, and wants cannot be overlooked or understated.

In short, planners and policy makers must be careful to scrutinize the values and motives that underlie their "objective" assessments of old people's residential environments, because it is not certain that these judgments will be consistent with those of old people. At the same time, subjective indicators are inadequate as the only evidence of need. Rather, a comprehensive examination of environmental quality must incorporate both objective and subjective analytical perspectives, each providing an important interpretative "check" on the other. Neither perspective is necessarily more correct, nor necessarily should be weighted more heavily than the other.

Beyond these general considerations, it is possible to identify three ways in which the findings of this book have practical applications.

(1) The findings make clear that to design new environments or improve the existing ones requires an understanding of how the "whole person" relates to his or her environment (Pastalan 1977). This implies that strategies of intervention must be sensitive not only to an old person's competence levels (e.g., perception-cognition impairments, life- and self-maintenance difficulties) but also be cognizant of the elderly person's life-styles, overall psychological well-being, attachment to community, reminiscing habits, and so on (see next section).

(2) The findings make clear that sizable numbers of elderly persons are experiencing unfavorable environmental outcomes. These constitute a "checklist" of items that should be addressed by appropriate program and planning responses. For instance, the difficulties that Evanston's elderly homeowners have in taking care of their dwellings emphasize the need for policies and programs designed to ease the burden of homeownership or to facilitate old people's relocation into more manageable residential accommodations (Struyk and Soldo 1980).

(3) Reports of how the environment affects Evanston's elderly also provide baseline data from which to estimate how old people

will evaluate environments or situations with new or different qualities. For example, there was virtual unanimity among the elderly that lack of privacy was never felt to be a problem. If comparable levels of privacy could not be realized in their future residences, personal discomfort would be a predictable result.

The Utility of Client-Oriented Therapies

An interactionist perspective allows for two diametrically opposite strategies by which to reduce or eliminate the harmful or noxious consequences of an environment. To recall, the interactionist argues that "situations (environments) are as much a function of the person as the person's behavior is a function of the situation" (Bowers 1973:327). In practical terms this implies that beneficial change may be accomplished by either manipulating the properties of the individual or manipulating the properties of the environment.

Consider the example of the auto-dependent elderly person living in a low-density suburb whose renewal application for a driver's license has just been turned down. In light of poor suburban public transit and the inherent limitations of walking as a transportation mode, the initiation of out-of-dwelling activities now becomes far more difficult and a once rewarding life-style becomes threatened. To effectuate change four types of solutions are possible: (a) modify the functioning of relevant social institutions—licensing bureau, state vehicle agency, etc.—so as to eliminate unjust and unfair age-discrimination practices responsible for the revoking of the old person's driver's license; (b) increase the level of bus services in suburban areas; (c) increase financial resources of the old person enabling him or her to afford taxi or paratransit service on a regular basis; and (d) relocate the elderly person to a more accessible location.

The first two solutions involve the manipulation of the old person's environment or situation; the third and fourth involve the manipulation of the old person's competency and behaviors. Both approaches have the potential of attaining the same goal: increasing the old person's mobility. Operationally or administratively, however, very different intervention strategies are clearly involved.

These alternative approaches are well illustrated by the current policy debate over how to provide low-rent apartment housing for poor people (including the elderly) in the United States. The traditional strategy involves building new public housing units that charge below market rents. The newer (proposed) strategy involves the distribution of cash vouchers to poor persons (akin to food stamps) so as to enable them to afford the present market rents of existing rental units. The first approach requires the manipulation of the environment so as to create new housing; the latter approach, the manipulation of the resources of the potential consumers so as to enable them to afford existing housing.

Policy-oriented research directed at improving the quality of old people's housing or community environment has generally emphasized the former approach: changing or modifying the qualities of the physical setting or social situation. For instance, the literature is replete with recommendations as to how to improve the architectural design of elderly-occupied housing or how to make units and buildings more defensible against crime (Newman 1973).

In contrast, the orientation of this book presents an opportunity to examine the potential of the individual as an agent of environmental change. It builds on earlier made assumptions of the individual as a purposively-behaving or goal-oriented being who actively rather than passively receives and processes environmental information and, although hampered by personal weaknesses and constraints, nonetheless seeks out environmental alternatives and initiates adaptive strategies that better satisfy needs and wants. From this perspective policy and planning responses should be directed towards heightening and mobilizing individual potentials and incentives. Importantly, this proposed individual focus does not imply any value judgment as to the superiority of one approach over another. Indeed, many environmental problems will only be solvable by changing the environmental attributes which are the source of the problem. Rather, the intent is to draw attention to less considered individual-oriented intervention strategies

Figure 11.1. Client-Oriented Therapies to Address Residential Environmental Problems

Mental and Behavioral State	Therapy Illustration
Designative representation of environment Problem: Social Isolation Solution: Increase awareness of existing environmental opportunities	Inform old people of the availability of special transportation services (e.g., dial-a-bus); introduce old people to members of senior center
Demands made of environment Problem: Need for smaller, less expensive, apartment accommodations Solution: Modify demands of existing environment to satisfy needs	Demonstrate to old person the merits of subletting extra room in dwelling to elderly boarder
Subjective values of environmental demands Problem: Dwelling environment evaluated as excessively boring, unstimulating Solution: Self-initiated modifications of dwelling's properties	Recommend new in-dwelling projects and activities; advise how to encourage visits of friends, neighbors, and relatives to old person's dwelling
Aspirations and expectations of achieving demands Problem: Pervasive dissatisfaction with all aspects of residential setting Solution: Change standards of comparison	Counsel old person as to psychological basis of dissatisfaction. Emphasize environmental accomplishments and achievements as against failures and disappointments
Individual-environment congruence Problem: All aspects of life and environment evaluated as unpleasant Solution: Increase general morale	Counseling designed to improve old person's self-concept and outlook on life
Self-awareness and memories Problem: Excessive reminiscing; preoccupation with past events and places Solution: Heighten person's awareness and perceptions of current environmental stimulation	Psychiatric care; reality orientation
Cognitive and behavioral competence Problem: Fatigue experienced while walking to nearby places Solution: Improve physical stamina	Encourage older person to enroll in senior-citizen-oriented physical fitness program

Figure 11.1. *(continued)*

Behavioral Relationships	Therapy Illustration
Residential behaviors	
Problem: Disgusted with cold weather, high heating bills; fatigue experienced when taking care of house.	Counseling sessions designed to improve old person's chances of successful move
Solution: Facilitate individual's ability to relocate to warmer climate into high-rise apartment or condominium complex	
Activity behaviors	
Problem: Confined to dwelling because of chronic illness or severe ambulatory impairment	Counseling designed to sensitize old person to potential satisfactions from in-dwelling activities; improve old person's communica-
Solution: Change attitude of old person to being in his/her dwelling environment	tion skills so as to increase potential visits to dwelling by family, friends, and neighbors

through which the impact of a residential environment on individual well-being can be effectively manipulated. Ideally both individual- and environment-oriented strategies should be initiated to improve the quality of old people's everyday settings, each complimenting and reinforcing the other.

One basis by which to identify alternative individual-focused strategies is to distinguish individual states and behaviors (chapters 5 to 7) that can be changed, modified, or reinforced. Solutions to environmental problems thereby consist of client-oriented therapies designed to manipulate the relevant individual properties. This book concludes with a brief and preliminary illustration of such therapies (figure 11.1).

Appendix A

Residential Environment Experiences Not Included in Final Factor Solution

Object Category	Experiential Items	Hypothetical Consequences
BEp	Enjoyed watching T.V. or listening to radio	Comfort, relaxation, leisure
PEs	Enjoyed company of pet	Relatedness, emotional comfort, companionship, relaxation
BEp	Annoyed because of higher grocery prices where shop	Emotional discomfort, anxiety, helplessness
PEs	Felt grocery store clerks were unfriendly	Emotional discomfort, anxiety
BEp	Estimated number of blocks in neighborhood	Restriction, anxiety, helplessness
PEs	Enjoyed being home alone	Self-acceptance, privacy, emotional comfort
BEp	Felt dwelling too big	Emotional and physical discomfort, anxiety, helplessness
UEp	Attacked while walking past year	Fear, anxiety, insecurity, helplessness, physical discomfort
UEp	Home robbed past year	Fear, anxiety, insecurity, helplessness, physical discomfort
UEp	Had item lost or stolen past year	Fear, anxiety, insecurity, helplessness, physical discomfort
SWp	Number of basic services needed	Dependency, helplessness, restriction
SSs	Enjoyed watching people go by in busy area	Novelty, variety, leisure, relaxation
PEs	Satisfaction with nearness of dwelling to family	Physical and emotional comfort, peace of mind
PEs	Enjoyed helping someone with chore of problem	Companionship, variety, involvement, relatedness, achievement
SSs	Necessary for happiness are people in neighborhood	Peace of mind, lack of conflict, social acceptance, reputation
PEs	Necessary for happiness are friends in community	Involvement, familiarity, relatedness, belongingness, social acceptance

Code	Description	Attributes
PEs	Necessary for happiness is dwelling's nearness to family	Physical and emotional comfort, peace of mind
LSs	Child divorced in past year	Emotional discomfort, anxiety
LSs	Spouse's death in past year	Loneliness, emotional and physical discomfort
LSs	Close relative's death in past year	Loneliness, emotional and physical discomfort
LSs	Relative's serious illness in past year	Emotional discomfort, anxiety
LSs	Friend's death in past year	Loneliness, emotional and physical discomfort
LSs	Child or relative moved away in past year	Loneliness, emotional and physical discomfort
BEp	Satisfaction with living near Chicago	Physical and emotional comfort, peace of mind, spontaneity, leisure
BEp	Necessary for happiness is living near Chicago	Physical and emotional comfort, peace of mind, spontaneity, leisure
SWp	Necessary for happiness are community services	Physical and emotional comfort, peace of mind, spontaneity, leisure
BEp	Necessary for happiness are the stores in community	Physical and emotional comfort, peace of mind, self-maintenance
BEp	Necessary for happiness are community places to have fun or relax	Physical and emotional comfort, peace of mind, self-maintenance
BEp	Necessary for happiness is nearness to desired community places	Relaxation, leisure, spontaneity, physical and emotional comfort
TC	Proud to live in community	Self-respect, achievement, social acceptance, involvement, belongingness
TN	Proud to live in neighborhood	Self-respect, achievement, social acceptance, involvement, belongingness
TD	Proud to live in dwelling	Self-respect, achievement, social acceptance, privacy, sense of permanence
TC	Satisfaction with community as place to live	Territorial control, belongingness, place orientation, sense of identity, self-respect
TN	Satisfaction with neighborhood as place to live	Territorial control, belongingness, place orientation, sense of identity, self-respect
TD	Satisfaction with dwelling as place to live	Territorial control, belongingness, place orientation, sense of identity, self-respect
TC	Necessity for happiness is community	Territorial control, belongingness, place orientation, sense of identity, self-respect
TN	Necessity for happiness is neighborhood	Territorial control, belongingness, place orientation, sense of identity, self-respect
TD	Necessity for happiness is dwelling	Territorial control, belongingness, place orientation, sense of identity, self-respect
BEp	Owners only: Caring for home too expensive	Anxiety, helplessness, emotional discomfort
BEp	Caring for home too much time	Emotional and physical discomfort
BEp	Caring for home too tiring	Fatigue, physical discomfort
NEp	Renters only: Bothered by insects or rodents	Emotional and physical discomfort, loss of status
BEp	Helpfulness of janitor	Emotional and physical comfort, security, independence
BEp	How clean and in good repair is building	Peace of mind, physical and emotional comfort, reputation, security

Appendix B

Further Background and Derivation of Variables Differentiating Individuals as Knowers

Personality Variables

Leary's Personality Variables

In Leary's system, personality is divided into sixteen areas of interpersonal behavior that are systematically related to each other and can be applied to any unit of observed, self-reported, or self-descriptive behavior. These sixteen areas are arranged along a circular continuum in which characteristics lying on opposite points of the perimeter represent psychologically opposite characteristics. These areas can then be combined to yield eight interpersonal octants, labeled by Leary as: *competitive-narcissistic, managerial-autocratic, responsible-hypernormal, cooperative-over-conventional, docile-dependent, self-effacing-masochistic, rebellious-distrustful,* and *aggressive-sadistic.* Each octant has several characteristic dispositions or behaviors that can be either self-descriptive or observed. Each of the octants has a moderate and an extreme pole; the moderate pole is adaptive and the extreme pole is pathological.

To assess each of the eight octants of personality, Leary developed an interpersonal checklist consisting of eight statements for each of the eight octants. The respondent is asked to select, from among the sixty-four statements, those that he feels describe himself. The self-selected items represent for Leary an expression of an individual's conscious description of himself and his world. This conscious self-description is distinct from that level of communication that Leary describes as "private symbolization," or that component of the personality tapped by projective instruments that may not be available to conscious awareness.

With some modification in phrasing to emphasize interpersonal relations, three statements were selected from the original Leary checklist for each of the sixteen categories, or six statements for each of the eight octants. In all, forty-eight statements formed the basis for the Self-Sort Task. Specific details concerning the modification of the original Leary instrument can be found in Tobin and Lieberman (1976) and Rosner (1968).

Respondents were asked to sort a shuffled deck of cards containing the forty-eight statements into two piles according to the following instructions:

> Here's something different. We'd like you to describe yourself. The statements in this deck of cards are ways people use to describe themselves. I want you to read each statement, and if it describes how you feel about yourself these days, put it in one pile. If you feel the statement is not like you, put it in a second pile. Please do this for each card.

Because of the great variability in the number of statements chosen as "like me," the percentage of total statements falling within each octant was computed. In this way, the respondents' scores could be compared with one another on a particular test regardless of the differences in their total number of responses. The proportion of statements selected per octant to the total number of statements chosen comprised the respondent's raw score. For example, if a respondent chose thirty self-sort statements, six of which were from the managerial-autocratic octant, then six out of thirty, or 20 percent, would be his raw score for that octant.

The eight octants provide a basis for generating two global dimensions: dominance-submission and affiliation-hostility. Formulas for computing these two dimensions are as follows:

Dominance-Submission score =
$$\%AP - \%HI + .7(\%NO + \%BC - \%FG - \%JK)$$
Affiliation-Hostility score =
$$\%LM - \%DE + .7(\%NO - \%BC - \%FG + \%JK)$$

Simply stated, the dominance-submission dimension is the difference between proportions of managerial-autocratic behaviors and self-effacing-masochistic behaviors, whereas affiliation-hostility is the difference between proportions of cooperative-overconventional behavior and aggressive-sadistic behavior. (Behaviors within the other four octants are added into Leary's formulas but they have less weight.)

McKechnie's Environmental Dispositions

Instructions to the respondent were as follows:

> Now I am going to read you some statements describing the way you may or may not feel. For each statement, please tell me whether you strongly agree, agree, disagree, or strongly disagree. On respondent's initiative, the statement was also coded as "neither agree nor disagree."

Each scale item was scored from 5 (strongly agree) to 1 (strongly disagree). Scale score equaled summed positive items minus summed negative items plus constant which was equal to six times the number of negative items in the scale (thereby eliminating the possibility of a negative total raw score). The specific items found in this study's three environmental disposition scales are shown below:

Urbanism

Statement	Reference No.[a]
Positive:	
Life in the city is more interesting than life on a farm.	(7)
I like the sounds of a city street.	(51)
Small-town life is too boring for me.	(85)
The cultural life of a big city is very important to me.	(158)
Negative:	
Cities are too noisy and crowded for me.	(38)
I often feel uneasy in a large crowd of people.	(39)

I often think of settling down on a
    farm someday.   (57)
Country people are more honest than
    city people.   (99)
Mental problems are more common
    in the city than in the country.   (177)

Stimulus-Seeking

Statement	Reference No.[a]

Positive:
I would enjoy driving a racing car.   (5)
It would be fun to move around and
    live in different parts of the coun-
    try.   (12)
I would enjoy traveling around the
    world on a sailing ship.   (21)
I have always been somewhat of a
    daredevil.   (103)
I need more variety in my life than
    other people seem to need.   (132)
I am an adventurous person.   (141)
I would like to live in a palace or a
    castle.   (163)
I like to be on the move, not tied
    down to any one place.   (176)

Negative:
I seldom vary the route I take to
    everyday destinations.   (145)

Antiquarianism

Statement	Reference No.[a]

Positive:
I enjoy browsing in bookstores.   (11)
I like places that have the feeling of
    being old.   (19)
Old sections of the city are more in-
    teresting than the new areas.   (52)
I like to read about the history of
    places.   (112)
Modern buildings are seldom as at-
    tractive as older ones.   (123)

I would enjoy watching movies made
   15 or 20 years ago.   (136)
I enjoy collecting things that most
   people would consider junk.   (155)

Negative:
I like modern furniture better than
   the more traditional styles.   (47)
I would like to live in a modern,
   planned community.   (59)

[a] McKechnie statement number.

Locus of Control

The locus of control items are as follows:

	Strongly Agree	Agree	Disagree	Strongly Disagree
There is really no way I can solve some of the problems I have. Do you	1	2	3	4
Sometimes I feel that I'm being pushed around in life. Do you	1	2	3	4
I have little control over the things that happen to me	1	2	3	4
I often feel helpless in dealing with the problems of life	1	2	3	4
There is little I can do to change many of the important things in life	1	2	3	4

Stage in Life

Functional Health

The functional health scale items are as follows:

1. Opening or closing jars?
2. Dressing and putting on your shoes?
3. Taking a bath or shower?
4. Cutting toenails?
5. Preparing a simple meal?
6. Cleaning and chores around the (house/apt./room)?
7. Climbing stairs?
8. Getting around the (house/apt./room)?
9. Eating?
10. Using a telephone?
11. Going short walking distances outside?
12. Riding in a regular bus?

Psychological Well-Being

Life Satisfaction Index A

Each of the twenty items in this index has three response alternatives: agree, disagree, or are you not sure. The total score is determined by assigning a zero to each incorrect or don't know response, and a one to each affirmative response. Accordingly, the scores on this scale may range from zero to twenty, with each item in the scale weighed equally. The properties of this instrument are described fully in Neugarten, Havighurst, and Tobin (1961) and D. L. Adams (1969).

Appendix C

Measurement Issues

The individual variables and the environmental experience variables were assumed to meet the requirements of true metric or interval-level scales or were constructed as dummy variables. In both instances, it was assumed that the measures had properties that enabled them to be analyzed by linear correlation analysis and ordinary least squares multiple regression analysis.

The use of discrete (or noncontinuous), ordered-metric scales, such as "community satisfaction," in a multiple regression analysis is more acceptable to some statisticians and social scientists than others. Labovitz (1972) and Cohen and Cohen (1975) contain arguments supporting the validity of this statistical treatment. In addition to defenses by statisticians, several other carefully executed empirical investigations used methodological approaches similar to that presented here.

Another fundamental methodological issue arises when multiple regression analysis is employed. This concerns the assumed shape of the mathematical function estimated when a set of independent variables are statistically related to a dependent variable. The use of multiple linear regression analysis and untransformed variables assumes that the relationships being evaluated are best described as linear. Empirical evidence supporting the "linear" assumption is found in Andrews and Withey (1976) and Campbell, Converse, and Rodgers (1976). Here, similar types of data and relationships were evaluated both by Pearson product-moment correlation coefficients, sensitive only to the linear component of a relationship, and by the eta statistic, sensitive to linear and curvilinear components. In the majority of instances, the researchers reported that the differences in the magnitudes of the coefficients were not noticeably large, that the ordering of the coefficients was virtually identical, and that the amount of variance explained was similar, irrespective of which measure of association was calculated. This led the researchers in both these studies to suggest that multiple linear regression analysis produces similar findings as multiple classification analysis and was therefore an appropriate statistical tool by which to evaluate such subjective indicator or quality-of-life survey data. In the present study, various sets of eta and Pearson r correlations were compared and a similar conclusion was reached.

It is true that several of the variable measures did not meet some of the statistical assumptions underlying multiple regression analysis. In particular, many of the variable distributions did not meet normality and homoscedasticity assumptions. More cautious readers may prefer to restrict their attention to the magnitudes of reported measures of statistical association (simple and standardized partial regression coefficients or beta weights) rather than to their significance levels. However, there was a very good match between levels of statistical significance and the magnitude of the beta values.

In an attempt to reduce the positive skewness of several of the environmental experiences treated as dependent variables, their seven-point scales were collapsed to four-point scales. Regression analysis findings were compared using both variable forms. There were some differences observed in the absolute sizes of the beta values of the independent variables, but, with few and relatively unimportant exceptions, neither their rank orderings or their levels of statistical significance changed.

Some care should be taken when interpreting the correlations and standardized partial regression coefficients of the individual variables that were measured as dummy variables. The reader is reminded that the magnitudes of these coefficients are, in considerable part, a function of the sample size of elderly persons analyzed. Both the means and standard deviations of dummy variable categories can be expressed as a function of the sample proportion of the persons contained in the total sample (e.g., percent female, or percent widowed, percent divorced-separated, and percent never married) (see Cohen and Cohen 1975:176–184). Consequently, the sizes of dummy variable coefficients cannot be compared directly with those found in other studies with different population-attribute proportions. Correlations between a dummy variable and a dependent variable is at a maximum when the categorical group is exactly half the total sample and then it declines toward zero or increases toward one (Cohen and Cohen 1975:177).

However, the correlation and standardized partial regression coefficients of dummy variables describing the same individual variables can be relatively safely compared from one analysis to another in *this* study. Aside from very small differences in case sizes due to the use of a listwise missing value option, the sample sizes and thus the proportion of individuals in the constructed dummy variable categories were constant across all analyses in the study. In the final-stage regression analyses containing dummy variables, the unstandardized regression coefficients were also reported. Their statistical interpretation is independent of the number of persons found in the particular dummy variable categories.

A data analytic approach such as this must continually question whether interpreted relationships between concepts or constructs legitimately follow from observed statistical relationships. The major issues surrounding measurement theory and models, particularly those related to survey research, are discussed elsewhere (for example, Bradburn and Caplovitz 1965; Campbell, Converse, and Rodgers 1976; and Andrews and Withey 1976). A central issue concerns the difficulties of drawing theoretical inferences (particularly of a causal nature) from empirical findings, when there is a hazard of confounding "true" conceptual relationships with measurement and modeling errors. To minimize this problem as much as possible, different variables were constructed to measure the same concept. Thus there was the possibility that different empirical findings could lead to the same conceptual or theoretical conclusion. More generally, conceptual interpretations that totally depended on a single empirical analysis were avoided. As a consequence, misplaced or erroneous interpretations arising from methodological weaknesses should have been minimized.

The Overcontrol of Direct Effects

After insignificantly correlated variables were dropped in the first statistical stage, often there remained in *each* variable category as many as seven or eight variables with significant direct effects on the dependent variable. After the second stage, there sometimes remained as many as 15 individual variables (in *all* variable categories) with significant direct effects. As the number of variables simultaneously analyzed in the same regression equation increases, the dangers of statistical overcontrol also increase. As succinctly defined by Campbell, Converse, and Rodgers, "to overcontrol is to adjust from view some contour of the data which is actually relevant in a substantive way to the more precise question being asked about reality" (1976:122). Consequently, variables having significant direct effects on a dependent variable when analyzed within a simple or "few variable" regression equation analysis, may display nonunique and trivial relationships with the dependent variable when many variables are controlled for in the multivariate analysis.

Thus arises the problem of multicollinearity, albeit with different degrees of severity. In the social and behavioral sciences, there is much subjectivity as to what magnitude of intercorrelation constitutes multicollinearity. Although multiple regression is, in fact, designed to handle low and moderately correlated independent variables, the analytical system may become overtaxed in situations when high intercorrelations exist between independent variables or, alternatively, when there are too many moderately correlated independent variables serving to depress the power and precision of parameter estimation. As Cohen and Cohen summarized: "The larger the k_A (the number of covariates) is made in a conscientious effort to cover an area, the greater the likelihood of redundancy and suppression among the independent variables in set A, thus reducing the power and precision of their estimation and increasing difficulty in their interpretation" (1975:377).

Researcher discretion inevitably must prevail when ascertaining whether the "redundancy and suppression" of an individual variable effect accurately represents the absence of a true conceptual relationship or merely some form of statistical overkill. Some situations are more straightforward than others. When the direct effects of sex and marital status, *both* having significant zero-order associations with a dependent variable, are assessed, it is informative to control for both variables to ascertain which has the nonspurious and direct effect on the dependent variable. A more ambiguous situation arises when the direct effects of a subjective income measure (e.g., concern about money) and an objective income measure (e.g., total household income) are assessed. Assume both have significant zero-order associations or significant simple regression relationships with a dependent variable, but they share a modest amount of variation with each other. When both variables are simultaneously controlled for in a regression analysis, each of the variables becomes insignificant. What is the researcher to do? He can retain both variables in the regression equation, but only at the cost of concluding that neither has any conceptual relevance for explaining the dependent variable. Alternatively, he can include only one of the variables in the equation under the assumption that the suppression effects were due to statistical causes. A very different approach would be to deal with the multicollinearity problem before it occurs through (1) a factor analytic approach by which a new representative covariate is calculated that represents the linear combination of two or more intercorrelated variables; (2) a scaling approach by which several variables are combined by some standard to form a single-scale measure; or (3) a hierarchical (stepwise) regression analysis by which variables are allowed to enter and leave the regression equation depending on prestated statistical criteria and hierarchical ordering. Space constraints do not permit a discussion of the advantages and disadvantages of these reduction approaches. In brief, however, the first two alternatives were rejected because in most cases the creation of a new variable would result in the undesirable loss of the conceptual clarity and integrity of the original variables (some of which were already constructed from variable combinations) and would increase the difficulty of variable replicability. The carte blanche hierarchical reduction process of stepwise multiple regression analysis was rejected because it was considered important to take on the responsibility of interpreting the conceptual relevance of particular variables. Also, in the majority of variable situations, it was impossible to impose— based on some causal structure hypothesis—an *a priori* hierarchical ordering of the variables. Failing to adopt the above approaches necessarily results in variable overcontrol decisions, which are resolved by the researcher's understanding of both his data and conceptual model. As Campbell, Converse, and Rodgers summed up the problem:

Whether one is overcontrolling in a given situation depends on the nature of the analytical question being asked. For some purposes, in examining a particular relationship, it might be important to control out the effects of a third factor which happens to be irrelevant to the question but which confounds the results. In dealing with exactly the same relationship, but with other purposes in mind, the same control might be quite self-defeating. The judgment thus depends on some conceptual understanding of the meaning of the influence which the third factor has upon the relationship. Without such understanding, the possibility of overcontrol cannot be evaluated. (1976:123)

Appendix D

Appendix D. Correlation Relationships (Pearson r's) Among Individual Differences

	1	2	3	4	5	6	7	8	9	10	11	12	13	14	15	16	17	18
1 LEARY DOMINANCE PERSONALITY																		
2 LEARY AFFILIATION PERSONALITY	---																	
3 URBANISM ENVIRONMENT DISPOSITION	15	---																
4 STIMULUS-SEEKING ENVIRONMENT DISPOSITION	21	-13	---															
5 ANTIQUARIANISM ENVIRONMENT DISPOSITION	---	---	---	---														
6 LOCUS OF CONTROL	21	-11	15	-12	---													
7 MALE (YES = 1, NO = 0)	09	-15	---	---	-19	---												
8 WHITE (YES = 1, NO = 0)	---	---	31	-11	09	15	---											
9 SEPARATED-DIVORCED (YES = 1, NO = 0)	---	---	-14	08	---	-10	---	-11										
10 WIDOWED (YES = 1, NO = 0)	---	---	---	---	-09	---	-28	---	-21									
11 NEVER MARRIED (YES = 1, NO = 0)	---	---	12	---	---	---	-11	08	---	-24								
12 TOTAL HOUSEHOLD SIZE	---	---	-11	---	---	---	20	-14	---	-45	-12							
13 ETHNIC STATUS	---	---	---	---	---	---	---	-25	---	---	---	---						
14 CATHOLIC RELIGION (YES = 1, NO = 0)	-09	---	---	---	---	---	---	13	---	---	---	---	-21					
15 JEWISH RELIGION (YES = 1, NO = 0)	08	---	17	---	-11	---	---	12	---	-09	---	---	-30	-12				
16 OTHER RELIGION (YES = 1, NO = 0)	---	---	09	11	---	---	---	---	13	---	---	---	---	-09	---			
17 NO RELIGION (YES = 1, NO = 0)	---	---	12	15	---	---	09	---	---	-09	17	---	---	-09	---	---		
18 TOTAL HOUSEHOLD INCOME	---	---	23	---	---	28	11	39	-11	-33	---	22	---	---	16	---	---	
19 LEVEL OF EDUCATION	09	---	31	---	---	24	---	41	---	-19	08	---	11	-13	11	08	---	52
20 DUNCAN SOCIOECONOMIC STATUS	---	---	35	---	---	21	---	55	---	-21	---	---	---	---	19	---	---	59
21 SIEGEL OCCUPATIONAL PRESTIGE	---	---	31	---	---	21	---	49	---	-21	---	---	---	---	17	---	---	56
22 SELF-RATED SOCIAL CLASS	14	---	26	---	08	15	---	24	---	---	---	---	10	-14	---	---	---	33
23 IMPACT OF HOUSING EXPENSE	---	---	-18	---	---	-26	---	-20	13	---	---	---	---	---	---	---	---	-29
24 CONCERN ABOUT HAVING ENOUGH MONEY	-09	---	-16	14	---	-30	---	-27	13	---	---	08	---	---	---	---	---	-25
25 MONEY SITUATION COMPARED TO 2 YEARS AGO	-09	---	---	08	---	-12	---	---	09	---	---	---	---	---	---	---	---	-19
26 MONEY SITUATION COMPARED TO 10 YEARS AGO	---	---	12	14	---	-11	15	---	10	---	---	-14	---	---	13	---	---	-10
27 ENOUGH MONEY FOR THINGS	---	---	18	---	---	10	20	---	29	-12	---	---	-11	---	---	---	---	27
28 SELF-RATED HEALTH	-20	---	-19	---	-13	-30	---	-15	---	---	---	---	---	---	---	---	---	-16
29 SELF-RATED HEARING DIFFICULTIES	-11	---	-09	---	---	---	---	---	---	---	---	---	---	---	---	---	---	---
30 SELF-RATED SEEING DIFFICULTIES	---	---	-10	---	-11	---	---	---	---	---	---	---	---	---	---	---	---	-11
31 FUNCTIONAL HEALTH	-17	---	---	-10	---	-18	-15	---	---	14	---	---	---	---	---	---	---	---
32 SELF-RATED CHANGE IN FUNCTIONAL HEALTH	-18	12	-09	-08	---	-14	-14	---	---	17	---	---	---	---	---	---	---	-14
33 HAD SERIOUS ILLNESS (YES = 1, NO = 0)	---	---	---	---	---	---	---	10	---	---	---	---	---	---	---	---	08	---
34 HAD MINOR ILLNESS (YES = 1, NO = 0)	---	---	---	---	---	---	---	---	---	-09	---	---	---	---	11	---	---	---
35 STOPPED ACTIVITY (YES = 1, NO = 0)	---	---	---	---	---	---	---	---	---	---	---	---	---	---	09	---	---	---
36 VOLUNTARY RETIREMENT (YES = 1, NO = 0)	---	---	---	---	---	---	---	---	---	---	---	---	---	---	09	---	---	---
37 FORCED RETIREMENT (YES = 1, NO = 0)	---	---	---	11	---	---	15	-09	13	-11	---	---	---	---	---	19	---	-09
38 EMPLOYED (YES = 1, NO = 0)	17	---	---	12	-09	---	19	-11	---	-15	---	12	---	09	---	---	---	15
39 HOW HAPPY ARE YOU THESE DAYS	14	---	---	---	---	31	---	---	---	---	---	---	---	---	---	---	---	12
40 LIFE SATISFACTION	20	---	13	---	---	39	---	10	---	-14	---	---	---	---	---	---	---	22
41 DURATION IN RESIDENCE	11	---	---	-10	16	---	---	-15	---	-10	10	---	---	---	---	---	---	---
42 DURATION IN COMMUNITY	09	---	---	---	---	11	---	-12	---	-11	12	---	---	---	---	---	-10	---
43 TENURE STATUS (OWN = 1, RENT = 0)	---	---	---	---	---	---	---	-12	-13	-13	21	---	---	---	---	---	---	25
44 ACTIVITY LEVELS	15	---	23	14	---	23	19	28	---	-24	---	---	---	---	11	---	---	38
45 ACTIVITY SPACE SIZE	09	---	20	---	-10	11	---	20	11	-15	---	---	---	---	23	09	---	22
46 CHANGE IN ACTIVITY	12	---	22	---	---	17	---	14	---	---	---	---	---	---	14	---	---	24

NOTE: Decimal points have been omitted. All variable relationships are significant at .05 level or less except those denoted by a dashed line. Where a dashed line is indicated, correlation coefficient had value of less than .08.

NOTES

1. An Overview

1. For overviews, see Binstock and Shanas 1976; Birren and Schaie 1977; Birren and Sloane 1981; Busse and Blazer 1980; Datan and Lohmann 1980; Eisdorfer 1981; Finch and Hayflick 1977; Howells 1975; *Journal of Social Issues* 1980; Kimmel 1980; Lowy 1980; Neugarten 1968; Palmore 1980; and Poon 1980.

2. For overviews, see *The Gerontologist*, 1968, 1969; Pastalan and Carson 1970; Lawton and Nahemow 1973; Lawton, Newcomer, and Byerts 1976; Carp 1976b; Windley 1977; Lawton 1977a; Golant 1979a; Lawton 1980; Windley and Scheidt 1980; Parr 1980; and Howell 1980.

2. Selecting a Population and Setting: The Scholar's Dilemma

1. Maddox and Wiley (1976) and see note 2 in chapter 1.

2. The decision to use the very recently published Haines reverse telephone-address directory as a sampling frame was made in order to avoid any sampling approaches that would draw population inferences from the 1970 published census data that was already eight years out of date. Nevertheless, several comparisons were made of the sampling and population distributions of selected variables describing Evanston's older residents. There was the expectation that some discrepancies noted between the two sets of distributions would be due to the different data collection periods. The sampling distributions of sex, occupation, and household size were very similar to the comparable census population distributions. However, the sample contained higher than expected percentages of the over age 75, black, widowed, and better educated persons. The lack of a reliable set of population distribution estimates for 1978 also prevented any statistical weighting of the variable sampling distributions reported in this study.

3. It was initially estimated that an elderly person would reside in approximately 25 percent, or 6,793, of Evanston's households.

4. Many reasons may be given for why individuals refuse or are unavailable to be interviewed that have little to do with their chronological age or stage in life. Additionally, to account for the interview completion rate of old people, two factors appear prominent. The first is a function of the physical and psychological health status of the old person. The very act of responding to more than 100 close-ended interview questions for over 90 minutes is itself a test of both the physical

stamina and the cognitive abilities of the old person. By default, the collection of data via such a survey research methodology eliminates from a study the extremely physically frail or weak elderly and those with cognitive impairments that would prevent lucid and rational responses. A second factor underlying the interview completion rate of old people becomes particularly evident when administering interviews in a middle-class community occupied by relatively healthy old people. Old people who are active, either because they are still in the labor force or because they are vigorously pursuing leisure and spare-time activities outside their homes, are less likely to be at home to receive an interviewer (despite at least five callback attempts to make contact) or will report that they simply do not have the time to be interviewed. Unfortunately, the interview report procedures did not allow for a systematic analysis of the impact of these very different completion rate factors. To some extent they will offset each other, but this was not ascertained.

5. Verification was conducted on 20 percent of each interviewer's work. All major errors in the interviews were corrected. All completed interviews were edited, coded, and keypunched in computer-readable form, and all data were machine cleaned for legal codes and contingency patterns. All stages of the survey, including sampling, questionnaire design evaluation, administering of the interviews, coding, and initial computer work, were carried out by professional trained personnel of the Survey Research Laboratory in its offices at the University of Illinois, Chicago Circle Campus. The laboratory, in addition to its extensive expertise in survey analysis in general, also had previous experience in the administering of surveys to elderly populations. The survey, which I wrote and designed, was subjected to several critical reviews by professional staff of the Survey Research Center. Several constructive revisions of the interview schedule resulted from these meetings. I will provide copies of the interview schedule upon request.

3. REPRESENTATIVENESS OF RESEARCH SITE

1. The section on the quality of life in Evanston is an abbreviated version of earlier work: Golant and McCutcheon (1980). Complete variable descriptions, data source references, factor solutions, and more detailed descriptions of methodology and findings are found in this source.

2. According to 1970 U.S. Bureau of the Census geographical classifications, a Standard Metropolitan Statistical Area (SMSA) consists of a county or group of contiguous counties that contain at least one city of 50,000 or more residents or two contiguous cities with a combined population of at least 50,000. Contiguous counties are included in a SMSA if they are socially and economically integrated with the central city.

3. Obviously, there are important sources of variation in the quality of life that simply will not be found in any one SMSA. These include, for example, climatic variations, regional development or economic base variations, and religious, ethnic, and racial subcultural variations.

4. Crude in the sense that within each of these large geographic areas there is considerable population and territorial heterogeneity.

5. The central city (City of Chicago) is located within Cook County, one of the six counties of the Chicago SMSA. The remainder of this county (other than the City of Chicago) is referred to as Suburban Cook County.

6. I will supply complete variable descriptions and data sources upon request.

7. I will supply the mapped factors upon request.

8. By virtue of the varimax rotation in the factor analysis, these seven independent variables are statistically unrelated to each other (in actuality the intercorrelations among the seven sets of derived factor scores ranged from -0.07 to $+0.09$). Consequently, the standardized partial regression coefficients (beta weights) reported in the multiple regression equations are equivalent to the simple standardized regression coefficients (and also to the zero-order correlations), which would be obtained if each independent variable was regressed alone on a dependent variable.

9. The index of dissimilarity expresses that proportion of a population subgroup y that would have to relocate among a set of n subareas to have a distribution equal to that of another subgroup x.

10. The size of the areal unit or parcel over which the index of dissimilarity is calculated influences the statistical magnitude of the index. Residential distributions measured over census blocks on the average yield larger index measures than census tracts. This is because the smaller block units are more likely to contain populations that are homogeneous with respect to some trait. Thus they will contain greater shares of a particular population subgroup.

11. When analyzing the residential segregation patterns of these different age groups, it was assumed that the under age 18 population was most likely to occupy the same households (residences) as persons in the age group 25–44 (most likely engaged in child-raising).

12. Available from me upon request.

4. Conceptualization and Measurement of Experiential Environment

1. Downs and Stea distinguish two modes of acquiring information from the environment:

> "Direct sources involve face-to-face contact between the individual, and for example, a city, and information literally floods the person from all of his sensory modes . . . Above all, he is 'learning by doing' via a trial and error process. Reinforcement and checking are continuous: erroneous beliefs about locational and attribute information are rapidly corrected by feedback from spatial behavior.
>
> Vicarious information about the city is by definition secondhand. It is literally and metaphorically 'seen through someone else's eyes.' This is true of verbal description, a cartographic street map, a T.V. film, a written description, a color photograph, or a painting" (1973:23).

2. A wide assortment of techniques may be employed to elicit and record an individual's environmental responses (see Lang et al. 1974).

3. For good discussions of the more well-known and well-documented factors underlying data input quality, see Marans 1975 and Bradburn and Caplovitz 1965.

4. A fundamental problem is that most objects found in the everyday residential environment cannot be designated by a small, simple set of attributes or properties. Even supposing the existence of such a set, the denotative qualities of these attributes will not be perceived or recognized similarly by all respondents. Con-

sequently, unless very specific, denotatively unambiguous attributes are identified for investigation, there will always be uncertainty as to exactly what object qualities are eliciting an individual's affective or evaluative responses. For the researcher seeking to verify the objective characteristics of an environmental object, two alternatives define the *range* of research strategies: to study a more complete set of attributes denoting a very few number of environmental objects, or to study only a very few select attributes describing a relatively complete population of objects.

5. Fishbein and Ajzen (1975:11) argue that the concepts of "affect" and "evaluation" are synonymous. They maintain that there is little empirical distinction between, for example, (1) feeling good about an object, and (2) evaluating the object as good.

6. For a discussion of the learning theory basis of belief strength (that is, the object-attribute association), see Fishbein and Ajzen (1975:11–52).

7. I am sensitive to the criticism that these examples measure belief content more than they measure belief strength, using the terminology of Fishbein and Ajzen (1975). If true, it is assumed in effect that the belief content measures are significantly correlated with the appropriate belief strength measures.

8. The "yes-no" response in the sample question represents a special case of either a zero or 100 percent probability of the existence of an event.

9. In the computation of the principal-factor solution, the diagonal elements of the correlation matrix (of 64 experiences) were replaced by communality estimates (the squared multiple correlation between a given variable and the rest of the variables in the matrix). An iterative procedure was then carried out for improving the estimates of communality by a method described in Nie et al. (1975:480). Final communality estimates reached by this interactive convergence required 44 iterations.

5. Conceptual Model of Individual Differences Underlying Environmental Experiences

1. It is "partial" in three ways: first, it is unlikely that any set of proposed individual variables fully depicts the manifold of personal factors underlying environmental experiences; second, the conceptualization of the experiential environment is a necessarily selective and incomplete portrayal of an individual's transactional outcomes; and third, no assessment is undertaken of the direct influences of the objective environment on the individual's cognitive, motivational, and behavioral states.

2. An excellent collection of papers (Magnusson 1981) containing several detailed interactionist interpretations of the individual and the environment (situation) came to my attention too late to be incorporated in the final manuscript.

6. Elderly Individuals as Knowers of Their Environment

1. It is nonetheless a fact that researchers make comparable inferences all the time from such sociological and demographic constructs in the course of explaining variable relationships. However, these authors usually make no attempt to ca-

tegorize their inferences within any conceptual model or to systematically compare their inferences to those of other studies.

2. There were some reservations about identifying an individual's marital status within a category depicting lifelong traits. It is evident that widowhood is an event that often takes place in old age and that for many it is a recently acquired status. Although true, the number of recent elderly widows is relatively small. About 73 percent of aged 60 and older widows in the study lost their spouses more than five years earlier; about 52 percent lost their spouses more than ten years earlier. Thus, for the majority of elderly in the sample widowhood was not a recent event. The identification of the other marital status categories as lifelong is clearer: 95 percent of older married people had this status more than 10 years; and 83 percent of separated or divorced people had this status for more than 10 years.

Similar reservations are held about identifying household size within a category depicting lifelong traits. As subsequent empirical analyses will suggest, there is justification for the categorization of both marital status and household size as stage-in-life variables.

The identification of marital status and household size as individual variables also raises the difficult-to-resolve issue of where the boundaries of the individual end and those of the environment or situation begin (Raush 1979).

3. The age distribution of the elderly persons interviewed in this study was as follows: 60–64 (19%); 65–69 (20%); 70–74 (23%); 75–79 (18%); and 80 and older (20 %).

7. The Behavioral Relationships of Elderly Individuals with Their Environment

1. Following Campbell, Converse, and Rodgers, a *community* is defined as a "local politically defined unit in which the individual resides: the city or town for most people; the county for persons living in rural areas" (1976:22). The first question of the interview schedule clearly established old people's designation of their "community" as Evanston.

2. Representative are Chapin's (1974:70) 12-class system of classification and Barker's (1968:52–66) classification system consisting of 11 "action patterns."

3. However, chapter 10 specifically considers the "social activity" of old persons, focusing on their interpersonal behavioral relationships with family, friends, relatives, and neighbors.

4. Of related concern is the selection of alternative types of behavioral observations (see Jaccard 1979:74–75).

5. For example, the behavior episodes of a girl entering a drugstore included: entering drugstore, looking at comic, moving toward stool, and choosing treat (soda). Barker and his associates observed that during an 11-minute period, the girl engaged in 25 episodes of behavior.

6. *Home range* should not be confused with the concept of *territory*, which has a very different connotation, conveying possession, protection, and defense (see chapter 8).

7. In a 1976 review of attitude-behavior literature, a mere one-half page of a 45-page article was devoted to a discussion of attitudes as a consequence of human action (Schuman and Johnson 1976).

8. In these and related studies, "activity" is conceptualized in different ways even within the same measurement instrument. Thus, this generalization must be tempered by the recognition that other definitions of activity behavior might yield different findings. Barker's specification of five behavior mechanisms making up a unit of activity can be used to illustrate. Is the old person who spends his days updating his stamp collection, analyzing chess solutions, and playing poker "active"? Yes, if by active one means manipulation and thinking; no, if one means gross motor activity or locomotor behavior; and no, if social role activity is meant. Is the elderly man who frequently works in his yard and workshop "active"? Yes, if by active one means gross motor activity; no, if one means locomotor activity; and no, if one means social role activity.

9. Considerable confusion exists as to whether low activity can be equated with disengagement and high activity with engagement (see Hochschild 1975 for a discussion of this and other issues). The authors of the disengagement theory portrayed disengagement as a decline in the individual's social role activity and investment of ego energy in the outside world. However, subsequent literature containing empirical tests of the theory was often unclear as to whether both interpersonal and noninterpersonal activity are included as social activity. Maddox (1963) attempted to clarify. Also, it is often unclear whether activity or engagement refers to social role activity, thereby implying the number and complexity of an individual's roles, or to the individual's level of activity in his social roles. If referring to the latter, the person could be engaged if he has only one role, but is intensely active in it; however, by the former criterion, the person would be disengaged. A later attempt at clarification by one of the authors of the original theory illustrates the potential confusion: "Activity and engagement are not in the same dimension. A disengaged person often maintains a high level of activity in a small number and narrow variety of roles, although it is doubtful if it is possible to be at once firmly engaged and inactive" (Cumming 1976:38).

10. Psychological disengagement is manifested by an individual's displaying a decrease in ego energy (Rosen and Neugarten 1960)—that is, a decline in the ability "to integrate wide ranges of stimuli"; less readiness "to perceive or deal with complicated, challenging or conflictual situations"; a reduced tendency "to perceive or to be concerned with feelings and affects as these play a part in life situations"; and a reduced tendency "to perceive vigorous and assertive activity in the self and in others" (Havighurst, Neugarten, and Tobin 1968:166). Research suggests that psychological disengagement may precede social disengagement or activity decline and thus persons who still display high levels of activity may have already started to disengage psychologically. Overall, however, the evidence supports the proposition that individuals with low or declining social activity are more likely to be psychologically disengaged than individuals displaying higher levels of social activity (see Kuhlen 1968:122–123; and Neugarten, Havighurst, and Tobin 1968:174).

8. The Types and Meaningfulness of Territorial Environment Experiences

1. It can be pointed out that most "neighborhood" studies do not take the trouble to examine their subjects' designative interpretations of their neighborhoods. They assume that individuals' estimations of the size and boundaries of their

neighborhoods vary, but never describe the variability in either quantitative or qualitative terms. Such a specification is believed to be important if the generality of relevant findings is to be judged.

2. Another University of Michigan national study, using a somewhat different "satisfaction" measure (an affective-evaluative rating scale), reached very similar findings (Andrews and Withey 1976, Exhibit 9.2).

3. The positive relationship between age and residential satisfaction was not supported by at least one study. Abu-Lughod and Foley (1960) found that in a sample of all age groups, the highest rate of dissatisfaction with suburban living was recorded for persons aged 50 and older.

4. The reader should be cautioned that identical distributions do not necessarily imply that the *same* old people identically responded to the respective questions. For example, although the response distributions, "pride in community" and "pride in dwelling," appeared identical, the correlation between the two experiences was only .62.

5. Environmental experiences with F-levels just short of being statistically significant were also sometimes included if they improved understanding of the meanings underlying a particular territorial experience.

6. The inclusion of "home robbed" as a "community" experience was believed to be justified in that crime is often viewed as either a community or neighborhood problem. This is apt to be true in Evanston where the incidence of community crime is relatively high.

7. If neighborhood and dwelling experiences are considered as possible correlates, the level of explanation increases substantially. However, by eliminating their effects from this analysis, it was possible to focus more sharply on the role of community-specific meanings that were not confounded by neighborhood and dwelling aspects.

8. To some extent, measurement effects may have inflated the strength of the observed association between neighborhood satisfaction and satisfaction with neighbors. Both experiences were measured along identical seven-point scales. However, in light of the observed strength of the other two social experiences, the conclusion regarding the importance of a satisfying social situation appears justified.

9. In all statistical stages, missing values were dealt with by what is commonly referred to as the listwise value option. The variable with the largest amount of missing data determines the maximum number of cases (individuals) on which a set of correlation or regression coefficients is calculated. In practice, however, missing values constituted less than 2.5 percent of any variable's cases. The one important exception was the variable, "total household income," which had 20 missing cases (persons).

10. I will supply the findings from stages one and two on request.

11. Whether "how happy are you these days" or "life satisfaction" significantly influenced any one of the three territorial experiences was determined in the second statistical stage. Here, the direct effects of both psychological well-being variables were simultaneously controlled for. That only one of the two psychological well-being variables had significant direct effects was understandable, given that they were substantially intercorrelated (.48). However, if *either* "happiness" or "life satisfaction" was included in any one of the three (community, neighborhood, or dwelling) multiple regression analyses, it remained statistically significant. It was

therefore reasonable to conclude that *either* happiness or life satisfaction had significant direct effects on community, neighborhood, and dwelling satisfaction. This analytical situation was very much a product of the researcher's decision to measure the same concept, "psychological well-being" or "congruence," by two different variables that shared common variance.

12. In this and subsequent analyses, "duration in community" was proposed as a residential behavior variable underlying community territorial experiences, whereas "duration in residence" (or dwelling) was proposed as a residential behavior variable underlying neighborhood and dwelling territorial experiences.

13. The simple Pearson correlations between race and dwelling satisfaction and race and community satisfaction were .039 and −.005 respectively, both statistically insignificant at the .05 level.

14. In the second-stage multiple regression analyses, the simultaneous effects of race, marital status, and sex were tested. When community satisfaction was the dependent variable, only sex status remained statistically significant; when neighborhood satisfaction was the dependent variable, only race and widowed status remained statistically significant; and when dwelling satisfaction was the dependent variable, only divorced-separated status was close to remaining statistically significant.

15. Muliple regression analyses in the second statistical stage assessed the simultaneous effects of the five socioeconomic individual variables (shown in table 8.5) on each of the three territorial experiences.

16. All three activity behavior variables were tested in the second-stage multiple regression analyses for their direct effects on each of the three territorial experiences, but only "activity level" had significant direct effects.

17. The simple Pearson correlation between tenure status and duration in residence was .47. Neither of the two residential behavior variables were highly intercorrelated with any other of the individual variables in the dwelling satisfaction multiple regression equation.

18. A reciprocal relationship probably exists in reality: individual happiness leads to positive environmental experiences, which in turn lead to individual happiness.

19. This relationship was just short of being significant at the .05 level. However, this reflected the small number of old people who reported being "forced out of their jobs."

20. A careful consideration of the analyses did not suggest that the answer lies in statistical decisions (for example, different "control" variables).

21. However, if the life satisfaction variable was included in any of the three (community, neighborhood, or dwelling pride) multiple regression equations—without controlling for the happiness variable—it too was statistically significant.

22. The other psychological well-being measure, "how happy are you these days," was insignificantly correlated with either dwelling or neighborhood memories.

9. THE TYPES AND MEANINGFULNESS OF PHYSICAL ENVIRONMENT EXPERIENCES

1. One experience not contained in the factor analyzed experiential environment was considered sufficiently important to deserve more detailed investigation, "number of basic services used."

2. The social scientist with situationist leanings might offer a different interpre-

tation, which is that elderly people who are longtime residents are more likely to live in older neighborhoods that, in turn, are more likely to have physically run-down dwellings. Thus, the greater annoyance of the longtime resident may be elicited by objectively verifiable poor neighborhood conditions.

3. "Helpfulness of janitor" was classified as an experience in the physical environment because it involved a transaction with an attribute of the building environment. However, a legitimate argument can be made for its classification as a social experience because it also involves a transaction with an attribute of the resident's personal environment (see figure 4.2).

4. As an aside, this interpretation is theoretically and practically more appealing than implied by the reciprocal relationship, which suggests that store satisfaction leads to a person feeling more satisfied with his life.

5. This discussion is restricted largely to more potentially violent "blue-collar" crimes. The increasingly significant and greatly underreported "white collar" crime is excluded. This involves various forms of fraudulent, unethical, and misleading schemes designed to obtain money illegally from older people.

6. Comparing crimes/1,000 elderly versus crimes/1,000 nonelderly obviously assumes that the young and old are similar "at risk" populations. However, old people in contrast with young people have lower activity levels, are more likely to be housebound, and experience a larger number of annual disability days.

7. The simultaneous effects of the marital status variables on the three crime experiences were also assessed by multiple regression analysis. This enabled the crime experiences of the separated-divorced, never married, and widowed elderly to be compared with those of the married elderly (the reference category).

8. Statistically, this results from the psychological well-being variables sharing common variance with health status, perceived locus of control, and household income individual variables (see Appendix D).

9. The actual wording of the interview question was: "Here is a list of services available to older people in Evanston. I would like to know if you are in need of such services now."

10. It is also possible that old people who do not report having a good time in their community have life-styles that usually take them outside their community setting.

10. THE TYPES AND MEANINGFULNESS OF SOCIAL ENVIRONMENT EXPERIENCES

1. Generalizations from this large body of research are sometimes made difficult because researchers assign different conceptual and measurement properties to their social activity variables. A not uncommon source of ambiguity is whether social behavior is intended to measure the social role activity of old people or old people's level of activity in particular social roles (see also chapter 7).

2. Old people in the study were initially asked, "About how many of your neighbors do you visit with?" Those answering "none" were recorded as "never visiting with their neighbors."

3. Michelson's (1970) review of the literature suggested that "neighbors" may also be visited in public settings such as taverns that are found outside the neighborhood.

4. The classic work on privacy by Westin (1967) treated this concept more broadly.

In addition to the state of "solitude" or aloneness, which is the primary focus in this study, privacy involves three other states, "intimacy," "anonymity," and "reserve."

5. Exceptions do exist. Criminals defined as physical objects in the urbanized environment can evaluate or "size up" their potential victims. Thus the criminal's assessment of an old person's physical competence may be highly relevant for understanding the origins of the old person's crime experiences.

6. A principal-components rotated factor analysis of these five sociopsychological support items confirmed the existence of these two independent dimensions of sociopsychological supports. The overall sociopsychological support scale was formed by summing the scores of all five support items; the expressive support scale was formed by summing the scores of the two relevant emotional support items; and the instrumental support scale was formed by summing the scores of the three relevant material support items. For each scale, a high score indicated greater support availability, and item-scale correlations were statistically significant at the .000 level.

7. The occurrence of certain of these stressful events will much depend on the old person's demographic characteristics and social environment. For instance, the stress of widowhood is not experienced by the never-married or the separated-divorced elderly. The never-married elderly or the married elderly without children never experience the stressful events usually connected with parenthood. Old people with few close friends are less likely to experience stress due to the illness, death, or relocation of a friend.

8. These researchers provided empirically derived stress and social readjustment scores for various events. However, the predicted impact of these events was not estimated for populations in different stages of their lives.

BIBLIOGRAPHY

Abelson, R. P. et al. 1968. *Theories of Cognitive Consistency: A Sourcebook.* Chicago: Rand McNally.

Abu-Lughod, J. and M. M. Foley. 1960. Consumer strategies. In N. N. Foote et al. eds., *Housing Choices and Housing Constraints*, pp. 71–271. New York: McGraw Hill.

Adams, D. L. 1969. Analysis of a life satisfaction index. *Journal of Gerontology*, 24:470–474.

Adams, J. S. 1969. Directional bias in intraurban migration. *Economic Geography*, 45:302–323.

Altman, I. 1975. *The Environment and Social Behavior.* Monterey, Calif.: Brooks/Cole.

Altman, I. and M. M. Chemers. 1980. *Culture and Environment.* Monterey, Calif.: Brooks/Cole.

Altman, I. and J. F. Wohlwill, eds. 1978. *Children and the Environment.* New York: Plenum Press.

American Law Institute. 1936. *Restatement of the Law of Property.* Vol. 1: *Introduction and Freehold Estates.* St. Paul, Minn.: American Law Institute.

Anderberg, M. R. 1973. *Cluster Analysis for Applications.* New York: Academic Press.

Andrews, F. 1981. Comments. In D. F. Johnston, ed., *Measurement of Subjective Phenomena*, pp. 21–30. Special Demographic Analyses, CDS-80-3. Washington, D.C.: GPO.

Andrews, F. M. and S. B. Withey. 1976. *Social Indicators of Well Being.* New York: Plenum Press.

Antonucci, T. 1976. Attachment: A life-span concept. *Human Development*, 19:135–142.

Antunes, G., F. L. Cook, T. D. Cook, and W. G. Skogan. 1977. Patterns of personal crime against the elderly: Findings from a national survey. *The Gerontologist*, 17:321–327.

Arling, G. 1976. The elderly widow and her family, neighbors, and friends. *Journal of Marriage and the Family*, 38:757–768.

Ashford, N. and F. M. Holloway. 1972. Transportation patterns of older people in six urban centers. *The Gerontologist*, 12:43–47.

Atkin, C. K. 1976. Mass media and the aging. In H. J. Oyer and E. J. Oyer, eds., *Aging and Communication*, pp. 99–118. Baltimore: University Park Press.

Audain, M. J. and E. Huttman. 1973. *Beyond Shelter*. Ottawa: The Canadian Council on Social Development.

Bach, R. L. and J. Smith. 1977. Community satisfaction, expectations of moving and migration. *Demography*, 14:147–167.

Barker, R. G. 1968. *Ecological Psychology*. Stanford, Calif.: Stanford University Press.

Barker, R. G. 1978. Stream of individual behavior. In R. G. Barker and Associates, eds., *Habitats, Environments, and Human Behavior*, pp. 3–16. San Francisco: Jossey-Bass.

Bell, W. 1958. Social choice, life styles, & suburban residence. In W. M. Dobriner, ed., *The Suburban Community*, pp. 225–247. New York: Putnam.

Bem, D. J. 1967. Self-Perception: An alternative interpretation of cognitive dissonance phenomena. *Psychological Review*, 74:183–200.

Bengston, V. L. and N. E. Cutler. 1976. Generations and intergenerational relations: Perspectives on age groups and social change. In R. H. Binstock and E. Shanas, eds., *Handbook of Aging and the Social Sciences*, pp. 130–159. New York: Van Nostrand Reinhold.

Berry, B. J. L. and Q. Gillard. 1976. *The Changing Shape of Metropolitan America*. Cambridge, Mass.: Ballinger.

Berry, B. J. L., C. A. Goodwin, R. W. Lake, and K. B. Smith. 1976. Attitudes toward integration: The role of status in community response to racial change. In B. Schwartz, ed., *The Changing Face of the Suburbs*, pp. 221–264. Chicago: University of Chicago Press.

Berry, B. J. L. and J. D. Kasarda. 1977. *Contemporary Urban Ecology*. New York: Macmillan.

Bild, B. R. and R. J. Havighurst. 1976. Senior citizens in great cities: The case of Chicago. *The Gerontologist*, 16:1–88.

Binstock, R. H. and E. Shanas, eds. 1976. *Handbook of Aging and the Social Sciences*. New York: Van Nostrand Reinhold.

Birch, D. et al. 1973. *America's Housing Needs: 1970 to 1980*. Cambridge: Joint Center for Urban Studies, M.I.T. and Harvard University.

Birren, J. E. and K. W. Schaie, eds. 1977. *Handbook of the Psychology of Aging*. New York: Van Nostrand Reinhold.

Birren, J. E. and R. B. Sloane, eds. 1980. *Handbook of Mental Health and Aging*. Englewood Cliffs, N.J.: Prentice Hall.

Blau, Z. S. 1973. *Old Age in a Changing Society*. New York: New Viewpoints/Franklin Watts.

Blenkner, M., M. Bloom, and M. Nielsen. 1971. A research and demonstration project of protective services. *Social Casework*, 52:483–499.

Bloom, B. S. 1964. *Stability and Change in Human Characteristics*. New York: Wiley.

Boal, F. W. 1976. Ethnic residential segregation. In D. T. Herbert and R. J. Johnston, eds., *Spatial Processes and Form*, 1:41–80. New York: Wiley.

Bogue, D. J. and E. J. Bogue, 1976. *Essays in Human Ecology*. Chicago: Community and Family Study Center, University of Chicago.

Botwinick, J. 1973. *Aging and Behavior*. New York: Springer.

Bourne, L. 1967. *Private Redevelopment of the Central City*. Chicago: Department of Geography, University of Chicago.

Bowers, K. S. 1973. Situationism in psychology: An analysis and a critique. *Psychological Review*, 5:307–337.

Bradburn, N. M. and D. Caplovitz. 1965. *Reports on Happiness*. Chicago: Aldine.

Brail, R. K., J. W. Hughes, and C. A. Arthur. 1976. *Transportation Services for the Disabled and Elderly*. New Brunswick, N.J.: Center for Urban Policy Research, Rutgers University.

Brehm, J. W. and Cohen, A. R. 1962. *Explorations in Cognitive Dissonance*. New York: Wiley.

Brickel, C. M. 1980. A review of the roles of pet animals in psychotherapy and with the elderly. *International Journal of Aging and Human Development*, 12:119–128.

Broadbent, G. 1973. *Design in Architecture*. London: Wiley.

Brody, E. 1977. *Long-Term Care of Older People*. New York: Human Sciences Press.

Brostoff, P. M., R. B. Brown, and R. N. Butler. 1972. The public interest: Report No. 6, "Beating up" on the elderly: Police, social work, crime. *Aging and Human Development,* 3:319–322.

Brown, L. A. and E. G. Moore. 1970. The intra-urban migration process: A perspective. *Geografiska Annaler,* 52:1–13.

Bruner, J. S. 1966. On cognitive growth. In J. S. Bruner, R. R. Olver, and P. M. Greenfield, eds., *Studies in Cognitive Growth,* pp. 1–67. New York: Wiley.

Buckley, W. 1967. *Sociology and Modern Systems Theory.* Englewood Cliffs, N.J.: Prentice-Hall.

Bultena, G. 1969. Rural-urban differences in the familial interaction of the aged. *Rural Sociology,* 39:5–15.

Busse, E. W. and D. G. Blazer, eds. 1980. *Handbook of Geriatric Psychology.* New York: Van Nostrand.

Butler, E. W. and E. J. Kaiser. 1971. Prediction of residential movement and spatial allocation. *Urban Affairs Quarterly,* 6:477–494.

Butler, R. N. 1975. *Why Survive.* New York: Harper and Row.

Buttimer, A. 1972. Social space and the planning of residential areas. *Environment and Behavior,* 4:279–318.

Byerts, T. O., ed. 1975. Symposium—The city: A viable environment for the elderly? Phase I. *The Gerontologist,* 15:13–46.

Byerts, T. and D. Conway. 1972. *Behavioral Requirements for Housing for the Elderly.* Washington, D.C.: American Institute of Architects.

Campbell, A., P. E. Converse, and W. L. Rodgers. 1976. *The Quality of American Life.* New York: Russell Sage Foundation.

Campbell, D. T. and J. C. Stanley. 1963. Experimental and quasi-experimental designs for research on teaching. In N. L. Gage, ed., *Handbook of Research on Teaching,* pp. 171–246. Chicago: Rand-McNally.

Cantor, M. H. 1976. Effect of ethnicity on life styles of the inner-city elderly. In M. P. Lawton, R. J. Newcomer, and T. O. Byerts, eds., *Community Planning for an Aging Society,* pp. 41–58. Stroudsburg, Pa.: Dowden, Hutchinson, & Ross.

Cantril, H. 1950. *The "Why" of Man's Experience.* New York: Macmillan.

Cantril, H. 1965. *The Pattern of Human Concerns.* New Brunswick, N.J.: Rutgers University Press.

Carp, F. M. 1965. Effects of improved housing on the lives of older people. In F. M. Carp, ed., *Patterns of Living and Housing of*

Middle Aged and Older People, pp. 147–159. Public Health Service Publication No. 1496. Washington, D.C.: GPO.

Carp, F. M. 1966. *A Future for the Aged.* Austin: University of Texas Press.

Carp, F. M. 1971. Walking as a means of transportation for retired people. *Gerontologist*, 11:104–111.

Carp, F. M. 1976a. Urban life-style and life-cycle factors. In M. P. Lawton, R. J. Newcomer, and T. O. Byerts, eds., *Community Planning for an Aging Society*, pp. 19–40. Stroudsburg, Pa.: Dowden, Hutchinson, & Ross.

Carp, F. M. 1976b. Housing and living environments of older people. In R. H. Binstock and E. Shanas, eds., *Handbook of Aging and the Social Sciences*, pp. 244–271. New York: Van Nostrand Reinhold.

Cath, S. H. 1975. The orchestration of disengagement. *International Journal of Aging and Human Development*, 6:199–213.

Cavan, R. S., E. W. Burgess, R. W. Havighurst, and H. Goldhammer. 1949. *Personal Adjustment in Old Age.* Chicago: Science Research Associates.

Chapin, F. S., Jr., 1974. *Human Activity Patterns in the City.* New York: Wiley.

Chapin, F. S., Jr. and R. K. Brail. 1969. Human activity systems in the metropolitan United States. *Environment and Behavior*, 1:107–130.

Chein, I. 1954. The environment as a determinant of behavior. *Journal of Social Psychology*, 39:115–127.

Chen, Y. P. 1973. *A Pilot Survey Study of the Housing-Annuity Plan (HAP).* Los Angeles: UCLA Graduate School of Management.

Chermayeff, S. and C. Alexander. 1963. *Community and Privacy.* New York: Doubleday.

Clark, A. R. 1975. Age segregation in nine cities, 1960 to 1970. *Proceedings of the Association of American Geographers*, 7:55–59.

Clemente, F. and M. B. Kleiman. 1976. Fear of crime among the aged. *The Gerontologist*, 16:207–210.

Cohen, J. and P. Cohen. 1975. *Applied Multiple Regression/Correlation Analysis in the Behavioral Sciences.* Hillsdale, N.J.: Lawrence Erlbaum.

Coleman, R. P. 1978. Attitudes toward neighbors: How Americans choose to live. *Working Paper No. 49.* Cambridge: Joint Center for Urban Studies of M.I.T. and Harvard.

Conklin, J. E. 1972. *Robbery and the Criminal Justice System.* Philadelphia: Lippincott.

Cooley, C. H. 1902. *Human Nature and the Social Order.* New York: Scribner.

Cowgill, D. O. 1978. Residential segregation by age in American metropolitan areas. *Journal of Gerontology,* 33:446–453.

Craik, K. H. 1970. Environmental psychology. In T. H. Newcomb, ed., *New Directions in Psychology,* pp. 3–121. New York: Holt, Rinehart, & Winston.

Craik, K. H. 1971. The assessment of places. In P. McReynolds, ed., *Advances in Psychological Assessment,* 2:40–62. Palo Alto, Calif.: Science and Behavior Books.

Cumming, E. 1976. Further thoughts on the theory of disengagement. In C. S. Kart and B. B. Manard, eds., *Aging in America,* pp. 19–41. Port Washington, N.Y.: Alfred.

Cumming, E. and W. Henry. 1961. *Growing Old: The Process of Disengagement.* New York: Basic Books.

Cumming, J. and E. Cumming. 1963. *Ego and Milieu.* New York: Atherton Press.

Cutler, S. 1975. Transportation and changes in life satisfaction. *The Gerontologist,* 15:155–159.

Dalkey, N. C. 1973. Quality of life. In Environmental Protection Agency, ed., *The Quality of Life Concept: A Potential New Tool for Decision-Makers,* pp. 191–201. Washington, D.C.: GPO.

Dalkey, N. C. and D. L. Rourke. 1973. The delphi procedure and rating quality of life factors. In Environmental Protection Agency, ed., *The Quality of Life Concept: A Potential New Tool for Decision-Makers,* pp. 209–221. Washington, D.C.: GPO.

Datan, N. and N. Lohmann, eds. 1980. *Transitions of Aging.* New York: Academic Press.

DeGrazia, S. 1961. The uses of time. In R. W. Kleemeier, ed., *Aging and Leisure,* pp. 113–153. New York: Oxford University Press.

Dewey, J. *Psychology.* 1891. New York: Harper & Row.

Dogan, M. and S. Rokkan. 1969. *Quantitative Ecological Analysis in the Social Sciences.* Cambridge: M.I.T. Press.

Doxiadis, C. A. 1968. *Ekistics, an Introduction to the Science of Human Settlements.* New York: Oxford University Press.

Doxiadis, C. A. 1974. *Anthropopolis: City for Human Development.* Athens: Athens Publishing Center.

Dowd, J. J. 1975. Aging or exchange: A preface to theory. *Journal of Gerontology*, 30:584–594.

Downs, R. M. and D. Stea. 1973. Cognitive maps and spatial behavior: Process and products. In R. M. Downs and D. Stea, eds., *Image and Environment: Cognitive Mapping and Spatial Behavior*, pp. 8–26. Chicago: Aldine.

Duncan, G. J. and S. J. Newman, 1976. Expected and actual residential mobility. *Journal of the American Institute of Planners*, 42:174–186.

Duncan, O. D. 1961. A socioeconomic index for all occupations. In A. Reiss et al., *Occupations and Social Status*, pp. 139–161. New York: Free Press.

Duncan, O. D. and B. Duncan. 1955a. A methodological analysis of segregation indexes. *American Sociological Review*, 20:210–217.

Duncan, O. D. and B. Duncan. 1955b. Residential distribution and occupational stratification. *American Journal of Sociology*, 60:493–503.

Edelhart, G. 1966. Consistency of self-concept, across instruments. Master's thesis. Chicago: Committee on Human Development, University of Chicago.

Eisdorfer, C., ed. 1980. *Annual Review of Gerontology and Geriatrics*. Vol. 1. New York: Springer.

Endler, N. S. and D. Magnusson, eds. 1976. *Interactional Psychology and Personality*. New York: Wiley.

Erikson, E. H. 1963. *Childhood and Society*. 2d ed. New York: Norton.

Faris, R. E. L. and H. W. Dunham. 1939. *Mental Disorders in Urban Areas*. Chicago: University of Chicago Press.

Finch, C. E. and L. Hayflick, eds. 1977. *Handbook of the Biology of Aging*. New York: Van Nostrand Reinhold.

Fine, J., N. D. Glenn, and J. K. Monts. 1971. The residential segregation of occupational groups in central cities and suburbs. *Demography*, 8:91–102.

Firey, W. 1945. Sentiment and symbolism as ecological variables. *American Sociological Review*, 10:140–148.

Fischer, C. S. and R. M. Jackson. 1976. Suburbs, networks, and attitudes. In B. Schwartz, ed., *The Changing Face of the Suburbs*, pp. 279–307. Chicago: University of Chicago Press.

Fishbein, M. 1963. An investigation of the relationships between beliefs about an object and the attitude toward that object. *Human Relations,* 16:233–240.

Fishbein, M. and I. Ajzen. 1975. *Belief, Attitude, and Behavior.* Reading, Mass.: Addison-Wesley.

Fiske, D. W. and S. R. Maddi, eds. 1961. *Functions of Varied Experience.* Homewood, Ill.: Dorsey.

Foley, D. L. 1964. An approach to metropolitan spatial structure. In M. M. Webber, ed., *Explorations into Urban Structure,* pp. 21–78. Philadelphia: University of Pennsylvania Press.

French, J. R. P., W. Rodgers, and S. Cobb. 1974. Adjustment as person-environment fit. In G. V. Coelho, D. A. Hamburg, and J. E. Adams, eds., *Coping and Adaptation,* pp. 316–333. New York: Basic Books.

Fried, M. and P. Gleicher. 1961. Some sources of residential satisfaction in an urban slum. *Journal of the American Institute of Planners,* 27:305–315.

Fromm, E. 1947. *Man for Himself: An Inquiry into the Psychology of Ethics.* New York: Rinehart.

Furby, L. 1978. Possessions: Toward a theory of their meaning and function throughout the life cycle. In P. B. Baltes, ed., *Life-Span Development and Behavior,* 1:298–331. New York: Academic Press.

Gans, H. 1967. *The Levittowners: Ways of Life and Politics in a New Suburban Community.* New York: Random House.

Geddes, R. and R. Gutman. 1977. Assessment of the built-environment for safety: Research and practice. In L. E. Hinkle, Jr. and W. C. Loring, eds., *The Effect of the Man-Made Environment on Health and Behavior,* pp. 143–195. Atlanta, Ga.: Center for Disease Control, Public Health Service, U.S. Dept. of Health, Education, & Welfare.

Gelwicks, L. E. 1970. Home range and use of space by an aging population. In L. A. Pastalan and D. H. Carson, eds., *Spatial Behavior of Older People,* pp. 148–161. Ann Arbor: Institute of Gerontology, University of Michigan.

Gerontologist. 1968. Vol. 8.

Gerontologist. 1969. Vol. 9.

Gibson, J. J. 1960. The concept of the stimulus in psychology. *American Psychologist,* 15:694–703.

Golant, S. M. 1971. Adjustment process in a system: A behavioral model of human movement. *Geographical Analysis,* 3:204–220.

Golant, S. M. 1972. *The Residential Location and Spatial Behavior of the Elderly: A Canadian Example.* Department of Geography Research Paper No. 143. Chicago: Department of Geography, University of Chicago.

Golant, S. M. 1976a. Housing and transportation problems of the elderly. In J. S. Adams, ed., *Urban Policymaking and Metropolitan Dynamics,* pp. 379–422. Cambridge, Mass.: Ballinger.

Golant, S. M. 1976b. Intraurban transportation needs and problems of the elderly. In M. P. Lawton, R. J. Newcomer, and T. O. Byerts, eds., *Community Planning for Aging Society,* pp. 282–308. Stroudsburg, Pa.: Dowden, Hutchinson, & Ross.

Golant, S. M. 1977. The housing tenure adjustments of the young and elderly. *Urban Affairs Quarterly,* 13:95–108.

Golant, S. M. 1977–78. Spatial context of aging persons. *International Journal of Aging and Human Development,* 8:279–289.

Golant, S. M., ed. 1979a. *Location and Environment of Elderly Population.* New York: Wiley.

Golant, S. M. 1979b. Rationale for geographic perspectives on aging and the aged. In S. M. Golant, ed., *Location and Environment of Elderly Population,* pp. 1–14. New York: Wiley.

Golant, S. M. 1980. Locational-environmental perspectives on old-age-segregated residential areas in the United States. In R. J. Johnston and D. T. Herbert, eds., *Geography and the Urban Environment.* Vol. 3, pp. 257–294. New York: Wiley.

Golant, S. M. 1982. Individual differences underlying the dwelling satisfaction of the elderly. *Journal of Social Issues,* 38:121–133.

Golant, S. M. 1984. The effects of residential and activity behaviors on old people's environmental experiences. In I. Altman, J. Wohlwill, and M. P. Lawton, eds., *Human Behavior and the Environment: The Elderly and the Environment,* pp. 239–278. New York: Plenum Press.

Golant, S. M. and R. McCaslin. 1979a. A functional classification of services for older people. *Journal of Gerontological Social Work,* 13:187–209.

Golant, S. M. and R. McCaslin. 1979b. A social indicator model of the elderly population's social welfare environment. In S. M. Golant, ed., *Location and Environment of Elderly Population,* pp. 181–196. New York: Wiley.

Golant, S. M. and A. McCutcheon. 1980. The external validity of community research findings. *Social Indicators Research,* 7:207–235.

Golant, S. M., G. Rudzitis, and S. Daiches. 1978. The migration of the older population from central cities in the United States. *Growth and Change,* 9:30–35.

Goldscheider, C., M. Van Arsdol, and G. Sabagh. 1966. Residential mobility of older people. In F. M. Carp, ed., *Patterns of Living and Housing of Middle Aged and Older People,* pp. 65–82. Public Health Service Publication No. 1496. Washington, D.C.: GPO.

Goldsmith, J. and S. S. Goldsmith, eds. 1976. *Crime and the Elderly.* Lexington, Mass.: Heath-Lexington.

Golledge, R. G. 1978. Learning about urban environments. In T. Carlstein, D. Parkes, and N. Thrift, eds., *Timing Space and Spacing Time,* 1:76–98. London: Edward Arnold.

Golledge, R. G. and G. Rushton, eds. 1976. *Spatial Choice and Spatial Behavior.* Columbus: Ohio State University Press.

Golledge, R. G. and G. Zannaras. 1973. Cognitive approaches to the analysis of human spatial behavior. In W. H. Ittelson, ed., *Environment and Cognition,* pp. 59–94. New York: Seminar Press.

Gordon, C. and C. M. Gaitz. 1976. Leisure and lives: Expressivity across the life span. In R. H. Binstock and E. Shanas, eds., *Handbook of Aging and the Social Sciences,* pp. 310–341. New York: Van Nostrand Reinhold.

Graney, M. J. and E. E. Graney. 1974. Communications activity substitutions in aging. *Journal of Communication,* 24:88–96.

Gurin, G., J. Veroff and S. Feld. 1960. *Americans View Their Mental Health.* New York: Basic Books.

Gutowski, M. 1978. *Housing Related Needs of the Suburban Elderly.* Washington, D.C.: The Urban Institute.

Hartmann, H. 1958. *Ego Psychology and the Problem of Adaptation.* New York: International Universities Press.

Hartup, W. W. and J. Lempers. 1973. A problem in life-span development: The interactional analysis of family attachments. In P. B. Baltes and K. W. Schaie, eds., *Life-Span Developmental Psychology: Personality and Socialization.* pp. 235–252. New York: Academic Press.

Havighurst, R. J. 1961. The nature and values of meaningful free-time activity. In R. W. Kleemeier, ed., *Aging and Leisure,* pp. 309–344. New York: Oxford University Press.

Havighurst, R. J. and R. Albrecht. 1953. *Older People*. New York: Longmans, Green.

Havighurst, R. J. and R. Glasser. 1972. An exploratory study of reminiscence. *Journal of Gerontology*, 27:245–253.

Havighurst, R. J., B. L. Neugarten, and S. Tobin. 1968. Disengagement and patterns of aging. In B. L. Neugarten, ed., *Middle Age and Aging: A Reader in Social Psychology*, pp. 161–172. Chicago: University of Chicago Press.

Heimsath, C. 1977. *Behavioral Architecture*. New York: McGraw-Hill.

Helson, H. 1964. *Adaptation-Level Theory*. New York: Harper and Row.

Herbert D. T. and R. J. Johnston, eds. 1976. *Spatial Processes and Form*. Vol. 1. New York: Wiley.

Hinkle, L. E., Jr. 1977. Measurement of the effects of the environment upon the health and behavior of people. In L. E. Hinkle, Jr. and W. C. Loring, eds., *The Effect of the Man-Made Environment on Health and Behavior*, pp. 197–239. Atlanta, Ga.: Center for Disease Control, Public Health Service, U.S. Department of Health, Education, & Welfare.

Hochschild, A. R. 1975. Disengagement theory: A critique and proposal. *American Sociological Review*, 40:553–569.

Hodge, R. W., P. M. Siegel, and P. H. Rossi. 1964. Occupational prestige in the United States, 1925–1963. *American Journal of Sociology*, 70:286–302.

Holmes, T. H. and R. H. Rahe. 1967. The social readjustment rating scale. *Journal of Psychosomatic Research*, 11:213–218.

Howard, A. and R. A. Scott. 1965. A proposed framework for the analysis of stress in the human organism. *Behavioral Science*, 10:141–160.

Howell, S. D. 1980. Environments as hypotheses in human aging. In L. W. Poon, ed., *Aging in the 1980s*, pp. 424–432. Washington, D.C.: American Psychological Association.

Howells, J. G., ed. 1975. *Modern Perspectives in the Psychiatry of Old Age*. New York: Brunner/Mazel.

Hunt, J. 1963. Motivation inherent in information processing and action. In O. J. Harvey, ed., *Motivation and Social Interaction: Cognitive Determinants*. pp. 35–94. New York: Ronald Press.

Ittelson, W. H. 1973. Environment perception and contemporary perceptual theory. In W. H. Ittelson, ed., *Environment and Cognition*, pp. 1–19. New York: Seminar Press.

Ittelson, W. H., K. A. Franck, and T. J. O'Hanlon. 1976. The nature of environmental experience. In S. Wapner, S. B. Cohen, and B. Kaplan, eds., *Experiencing the Environment*, pp. 187–206. New York/London: Plenum Press.

Jaccard, J. 1979. Personality and behavioral prediction: An analysis of behavioral criterion measures. In L. R. Kahle, ed., *Methods for Studying Person-Situation Interactions*, pp. 73–92. San Francisco: Jossey-Bass.

Jakubs, J. F. 1977. Residential segregation: The Taeuber index reconsidered. *Journal of Regional Science*, 17:281–283.

James, W. 1902. *The Varieties of Religious Experience: A Study of Human Nature*. New York: Longmans, Greens.

Jessor, R. and S. L. Jessor. 1973. The perceived environment in behavioral science. *American Behavioral Scientist*, 16:23–50.

John, E. R. 1976. A model of consciousness. In G. E. Schwartz and D. Shapiro, eds., *Consciousness and Self-Regulation*, 1:1–50. New York: Plenum.

Johnston, D. F., ed. 1981. *Measurement of Subjective Phenomena*. Special Demographic Analyses, CDS-80-3. Washington, D.C.: GPO.

Johnston, R. J. 1976. Residential area characteristics: Research methods for identifying urban sub-areas—social area analysis and factorial ecology. In D. T. Herbert and R. J. Johnston, eds., *Spatial Processes and Form*, 1:193–235. New York: Wiley.

Journal of Social Issues. 1980. Vol. 2.

Kahana E., J. Liang, and B. J. Felton. 1980. Alternative models of person-environment fit: Prediction of morale in three homes for the aged. *Journal of Gerontology*, 35:584–595.

Kalish, R. A. 1976. Death and dying in a social context. In R. H. Binstock and E. Shanas, eds., *Handbook of Aging and the Social Sciences*, pp. 483–507. New York: Van Nostrand Reinhold.

Kalish, R. A. and F. W. Knudtson. 1976. Attachment versus disengagement: A life-span conceptualization. *Human Development.* 19:171–181.

Kantrowitz, N. 1973. *Ethnic and Racial Segregation in the New York Metropolis*. New York: Praeger.

Kasarda, J. D. and M. Janowitz. 1974. Community attachments in mass society. *American Sociological Review*, 39:328–339.

Kasl, S. V. 1972. Physical and mental health effects of involuntary relocation and institutionalization—a review. *American Journal of Public Health*, 62:379–384.

Kasl, S. V. 1977. Health and behavior: A review. In L. E. Hinkle, Jr. and W. C. Loring, eds., *The Effect of the Man-Made Environment on Health and Behavior of People*, pp. 65–127. Atlanta, Ga.: Center for Disease Control, Public Health Service, U.S. Department of Health, Education, & Welfare.

Kassabaum, G. E. 1962a. Housing for the elderly: Technical standards of design. *Journal of the American Institute of Architects*, 38:61–65.

Kassabaum, G. E. 1962b. Housing for the elderly: Site selection. *Journal of the American Institute of Architects*, 38:65–68.

Kassabaum, G. E. 1962c. Housing for the elderly: Functional program. *Journal of the American Institute of Architects*, 38:51–52.

Kastenbaum, R. and S. Candy. 1973. The 4% fallacy. *International Journal of Aging and Human Development*, 4:15–21.

Katz, S. et al. 1970. Progress in development of the index of ADL. *The Gerontologist*, 10:20–30.

Keller, S. 1968. *The Urban Neighborhood: A Sociological Perspective*. New York: Random House.

Kelman, H. C. 1974. Attitudes are alive and well and gainfully employed in the sphere of action. *American Psychologist*, 9:310–324.

Kemper, T. D. 1978. *A Social Interactional Theory of Emotions*. New York: Wiley.

Kimmel, D. C. 1980. *Adulthood and Aging*. 2d ed. New York: Wiley.

Koffka, K. 1935. *Principles of Gestalt Psychology*. New York: Harcourt Brace.

Kuhlen, R. G. 1968. Developmental changes in motivation during the adult years. In B. L. Neugarten, ed., *Middle Age and Aging*, pp. 115–136. Chicago: University of Chicago Press.

Kutner, B. 1956. *Five Hundred over Sixty*. New York: Russell Sage Foundation.

Kuypers, J. A. and V. L. Bengston. 1973. Competence and social breakdown: A socio-psychological view of aging. *Human Development*, 16:37–49.

Labowitz, S. 1972. Statistical usage in sociology: Sacred cows and ritual. *Sociological Methods and Research*, 1:13–38.

Land, K. C. 1969. Duration of residence and prospective migration: Further evidence. *Demography*, 6:133–140.

Land, K. C. 1975. Social indicator models, An overview. In K. C. Land and S. Spilerman, eds., *Social Indicator Models*. pp. 5–36. New York: Russell Sage Foundation.

Lang, J., C. Burnette, W. Moleski, and D. Vachon, eds. 1974. *Designing for Human Behavior: Architecture and the Behavioral Sciences*. Stroudsburg, Pa.: Dowden, Hutchinson, & Ross.

Langford, M. 1962. *Community Aspects of Housing for the Aged*. Ithaca, N.Y.: Cornell University Center for Housing and Environmental Studies.

Lansing, J. B. and E. Mueller. 1967. *The Geographic Mobility of Labor*. Ann Arbor: Institute for Social Research, University of Michigan.

Larson, R. 1978. Thirty years of research on the subjective well-being of older Americans. *Journal of Gerontology*, 33:109–129.

Lawton, M. P. 1970. Planner's notebook: Planning environments for older people. *Journal of the American Institute of Planners*, 36:124–129.

Lawton, M. P. 1972. Assessing the competence of older people. In D. Kent, R. Kastenbaum, and S. Sherwood, eds., *Research, Planning, and Action for the Elderly*, pp. 122–143. New York: Behavioral Publications.

Lawton, M. P. 1975. *Planning and Managing Housing for the Elderly*. New York: Wiley.

Lawton, M. P. 1977a. The impact of the environment on aging and behavior. In J. E. Birren and K. Warner Schaie, eds., *Handbook of the Psychology of Aging*, pp. 276–301. New York: Van Nostrand Reinhold.

Lawton, M. P. 1977b. Morale: What are we measuring? In C. N. Nydegger, ed., *A Guide to Effective Assessment*, pp. 6–14. Special Publication No. 3. Washington, D.C.: Gerontological Society.

Lawton, M. P. 1978. The housing problems of community-resident elderly. In R. Boynton, ed., *Occasional Papers in Housing and Community Affairs*, 1:39–74. Washington, D.C.: U.S. Dept. of Housing and Urban Development.

Lawton, M. P. 1980. *Environment and Aging*. Belmont, Calif.: Wadsworth.

Lawton, M. P., M. Kleban, and D. Carlson. 1973. The inner city resident: To move or not to move. *The Gerontologist,* 13:443–448.

Lawton, M. P. and L. Nahemow. 1973. Ecology and the aging process. In C. Eisdorfer and M. P. Lawton, eds., *Psychology of Adult Development and Aging,* pp. 619–674. Washington, D.C.: American Psychological Association.

Lawton, M. P., R. J. Newcomer, and T. O. Byerts, eds. 1976. *Community Planning for an Aging Society.* Stroudsburg, Pa.: Dowden, Hutchinson, & Ross.

Lawton, M. P. and B. Simon. 1968. The ecology of social relationships in housing for the elderly. *The Gerontologist,* 8:108–115.

Lazarus, R. S. 1966. *Psychological Stress and the Coping Process.* New York: McGraw-Hill.

Leary, T. 1957. *The Interpersonal Diagnosis of Personality.* New York: Ronald Press.

Lee, G. R. and M. L. Lassey. 1980. Rural-urban differences among the elderly: Economic, social, and subjective factors. *Journal of Social Issues,* 36:62–74.

Leff, H. 1978. *Experience, Environment, and Human Potentials.* New York: Oxford University Press.

Leighton, A. H. 1959. *My Name Is Legion: Foundations for a Theory of Man in Relation to Culture.* The Stirling County Study of Psychiatric Disorder and Sociocultural Environment I. New York: Basic Books.

Lerner, R. M. and C. D. Ryff. 1978. Implementation of the life-span view of human development: The sample case of attachment. In P. B. Baltes, ed., *Life-Span Development and Behavior,* 1:2–44. New York: Academic Press.

Levinson, B. M. 1972. *Pets and Human Development.* Springfield, Ill.: Thomas.

Lewin, K. 1951. *Field Theory in Social Science.* New York: Harper and Row.

Lewis, C. N. 1971. Reminiscing and self-concept in old age. *Journal of Gerontology,* 26:240–243.

Lieberman, M. A. 1975. Adaptive processes in late life. In N. Datan and L. Ginsberg, eds., *Life-Span Developmental Psychology: Normative Life Crises,* pp. 135–159. New York: Academic Press.

Lieberman, M. A. and A. S. Coplan. 1969. Distance from death as a variable in the study of aging. *Developmental Psychology*, 2:71–84.

Lieberman, M. A. and J. M. Falk. 1971. The remembered past as a source of data for research on the life cycle. *Human Development*, 14:132–141.

Lieberman, M., S. S. Tobin, and D. Slover. 1971. *The Effects of Relocation on Long-Term Geriatric Patients*. Final Report, Project No. 17-1328. Chicago: Illinois Department of Health and Committee on Human Development, University of Chicago.

Lieberson, S. 1962. Suburbs and ethnic residential patterns. *American Journal of Sociology*, 67:673–681.

Lingoes, J. C. 1972. A general survey of the Guttman-Lingoes nonmetric program series. In R. N. Shepard, A. K. Romney, and S. B. Nerlove, eds., *Theory and Applications in the Behavioral Sciences*, pp. 49–68. New York: Seminar Press.

LoGerfo, M. 1980–81. Three ways of reminiscence in theory and practice. *International Journal of Aging and Human Development*, 12:39–48.

Longino, C. F. 1982. Changing aged nonmetropolitan migration patterns, 1955 to 1960 and 1965 to 1970. *Journal of Gerontology*, 37:228–234.

Longino, C. F. and C. S. Kart. 1982. Explicating activity theory: A formal replication. *Journal of Gerontology*, 37:713–722.

Louis Harris and Associates, Inc. 1975. *The Myth and Reality of Aging in America*. Washington, D.C.: National Council on Aging.

Lowry, I. S. 1970. Filtering and housing standards. A conceptual analysis. In A. N. Page and W. R. Seyfried, eds., *Urban Analysis*, pp. 339–347. Glenview, Ill.: Scott, Foresman.

Lowy, L. 1980. *Social Policies and Programs on Aging*. Lexington, Mass.: Heath.

Lynch, K. 1960. *The Image of the City*. Cambridge: M.I.T. Press.

Lynch, K. and L. Rodwin. 1958. A theory of urban form. *Journal of the American Institute of Planners*, 24:201–214.

McGinnis, R. 1968. A stochastic model of social mobility. *American Sociological Review*, 33:712–722.

McKechnie, G. E. 1977. The environmental response inventory in application. *Environment and Behavior*, 9:255–276.

Maddox, G. L. 1963. Activity and morale: A longitudinal study of selected elderly subjects. *Social Forces*, 42:195–204.

Maddox, G. L. 1968. Persistence of life style among the elderly: A longitudinal study of patterns of social activity in relation to life satisfaction. In B. L. Neugarten, ed., *Middle Age and Aging*, pp. 181–183. Chicago: University of Chicago Press.

Maddox, G. L. and J. Wiley. 1976. Scope, concepts and methods in the study of aging. In R. H. Binstock and E. Shanas, eds., *Handbook of Aging and the Social Sciences*, pp. 3–34. New York: Van Nostrand Reinhold.

Madge, J. 1969. Aging and the fields of architecture and planning. In M. W. Riley, J. W. Riley, and M. E. Johnson, eds., *Aging and Society*, pp. 229–273. New York: Russell Sage Foundation.

Magnusson, D., ed. 1981. *Toward a Psychology of Situations: An Interactional Perspective.* Hillsdale, N.J.: Lawrence Erlbaum.

Malinchak, A. A. and D. Wright. 1978. The scope of elderly victimization. *Aging*, 281–282:11–16.

Mangum, W. P. 1982. Housing for the elderly in the United States. In A. M. Warnes, ed., *Geographical Perspectives on the Elderly.* New York: Wiley.

Marans, R. W. 1975. Survey research. In W. Michelson, ed., *Behavioral Research Methods in Environmental Design*, pp. 119–179. Stroudsburg, Pa.: Dowden, Hutchinson, & Ross.

Marans, R. W. and W. Rodgers. 1975. Toward an understanding of community satisfaction. In A. M. Hawley and V. P. Rock, eds., *Metropolitan America in Contemporary Perspective*, pp. 299–352. New York: Wiley.

Marcuse, P. 1972. *The Legal Attributes of Homeownership for Low and Moderate Income Families.* Working Paper No. 209-1-1. Washington, D.C.: The Urban Institute.

Markovitz, J. 1971. Transportation needs of the elderly. *Traffic Quarterly*, 25:237–253.

Maslow, A. H. 1954. *Motivation and Personality.* New York: Harper & Row.

Mehrabian, A. and J. R. Russell. 1974. *An Approach to Environmental Psychology.* Cambridge: M.I.T. Press.

Merriam, S. 1980. The concept and function of reminiscence: A review of the research. *The Gerontologist*, 20:604–609.

Michelson, W. 1970. *Man and his Urban Environment: A Sociological Approach.* Reading, Mass.: Addison-Wesley.

Midwest Research Institute. 1977. *Crimes Against the Aging: Patterns and Prevention.* Kansas City: Midwest Research Institute.

Milgram, S. 1970. The experience of living in cities. *Science,* 167:1461–1468.

Miller, J. G. 1978. *Living Systems.* New York: McGraw Hill.

Mischel, W. 1968. *Introduction to Personality.* New York: Wiley.

Mischel, W. 1973. Toward a cognitive social learning reconceptualization of personality. *Psychological Review,* 80:252–283.

Misra, S. K. 1970. *Human Needs and Physical Environment.* A Discussion Paper. Stockholm: Department of Building Function Analysis, The Royal Institute of Technology.

Montgomery, J. E. 1972. The housing patterns of older families. *Family Life Coordinator,* 21:37–46.

Moon, M. 1974. *The Measurement of Economic Welfare: Its Application to the Aged Poor.* New York: Academic Press.

Moore, G. T. 1979. Knowing about environmental knowing: The current state of theory and research on environmental cognition. *Environment and Behavior,* 11:33–70.

Moos, R. H. 1974. *Evaluating Treatment Environments: A Social Ecological Approach.* New York: Wiley.

Moos, R. H. 1976. *The Human Context: Environmental Determinants of Behavior.* New York: Wiley-Interscience.

Morrison, P. A. 1967. Duration of residence and prospective migration: The evaluation of a stochastic model. *Demography,* 4:553–561.

Morrison, P. A. 1972. Population movements and the shape of urban growth: Implications for public policy. In S. M. Mazie, ed., *Commission on Population Growth and the American Future.* Vol. 5: *Population Distribution and Policy,* pp. 281–322. Washington, D.C.: GPO.

Murray, H. A. 1938. *Explorations in Personality.* New York: Oxford University Press.

Musson, N. and H. Heusinkveld. 1963. *Buildings for the Elderly.* New York: Reinhold.

National Center for Health Statistics. 1974. Limitation of activity and mobility due to chronic conditions, United States, 1972.

Vital and Health Statistics, Series 10, No. 96. Rockville, Md.: U.S. Dept. of Health, Education, & Welfare.

Neff, J. A. and R. J. Constantine. 1979. Community dissatisfaction and perceived residential alternatives: An interactive model of the formulation of migration plans. *Journal of Population*, 2:18–32.

Nehrke, M. F. et al. 1981. Environmental perception differences between staff and elderly domiciliary residents. (Abstract). *The Gerontologist*, 21:271.

Nelson, L. M. and M. Winter. 1975. Life disruption, independence, satisfaction, and the consideration of moving. *The Gerontologist*, 15:160–164.

Neugarten, B. L., ed. 1968. *Middle Age and Aging*. Chicago: University of Chicago Press.

Neugarten, B. L. 1974. Age groups in American society and the rise of the young-old. *Annals of the American Academy of Political and Social Science*, 415:187–198.

Neugarten, B. L. 1977. Personality and aging. In J. E. Birren and K. W. Schaie, eds., *Handbook of the Psychology of Aging*, pp. 626–649. New York: Van Nostrand Reinhold.

Neugarten, B. L. and N. Datan. 1973. Sociological perspectives on the life cycle. In P. B. Baltes and K. W. Schaie, eds., *Life-span Developmental Psychology: Personality and Socialization*, pp. 53–69. New York: Academic Press.

Neugarten, B. L. and G. O. Hagestad. 1976. Age and the life course. In R. H. Binstock and E. Shanas, eds., *Handbook of Aging and the Social Sciences*, pp. 35–55. New York: Van Nostrand Reinhold.

Neugarten, B. L., R. J. Havighurst, and S. S. Tobin. 1961. The measurement of life satisfaction. *Journal of Gerontology*, 16:134–143.

Newcomer, R. J. 1976. An evaluation of neighborhood service convenience for elderly housing project residents. In P. Suefeld and J. A. Russell, eds., *The Behavioral Basis of Design*, 1:301–307. Stroudsburg, Pa.: Dowden, Hutchinson, & Ross.

Newman, O. 1973. *Defensible Space*, New York: Macmillan.

Newman, S. J. and G. J. Duncan. 1979. Residential problems, dissatisfaction, and mobility. *Journal of the American Planning Association*, 45:154–166.

Nie, N. et al. 1975. *Statistical Package for the Social Sciences*. 2nd ed. New York: McGraw Hill.

Niebanck, P. 1965. *The Elderly in Older Urban Areas*. Philadelphia: Institute for Environmental Studies.

Norberg-Schulz, C. 1971. *Existence, Space, and Architecture*. New York: Praeger.

Northwestern University, Center for Urban Affairs. 1972. *Evanston, Illinois—Selected Studies of Its People, Its Economy, and Its Human Services*. Evanston, Ill.: Center for Urban Affairs, Northwestern University.

Nydegger, C. N., ed., 1977. *Measuring Morale: A Guide to Effective Assessment*. Special Publication No. 3. Washington, D.C.: Gerontological Society.

Nystuen, J. D. 1963. Identification of some fundamental spatial concepts. *Papers of the Michigan Academy of Science, Arts, and Letters*, 48:373–384.

Osgood, C. E., G. J. Suci, and P. H. Tannenbaum. 1957. *The Measurement of Meaning*. Urbana: University of Illinois Press.

Palmore, E. B. 1968. The effects of aging on activities and attitudes. *The Gerontologist*, 8:259–263.

Palmore, E., ed. 1980. *International Handbook on Aging*. Westport, Conn.: Greenwood Press.

Pampel, F. C. and H. M. Choldin. 1978. Urban location and segregation of the aged: A block-level analysis. *Social Forces*, 56:1121–1139.

Parr, J. 1980. The interaction of persons and living environments. In L. W. Poon, ed. *Aging in the 1980s*, pp. 393–406. Washington, D.C.: American Psychological Association.

Pastalan, L. A. 1970. Privacy as an expression of human territoriality. In L. A. Pastalan and D. H. Carson, eds., *Spatial Behavior of Older People*, pp. 88–101. Ann Arbor: Institute of Gerontology, University of Michigan.

Pastalan, L. 1977. Designing housing environments for the elderly. *Journal of Architectural Education*, 31:11–13.

Pastalan, L. A. N.d. Relocation: A state of the art. Unpublished paper. Ann Arbor: Institute of Gerontology, University of Michigan.

Pastalan, L. A. and D. H. Carson, eds. 1970. *Spatial Behavior of Older People*. Ann Arbor: Institute of Gerontology, University of Michigan.

Patterson, A. H. 1977. Methodological developments in environment-behavior research. In D. Stokols, ed., *Perspectives on Environment and Behavior*, pp. 325–344. New York: Plenum.

Paykel, E., B. Prusoff, and E. H. Uhlenhuth. 1971. Scaling of life events. *Archives of General Psychiatry*, 25:340–347.

Pearlin, L. I. and C. Schooler. 1978. The structure of coping. *Journal of Health and Social Behavior*, 19:2–21.

Perin, C. 1970. *With Man in Mind*. Cambridge: M.I.T. Press.

Perry, C. 1929. *Regional Survey of New York and Its Environment*. Vol. 7: *Neighborhood and Community Planning*. New York: Regional Plan Association.

Pervin, L. A. 1978. Definitions, measurements, and classifications of stimuli, stimulations, and environments. *Human Ecology*, 6:71–105.

Pickvance, C. G. 1973. Life-cycle, housing tenure, and intra-urban residential mobility: A Causal Model. *Sociological Review*, 21:279–297.

Pocock, D. and R. Hudson. 1978. *Images of the Urban Environment*. New York: Columbia University Press.

Polanyi, M. 1946. *Science, Faith, and Society*. Chicago: University of Chicago Press.

Poole, M. A. and F. W. Boal. 1973. Religious residential segregation in Belfast in mid-1969: A multi-level analysis. In B. D. Clark and M. B. Gleave, eds., *Social Patterns in Cities*, pp. 1–40. London: Institute of British Geographers.

Poon, L. W. ed. 1980. *Aging in the 1980s*. Washington, D.C.: American Psychological Association.

Proshansky, H. M., W. H. Ittelson, and L. Rivlin. 1970. Freedom of choice and behavior in a physical setting. In H. M. Proshansky, W. H. Ittelson, and L. Rivlin, eds., *Environmental Psychology*, pp. 173–183. Chicago: Holt Rinehart, & Winston.

Rapoport, A. 1977. *Human Aspects of Urban Form*. New York: Pergamon Press.

Raush, H. L. 1979. Epistemology, metaphysics, and person-situation methodology: conclusions. In L. R. Kahle, ed., *Methods for Studying Person-Situation Interactions*, pp. 93–106. San Francisco: Jossey-Bass.

Rees, P. H. 1970. Concepts of social space: Toward an urban social geography. In B. J. L. Berry and F. E. Horton, eds., *Geo graphical Perspectives on Urban Systems,* pp. 306–394. Prentice Hall: Englewood Cliffs, N.J.

Rees, P. H. 1979. *Residential Patterns in American Cities: 1960.* Department of Geography Research Paper No. 189. Chicago: Department of Geography, University of Chicago.

Regnier, V. 1981. Neighborhood images and use: A case study. In M. P. Lawton and S. L. Hoover, eds., *Community Housing Choices for Older Americans,* pp. 180–197. New York: Springer.

Rogers, C. R. 1951. *Client-Centered Therapy: Its Current Practice, Implications, and Theory.* Boston: Houghton Mifflin.

Rosen, J. L. and B. L. Neugarten. 1960. Ego functions in the middle and later years: A thematic apperception study of normal adults. *Journal of Gerontology,* 15:62–69.

Rosenberg, M. J. 1956. Cognitive structure and attitudinal affect. *Journal of Abnormal and Social Psychology,* 53:367–372.

Rosencranz, H. A. and C. T. Pihlblad. 1970. Measuring the health of the elderly. *Journal of Gerontology,* 25:129–133.

Rosenmayr, L. and E. Kockeis. 1965. Housing conditions and family relations of the elderly. In F. M. H. Carp, ed., *Patterns of Living and Housing of Middle-Aged and Older People,* pp. 29–46. Public Health Service Publication No. 1496. Washington, D.C.: GPO.

Rosner, A. 1968. Stress and the maintenance of self-concept in the aged. Ph.D. dissertation, University of Chicago.

Rosow, I. 1961. The social effects of physical environment. *Journal of the American Institute of Planners,* 27:127–133.

Rosow, I. 1967. *Social Integration of the Aged.* New York: Free Press.

Rosow, I. 1974. *Socialization to Old Age.* Berkeley: University of California Press.

Rosow, I. and N. Breslau. 1966. A Guttman health scale for the aged. *Journal of Gerontology,* 21:556–559.

Rossi, P. H. 1955. *Why Families Move.* Glencoe, Ill.: Free Press.

Rowles, G. D. 1978. *Prisoners of Space?* Boulder, Col.: Westview Press.

Rowles, G. D. 1979. The last new home: Facilitating the older person's adjustment to institutional space. In S. Golant, ed., *Location and Environment of Elderly Population.* New York: Wiley.

Rudzitis, G. 1982. *Residential Location and the Older Population.* Department of Geography Research Paper No. 202. Chicago: Department of Geography, University of Chicago.

Saarinen, T. F. 1976. *Environmental Planning: Perception and Behavior*. Boston: Houghton Mifflin.

Samuels, M. S. 1978. Existentialism and human geography. In D. Ley and M. Samuels, eds., *Humanistic Geography*, pp. 22–40. Chicago: Maaroufa Press.

Sanoff, H. 1973. Youth's perception and categorizations of residential cues. In W. F. E. Preiser, ed., *Environmental Design Research*, 1:84–97. Stroudsburg, Pa.: Dowden, Hutchinson, & Ross.

Sargent, H. D., H. C. Modlin, M. T. Favis, and A. M. Voth. 1958. Situational variables. *Bulletin Menninger Clinic*, 22:148–166.

Sawrey, J. M. and C. Telford. 1967. *Psychology of Adjustment*. Boston: Allyn & Bacon.

Schneider, M. 1975. The quality of life in large American cities: Objective and subjective social indicators. *Social Indicators Research*, 1:495–509.

Schooler, K. K. 1976. Environmental change and the elderly. In I. Altman and J. F. Wohlwill, eds., *Human Behavior and Environment*, 1:265–298. New York: Plenum Press.

Schorr, A. L. 1970. Housing and its effects. In H. M. Proshansky, W. H. Ittelson, and L. G. Rivlin, eds., *Environmental Psychology*, pp. 319–333. Chicago: Holt, Rinehart, & Winston.

Schulz, R. and G. F. Brenner. 1977. Relocations of the aged: A review and theoretical analysis. *Journal of Gerontology*, 32:323–333.

Schuman, H. and M. P. Johnson. 1976. Attitudes and behavior. *Annual Review of Sociology*, 2:161–207.

Sells, S. B. 1963. Dimensions of stimulus situations which account for behavior variance. In S. B. Sells, ed., *Stimulus Determinants of Behavior*, pp. 3–15. New York: Ronald Press.

Shanas, E. 1979. The family as a social support system in old age. *The Gerontologist*, 1979. 19:169–174.

Shanas, E. et al. 1968. *Old People in Three Industrial Societies*. New York: Atherton Press.

Shaw, M. E. and P. R. Costanzo. 1970. *Theories of Social Psychology*. New York: McGraw-Hill.

Sherif, M. 1967. *Social Interaction: Process and Products*. Chicago: Aldine.

Shevky, E. and W. Bell. 1955. *Social Area Analysis: Theory, Illustrative Application and Computational Procedures*. Stanford: Stanford University Press.

Shibutani, T. 1968. A cybernetic approach to motivation. In W. Buckley, ed., *Modern Systems Research for the Behavioral Scientist*, pp. 330–342. Chicago: Aldine.

Siegel, P. M. 1971. Prestige in the American occupational structure. Ph.D. Dissertation. Chicago: Department of Sociology, University of Chicago.

Simmons, J. W. 1968. Changing residence in the city: A review of intraurban mobility. *Geographical Review*, 58:622–651.

Simon, H. 1957. *Models of Man*. New York: Wiley.

Skinner, B. F. 1953. *Science and Human Behavior*. New York: Macmillan.

Smith, B. W. and J. Hiltner. Intraurban location of the elderly. *Journal of Gerontology*, 30:473–478.

Smith, R. J. 1979. *Crime against the Elderly*. Washington, D.C.: The International Federation on Ageing.

Smith, T. W. 1979. Happiness: Time trends, seasonal variations, intersurvey differences and other mysteries. *Social Psychological Quarterly*, 42:18–30.

Speare, A., Jr. 1970. Home ownership, life cycle stage, and residential mobility. *Demography*, 7:449–458.

Speare, A., Jr. 1974. Residential satisfaction as an intervening variable in residential mobility. *Demography*, 11:173–188.

Spivak, M. 1973. Archetypal place. In W. F. E. Prieser, ed., *Environmental Design Research*, 1:33–46. Stroudsburg, Pa.: Dowden, Hutchinson, & Ross.

Stea, D. 1970. Home range and use of space. In L. A. Pastalan and D. H. Carson, eds., *Spatial Behavior of Older People*, pp. 138–147. Ann Arbor: Institute of Gerontology. University of Michigan.

Stern, W. 1938. *General Psychology*. New York: Holt, Rinehart and Winston.

Stokols, D. 1978. Environmental psychology. *Annual Review of Psychology*, 29:253–295.

Stotland, E. 1969. *The Psychology of Hope*. San Francisco: Jossey-Bass.

Struyk, R. 1977. Housing situation of elderly Americans. *The Gerontologist*, 17:130–139.

Struyk, R. M. and B. J. Soldo. 1980. *Improving the Elderly's Housing*. Cambridge, Mass.: Ballinger.

Sullivan, H. S. 1953. *The Interpersonal Theory of Psychiatry*. New York: Norton.

Sweeney, D. R., D. C. Tinling, and A. H. Schmale. 1970. Dimensions of affective expression in four expressive modes. *Behavioral Science*, 15:393–408.

Taeuber, K. E. 1981. Duration-of-residence analysis of internal immigration in the United States. *The Millbank Memorial Fund Quarterly*, 39:116–131.

Taueber, K. E. and A. F. Taeuber. 1969. *Negroes in Cities: Residential Segregation and Neighborhood Change*. New York: Atheneum.

Taylor, C. C. and A. R. Townsend, 1976. The local 'sense of place' as evidenced in North–East England. *Urban Studies*, 13:133–146.

Taylor, R. 1968. Purposeful and non-purposeful behavior: A rejoinder. In W. Buckley, ed., *Modern Systems Research for the Behavioral Scientist*, pp. 238–242. Chicago: Aldine.

Thibaut, J. W. and H. H. Kelley. 1959. *The Social Psychology of Groups*. New York: Wiley.

Thomae, H. 1979. The concept of development and life-span developmental psychology. In P. B. Baltes and O. G. Brim, Jr., eds., *Life-Span Development and Behavior* 2:281–312. New York: Academic Press.

Thomas, W. I. 1923. *The Unadjusted Girl*. Boston: Little, Brown.

Tibbetts, P. 1972. The transactional theory of human knowledge and action: Notes toward "behavioral ecology." *Man-Environment Systems*, 2:37–59.

Timms, D. W. G. 1971. *The Urban Mosaic*. Cambridge: Cambridge University Press.

Tobin, S. and M. A. Lieberman. 1976. *Last Home for the Aged*. San Francisco: Jossey-Bass.

Tolman, E. C. 1932. *Purposive Behavior in Animals and Men*. New York: Appleton-Century-Crofts.

Toney, M. B. 1976. Length of residence, social ties, and economic opportunities. *Demography*, 13:297–309.

Uhlenhuth, E. H. and E. S. Paykel. 1973. Symptom intensity and life events. *Archives of General Psychiatry*, 28:473–477.

U.S. Bureau of the Census. 1972a. *Census of Housing: 1970 Block Statistics*. HC(3)–68, Chicago, Illinois–Northwestern Indiana Urbanized Area. Washington, D.C.: GPO.

U.S. Bureau of the Census. 1972b. *Census of Population and Housing, 1970*. Chicago SMSA, Part 1, Final report. PHC(1)-43. Washington, D.C.: GPO.

U.S. Bureau of the Census. 1973. *Census of Housing, 1970: Housing of Senior Citizens.* Subject Reports. Final Report HC(7)-2. Washington, D.C.: GPO.

U.S. Bureau of the Census. 1976. Demographic aspects of aging and the older population in the United States. *Current Population Reports: Special Studies.* Series P-23. No. 59. Washington, D.C.: GPO.

U.S. Bureau of the Census. 1979. Social and economic characteristics of the older population, 1978. *Current Population Reports: Special Studies.* Series P-23, No. 85. Washington, D.C.: GPO.

U.S. Bureau of the Census. 1981. Geographical mobility: March, 1975 to March, 1980. *Current Population Reports, Series P-20,* No. 368. Washington, D.C.: GPO.

U.S. Department of Health, Education, & Welfare. 1976. *Health, United States, 1975.* DHRW Pub. No. (HRA)76–1232. Rockville, Md.: Health Resources Administration, National Center for Health Statistics.

Varady, D. P. 1980. Housing problems and mobility plans among the elderly. *Journal of the American Planning Association,* 46:302–314.

Veblen, T. 1899. *The Theory of the Leisure Class.* New York: Macmillan.

Wachtel, P. L. 1973. Psychodynamics, behavior therapy and the implacable experimenter: An inquiry into the consistency of personality. *Journal of Abnormal Psychology,* 82:324–334.

Wapner, S., B. Kaplan, and S. B. Cohen. 1973. An organismic-developmental perspective for understanding transactions of men in environments. *Environment and Behavior,* 5:255–289.

Webb, E. J., D. T. Campbell, R. D. Schwartz, and L. Sechrest. 1966. *Unobtrusive Measures.* Chicago: Rand-McNally.

Webber, M. M. 1963. Order and diversity: Community without propinquity. In L. Wingo, ed., *Cities and Space: The Future Use of Urban Land,* pp. 23–56. Baltimore: John Hopkins University Press.

Webber, M. M. 1964. The urban place and the nonplace urban realm. In M. M. Webber, ed., *Explorations into Urban Structure,* pp. 79–153. Philadelphia: University of Pennsylvania Press.

Weiss, R. S. 1973. *Loneliness: The Experience of Emotional and Social Isolation.* Cambridge: M.I.T. Press.

Welfeld, I. and R. J. Struyk. 1979. *Housing Options for the Elderly.* Occasional Papers in Housing and Community Development, No. 3. Washington, D.C.: GPO.

Westin, A. F. 1967. *Privacy and Freedom.* New York: Atheneum.

Wheatley, P. 1976. Levels of space awareness in the traditional Islamic city. *Ekistics,* 253:354–366.

White, R. W. 1970. Excerpts from motivation reconsidered: The concept of competence. In H. M. Proshansky, W. H. Ittelson, and L. G. Rivlin, eds., *Environmental Psychology,* pp. 125–134. New York: Holt, Rinehart, & Winston.

White, R. W. 1974. Strategies of adaptation: An attempt at systematic description. In G. V. Coelho, D. A. Hamburg, and J. E. Adams, eds., *Coping and Adaptation,* pp. 47–68. New York: Basic Books.

Wilcox, A. R. 1981. Dissatisfaction with satisfaction: Subjective social indicators and the quality of life. In D. F. Johnston, ed., *Measurement of Subjective Phenomena,* pp. 1–20. Special Demographic Analyses, CDS-80-3. Washington, D.C.: GPO.

Wilkening, E. A. and McGranaham. 1978. Correlates of subjective well-being in Northern Wisconsin. *Social Indicators Research,* 5:211–234.

Willems, E. P. 1977. Behavioral ecology. In D. Stokols, ed., *Perspectives on Environment and Behavior,* pp. 39–67. New York: Plenum Press.

Windley, P. G. 1977. Evaluative research: Housing and living arrangements for the elderly. In U.S. Department of Health, Education, and Welfare, Office of Human Development, *Evaluative Research on Social Programs for the Elderly,* pp. 118–136. Washington, D.C.: GPO.

Windley, P. G., T. O. Byerts, and F. G. Ernst, eds. 1975. *Theory Development in Environment and Aging.* Washington, D.C.: Gerontological Society.

Windley, P. G. and R. J. Scheidt. 1980. Person-environment dialectics: Implications for competent functioning in old age. In L. W. Poon, ed., *Aging in the 1980s,* pp. 407–423. Washington, D.C.: American Psychological Association.

Windley, P. G. and R. J. Scheidt. 1982. An ecological model of mental health among small-town rural elderly. *Journal of Gerontology,* 37:235–242.

Wiseman, S. M. 1980. Why older people move: Theoretical issues. *Research on Aging,* 2:141–154.

Withey, S. B. 1962. Reaction to uncertain threat. In G. W. Baker and D. W. Chapman, eds., *Man and Society in Disaster*, pp. 93–123. New York: Basic Books.

Wohlwill, J. F. 1976. Environmental aesthetics: The environment as a source of affect. In I. Altman and J. F. Wohlwill, eds., *Human Behavior and Environment*, 1:37–86. New York/London: Plenum Press.

Wohlwill, J. F. and I. Kohn. 1976. Dimensionalizing the environment manifold. In S. Wapner, S. B. Cohen, and B. Kaplan, eds., *Experiencing the Environment*, pp. 19–53. New York/London: Plenum Press.

Wolman, B. B., ed. 1973. *Dictionary of Behavioral Science.* New York: Van Nostrand Reinhold.

Wolpert, J. 1965. Behavioral aspects of the decision to migrate. *Papers and Proceedings of the Regional Science Association*, 15:159–169.

Wolpert, J. 1966. Migration as an adjustment to environmental stress. *Journal of Social Issues*, 22:92–102.

Wynn, F. H. and H. S. Levinson. 1967. Some considerations in appraising bus transit potentials. *Highway Research Record*, 197:1–24.

Yarrow, M. R. 1963. Appraising environment. In R. W. Williams, C. Tibbi ᵥ, ᴖnd W. Donahue, eds., *Processes of Aging*, 1:201–222. New York: Atherton Press.

Yeates, M. 1979. The need for environmental perspectives on issues facing older people. In S. M. Golant, ed., *Location and Environment of Elderly Population*. New York: Wiley.

Zablocki, B. and R. M. Kanter. 1976. The differentiation of life-styles. *Annual Review of Sociology*, 2:269–298.

Zajonc, R. B. 1960. The process of cognitive tuning in communication. *Journal of Abnormal Social Psychology*, 61:159–167.

Zajonc, R. B. 1980. Feeling and thinking preferences need no inferences. *American Psychologist*, 35:151–175.

Zelder, R. E. 1970. Racial segregation in urban housing markets. *Journal of Regional Science*, 10:93–105.

Zelder, R. E. 1977. On the measurement of residential segregation: Reply. *Journal of Regional Science*, 17:299–303.

Zimmer, B. B. 1955. Participation of migrants in urban structures. *American Sociological Review*, 20:218–224.

INDEX